WITHDRAWN

James Baldwin
Artist on Fire

also by W.J. Weatherby
Conversations with Marilyn

James

A Portrait by

Baldwin

Artist on Fire

W. J. WEATHERBY

DONALD I. FINE, INC.
NEW YORK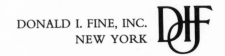

Library of Congress Cataloging-in-Publication Data

Weatherby, William J.
James Baldwin: artist on fire.

1. Baldwin, James, 1924- —Biography. 2. Authors,
American—20th century—Biography. 3. Civil rights
workers—United States—Biography. 4. Afro-Americans—
Civil rights—History—20th century. I. Title.
PS3552.A45Z94 1989 818'.5409 [B] 88-45852
ISBN 1-55611-126-6

Manufactured in the United States of America

10 9 8 7 6 5 4 3 2 1

Designed by Irving Perkins Associates

The author is grateful for permission to quote from the following works: *Notes of a Native Son* by James Baldwin. Copyright © 1955, renewed 1983 by James Baldwin. Reprinted by permission of Beacon Press. *Another Country* by James Baldwin. Copyright © 1960, 1962 by James Baldwin; *Blues for Mister Charlie* by James Baldwin. Copyright © 1964 by James Baldwin; *The Fire Next Time* by James Baldwin. Copyright © 1962, 1963 by James Baldwin; *Going to Meet the Man* by James Baldwin. Copyright © 1951, 1957, 1958, 1960, 1965 by James Baldwin; *If Beale Street Could Talk* by James Baldwin. Copyright © 1974 by James Baldwin; *Nobody Knows My Name* by James Baldwin. Copyright © 1954, 1956, 1958, 1959, 1960, 1961 by James Baldwin; *No Name in the Street* by James Baldwin. Copyright © 1972 by James Baldwin; *Tell Me How Long the Train's Been Gone* by James Baldwin. Copyright © 1968 by James Baldwin; *Go Tell It on the Mountain* by James Baldwin. Copright © 1952, 1953 by James Baldwin; *Giovanni's Room* by James Baldwin. Copyright © 1956 by James Baldwin. All reprinted by permission of Doubleday. Quotations from *The Unfinished Quest of Richard Wright* by Michel Fabre. Copyright © 1973 by William Morrow and Company, Inc. Reprinted by permission of William Morrow and Company, Inc.

For James Monroe Parker,
artist and friend of the Baldwin family,
to whom James Baldwin wrote, "Now *you* go
tell it, and help to create for
us another country."

"It now had been laid to my charge to keep my own heart free of hatred and despair."

James Baldwin,
Notes of a Native Son

Contents

Author's Note

THIS PORTRAIT of James Baldwin is based on conversations and interviews with more than one hundred people who knew him at various stages of his life, and on my own acquaintance with him over twenty-eight years. I remember very clearly the first time he really began to trust me. We met for a drink at Small's Paradise in Harlem, and at the sight of us a young black woman came rushing over. Baldwin braced himself, assuming she was one of his fans. But she rushed past him and embraced me. She was a barmaid I knew at another Harlem bar. He was always impressed when a white man was at home on his turf. Later he selected a book of my reportage about the civil rights movement as one of the best books of 1965 and thereafter trusted me as what he called an "accurate reporter." I often asked him questions about his life and work over the years, and filled several notebooks with his answers. He was a very open man, but occasionally he would say about something he told me, "Don't tell your journalist friends," or "Keep that until I'm dead."

If you dropped by his apartment you would become part of the crowd already there, and before the day was over you might find yourself dining with him at one of his favorite restaurants, attending a party in the Village or bar-hopping in Harlem. I enjoyed best those times when he was alone with his family, his mother and one or two of his brothers and sisters, sitting back like a patriarch, free from the public pressures. But this is not intended to be a personal account of our acquaintance but rather a portrait of the man. For that reason I have avoided too many personal references and merely attributed some of my memories to "a friend." I am not, however, to be confused with other friends who wished to remain unidentified. Although I was not a member of his most intimate circle, some of his intimate friends were willing to be interviewed provided their names were not mentioned. A few of them had almost total recall of the relationship apparently, but others seemed hardly aware of the never-ending struggle that was James Baldwin's life—a struggle, as he put it, to keep his heart "free from hatred and despair." Much of the interest in the story of his life is in following how well he succeeded.

—W.J.W.
New York City

1

Blues for Mister Baldwin

JAMES BALDWIN had a mystical view of his own life. He sometimes talked about the course that his life had taken as if he believed in fate, in destiny. He was a man who would wear an ancient Turkish silver ring because he had been told that it could ward off evil, and he once sent a friend a little stone from India, Scotch-taped to a letter, because he had been assured it had "magical powers." He rapped on wood for good luck all his life, and when his intelligence pointed one way and his instincts another, he invariably followed his instincts. His outlook was partly the result of his early religious upbringing, partly the effect of his extraordinary rise from extreme poverty in Harlem to international celebrity. After all he had been through, it must have seemed almost like a fairy tale come true, but he often wondered whether there would be a happy ending.

"I suspect, though I certainly cannot prove it," he wrote ten years before he died, "that every life moves full circle . . . toward revelation." Certainly Baldwin's own life moved full circle even to the extent that his funeral in Harlem on December 8, 1987, was held only a few blocks away from where he had been born sixty-three years before. As for the "revelation" he saw himself moving toward, this was closely related to his attitude toward experience and how it changes our perception of life—and especially our past. When as frequently happened he was described as a "spokesman" for American blacks, he always denied it. He was a "witness," he always replied. "Witness to whence I came, where I am. Witness to what I've seen and the possibilities that I think I see."[Life for him was a never-ending struggle between Good and Evil, as much inside a person as outside—that was certainly how he saw the racial situation in America]

He was fond of quoting Lambert Strether's famous advice in Henry James' *The Ambassadors:* "Live all you can; it's a mistake not to," which he said he interpreted as meaning "Trust life, and it will teach you, in joy and sorrow, all you need to know." If you played safe in Baldwin's opinion, you might never attain the deepest state of "revelation" about your own past when, as he expressed it, eventually "you begin to see, and even rejoice to see, what you always saw." He once advised one of his nephews, "Take no one's word for anything, including mine—but trust your experience. Know whence you came. If you know whence you came, there is really no limit to where you can go." He sometimes compared life to a handkerchief stuffed into a pocket that you slowly pull out through your experiences. If you live "with passion," the whole handkerchief should be out by the time you die and you need have no regrets. "Go for broke" and "Let it all hang out" were favorite sayings of his. He had the same attitude toward his writing: "One writes out of one thing only—one's own experience. Everything depends on how relentlessly one forces from this experience the last drop, sweet or bitter, it can possibly give."

How much James Baldwin took his own advice in coming full circle was suggested by the vast, very mixed congregation of over five thousand mourners at his funeral service—officially called "a celebration" of his life—in the Cathedral of St. John the Divine on Amsterdam Avenue at 112th Street, the edge of Harlem. Every aspect of his complex life, every level at which he had lived on both sides of the Atlantic was represented in the crowded benches and in the lines of people standing along the walls beneath the great vaulted ceiling and high stained-glass windows.[Side by side were the strangest contrasts from different periods

of his life—celebrities in politics and show business who had known him
as a fellow celebrity were sitting near graying classmates from his far-off
high school days, ex-lovers who were often jealous of their relationship
with the great man, and old comrades from the civil rights movement
of twenty years ago who had come to mourn him as they had mourned
Martin Luther King and Malcolm X and Medgar Evers and all the rest
of the dead heroes. Even Baldwin's lover's quarrel with his native land
was reflected there. The speakers who paid tribute to him were all fellow
black writers—Amiri Baraka, Toni Morrison and Maya Angelou—
except for the French cultural counsellor, Marc Perrin de Brichambaut.
Baldwin had been put under FBI surveillance by the United States
government whereas France had given him one of its highest honors,
making him a commander in its Legion of Honor in 1986. Not even
the New York literary establishment had given him any of its top
awards, such as the Pulitzer Prize or a National Book Award. Although
his last editor had been invited to speak but wasn't free, there was no
white American literary or political figure among the eulogizers of—as
a Baldwin family message described him—"our son, our brother, our
uncle, our father—our Jimmy—now ancestral." It left a sense of something missing in the celebration of his extraordinary life.

Certain writers are linked to a particular place and James Baldwin
was as much a part of New York's Harlem, often called the capital of
Black America in its great days, as Charles Dickens was of the East End
of London or Dostoevsky was of St. Petersburg. Even Harlemites who
had never seen Baldwin except on television felt they knew the little
man with the big, prominent eyes and the infectious, gap-toothed grin.
He had departed from Harlem when he was eighteen never to return
except for brief visits, but as a writer he never left. In book after book,
including those he was working on the last year, he returned obsessively
to the Harlem he had grown up in. Although he was criticized by some
black militants for not living there after he became famous, the ghetto
never had a more faithful literary son. He kept the faith—the Harlem
test—in all the ways that mattered. For many white Americans even
when they gave up listening, he remained the messenger with bad news
right up to the end.

You don't die in Harlem, you *pass,* an expression that has echoes from slave days of a release from bondage to somewhere better. No one understood all the nuances of the Harlem view of death better than Baldwin. Not only had he grown up in a minister's home, but he was a teenage preacher himself. Some Harlemites, especially those with Deep South roots, believe the spirit doesn't pass until after the funeral. So a wake was held the night before in his old apartment on West Seventy-first Street in the house he had bought for his mother from the proceeds of his first bestsellers. People sat recalling the Baldwin parties that had gone on there until daybreak, the rooms once echoing with laughter now in silent darkness except for a few candles flickering over his empty desk.

The highpoint of his funeral was not the "celebration" before the huge congregation that included an African drum salute, folk singing, a jazz trumpet solo and a recording of Baldwin reciting the prayer "Precious Lord." The real highpoint came with the last drive through the Harlem streets. In front, with a police escort, was the huge mahogany casket that looked far too big for his slight, frail body wasted from cancer unless you took into account the great spirit that had kept him going with the help of chain-smoking and bottles of Johnnie Walker scotch whisky. The casket was closed, but a glass panel showed the striking dark features topped by thinning gray hair, at rest at last. Immediately behind came the Baldwin family led by his old mother, Emma Berdis Baldwin, looking extraordinarily like her eldest son that day, and his younger brother David, who had shared so many of his journeys and played many roles in his life. Normally a cheerful, gregarious man, that day he was somber, grim-faced, as if struggling not to express his feelings. Then came the rest of his eight brothers and sisters, whom he had helped to bring up, as well as all his nephews and nieces to whom he was "Uncle Jimmy" and whose books were studied in their schools. Behind them was a long procession of over forty cars. Among the local people who came out of tenements and stores and bars along Amsterdam Avenue to watch the procession pass by were old Harlem grandmothers who remembered how the other kids used to shout after him, "Hey, Frog Eyes!" and they had watched from their apartment windows, remarking "That sure is a sorry little boy." And now he had come back a great man to be honored.

The Harlem that James Baldwin passed through for the last time was superficially different from the Harlem he had grown up in. There were more vacant lots, more abandoned buildings, the desolation that came from the greatly increased drug trade and from so-called urban renewal that tamed the ghettoes. The towering state office building had cleared one of the most famous blocks of 125th Street. The Black Nationalist Bookstore, once a local literary hangout, was gone. The Hotel Theresa, the scene of so many legendary Harlem dramas, was closed. So was Small's Paradise, where Baldwin's publisher, Dial Press, had held a huge party to launch his novel, *Another Country*—a party still talked about twenty-six years later—and where he liked to stop by for a late-night drink and chat to the jazz musicians who often ended their night there. Wells' Restaurant and Bar on the opposite side of Seventh Avenue, now Adam Clayton Powell Boulevard (When would there be a Baldwin Boulevard?), was gone, too, and so was Count Basie's down the block.

But enough still remained, even corner grocery stores where Baldwin had been sent as a boy, and storefront churches he had known in his preaching days. His "turf" was bounded by Lenox Avenue on the west, the Harlem River on the east, 135th Street on the north, and 130th Street on the south. "We never lived beyond these boundaries; this is where we grew up," he once recalled.

As the long slow funeral procession reached this area of Harlem, there were the same faded houses with windows "like a thousand blinded eyes" that the young Baldwin had noted in his early writing. This was the environment young "Frog Eyes" had known, he once said, like his hand. At last the huge casket neared the corner of 135th Street and the procession paused for a moment. Down the street stood Harlem Hospital, where he had been born on August 2, 1924. The circle of his life then seemed to be complete. It was both the end of his story and the beginning, and looking at the gray decaying landscape of the ghetto that had seemed like a prison to the young Jimmy Baldwin, you could appreciate how far he had come in his sixty-three years—and what it had cost him. It was the moment of revelation.

2

"Frog Eyes"

"I REALLY have the same name as you," James Baldwin once informed his friend and fellow novelist James Jones, the author of *From Here to Eternity.* He told other people, too, that his real name was James Jones even though he had by then become internationally famous as James Baldwin. The title of his bestselling collection of essays, *Nobody Knows My Name,* always had an ironic double meaning for him.

His illegitimacy obsessed him from the time he first learned about it in his boyhood right to the end of his life. Emile Capouya, his best friend at De Witt Clinton High School in the Bronx, recalled an intense conversation after school when Baldwin was about sixteen. "He talked about finding out he was illegitimate. I think he had long suspected it, but it had recently been confirmed. He was very emotional, very tearful, and I laughed to try to jolly him out of it because he took it so seriously. I told him a wise child knows his own father. He didn't blame his mother in any way for bringing him into the world illegitimate, he was always very tender about her. But when he talked to me, he didn't know who his father was." Even after he became well-known, as secure as he was ever likely to be, he often still brooded about it with trusted friends.

The mystery has never been cleared up even now that his life is over.

He had assumed his mother's husband, David Baldwin, was his father, but a conversation he apparently overheard in his teens put him right— he was a bastard child. It explained to him why David Baldwin rarely seemed pleased with him. He was legally only his stepfather, he had been born in sin. But as Baldwin put it in later years, when he viewed his stepfather more sympathetically, David Baldwin was really his father in every way except "biological." In many of his essays he continued to refer to David Baldwin as "my father."

Jesuit priests say give us a boy for his first seven years and you can have him forever after. James Baldwin was under his stepfather's influence far longer than that—from the age of three when David Baldwin married his mother (he "did not arrive on *my* scene, really, until I was more than two years old") to the age of eighteen. His stepfather was undoubtedly the most important influence on his life.[Baldwin wrote: "He formed me, and he raised me, and he did not let me starve." He also said: "No matter that he was not my biological father. He claimed me as his son. He gave me myself. I may not always like that self, have many quarrels with it—yet, here it is, and here I am, and I would not be here had it not been for him."] It was from David Baldwin that he acquired his detailed knowledge of the Bible, which was to affect his thinking and his style until he died. It was from David Baldwin that he learned he was "ugly," which made him painfully shy and uncertain of himself for years. When his stepfather insulted his big, prominent eyes, he was angry because he had his mother's eyes and therefore he wasn't under attack as much as his mother] "No doubt, he was also attacking my real, and unknown, father." It was from his relationship with David Baldwin that he developed his obsession about rebelling against father figures that was to make his relations with such older celebrities as Richard Wright and Elia Kazan so difficult. In talks with friends he also occasionally wondered whether his stepfather's aggressive, often cruel dominance encouraged his homosexuality. "I wished to rebel in every way," he recalled.

Baldwin's first memory of his stepfather was strangely happy. David Baldwin was standing in the kitchen, drying the dishes. Little Jimmy was in his mother's arms, dressed to go out. He stared at David Baldwin over his mother's shoulder, and his stepfather smiled back. He also remembered sitting on his stepfather's knee in the first church he attended, the Abyssinia Baptist Church on 138th Street. These memories soon became like a vanished vision of the Garden of Eden. As he grew bigger and more aware of the mood around him, David Baldwin changed into someone to fear and even hate. ["He frightened me so much that no man has ever frightened me since." His stepfather once gave him his last dime to go to the local store for kerosene for the stove in the winter and he slipped on the icy street and lost the dime. David Baldwin beat him with an iron cord until he lay half-conscious on the floor. Yet he didn't think his stepfather showed favoritism—"he did not beat me worse than the others because I was not his son."] If David Baldwin was not denouncing "white devils" or making New York seem like Sodom and Gomorrah, he was reminding young Jimmy how little he had to offer the world. Jimmy learned he was not only poor and black but the ugliest child his stepfather had ever seen, with a weak little body and pop eyes. He was even left-handed! The boy used to cry himself to sleep at being so unlucky. It never occurred to him to doubt his stepfather. In *Go Tell It On the Mountain,* he described the boy based on himself dreaming of being "beautiful, tall and popular." He would become "a poet or a college president or a movie star," and he would drink expensive whisky and smoke Lucky Strike cigarettes. He wasn't to know that in less than thirty years, much of this fantasy life would come true.

But if David Baldwin wasn't his father, then who was? When he asked his mother casually if she had ever been married before, she guessed what he was after and brushed him off. He later told Fern Eckman, a writer for the New York *Post:* "My mother used to say I was just like him. Whenever she said that, she looked very worried: 'Just like him—just like your father.' That was when she would, you know, slap me—or something." At first he assumed she meant he was like David Baldwin. "But I knew very well—somewhere—that that was not what she meant." In *A Rap On Race* with anthropologist Margaret Mead, he said he didn't know anything about his ancestors. "I just know I have an English name, and God knows how I got that!" Margaret Mead said bastards specialized in knowing who their fathers were, and

Baldwin replied, "Because it is much more important," but he didn't mention he was illegitimate. The "rap" took place in 1970. What he told me several times in the sixties and seventies was that he didn't know who his father was. I had the impression he knew very little, that it was a subject his mother didn't like to talk about and treated as closed. A friend in publishing who knew him to the end said his mother wouldn't tell him who his father was. David Adams Leeming, a close confidant who was with Baldwin in the final weeks and was chosen by him to write his authorized biography, told me he didn't know who Baldwin's father was, but would try to sit down with his mother and ask her before writing his official account of Baldwin's life. I have known Mrs. Baldwin almost as long as I knew her eldest son, but I didn't wish to confront her with a question she might find unpleasant, and so I wrote to her but received no reply. I then asked his sister, Gloria Karefa-Smart, who for years acted as his secretary, and she replied flatly, "There is no information about that." When I inquired if he had ever met his father, she said "If he did, he was too young to remember it."

Mrs. Baldwin's maiden name was Emma Berdis Jones, and she moved to New York from Maryland after World War I, gave birth to a son she named James Arthur in Harlem Hospital on August 2, 1924, and married David Baldwin three years later in 1927. Presumably in claiming to be really James Jones, Baldwin meant that on his birth certificate he was given his mother's maiden name as his surname.

James Baldwin used to speculate about what it must have been like for his mother, a sensitive, very religious woman, to be alone in Harlem in the mid-twenties, a far less tolerant period than today, with an illegitimate child. She needed the missing father not only for support but to give her respectability. Did he abandon her or did he die? Baldwin once told me that his portrait of Richard in *Go Tell It On the Mountain,* who kills himself after suffering police brutality and whose pregnant girlfriend later marries a stern, forbidding evangelist very much like David Baldwin, was an idealized picture of his father. It was an example of how much he dreamed about what his father was like.

Such was Baldwin's power to dramatize events in his own life, however, [there are old friends in Harlem who doubt that he really was illegitimate and believe that David Baldwin was his real father.] One reason given is that Baldwin's black skin was like David Baldwin's whereas his mother has a much lighter complexion. Another is that he called David Baldwin "my father" or "Daddy" in his later essays. Some skeptics also think that for Baldwin to be illegitimate on top of all the other handicaps he surmounted was overdoing it, was too much like the Dickens romances he read as a boy—Jimmy Baldwin as Oliver Twist. But, however much Baldwin might dramatize, in my experience of him he was invariably truthful in his recollections. As he many times said he was illegitimate to many people, I believe he was, but who his father was and what happened to him may never be known unless Mrs. Baldwin breaks her silence. What is important, anyway, is the effect of being illegitimate on him—it was yet more proof to "Frog Eyes" of his misfortune—and that by the time he was three, David Baldwin was his acting father and remained so for the next fifteen years until he was grown up and ready to leave home.

It is easy to be unfair to David Baldwin. It took Baldwin himself half a lifetime to transform his fear and hatred of the man into a grudging appreciation and love. In many ways his stepfather resembled an Old Testament prophet and the America he came from seems almost as remote now as biblical times. His mother had been a slave and he was of the first generation of free men, though there were soon severe limitations on that freedom. Born in New Orleans, he moved north with thousands of other blacks after World War I to get away from continuing racial oppression, only to find that segregation was enforced—more subtly but the result was much the same—in New York, too. Slowly David Baldwin's bitterness dominated his thoughts—even his religion became a means of obtaining revenge against the "white devils"—and it soured his life, his old friends dropped him, and he was finally driven to paranoia. His growing isolation and his cruelty to the children were symptoms of his illness, though no one recognized it until it was too late. James Baldwin often talked about the double life blacks had to live in those days—playing a role for white employers, able to be themselves only at home. With a man like David Baldwin, the two roles gradually merged and he saw "white devils" everywhere. He had an exhausting factory job in faraway Long Island during the week and preached in Harlem storefront churches on Sundays, but his bitter, angry sermons eventually drove away many in his congregations and he preached at smaller and smaller churches. Increasing the financial burden on him, his family grew almost every year. He had brought with him his old mother and a son, Samuel, from an earlier marriage. Then Mrs. Baldwin had eight more children, three boys—George, Wilmer and David—and five girls—Barbara, Gloria, Ruth, Elizabeth and Paula Maria—and even though [she went out cleaning for people between babies, it was a constant struggle to pay the rent and buy enough food.] They got cans of corned beef and prunes from home-relief workers. "While I won't speak for my brothers and sisters, I can't bear corned beef hash or prunes even today," Baldwin wrote two years before he died. He often said he grew up feeling he'd never had enough to eat. David Baldwin "had trouble keeping us alive." Part of his stepfather's problem was "he couldn't feed his kids, but I was a kid and I didn't know that." Baldwin remembered going to the Cotton Club in Harlem at Thanksgiving with his brother George to line up in the street for free Thanksgiving dinners.

The Harlem he had been born into was still very much a community. [Drugs were still largely underground, it was drunks not drug addicts that young Jimmy Baldwin saw on the streets. The majority of the people came from the South, often called the Old Country, with a strong family and church tradition and a sense of neighborliness.] If neighbors found him doing something wrong, Baldwin recalled, they would "whip my behind and carry me, howling, to my house."[Harlem also had a much more racially mixed population than in later years.] Baldwin grew up among Finns, Jews, Poles, West Indians "and various other exotics." It was the Depression, and although the stock market crash hadn't meant much to families like the Baldwins, its effects were soon felt. Black and white could be found eating as much as they could hold in Father Divine's restaurants for fifteen cents. Jimmy Baldwin said he fought every campaign of the Italian-Ethiopian War with the oldest son of the Italian fruit-and-vegetable vendor who lived next door. They also shared spaghetti dinners. There were, in fact, two Harlems for Jimmy Baldwin. He told Julius Lester who interviewed him for the New York *Times Book Review,* "There were those who lived on Sugar Hill and there was the Hollow, where we lived. There was a great divide between the black people on the Hill and us. I was just a ragged, funky black shoeshine boy and was afraid of the people on the Hill, who, for their part, didn't want to have anything to do with me." There had been a Harlem Renaissance in the twenties with all kinds of artistic events and night life that had drawn people from all over New York, but it had hardly touched the Baldwin family, whose stern patriarch had condemned it all as sinful catering to the "white devils."

The first home Baldwin remembered was on Park Avenue at 131st Street near the railroad tracks. He recalled playing on the roof and in a garbage dump near the river when he was allowed out. When he returned thirty years later, a housing project had replaced the house he grew up in, but much of the street looked the same as it had when he was a boy. "The grocery store which gave us credit is still there, and there can be no doubt that it is still giving credit." When he passed by, "the Jewish proprietor was still standing among his shelves, looking sadder and heavier but scarcely any older." Farther down the block stood the shoe-repair store "in which our shoes were repaired until reparation became impossible and in which, then, we bought all our 'new' shoes. The Negro proprietor is still in the window, head down, working at the leather." When Baldwin turned east on 131st Street and Lenox Avenue, there was a soda-pop joint, then a shoeshine "parlor," then a grocery store, then a dry cleaners, then at last the houses where the people lived "who watched me grow up, people who grew up with me, people I watched grow up along with my brothers and sisters."

At first his home was dominated by the presence of David Baldwin's bedridden mother, Barbara, the ex-slave. She was a pale, gaunt old woman who used to scold her son for the way he treated little Jimmy, and it had an effect because David Baldwin seemed "a little afraid of her." To have such a protector meant a lot to the little boy, and he was heartbroken when she passed. As she lay dying, she called for him to come to her and she gave him an old, round metal box she said was full of candy. After the funeral, he opened it eagerly only to find she had forgotten that it was really full of needles and thread.

His stepfather's son, Samuel, also didn't remain long. He was nine years older than Jimmy and took him out to places like Coney Island. But he was continually rowing with his father. One night when he came home late, Daddy was there to greet him, they had a terrible argument, and Samuel left home never to return although he was still only a teenager. He swore his father would never see him again and he never did.] David Baldwin wrote to him when he finally traced him, but he never replied. When Jimmy was able to write, his stepfather dictated letters to him, but Samuel never answered though he sometimes wrote to Jimmy. David Baldwin slowly accepted that he was never going to see Samuel, his darling, anymore, "and this broke his heart and destroyed his will and helped him into the madhouse and the grave—my only intimation, perhaps, during all those years, that he was human."

The taunts about ugliness grew worse after Samuel left. It was as if his stepfather was taking his heartbreak out on him. It left a permanent mark. He grew up convinced he *was* ugly and was forever defensive about his appearance, eagerly seeking friendships at school and later sexual relationships as if to show that he was wanted, that he couldn't be *that* ugly if people were attracted to him. But it was something that was on his mind until the end of his life. Two years before he died, he recalled that his stepfather kept him in short pants much longer than he should have. It was one reason why some of the older kids called him "sissy." That and the constant references to his appearance "meant that the idea of myself as a sexual possibility or target, as a creature capable of desire, had never entered my mind. And it entered my mind, finally, by means of the rent made in my short Boy-Scout pants by a man who had lured me into a hallway, saying that he wanted to send me to the store. That was the very last time I agreed to run an errand for any stranger." But he drew the moral, too, that he wasn't too ugly to be desired.

David Baldwin's domestic routine was as strict as a prison's; Samuel hadn't been able to stand it and had escaped, but Jimmy was too young for that, and besides, his mother was there. With the same quick intelligence and small physique as himself, Mrs. Baldwin did her best to keep the peace between her husband and the children. Often she diverted his wrath from them to her. [Jimmy and the other children as they grew up didn't like to see him come home. They were supposed to remain inside when they weren't going to church or to the store. Playing in the streets with the other kids was considered the first step to hell and damnation]

Young Jimmy sat for hours at the living-room window observing the life in the street below. He was sometimes permitted to go on the fire escape and even the roof where there was a much wider view of the neighborhood, but he wasn't allowed to hang out on the stoop. But David Baldwin was gone for much of the day and so was Mrs. Baldwin. "I hit the streets when I was about six or seven, like most black kids of my generation, running errands, doing odd jobs," he remembered. He sometimes met Mrs. Baldwin returning from a cleaning job late at night at the subway. She was paid by the day so then they could eat. Sometimes he accompanied her to a store, where she would talk the proprietor into giving her credit and Jimmy would help her carry the food home. The little boy became very much attached to his mother, and later one critic even went so far as to define his feelings as "an unmistakably Oedipal pattern." But he had to share her love with the other children. When he became famous, a reporter asked Mrs. Baldwin which was her favorite of her nine children, obviously expecting her to name the celebrity of the family. "I have no favorites," she replied. But certainly at that time Jimmy was her special ally in helping to bring up the other children. He changed their diapers, scrubbed them, slapped them, took them to school when the time came, scolded them—and loved them. It was as if he was trying to make up for the love they missed from their father. When he became famous, he made sure they shared the benefits.

Mrs. Baldwin told a reporter, "He was my right arm. He took care of them all. Of course, he wasn't a girl, but he was very dependable. He'd get them to bed and then say, 'Is there anything else I could do for you, Mama?' He's been like a second father. I can't say he really was sickly, but he was on the delicate side. He never had the vitality most boys have in growing up. He never got into trouble with other boys— he was too shy."

But in an incident he described many times, notably in his last novel, *Just Above My Head,* he could get into trouble with the police just through being black. Two white cops stopped him and took him on a vacant lot and roughed him up, calling him "nigger."

It was reading that saved him. It was an escape from his stepfather, his home life, the Harlem streets, the other boys, the cops. A book could take him far away, he soon learned. By the age of thirteen he had read everything in the Harlem libraries and had started going down to the main library on Forty-second Street. He went at least three or four times a week to the local libraries to return home with a pile of books each time. "I read books like they were some weird kind of food," he said. They taught him that his problems were not unique. The hunchback of Notre Dame had been even uglier than Frog Eyes! The East End of London that Charles Dickens described was even worse than Harlem! *A Tale of Two Cities* and *Uncle Tom's Cabin* became his favorites and he reread them so many times his mother hid them in case excessive reading weakened his prominent eyes, but he persuaded her they did him no harm. He often recalled sitting with a book in one hand and the latest baby held in the other. "I was playing substitute mother," he said, and he wondered if that, too, encouraged his homosexual traits. Much later in his life when he and his brother David were drinking with a publisher's publicity director, she asked him how long he had known he was homosexual and how the family had responded. David answered for him. "Honey, I knew when Jimmy was a little boy," he said. "Of course we just knew." In *Go Tell It On the Mountain,* Baldwin describes a brother mocking him in a "shrill, little-girl tone" and how he tried to reply in a deep masculine voice. It would be years before he was quite clear about his sexual identity.

He said he hated to see his mother become pregnant because it took her away from him to the hospital and left him more at the mercy of his stepfather. Books became even more important at such times. Dickens' colorful foreign scenes fascinated him, especially the revolutionary background of *A Tale of Two Cities.* The southern setting of *Uncle Tom's Cabin* reminded him of the talk of his southern relatives who came by the apartment. He was particularly fond of one of his aunts who stood up to his stepfather and made him hang a picture of Louis Armstrong on the wall. The memories of David Baldwin's mother had gone back almost as far as the period of *Uncle Tom's Cabin.* There was much he couldn't understand in the books, but he continued to reread them until they became as familiar as old friends. Later he credited Dickens' "bravura" as one of the influences on his style, but his attitude toward *Uncle Tom's Cabin* changed and he dismissed it in an essay he wrote years later.

His first school was PS 24 near his home, and there he made another discovery. His quick mind was an asset that could make up for his handicaps. He could outsmart the bigger boys both in and out of the classroom. Intelligence could be as useful as good looks. This discovery meant so much to him that he vividly recalled it fifty years later in *Just Above My Head.* He never forgot the moment when he realized that Frog Eyes had a chance of making it in the world. It was like the first major tug on that pocket handkerchief he saw as his life. Altogether he attended three schools and it was like a steady progression to self-confidence and independence. At first, however, he got on far better with the teachers than the other boys, who mocked him as "Popeye" and "Frog Eyes," joked about his worn, ill-fitting clothes and haircut, and tried to bully him. So he began by loathing school and remained defensively silent and watchful, seldom even smiling.

He was astonished to find the principal of PS 24 was black, a well-known woman named Mrs. Gertrude E. Ayer, the first black principal in the history of New York City schools—the only one until 1963. "She liked me," he remembered. "And in a way I guess she proved to me that I didn't have to be entirely defined by my circumstances," whatever his stepfather said. He soon became a star of the school magazine. He was assigned a story about the history of Harlem for which he did research in the main public library downtown on Forty-second Street. The teacher who accompanied him had an encounter with his stepfather that made little Jimmy so nervous he vomited on the way to the library. The essay he produced showed none of his nervousness. He didn't allow himself to be overwhelmed with facts but selected cleverly in a style of surprising self-confidence. "Harlem—Then and Now" began: "I wonder how many of us have ever stopped to think what Harlem was two or three centuries ago? . . ." He also won a prize for a short story in a church newspaper. It was about the Spanish revolution and was slightly censored by a lady editor. It was his first published work. He also received a letter of congratulations from the mayor of New York for a song he submitted. Paper was expensive, so much of this early writing was done at home on paper bags. It became an even better way of escape—a greater "consolation"—than reading. No one cared what a writer looked like. He could be "as grotesque as a dwarf and that wouldn't matter." Perhaps this was the way to save himself and his family. He had already discovered he wouldn't make a businessman. "I had been born, apparently, with some kind of deformity that resulted in a total inability to count. From arithmetic to geometry, I never passed a single test." He saw himself as "an exceedingly shy, withdrawn and uneasy student. Yet my teachers somehow made me believe that I could learn. And when I could scarcely see for myself any future at all, my teachers told me that the future was mine . . . everything was up to me." But he knew from his experience as Frog Eyes that "every child's sense of himself is terrifyingly fragile." No child "can do it alone."

Help arrived from a young white teacher from the Midwest whose innocent, open face concealed a keen social conscience and a determination to help where she could. Her name was Orrin Miller, nicknamed Bill, and she set about widening the horizon of the shy, brilliant little boy. He had written a short play and she staged it at the school. She talked to him about books as if he were a grownup and about current news events in Spain and Ethiopia and Italy and about the Nazis in Germany who were beginning to dominate Europe. She described the world's social and economic arrangements that produced so much poverty. He even took part in public demonstrations with her. He marched in one May Day parade, carrying banners and shouting slogans like *East Side, West Side, all around the town, we want landlords to tear the slums down!* He didn't know anything about socialism or communism, he said, but he knew a lot about slums. Bill Miller didn't discuss racial prejudice much with him, probably feeling that she had neither the right nor the authority, "and also knowing that I was certain to find out." She said she would take him to see a "real" play. This offended him a little— hadn't his play been a real one? Years later her remark still rankled because he described it as tactless. But he knew from the beginning that Bill Miller was special. "It is certainly partly because of her . . . that I never really managed to hate white people," he wrote in later life. "Bill Miller was not at all like the cops who had already beaten me up, she was not like the landlords who called me nigger, she was not like the storekeepers who laughed at me." But theatergoing was forbidden in the Baldwin household, so young Jimmy arranged for her to talk to David Baldwin. Before she arrived, David Baldwin wanted to know what interest she could possibly have in a boy like him. Young Jimmy cunningly suggested it had something to do with education, a word that always impressed his stepfather. Bill Miller arrived very determined and David Baldwin agreed very reluctantly to let Jimmy go with her. She began to take him to plays and films regularly, and when David Baldwin was laid off from his factory job, she helped with food and other things through a long hard winter. Mrs. Baldwin paid her the highest compliment she knew—she was "a Christian"—but although she and Jimmy were friendly for several years, David Baldwin never trusted her. He also warned Jimmy about his white friends at school because white people, he said, would do anything to keep a Negro down. But Jimmy, like Samuel before him, had begun to rebel against and argue with his stepfather. They had some bitter arguments, with Mrs. Baldwin between them trying to keep the peace. Jimmy credited David Baldwin with teaching him to fight, to have determination and not give up. He had to be cunning to outwit his stepfather and survive in Harlem, where you couldn't even trust the police.

Among the films he saw with Bill Miller was "20,000 Years in Sing-Sing" with Bette Davis, and he was astounded to see this famous white movie star had pop eyes just like him. And was *ugly*. He raced home to tell his mother. In his outings with Bill Miller, he enjoyed a new freedom. His stepfather had less control over him. He began to try to earn a little money for his mother, shining shoes or selling bags downtown on the streets after school. The white world downtown was so much cleaner with much better garbage collection than Harlem. He had a favorite hill in Central Park on which he could stand and look one way and see Harlem and look the other and see downtown—the two worlds of black and white that were to be his life. David Baldwin even began to send him to pay his union dues downtown to save himself from dealing with the "white devils." The first "real" play Bill Miller took him to was Orson Welles' production of *Macbeth,* set in Haiti with an all-black cast at the Lafayette Theater, then on 132nd Street and Seventh Avenue near his home. He was then twelve. "I don't think that the name *Shakespeare* meant very much to me in those years. I was not yet intimidated by the name—that was to come later." He had read the play and was unprepared for the change to Haiti and actors black "like me."[Bill Miller had chosen the first play he was to see more carefully than he realized. She wanted him to have the inspiration of seeing black players]

He graduated from PS 24 and moved on to PS 139, known as Frederick Douglass Junior High School. There, too, he was soon spotted as outstanding. He contributed a short story, editorials and sketches to the school magazine, The Douglass Pilot, and wrote the lyrics for a school song. He also studied with the well-known black poet, Countee Cullen, who was the adviser to the Douglass literary club. Countee Cullen, a romantic strongly influenced by Keats, had been a leading figure in the Harlem Renaissance. He was a New Yorker, a minister's son who had studied at New York and Howard universities. He published his first collection of poetry, *Color,* while he was still an undergraduate in 1925, the year after Baldwin was born. A Guggenheim Fellowship took him to Paris. He began teaching in Harlem schools in 1934 when Baldwin was at his first school. He knew several of Countee Cullen's poems and meeting him—a successful professional black writer who had turned his experience into poetry—made young Jimmy more serious about his own writing. When he showed some of his poetry to Countee Cullen, the poet told him it sounded too much like an imitation of Langston Hughes' poetry. So he gave up writing poetry for the time being to concentrate on fiction. He cooled on the idea of writing a black *Oliver Twist,* of being another Dickens. The imitations set in faraway romantic places ceased, and instead he looked at his own experience as a subject. He would write about his family and about Harlem. Writing became therapy for him. He wanted to purge himself of his feelings about his stepfather, his souring hatred of him and wild fantasies of getting revenge that left him so guilt-ridden. He began to write about a ten-year-old black boy named Teddy and his scheme to maneuver a poisoned communion cup before the deacon, his father, on Pentecost Sunday. Baldwin later called it the "first version" of *Go Tell It On the Mountain* and said it failed because Teddy's ingenuity wasn't equal to the task of murdering his father—nor was young Jimmy to the task of writing it successfully. He was too close to his subject, too much a part of it, and he hadn't yet acquired the technique to achieve any distance or cope with a complicated plot. But he was "appalled" by what he had imagined and "ashamed" of what it revealed about his state of mind. He agonized over the question of whether he really hated his stepfather so much. Writing obviously didn't provide the outlet, the therapy, he badly needed. There was only one other way to handle it. He had to confess his sins and be saved. But that couldn't happen in his stepfather's church. He had to look for someone else—a stranger he could respect—to help him.

On top of the guilt feelings about his stepfather, he had to cope with his first sexual experiences that made him feel even more like a sinner. In *Go Tell It On the Mountain,* he recalled "he had sinned with his hands a sin that was hard to forgive. In the school lavatory, alone, thinking of the boys, older, bigger, braver, who made bets with each other as to whose urine could arch higher, he had watched in himself a transformation of which he would never dare to speak." He also found himself very confused as to his feelings, attracted as he was by the boys as much as the girls. The Devil was busy tempting him. He *had* to do something about it.

"I underwent," he wrote in *The Fire Next Time,* "during the summer that I became fourteen, a prolonged religious crisis." He became "for the first time in my life, afraid—afraid of the evil within me and afraid of the evil without." It was as if all his confused guilt feelings had made him see the "menace" around him for the first time and the growing danger that instead of fulfilling his dreams of becoming a writer he might join the whores and pimps and racketeers on Lenox Avenue as his stepfather kept predicting. Even his schoolfriends scared him. They were beginning to drink and smoke and embark on their "sexual careers," and he sensed in them "a curious, wary, bewildered despair, as though they were now settling in for the long, hard winter of life." Would he soon be like them? He knew he couldn't save himself alone.

So one Saturday in 1938 a friend at school who had already been saved took him to his church, Mount Calvary of the Pentecostal Faith, to meet the pastor—"an extremely proud and handsome woman" in her late forties. She was sitting in resplendent robes like a high priestess. Her name was Mother Horn and she was famous in Harlem. "Whose little boy are you?" she asked Jimmy Baldwin. This was the same question he had been asked by pimps and racketeers who wanted to draw him into their way of life. It was his good luck, he decided later, that he "found myself in the church racket instead of some other, and surrendered to a spiritual seduction long before I came to any carnal knowledge. For when the pastor asked me, with that marvelous smile, 'Whose little boy are you?' my heart replied at once, 'Why, yours.' " He was to use his memory of her later in portraying Sister Margaret in his first play, *The Amen Corner.*

It wasn't long before all his bottled-up guilt and fear came roaring out at one of her church services, and he fell to the floor before the altar, screaming, as he had seen others do so many times, pleading for forgiveness. "It was the strangest sensation I have ever had in my life—up to that time, or since," he wrote twenty-five years later in *The Fire Next Time.* In the spiritual anguish he experienced, he was soon free of his torment of the previous few months. The highly emotional act was like a release, a physical giving up of the Devil. He was saved from his sins, from all temptations. But merely to join the church and be a loyal member of the congregation wasn't enough. "I also intended to best my father on his own ground"—his stepfather, that is. Still only fourteen, he became a preacher, a "Young Minister," and was soon in the pulpit regularly on Sundays for the next three years at the nearby Fireside Pentecostal Assembly. When his mother was told of his new role, she was amazed. It was certainly hard to imagine little Frog Eyes with his painful shyness as a public preacher facing a crowd, but in fact as soon as he stepped into the pulpit, he seemed to become another person. He considered the pulpit a stage and steeled himself to perform like the actors he had seen with Bill Miller. He didn't even write out his sermons, but just depended at the most on a few scribbled notes, which he might not even refer to. "I would improvise from the texts, like a jazz musician improvises from a theme," he told the Paris Review in 1984. "I never wrote a sermon—I studied the texts. I've never written a speech. I can't *read* a speech. It's kind of give and take. You have to sense the people you're talking to. You have to respond to what they hear." He had watched so many preachers, including his fire-and-brimstone stepfather, that he knew how they worked up a congregation. His well-controlled, articulate way of speaking that the other kids mocked was an advantage in preaching. It sounded classy from a mere youth. He aroused the maternal instincts of the middle-aged ladies in the church. At his age he must have been specially chosen to bring the Word, and yet he looked so frail and in need of protection. His first sermon was successful enough to give him the confidence to come back the following Sunday. He soon discovered "my youth quickly made me a much bigger drawing card than my father," and he used his success to further break David Baldwin's hold over him.

How could his stepfather treat him like a child, a sinner, to be punished, when he was now a fellow preacher? David Baldwin even dictated a letter to his son, Samuel, who was now in California, as if it would have more chance of a reply coming from the new young preacher. Jimmy even dared to preach a sermon on his stepfather's favorite text, "But as for me and my house, we will serve the Lord," and proudly gave it quite a different interpretation from his stepfather's. He gained more privacy in the crowded home because he could always claim to be preparing his sermons as well as his school homework. He found his life at home changing, becoming more free as David Baldwin's mental illness worsened. In all the excitement of being a teenage star at the church, it was a long time before he realized he "had escaped from nothing whatever." Nothing seemed to go too well even there for him. He became friendly with a girl in the church, but she had a breakdown—"went mad"—and she was taken to a mental hospital. He visited her in the women's wing, and when he came out into the courtyard outside, he saw all the women patients watching him through the bars with an "unspeakable, despairing, captive avidity." The church and such a world seemed to be on different planets.

[At the same time he moved on to a new school, his last one—the prestigious De Witt Clinton High School in the Bronx. He later said appreciatively of his Douglass years that a teacher had guided him from the sentimental, over-written horrors he began with to something approaching an intelligent style. He also joked about his often bad health.] He had been supposed by all to have one foot in the grave and he staggered about looking like a cross between the Ancient Mariner and

Bette Davis in the last reel of "Of Human Bondage." A teacher had taken one look at him and promptly bought a gallon of cod liver oil and poured it down his throat. It had brought him back from the "pearly gates."

[He welcomed the change in schools because he had ended his friendship with Bill Miller, and it took him farther away with little chance of seeing her. He had gone down to the dedicated young teacher's home on Twelfth Street in the Village to tell her that as a Young Minister he could no longer go to such sinful places as theaters and moviehouses with her. He never forgot her quiet reply: "I've lost a lot of respect for you."] He couldn't convey to her why he had done it, the guilt and hysteria and need for security that perhaps only a church could give him at this time in his life. Being saved had cost him his old friend. She couldn't understand how strict the church leaders were, especially about white people. He had been taught by his mother to stand up and give his seat to a woman on crowded subway trains. Some of the preachers now told him that he must never give his seat to a white woman. He solved the problem by never sitting down on trains. But he thought about it a lot—whether a woman's color was more important than her being a woman. It was like private warfare, but he couldn't tell Bill Miller.

The new school was in the northern part of the Bronx and so he had to take a long subway ride each day. He enjoyed getting out of Harlem to cleaner, tree-lined streets. He found himself in a brilliant, highly competitive class, which included Emile Capouya and Sol Stein, who were later to become distinguished book editors and publishers, and Richard Avedon, who was to earn an international reputation as a photographer and collaborate with Baldwin on a book, *Nothing Personal.* All white boys. Baldwin found the competition was good for him, though in the early days of his preaching he didn't give much time to his homework and his grades showed it. But he was soon contributing to The Magpie, the school magazine. Three short stories—"The Woman at the Well," "Mississippi Legend" and "Incident in London"—showed a big improvement in technique, even the titles showed the influence of the films he had seen with Bill Miller, and the stories' religious overtones reflected the experience he was going through as a Young Minister. He also interviewed his old literary adviser, Countee

Cullen, for The Magpie and entitled it "Rendezvous with Life," as if his mind was already on graduating and getting out into the big world. He had published some poems in The Magpie—perhaps he could become a full-time poet!—but Countee Cullen warned him, "Poetry is something which few people enjoy and which fewer people understand. A publishing house publishes poetry only to give the establishment tone. It never expects to make much money on the transaction. And it seldom does." The young interviewer reacted dramatically: "Yours truly, who had been under the impression that one simply published a book, and sat back and watched the shekels roll in, sat aghast. 'I never knew that,' I said. 'I guess a teaching job comes in pretty handy, then.'" Countee Cullen said it did, but he also liked to teach. He recommended to the fledgling writer three things for success: "Read and write—and wait." Jimmy Baldwin asked if he had found much prejudice against blacks in the literary world. "Mr. Cullen shook his head." Playing interviewer seemed a long way from his role as Young Minister.

He credited Emile Capouya with being his best friend at De Witt Clinton. They were both on the staff of The Magpie and Capouya had a high, unbending idealism that appealed to the Young Preacher. A young poet and well-read even at that age, Capouya was the son of immigrants from Spain and Russia with a Jewish heritage. He described Jimmy Baldwin nearly fifty years later as "the most remarkable young man I have ever known." He could still remember an extraordinary short story Jimmy Baldwin had written for The Magpie. It was set in the Deep South, where Jimmy had never been, although he had heard tales of the South from his relatives. In the story he described how a southern redneck said, "Niggers are gettin' uppity" and Capouya told him nobody would talk that way. Baldwin replied, "I'm afraid you don't know," and Capouya commented later, "And of course he was right." He described the young Jimmy Baldwin as "an obvious genius. He was also still very holy in those days." But that wasn't to last much longer.

Capouya recalled that The Magpie was run by an English teacher, Wilmer T. Stone, a southerner and a radical "of a resigned kind—resigned because he knew the world wasn't going to change overnight." Capouya said Jimmy Baldwin "was fluent and relaxed with him because he knew he was in the presence of a friend. He took a special interest in Jimmy not because he was black but because he was talented."

Capouya was aware that David Baldwin gave Jimmy a hard time at home "partly because he was illegitimate and there was a special sense of sin." Jimmy tended to see everything in biblical terms, quoting from the Old and New Testaments frequently to back up his opinions in arguments with his friends. It often annoyed him that his friends, several of them skeptical Jewish intellectuals, were not as impressed with his biblical references as he was. But these heated disagreements with his peers at school eventually affected his attitude toward his Sunday preaching.

It was through Emile Capouya that Baldwin met a man who was to be a major influence on him. When Capouya was sitting in Washington Square Park in the Village, he started talking with a black artist named Beauford Delaney. He went back with Delaney to his nearby studio at 181 Greene Street to see his paintings, which he found "very strong." Delaney was "the first real-life painter I had met who was a true artist," Capouya told me. Although he doesn't remember doing so, according to Jimmy Baldwin he went back to school the next day and "told me about this wonderful man he had met, a black—then Negro or colored—painter, and said that I must meet him and he gave me Beauford Delaney's address."

Baldwin at that time had a laboring job after school in a Dickensian sweat shop on Canal Street in the Village, and he was getting on so badly at home with his stepfather that he welcomed going somewhere after work. He remembered feeling terrified as he climbed up all the narrow, gloomy stairs to Delaney's studio and knocked. A short, round, brown-skinned man with extraordinarily penetrating eyes appeared. "Emile sent me," said Baldwin shyly, and that was the start of a close friendship that lasted nearly forty years until the artist's last illness. Delaney was in his late thirties when they met. He had been born in Knoxville, Tennessee, and came north in 1924, the year Baldwin was born, to study at art schools in Boston. By coincidence he had known Jimmy Baldwin's old literary adviser, Countee Cullen, when the poet was studying for a master's degree in English at Harvard. He arrived in New York in 1929 attracted by all he had heard about the Harlem Renaissance. He had his first one-man show at the 135th Street branch of the New York Public Library in 1930. He painted portraits of such black celebrities as W.E.B. Du Bois, the historian and radical political scientist, and W.C. Handy, the composer and music publisher known as the "Father of the Blues." He also became friendly with Henry Miller, who wrote an essay about him entitled "The Amazing and Invariable Beauford Delaney." But that was in 1945, five years after Delaney first met Jimmy Baldwin.

Emile Capouya said that he had recognized from Delaney's manner that he was homosexual and therefore doubted he would have urged Jimmy Baldwin to visit him, knowing that Jimmy was having problems about his sexual identity. But he didn't think the two had a homosexual relationship at that time "because Jimmy hadn't made up his mind about his homosexual nature. He was still thinking of sex with girls." In an introduction Baldwin wrote for the catalogue of an exhibition of Delaney's paintings in France in 1964, he called Delaney a great painter and added: "I do know that great art can only be created out of love, and that no greater lover has ever held a brush."

Beauford Delaney's small studio with a black stove and paintings everywhere and music always playing—the kind of music Baldwin's stepfather would never have in the house but was part of the Harlem culture—Ma Rainey, Louis Armstrong, Bessie Smith, all the greats of the twenties and thirties—became a second home for Jimmy Baldwin. He and the artist began to go to concerts the way he had gone to theaters and movies with Bill Miller. One of Beauford Delaney's great favorites was Marian Anderson—he later painted a huge portrait of her from memory—and he often bought standing-room tickets (the cheapest) at the Metropolitan Opera or Carnegie Hall just to hear her. Jimmy Baldwin often accompanied him. Attempts had been made to prevent her from singing in Washington, D.C., because she was black, so Eleanor Roosevelt, then the First Lady, had arranged for her to sing on the steps of the Lincoln Memorial. Baldwin commented, "This was a quite marvelous and passionate event in those years, triggered by the indignation of one woman who had clearly, it seemed to me, married beneath her." So much for Franklin D. Roosevelt.

Baldwin credited Beauford Delaney with teaching him how to see clearly, a vital attribute for a writer. He remembered standing on a street corner in the Village with Delaney, waiting for the light to change, and the artist pointed down and said, "Look." Baldwin looked and all he saw was water—a puddle. "Look again," Delaney said. Baldwin did so, and he saw oil on the water and the nearby houses reflected in the puddle. "It was a great revelation to me. I can't explain it. He taught me how to see, and how to trust what I saw. Painters have often taught writers how to see. And once you've had that experience, you see differently." But Delaney did more than teach him a clear vision, he taught him to question the meaning of what he saw. As Baldwin explained it, "the sunset one saw yesterday, the leaf that burned, or the rain that fell, have not really been seen unless one is prepared to see them every day." You had to experience consistently at a deep level. He discussed everything with Delaney as once he had done with Bill Miller. The artist shared all his experiences with the shy youth. Such conversations also helped convince the teenage preacher he no longer believed in his own sermons. His preaching, it seemed, had become a mere act. He wondered how long he could keep it up.

He and Emile Capouya also had lengthy discussions about religion. "I never heard him preach," Capouya recalled, "but in the Magpie office he gave renditions, played the tambourine, shuffled and then went into a 'trance.'" Making fun of his sermons in this way showed the change in him. Yet Capouya also remembered the guilt Baldwin felt when he sneaked into a moviehouse—"he thought he was bound for hell." He always liked to compare himself in such a situation to "Bette Davis in the last reel of 'Of Human Bondage.'" He also enjoyed doing imitations of Bette Davis long before it was a popular turn among New York show business people. "Frog Eyes" tended to identify with her.

Another school friend, Sol Stein, who was also to become a writer as well as a publisher and was to help to assemble Baldwin's first collection of essays, *Notes of a Native Son,* didn't remember him as being shy, just physically very small. As Sol Stein's family lived close to the school, he was impressed by how far Jimmy Baldwin had to travel each day. But De Witt Clinton had a well-deserved reputation, and Sol Stein remembers his experiences there better than his later years in college. Wilmer Stone used to read the young Magpie authors' work back to them as if it were the telephone directory, Sol

Stein said. The teacher's point was that "the language had to carry it and you couldn't fake it by dramatizing it. It was excruciatingly painful to hear him read out your stuff that way." Jimmy Baldwin, used to the dramatizing of the pulpit, suffered especially, though it was a good discipline for the elegant prose writer he was to become. Sol Stein sometimes invited him to his home. His young sister became very fond of Baldwin and looked forward to his visits. "Jimmy was pretty well past his hallelujah period then." Stein also met Jimmy's young brothers and sisters. "I learned Jimmy was the only illegitimate one of the nine. He talked to me about it and said his mother had never wanted to tell him who his real father was. If Jimmy ever did meet him, he didn't know he was his father. But even very early the difference between Jimmy and the others was obvious. With Jimmy there was a ferocious involvement with language. One of the oversights in what is written about him is the degree to which he transformed the way black speech is conveyed in fiction. It always used to be put in dialect and bad dialect at that. Even his early pieces all had an intellectual grasp of whatever he was writing about that was beyond the interests of the others in his family. They were obviously always very interested in Jimmy and looked up to him. His mother, Berdis, is a very impressive woman, so one could only assume that Jimmy's father was an extraordinary man in whatever he could hand out genetically. I could tell Jimmy was obsessed with his father by the way he raised it with me and wanted to talk about it.

"He had no reservations about talking about things that didn't usually get talked about in those days. I remember once he told me at school in his late teens he had got gonorrhea from a girl. He talked about it in the past tense. He might have been making it up to put down women, but I don't think so. I assumed from day one of knowing him that Jimmy's preferences were gay. I never had a sense from Jimmy as one did from other kids at that age that he was making up a biography for himself. What he said came across as accurate and was either skilled storytelling or was simply honest. Jimmy was obviously greatly influenced by the Bible, but he didn't get his precision from the Bible, which is evocative rather than precise. Jimmy seemed to make a great effort to be precise from the beginning. When he looked back at his sermonizing and speechifying, the actual conduct of services that is echoed in the oratory of Jesse Jackson today, it seemed imprecise and emotional. But writing isn't catharsis, it's orchestration. I think if you look at Jimmy's early writing when his writer's mind was first maturing, you have something that is very different from the Bible and what outsiders hear of the sermons in the fervent black churches. Jimmy was over a year older and I was always aware of that. The fact my family had once lived in Harlem perhaps helped Jimmy and me to understand each other better. He was marvelous with children. My sister used to say it was a pity he was gay. But then he had the attitude it was a pity some people he liked were not gay. But in our school days he used to tell me about teenage sexual experiences with girls. He did have a bad experience with a white radical City College girl. Some of them cap their sex lives by having a fling with a black. He felt she had used him and he had used her."

Baldwin had begun to carry on a double life, a life of deception— sinner during the week and saintly Young Minister on Sundays—and it was beginning to create a new tension in him that was hard to live with. Another crisis was looming ahead. Although he talked about most of his experiences with his close friends at school, there was one relationship he didn't talk about. It must have begun about the time he overheard the conversation definitely confirming he was illegitimate. Although remarks of his stepfather had made him suspect it and he had pestered his mother with questions about her past, this was the first time he was sure. It was when he mentioned it to Emile Capouya and burst into tears. One wonders if it put him in an I-don't-care mood, an I'll-get-back-at-the-world attitude, and that was why he embarked on such a potentially dangerous relationship. But all we know for sure is that soon after he turned sixteen, he met a Harlem racketeer, a man in his late thirties, who "fell in love with me." Baldwin wrote over forty years later, "I will be grateful to that man until the day I die," and, in fact, close to the end of his life he was planning a novel—a love story—based on this relationship. He even showed the man all his secret poetry, there was no one else he was that close to. He recalled in 1985, "Even now, I sometimes wonder what on earth his friends could have been thinking, confronted with stingy-brimmed, mustachioed, razor-toting Poppa and skinny, pop-eyed Me when he walked me (rarely) into various shady joints, I drinking ginger ale, he drinking brandy. I think I was supposed to be his nephew, some nonsense like that, though he was Spanish and Irish, with curly black hair. But I know that he was showing me off and wanted his friends to be happy for him." Some of the feeling in the relationship was conveyed in the similar affair between a youth and an older man in *Just Above My Head*. Baldwin called the youth Arthur, his own middle name. He described how much being so loved meant to little Arthur, another Frog Eyes, and how it boosted his self-confidence.

But during this affair, Jimmy Baldwin was still playing the role of saintly Young Minister on Sundays, and as Harlem was a close, inter-related community, inevitably there was gossip about him. Baldwin recalled that "though I loved him, too—in my way, a boy's way—I was mightily tormented." It was a "sinful" relationship and also one that made him face his homosexuality, but he was not yet ready to deal with that. Torn between the affair and the pulpit, he eventually gave up both. But the affair ended first. He had to end the gossip. He didn't want it to reach his family. But he found it increasingly difficult to prepare his sermons and deliver them with the right air of sincerity. He started canceling church engagements and preaching as rarely as possible. Some church members gossiped that their teenage star was "cooling off."

He talked it over with Emile Capouya. As Baldwin remembers it in *The Devil Finds Work*, he knew he could not remain a Young Minister, but he couldn't bring himself to leave, to explain to his brothers and sisters—and his mother. His stepfather was then almost past com-municating with, out of touch with reality and beginning his descent into madness. He sat at the living-room window, his silence occasionally broken by hallelujahs and old church or southern songs. Emile Capouya, according to Baldwin, took him to a Russian movie downtown at the Irving Place Theater to help him leave the church. Baldwin hadn't been to a film or a theater for a long time. In the film there was a tambourine, which Baldwin played in church, and it triggered a collapse. He began to weep, suddenly terrified, and Capouya led him out to the darkness of nearby Herald Square and challenged him. What he was doing, Capouya said, was hypocritical. He had no right to preach the Gospel if he no longer believed in it. Therefore on Sunday when he was due to spend all day at church, Capouya said he would buy two tickets for a Broadway matinee and wait for him on the steps of the public library on Forty-second Street at two P.M. If he didn't come, Capouya said according to Baldwin, he would never speak to him again.

After Baldwin's death Capouya couldn't remember making any such challenge and said he wouldn't have had the money for a Broadway play. "But kids are so crazy I could have challenged him even though it was a foul thing to do as he was already between a rock and a hard place. But kids do that sort of thing, I can't disavow that. But Jimmy had a very *constructive* memory. He liked to dramatize. It's quite possible I challenged him, but it wouldn't have been a Broadway play, just a cheap moviehouse, perhaps another Russian film. The war had started and the Russians were our allies and the Russian films downtown were very cheap."

Baldwin remembered Bill Miller's remark, *I've lost a lot of respect for you.* Perhaps in the last few months he had begun to lose respect for himself. But accepting Capouya's challenge meant there was only one other way to go—to commit himself "to the clear impossibility of becoming a writer, and attempting to save my family that way." He had a last conversation with his stepfather, "the one time in all our life together when we had really spoken to each other." They were walking to church. David Baldwin suddenly said, "You'd rather write than preach, wouldn't you?"

Jimmy Baldwin was astonished by the question. His stepfather knew what was in his mind. "Yes," he answered. That was all he said. He knew his stepfather's attitude—that to be a writer was an impossible ambition for a black youth in the world of the "white devils," that he'd only get himself hurt or worse contesting the white man's definitions. It was no use Jimmy pointing out that there were black writers who had survived successfully—Countee Cullen whom he knew, Langston Hughes who lived in Harlem, and just recently a new writer named Richard Wright whose novel, *Native Son,* had been a bestseller, the first book by a black writer to be selected by a major book club. He would write his novel about Harlem, about his family, about his stepfather, and become famous, too.

For his last sermon he chose as the text "Set thy house in order," addressing himself. He went to the church for the last time hoping for a reprieve, to get away without being noticed when he had to, but as young Brother Baldwin, he had to sit in the front row and the pastor didn't begin his sermon until about 1:15 P.M. To reach Forty-second Street by 2:00 P.M. he'd have to leave in the middle of the sermon. At 1:30 P.M. he got up and tiptoed down the aisle, watched by the whole congregation. The pastor's little son followed him out and said, "Daddy wants you back inside." Baldwin told the boy he had an appointment. Then the pastor himself came out and ordered him back inside. His tone angered Baldwin, who said, "I've already told you I have a date." And off he went downtown to meet Emile Capouya. We don't know if he ever tried to explain to the pastor why he would never be back, but years later he tried in his first play, *The Amen Corner,* when the rebellious son tells Sister Margaret, the pastor of the church and also his mother, "Mama, if a person don't feel it, he just don't feel it . . . I don't want to tell no more lies . . . If I stayed here, I'd end up worse than Daddy because I wouldn't be doing what I know I got to do."

So he left the church, though he knew that in some ways, "on the blindest, most visceral level," he would never leave. "Nothing that has happened to me since," he wrote in *The Fire Next Time,* "equals the power and the glory that I sometimes felt when, in the middle of a sermon, I knew that I was somehow, by some miracle, really carrying, as they said, 'the Word'—when the church and I were one." But it had been a long time since he had felt that way. Yet to the end of his life, nothing stirred his emotions quite like the church music he had grown up with. The sound of a tambourine could make his heart beat faster and he loved to sing the songs he had known as a young preacher. "I had made the break," he told me, "but there were some things I couldn't ever give up. They're in my blood, you know. I've lived with them all my life."

But having left the church at last, he couldn't remain at home. As an ex-preacher his position in that religious household would be impossible. It was the kind of situation that he was to find himself in throughout his life. When the pressures grew unbearable, he had to get away. But where could he go now, at eighteen, with no money? He couldn't move to another part of Harlem. "I was icily determined never to make peace with the ghetto." Downtown was mostly white and therefore the risks were much greater. Was he ready for that yet? "I would die and go to hell before I would let any white man spit on me, before I could accept my place in this Republic." He had graduated from De Witt Clinton, but months late after failing several courses that didn't interest him. His mind hadn't been on his schoolwork. So now he hung in limbo, not knowing precisely where he belonged or where he could escape to. He needed a job, he had to continue to provide his mother with money to help feed the family. Some of the other children were old enough now to have jobs after school. George, Wilmer and David were going round on a horse-and-wagon selling vegetables. They were talking of going in the army when they were old enough. World War II had brought plenty of opportunities for work. Jimmy would certainly have been drafted into the army except that as the eldest of nine children with an ailing father, he was exempted. He was free to find his own way—or as free as he was ever likely to be in the foreseeable future.

3

Baptism of Fire

EMILE CAPOUYA helped him to escape. After graduating, Capouya had obtained a job laying railroad track for the army in Belle Mead, New Jersey. He offered to recommend Jimmy Baldwin. Slightly built, only five feet six inches fully grown, Baldwin didn't seem to have the physique for such work, but he eagerly accepted Capouya's offer. The job paid nearly three times the $27.50 a week his stepfather earned at the factory and his stepfather took it badly—"his authority was being eroded." But with that pay, Jimmy could not only cover his own living expenses but also send a fair sum to his mother.

What Jimmy Baldwin wasn't prepared for was New Jersey's crude, segregated lifestyle. Until then, although he had after-school jobs in the predominantly white Greenwich Village, he had always lived in Harlem, an environment where blacks were in the majority. The occasions when racism had affected him directly, such as the incident involving the two policemen, were rare. His attitude was probably still well summed up by his reply when his mother had asked him if his teacher was colored or white. "A little bit colored and a little bit white," he had told her. His stepfather's dire warnings about "white devils" had seemed like sick talk in the safety of his home. But in New Jersey, only a short distance away across the Hudson River, the whole situation was suddenly reversed. He was completely vulnerable as the black outsider in a white community and he had no family home as a refuge. He was used to the greater freedom of New York City and found New Jersey's stricter segregation impossible to accept. He no doubt had this experience in mind when he was writing about the independent youth from the North who goes south with violent consequences in his play, *Blues for Mister Charlie.* Baldwin recalled in *A Rap On Race* how he had worked with people from Georgia, Alabama and Mississippi, the most racist of the southern states. "I talked the way I always talked, acted the way I always acted, and I just couldn't believe what happened—the kind of fury that erupted." When he caught out a white man from Georgia in a lie and called him a liar, the man's face turned purple. "That man wanted to kill me. If I had been alone I think he would have." Although Emile Capouya's presence protected him at first, his New Jersey experience was to become like a baptism of fire. "Fire" was his favorite metaphor for the effects of racism, but when he warned white Americans of the possible consequences in *The Fire Next Time,* he did so feeling that he had already been through the fire himself—in New Jersey. To the end of his life he spoke of that period with horror. "That whole year, that whole time, is something that I've never been able to write about," he told Margaret Mead, though he did mention it briefly in an essay on his stepfather.

Emile Capouya recalled, "A big warehouse had been built for military purposes on one hundred or so acres and it needed a lot of track to serve it. There were ten men in a gang laying track. Jimmy was slightly built but quite muscular. But he never learned how to use a pick or a shovel. When he walked he trailed the shovel behind him like a pup on a leash. It was very funny to see. I was six feet and I could carry a great deal of rail, but Jimmy was much smaller and it was harder for him. We lived in Rocky Hill at the house of a remarkable Irishman named Tom Martin. He was a great influence on us, a man of character much older than us—he was about thirty. He was interested in poetry and was a pretty good poet himself. He had five children, but he drank a lot and eventually died mainly through drink. It was a good environment for Jimmy and me, and I think he did his best to protect Jimmy. Jimmy and I slept in the same room. I was over half a foot taller and one night I got into my bed and I joked to him, 'Jimmy, I feel awful tired. Tuck me in like a mother.' He replied, 'So tuck you.' He was a terribly funny guy and a very clean person. I remember I once said, 'You hurt me to the quick,' and he replied, 'My quick will never be the same.' He always had a pleasant witticism.

"Jimmy was always much more social than I was. He was never homosexual in the period I knew him, at least to my knowledge. He wasn't decided about that sort of thing until later. When he was eighteen or nineteen, girls were all over him. A white girl came over to Rocky Hill to see him. White girls called up all the time to speak to him. I don't remember his writing anything in New Jersey. He was probably too tired. I think when he went to New Jersey, it was his first experience of open racial hostility, but I didn't share his experiences. He got out much more than I did. He told me about a dreadful time he had in Princeton, a town very southern in character, more courtly and more savage than the New York he was used to. It was close to Rocky Hill and something dreadful happened to him there and he reacted violently—after all these years I forget the details."

The incident Capouya referred to came as the climax of a long series of racial incidents. In the face of open hostility, especially when he was with a white woman, Jimmy Baldwin refused to back down. Shy he might be, but he certainly wasn't lacking in courage. "I had scarcely arrived before I had earned the enmity, which was extraordinarily ingenious, of all my superiors and nearly all my co-workers," Baldwin recalled. He went to a self-service restaurant for a hamburger and a coffee only to be told Negroes weren't served there. "Once I was told this, I determined to go there all the time. But now they were ready for me and, though some dreadful scenes were subsequently enacted in that restaurant, I never ate there." He faced the same treatment in bars, bowling alleys, diners and places to live. "I was always being forced to leave." He was a one-man civil rights movement twenty years before his time.

Burton Bendow, another friend from De Witt Clinton days, said, "It was a tough scene for Jimmy to deal with. A group of women working on the payroll called themselves the contingent from Atlanta. They were very southern white and were against blacks and probably put Jimmy in his place. That part of New Jersey was known as New Georgia so I'm sure Jimmy did suffer. But I'm also sure he never felt any of that in high school where most of his friends were white. It must have been a shock to face such open hostility."

Capouya recalled that eventually Baldwin was fired. "I'm not sure why. Maybe the Irish foreman observed him trailing his shovel. The foreman was a tough little Irishman with a crazed look and I think he probably saw Jimmy and told him on the spot, 'You're fired!' " Baldwin remembered it more dramatically. "I was fired once, and continued, with the aid of a friend from New York, to get back on the payroll; was fired again, and bounced back again. It took a while to fire me for the third time, but the third time took." His official explanation was that he was fired "for not conforming to their conception of a good American laborer—the ostensible reason was that I took too much time for lunch, which was true." This explanation made Capouya chuckle. "That was Jimmy making the best of it."

The out-of-work laborer also claimed to be "in love" and with a girlfriend of Capouya's, apparently. She was a twenty-four-year-old woman named Jessie, six years older than Baldwin, who had been married and divorced. She was keenly interested in politics and had become a Trotskyite. Baldwin claimed never to have felt the same way about anyone before. But Jessie decided that the difference in their ages was too much to his disadvantage. "If any one of us got hurt in this," she told him, "you would be the one to be hurt most. I'm not sure that I'm really in love with you." Her uncertain feelings were the only obstacle, Baldwin said, and he confessed to being "sick with loneliness when I'm without her" and "sick with love when I'm with her." He described her as a "wonderful kid" and pondered what he should do. She was the only girl he had ever met "whom I really respect intellectually." She had enormous green eyes and a long slender figure, but she wasn't "in the least pretty." Capouya knew nothing about this relationship until after Baldwin's death. "I remember Jimmy met her with me

37

because she came over to Belle Mead several times," Capouya said, "but I didn't know he began seeing her. He never mentioned it to me. I went off to sea later that year—1942—and when I came back I asked her if she had been sleeping with anyone in my absence and she mentioned one person. She said he was a poet. Jimmy wrote poetry, good poetry, but she didn't mention his name. You must remember there was a bohemian atmosphere among radicals in those days." Being in love, however, didn't help Jimmy Baldwin's writing. "For the most part junk," was the way he described what he had written in New Jersey and he wondered if he had dried up. He was becoming frightened, he said, that he might be "through at eighteen."

By then all the pressures on him, but mainly his racial experiences, had resulted in an explosion that really scared him. A white friend from New York took him to a movie and to have a few drinks in Trenton, the nearest big town. They went into a diner for a hamburger and met the familiar reception—no Negroes. They walked out, but it was the last straw for Jimmy Baldwin. A seething anger took over. The white passersby in the streets seemed to be pressing toward him, threatening him, wanting to crush him. He left his friend and pushed his way into a fashionable restaurant full of white faces. All of his fury was directed at a white waitress who barred his way. She told him the restaurant didn't serve Negroes. Her obvious fear of him merely intensified his rage. On a table was a mug half-full of water and he seized it and hurled it at her. She ducked and it shattered a mirror behind the bar. The noise brought Baldwin to his senses. "I realized what I had done, and where I was, and I was frightened." He ran into the street. The police soon arrived, but his friend, who had waited outside, directed them the wrong way. Baldwin felt as if he had contracted a dread disease known to all blacks—a rage in the blood, a fever of hatred you could learn to live with or surrender to and be destroyed by. "This fever has recurred in me, and does, and will until the day I die." He realized his life was in danger "and not from anything other people might do but from the hatred I carried in my own heart."

In the midst of these experiences he had kept away from Harlem. The last time he had been home, his stepfather was missing. Searching for him in the streets, he found the old man sitting on a wall in a daze not knowing where he was. Even in his fear of this man he had been in awe of him, admiring his handsome, dignified appearance, which reminded him of an African chief, and also his great pride in the face of so many difficulties. He was upset to see him so broken, out of his mind. So he kept away from home, just sending money back, until he received an urgent message from his mother to return at once. His stepfather had refused to eat, claiming his family was trying to poison him, and he had had to be committed to Central Islip Hospital, a state mental institution on Long Island. The doctors discovered he had tuberculosis, and the disease of his mind was allowing the disease of his body to destroy him. He was fed intravenously, but it was clear there was no hope for him.

Baldwin packed his bags and took the next train back to New York. He was the head of the family now, and the responsibility scared him. What made the situation seem even worse was that he discovered his mother was pregnant again. It distressed and angered him, he said, because it meant more expense at a time when his stepfather was dying and his own personal finances "had come to a desperate pass." He got a job in a meat-packing factory at twenty-nine dollars a week and lived at home. It became obvious, he said, that "barring a legacy, I could do nothing for the family, and as long as I tried to help the family, I could do nothing for myself." A tense routine developed. He went to work, he came home, and then he went out again and didn't return until very late. Nothing seemed quite real as if their world was suspended waiting for his stepfather to die and the new baby to be born. The baby seemed reluctant to come into the world. "I don't believe that a single one of us arrived in the world, or has since arrived anywhere else, on time." It was also a period of great unrest in Harlem, partly as a result of the war and the segregation that black soldiers and black factory workers had experienced. The fever that Baldwin had contracted had reached plague proportions in the black ghetto. Policemen were at every corner, on foot or on horseback. It was in this tense, explosive atmosphere that Jimmy and his stepfather's older sister went to see him in the Long Island hospital, a long ride by train and bus.

"I had told my mother that I did not want to see him because I hated him," Baldwin recalled. "But this was not true. It was only that I *had* hated him and I wanted to hold on to this hatred. I did not want to look on him as a ruin." It was a hot, late July day, and Jimmy and his aunt argued over his smoking cigarettes to release some of the tension. David Baldwin lay in the hospital "all shriveled and still, like a little black monkey." There was a whistling sound in his throat; he couldn't speak. "He was not really in that room with us, he had at last really embarked on his journey."

In the morning came a telegram announcing he was dead, and a few hours later his last child—another daughter—was born. It was left to Jimmy to choose a name for her—Paula Maria. He then had to worry about how to pay for the funeral. He said later that he came as close to a nervous breakdown as he would ever come. He wandered about the city hardly knowing where he was, trying to work out how to bury a body and feed a family on his pay. By contacting other relatives through innumerable phone calls, he eventually raised enough to cover the funeral expenses.

The day of the funeral was Jimmy's nineteenth birthday. He spent most of the early part of the day at the downtown apartment of a girlfriend—Jessie?—celebrating his birthday, drinking whiskey. His girlfriend had planned to take him out to a big dinner and a nightclub, and Jimmy decided he would join her as soon as the funeral service was over. She ironed a black shirt for him, and dressed in that and the darkest pants and jacket he had, he returned uptown feeling "slightly drunk." It seemed a very long service to him. The minister depicted his stepfather as a thoughtful, patient, forbearing person—"a man whom none of us had ever seen," Baldwin commented. But it was "better not to judge the man who had gone down under an impossible burden," he decided, probably because he had begun to feel some of that burden himself. He tried to hide the whiskey smell on his breath with chewing gum and think of only pleasant memories, but "I remembered our fights, fights which had been of the worst possible kind because my technique had been silence." The children went up to view the open casket. He had thought they were too young, but had been overruled, "and there they were, bewildered and frightened and very small." He hadn't wanted to go up himself. His stepfather's face didn't look like him at all. Yet his life filled the room, and further up the avenue outside was his newborn daughter, Paula Maria—"life and death so close together, and love and hatred . . ."

Baldwin went back downtown to celebrate his birthday and try to forget. That night a black soldier got into a fight with a white policeman in the lobby of Harlem's Hotel Braddock and was shot. A rumor spread through the ghetto that the soldier was dead and he had been killed protecting a black woman. It was like tossing a lighted match into a can of gasoline, Baldwin said. While the body of David Baldwin lay in the mortician's chapel, a mob gathered in front of the Hotel Braddock, and Harlem erupted. East and west along 125th Street and for the whole length of Lenox, Seventh, and Eighth avenues through Harlem, crowds smashed open bars, stores, pawnshops and restaurants. The next morning David Baldwin was driven to the graveyard along streets littered with broken glass. Jimmy Baldwin stared out at the aftermath of the violent riot and remembered his stepfather's forecast of an impending apocalypse. "He had lived and died in an intolerable bitterness of spirit and it frightened me, as we drove him to the graveyard through those unquiet, ruined streets, to see how powerful and overflowing this bitterness could be and to realize that this bitterness now was mine." His experiences in New Jersey, he knew then, had made him "aware of the meaning of all my father's bitter warnings." He was afraid that the bitterness which had helped to kill his stepfather could also kill him. Could he find a stronger antidote to the poison than his stepfather had found? "That bleakly memorable morning I hated the unbelievable streets and the Negroes and whites who had, equally, made them that way. But I knew that it was folly, as my father would have said, this bitterness was folly. It was necessary to hold on to the things that mattered. The dead man mattered, the new life mattered; blackness and whiteness did not matter; to believe that they did was to acquiesce in one's own destruction. Hatred, which could destroy so much, never failed to destroy the man who hated."

As Jimmy Baldwin followed his stepfather's casket through the ruined streets he had grown up in, he had a moment of what he would later call "revelation." You had to accept, "totally without rancor," life as it was and human beings as they were, which meant injustice was a commonplace. But at the same time you also had to accept that "one must never, in one's own life, accept these injustices as commonplace but must fight them with all one's strength." It meant keeping your heart free of hatred and despair and not succumbing to the fever, the rage in the blood that he had experienced in New Jersey and that the destruction in Harlem now reflected. How well you achieved that discipline depended on the course of your life in the future. This was a philosophy that Baldwin would believe in and try to live by until he died.

He went back to work, but fainted the first day and was fired. He got a similar job a few days later, but "the knowledge that I had to spend so many hours a day there filled me with a choking desire to scream." He fled from one job after another, often without waiting to be paid what he was owed. Nor could he stay home for long. He soon grew restless in a moviehouse, he couldn't sleep. He spent his nights roaming the Village cafeterias and bars and borrowed where he could and "went slightly mad." He was obsessed by a need to fill all his time with crowds, lights, laughter, and never, never be alone. Finally a friend gave him a good "tongue-lashing" about his crazy behavior and it woke him up. He got a "pretty awful" job as an elevator attendant in a department store. It was dull, but at least "you do learn a lot about people." He also began to write again—more poetry than prose. He was reading Shakespeare, Milton, Chaucer and T.S. Eliot, whose "Love Song of J. Alfred Prufrock" seemed to him "poetry as she is seldom written." His own poems that included "Three AM," "On Hearing Handel's Messiah" and "Nat'l Anthem: 1943" seemed strongly influenced by what he was reading. Presumably the affair with Jessie was over because he told a friend, "I was not in love with anyone then—thank God." He said he was just very casually playing the field and keeping his eyes open. He felt he had learned so much about living through his mistakes and concluded that all of us are so important "and so tragically unimportant." He had also been visiting museums and decided he liked Degas and Rembrandt and hoped to enroll in an acting school. He might even get to play Othello—"Wouldn't *that* be a break for Shakespeare?"

He was slowly moving toward a big decision—that he had to move out of his home for a second and last time, and that his survival depended on becoming a writer—he was sure of that now. He told the Paris Review many years later that he realized when his stepfather died "I had to make a jump—a leap." Beauford Delaney, who had helped him with the funeral expenses, encouraged him to move to the Village. That was where he should "leap" to. It certainly appeared a more congenial setting for a writer. Many would-be artists from all over the country flocked there. It was seemingly the most tolerant, easygoing area in New York City. In the summer, painters displayed their pictures along Sixth Avenue and the side streets, musicians played their guitars in Washington Square Park, there were all-night coffee shops along Macdougal and Bleecker streets where you could play chess twenty-four hours a day, and in favorite bars like the Riviera, the White Horse, the Cedar Tavern and the San Remo artists of all kinds drank, argued, looked for lovers and made business contacts. The presence of Beauford Delaney was a big attraction for Jimmy Baldwin. Even when working long hours in New Jersey, he had come over to see his artist friend and go to a concert with him. "It helped to keep me sane," he said. After a series of dull jobs, he settled for a better paying one as a waiter in a West Indian restaurant known as the Calypso on Macdougal Street. The owner was a hearty Trinidadian woman named Connie Williams whose strong personality and common sense appealed to him, and they became friends. He rented a small room in the Village and late at night, after the Calypso closed and he had made a round of his favorite bars, he settled down to try to write.

He struggled over another version of his family's story—the title was *Crying Holy* and then *In My Father's House*—but he kept tearing up pages and starting again. His feelings about his stepfather prevented him from portraying him clearly. He didn't want to write out of hatred, but what were his *true* feelings for the man? He also had his racial and sexual experiences to deal with. How could he dramatize his attitude toward the white world and toward homosexuality? His head seemed to contain a chaos of experience and emotion that resisted any clear pattern, yet art, he knew, depended on selection. He worked hard to improve his technique. When he read now, it was to study how other writers achieved their effects. The new black writer, Richard Wright, particularly interested him. Wright described a black scene convincingly without slavishly reproducing the way people talked, which had made the dialogue of some of the older black writers dated and almost unreadable. He concluded that in dialogue that was really effective "you try and make people say what they would say if they could and then you sort of dress it up to look like speech." He was also trying to achieve a prose style that was elegant, had his own rhythm, but was also precise, using as simple words as possible so that anyone might understand him. It was an ambitious aim and, however late he stayed up, success still eluded him. His busy social life also got in the way. Sometimes he was too tired to write.

Emile Capouya had been fired from the railroad job soon after Baldwin, and they had a reunion in a Village bar. It was dimly lit, like most Village bars, and over a drink Jimmy Baldwin confided that he had been uncertain about his sexual identity, as Capouya knew, but he was uncertain no longer. He had decided quite definitely he was a homosexual. Capouya was surprised. "I thought he was a man who had flirted with homosexuality, but I had it the wrong way round. He was not in horror of women, though, like many homosexuals. I don't know what or who influenced him. I don't know whether it was his natural bent or the influence of the culture he found himself in. His milieu in Harlem included a lot of dancing and music and art, but for all that, his literary turn was perhaps looked on as sinful because it was worldly and because the whole atmosphere of Harlem was fairly male-oriented. Writing may have been considered effeminate even by his family."

When Baldwin told his mother he intended to be a writer, Mrs. Baldwin was surprised and concerned for him as she had been when he went to work in New Jersey. She no doubt would have preferred that he stay safely at home with the rest of the family in Harlem. But perhaps she already sensed that her eldest son was to have an extraordinary life, one that was eventually to transform her own and take her out of Harlem, too.

Baldwin later credited his experiences with white women and long talks with Beauford Delaney for "bringing me to my senses and clearing my head." In his essay "Here Be Dragons," published in 1985, he recalled being sexually involved with two white women in the Village. Apart from sex—"sometimes it was great, sometimes it was just moaning and groaning"—he wasn't sure what they wanted from him. Did they wish to "civilize" a black boy or humiliate their parents? He grew tired of "speculations concerning the size of [my] organ: speculations sometimes accompanied by an attempt at the laying-on of hands." He was being treated, he felt, merely as black, they didn't really see *him*.

About this time he had a strange encounter with the FBI in Woodstock in upstate New York, where he was living in a cabin in the woods in an artists' colony, writing and earning a little through a Village friend as an artists' model. He was eating in a diner when two FBI agents walked him out and stood him against a wall. He learned eventually they were looking for a youth named Teddy who had deserted from the Marines. They showed Baldwin photographs, threatened him and searched his cabin. He had met Teddy at a Village party, but had no idea where he was. Eventually the FBI agents left Baldwin alone, but he was "terribly frightened." Also angry.

By then he had discovered the Village's appearance of tolerance could be deceptive. He was one of the few blacks living in the Village and he found himself thrown out of some bars, involved in shouting matches and sometimes even fights with drunken whites, and pursued by other whites who came out of the closet after dark. "I was far too terrified to be able to accept their propositions, which could only result, it seemed to me, in making myself a candidate for gang rape." He had "a very brief, intense affair" with a man who was on drugs and who died soon after. Another man told him later, "My God, Jimmy, you were moving so fast in those years, you never stopped to talk to me." Baldwin replied, "That's right, baby, I didn't stop because I didn't want you to think that I was trying to seduce you." The other said, "Man, why didn't you?" Baldwin was eager, vulnerable, lonely and still terribly shy. "I was afraid that I already seemed and sounded too much like a woman," he recalled, but he "certainly needed all the friends I could get." He went through a phase of trying to prove he wasn't a "nigger"—straightening his hair, modulating his voice even more, developing elegant table manners. None of it helped him to avoid the local discrimination. However much

45

he tried to please, he was still a "nigger." This realization drove him to the opposite extreme—he would give up on trying to come to terms with the square, established white world of the Village.

The gay world—then called "queer"—was mainly underground. The few openly gay bars were in parts of the Village down by the river that were considered too lonely, dark and potentially dangerous for most people to venture there. Baldwin found himself a star there, exotic, simply because he was usually the only black. The passes and propositions were apparently flattering to "Frog Eyes," and for a time the freedom of brief relationships with no responsibilities went to his head, and in looking back at that time he referred to it as his "season in hell." He realized he "had endured far too much debasement willingly to debase myself." An Italian in his mid-twenties helped him to draw back from this wild nightlife. His new friend, on whom he partly based Vivaldo in *Another Country,* threatened to kill anyone who touched Baldwin, and his situation slowly "stabilized itself."

An introduction to another new friend, who was to be a great influence on his literary life, also helped to boost his morale. He had heard that Richard Wright was living in Brooklyn, and he wangled an invitation to his house through a woman friend named Esther. Baldwin then was twenty, Wright thirty-six. Wright had been one of his idols since high school, the greatest black writer in the world for him then. Langston Hughes and his old literary adviser, Countee Cullen, were the only other black writers whose work he knew well, but they didn't interest him much until Wright showed him how to read them with more understanding. Wright also guided him about which earlier black writers to study, notably Jean Toomer. The black middle-class, which produced many of the writers, was essentially an abstraction to him, as remote as the well-off on Sugar Hill in Harlem, but Wright's work touched his own life, the tenements, the rats, the street people, the churches. "I found expressed, for the first time in my life, the sorrow, the rage and the murderous bitterness which was eating up my life and the lives of those around me. His work was an immense liberation and revelation for me."

This was what Jimmy Baldwin wanted to tell Richard Wright when he went to Brooklyn to meet him. He expected to get on well with him. Wright had been born in Mississippi with no more advantages than Baldwin, a rural working-class black southerner who had become a writer through sheer talent and determination. Wright used to recall that his family began with his grandparents born in slavery; his own birth was never officially recorded. Baldwin could identify with that. He went to see him on a very cold winter's day—"I was broke, naturally, shabby, hungry and scared." Wright was waiting for him in a long living room, a round man with a light southern accent and a boyish, diffident grin, not at all the heroic figure Baldwin had imagined. "Hey, boy!" Wright said in a friendly tone. He introduced Baldwin to his wife, Ellen, and then the two sat together over a bottle of bourbon. Baldwin hadn't then started his drinking career seriously and was afraid the liquor on his empty stomach might cause him to throw up. At least it relaxed him enough to respond when Wright kindly inquired about his writing. He told Wright about the novel he was working on, "madly improvising, one jump ahead of the bourbon, on all the themes which cluttered up my mind." Wright immediately offered to read what Baldwin had written. This was what Jimmy Baldwin had come for—to see if Wright would take him seriously as a writer. He rushed back to his little room in the Village, locked the door, ignored the knocking of friends and worked through the night trying to expand what he had done into the sixty or seventy pages he had claimed to have completed. Then next day, on the way to work at the Calypso, he mailed it in a bulky package to Wright.

The following few days dragged. What would he do if Richard Wright said it was a mess and showed no talent whatever? Would he give up and try to be a jazz musician or a painter, two earlier ambitions? Wright, generous as always with young writers, replied quickly and "very kindly and favorably," and offered to help Baldwin to get a Eugene F. Saxton Fellowship, which was administered by the publishing company of Harper & Brothers. One received a $500 grant and also Harper would publish one's novel if they accepted it after it was finished. Another short anxious wait was followed by good news— Baldwin had been awarded a fellowship, the first of several grants that helped to sustain him until he could live off his writing. Richard Wright had used his influence with Edward Aswell, his editor at Harper, who was one of the directors of the Eugene F. Saxton Foundation. On November 21, 1945, Aswell informed Wright the decision over young Baldwin was a unanimous one. He added that he was sure Wright would have been touched by Baldwin's reaction to the good news. "He was so overcome with joy that he could hardly speak. He came to my office the next day to get his check and I took an instant liking to him. It seems to me that the job he is doing is an important one and that he has the requisite integrity to carry it out."

It was hard to tell who was more pleased, Baldwin or Wright. Baldwin remembered that Wright "was very proud of me then, and I was puffed up with pleasure that he was proud, and was determined to make him prouder still." After sharing the money with his mother, Baldwin promptly settled down to finish *In My Father's House.* Harper's were hoping they had found another Richard Wright and kept in touch with Baldwin as he struggled with the novel. When Harper's president, Frank S. MacGregor, invited him to dinner, he asked Jimmy Baldwin to suggest a restaurant. Baldwin had been having trouble at the San Remo, an Italian bar and restaurant on the corner of Macdougal and Bleecker streets that he passed on the way to work. Every time he tried to stop there for a drink he was asked to leave. Shades of New Jersey! So he suggested to Harper's president they dine there. Baldwin entered prepared for trouble, but after one look at his imposing white companion, the management seated and served them, and Baldwin was never bothered again. When a group insulted him on the street, he took refuge in the San Remo, the owners turned the lights out, and they all sat in the back room until the group outside dispersed. "They had fought me very hard to prevent this moment, but perhaps we were all much relieved to have got beyond the obscenity of color." Now they accepted him, they introduced him to their families, and showed no interest "in whatever my sexual proclivities chanced to be."

But work on the novel was not going well. He still hadn't solved the problem of portraying his stepfather—was it to be done with hatred or love? The story was told through several characters and seemed to get lost in detail. But he *had* to finish it and get it published. He would present Richard Wright with the first copy. Perhaps he might even dedicate it to him. Baldwin labored night after night straining to bring some order to the chaos of characters and situations and conflicting viewpoints. It was then that he learned that in writing, as he was often to say later when struggling over a book, the will is not enough. He *couldn't* finish the novel satisfactorily however much he willed it. He talked about it to other would-be writers in the bars, he listened to too much advice, it merely confused him more. He fell back on trying to imitate Richard Wright—if they wanted another Wright, he'd give them one!—but that didn't work either. "Instinctively I knew that wasn't the direction to go in. Richard and I were two very different people, two very different writers. I knew I had to find myself as a writer even if it cost me this book. I became paralyzed. I couldn't go on with it. I felt it was irreparably ruined—and I with it." He showed what he had to Harper's and his worst fears were confirmed—they turned it down. He then forced himself to submit it to another publisher, Doubleday, and he told a friend, "The prospects are reasonably bright," but it was rejected there, too. All his dreams came crashing down, "a kind of desolate demoralization" overcame him and he began to drink heavily.

He couldn't face Richard Wright. He was deeply ashamed of his failure and was sure Wright would be ashamed of him, too. What was supposed to be his triumph had turned into his worst defeat. He went into hiding, running from what he saw as his disgrace. It is hard to exaggerate the effect of this rejection on Baldwin. It must be put in the same class as David Baldwin's rejection of him as "ugly." Working long hours, forever short of money, a continual target as a black or as a "faggot," about all he had to keep him going was his pride, and this humiliation was a tremendous blow to it. Perhaps he wasn't destined to make it as a writer, he reflected desperately. Perhaps his future lay with the drunks and junkies and panhandlers on Lenox Avenue. If he could have talked it over with Richard Wright he would have found help because Wright had gone through similar problems himself in completing his own first novel. But pride wouldn't let Baldwin get in touch with him. They were too different, their ages were too far apart and Wright was a success and he was a failure.

When at last he did come out of hiding, he didn't return to writing for a long time. Burton Bendow, his friend from De Witt Clinton days, met him for lunch, but Jimmy didn't discuss his problems. "We dined at Frank's Restaurant on 125th Street, a Victorian mahogany-paneled place with ancient Harlem waiters, a good menu and reasonable prices," Bendow recalled. "We had reached the coffee stage following our usual London broil. Jimmy told the waiter he'd take his coffee black, I said I'd take mine white. Jimmy laughed. 'Chauvinistic, aren't you?' he said. I was at Columbia University then and I think he was working as a waiter in the Village. Successful, cultivated Negroes were rarer then than now and most of his friends were white. He had friends and family in Harlem, of course, ties to earlier days. He associated with the world of the white Village bohemians and emotionally with other blacks."

Gradually he slipped back into his Village social rounds again. He dreaded anyone in the Village bars asking about his novel, but he learned to shrug off inquiries. Beauford Delaney and Connie Williams at the Calypso were a big help in boosting his morale, so were the jazz musicians he knew who called him "the Kid." Their example was "an enormous protection" in this difficult, dangerous time. He was surrounded by examples of would-be writers and even once-famous writers who had given up. There was a well-known poet of the twenties and thirties who went around the bars cadging drinks, another literary "relic" was lost on opium, a young writer Baldwin used to drink with suddenly committed suicide. The Village for someone in his position was "an alabaster maze perched above a boiling sea. To lose oneself in the maze was to fall into the sea." The jazz musicians helped to keep him away from dope. Occasionally he smoked marijuana with Beauford and his friends, but he found he couldn't write if he was "high." When he tried, his writing seemed "the greatest pages the world had ever seen," but in the morning he had to tear them all up. Above all he learned from Beauford and Connie and the musicians that they "expected me to accept and respect the value placed upon me." Beauford Delaney became his model, "the first walking, living proof, for me, that a black man could be an artist." Baldwin said Beauford was his master and he was his pupil. "He became, for me, an example of courage and integrity, humility and passion. An absolute integrity: I saw him shaken many times and I lived to see him broken, but I never saw him bow."

He slowly recovered from his failure—the latest crisis—enough to start thinking about writing again. His obstinacy helped. He wasn't going to roll over and give in! What would his family do? He'd start again with less ambitious pieces—short stories, essays, even journalism for the weeklies—before he attempted another novel. He'd learn his craft more thoroughly before risking another humiliation. "My pride was massive in those days," he once told me. "It had to be to survive." In 1985 when Baldwin reminisced about his start as a professional writer in the introduction to *The Price of the Ticket,* he recalled having applied for jobs at two black newspapers in New York "and had simply been laughed out of the office: I was a shoeshine boy who had never been to college. I don't blame these people, God knows that I was an unlikely cub reporter: yet, I still remember how deeply I was hurt." He fared better at the liberal New York paper, *PM,* that had token blacks on its staff, and he landed a job as a messenger. He found his career there "very nearly as devastating" in a different way as his experiences in New Jersey. "If the black newspapers had considered me absolutely beyond redemption, *PM* determined to save me: I cannot tell which attitude caused me the more bitter anguish." He felt "patronized and condescended to" as if he had no identity of his own.

Baldwin didn't recall at the end of his life in *The Price of the Ticket* how he found his way to the first publishers of his work—Randall Jarrell of The Nation, Sol Levitas of The New Leader, Elliott Cohen and Robert Warshow of Commentary, and Philip Rahv of Partisan Review. "These men are all dead now and they were all very important to my life. It is not too much to say that they helped to save my life." Baldwin told me in 1961 on the publication of *Nobody Knows My Name,* which put together many of the essays he had written for these publications, that he deliberately hung out in Village bars frequented by journalists and editors in the hope of making useful contacts, and he said he was quite brazen after a few drinks about approaching them. His idea was to write about his main experiences—Harlem or the Village; he didn't think he could face writing about New Jersey even then. Some young writers made a few dollars reviewing books. Perhaps he could do that. Now World War II had ended, restrictions were easing, providing new opportunities. He also met editors through socialist connections. One of his great Village friends, a young black about his own age named Eugene Worth, was a member of the Young People's Socialist League and persuaded Jimmy Baldwin to join. With his usual enthusiasm, Jimmy soon "outdistanced" his friend by becoming a Trotskyite, an anti-Stalinist when the U.S. and Stalin's Russia were still allies. "My life on the Left is of absolutely no interest," summed up Baldwin in *The Price of the Ticket.* "It did not last long. It was useful in that I learned that it may be impossible to indoctrinate me; also revolutionaries tend to be sentimental and I hope that I am not." This attitude led to many heated arguments with his friend Eugene, but it was during this period that he met the editors who were to help him launch his career.

His first professional work to be published was a review of Maxim Gorki's *Best Short Stories* headed "Maxim Gorki as Artist" in The Nation of April 12, 1947. Probably the choice of the book came from identifying him with the Young People's Socialist League and its interest in everything Russian. But Jimmy Baldwin was already familiar with some of the Russian literary classics. Back in the days when he used to read a book while holding the latest baby, he had read Dostoevsky's *Crime and Punishment* with such intensity his stepfather had remarked on it as if it proved he was "strange," and he knew Tolstoy's *Anna Karenina* so well he could quote passages. If he wasn't as familiar with Maxim Gorki's writing, no reader would have known it from the self-confident review he wrote for his début and that The Nation called "precociously talented" and led eventually to his becoming a member of The Nation's editorial board. He began by dismissing the translation as "most uneven" and summing up Gorki as "incomplete" as an artist with a narrow range. His "failure" was often that he didn't speak as his characters, taking the reader inside them, but spoke *for* them, more reporter and judge than artist and prophet. And in Gorki's· failure, Baldwin found "the key to the even more dismal failure of present-day realistic novelists." Summed up the fledgling reviewer: "If literature is not to drop completely to the intellectual and moral level of the daily papers, we must recognize the need for further and honest exploration of those provinces, the human heart and mind, which have operated, historically and now, as the no-man's land between us and our salvation." The last sentence has a rhetorical ring worthy of his preaching days, but it was a start and he was in good company—the review printed above his was of a book about the press by A. J. Liebling, a star of The New Yorker.

His début was noticed and soon he was also reviewing books regularly for The New Leader. Baldwin in *The Price of the Ticket* pays a special tribute to Samuel "Sol" Levitas, the editor of The New Leader, and his Woman Friday, Mary Greene. "It was a very great apprenticeship," he commented. Sol Levitas disciplined him as a writer, making him produce a certain number of words to a deadline. Baldwin took it as a vote of confidence in him and "I swore that I would give him my very best shot." Sol Levitas, whom he called "the Old Man," even to his face, paid him ten to twenty dollars a review, and Mary Greene "would sometimes coerce him into giving me a bonus." He was generally given any books that were remotely to do with racism, but he was by no means restricted to that subject because he was black. In the September 27, 1947, issue, for example, he reviewed a novel about schizophrenia, *The Sling and the Arrow,* by Stuart Engatrand. "Here is no illumination, no pity, no *terror,*" he wrote. "One closes this neat and empty volume untouched, indifferent." The review is interesting today mainly for the glimpses it provides of the reviewer. "Here is a dilemma known to all of us," he remarked in listing a character's problems— terrible guilt, the compulsion to be accepted, helplessness in the face of the war within him. Baldwin then added: "The contemporary sexual attitudes constitute a rock against which many of us founder all our lives long: no one escapes entirely the prevailing psychology of the times. Perhaps the failure of *The Sling and the Arrow* can partially be traced to its implicit acceptance of the popular attitude." Baldwin's best-known review, however, appeared in the April 10, 1948, issue, and he thought well enough of it to include it in his collected essays, the only one of his early book reviews he did reprint. The book reviewed was

Ross Lockridge's huge 1,066–page novel, *Raintree County,* about the American Dream—and Down South. Baldwin dismissed it as being "as amorphous as cotton candy under the drumming flow of words" with a superficial affirmation about America. Lockridge's later suicide led Baldwin to write a postscript suggesting the novelist's death "admits an uncertainty and a desperation the entire country would conspire to deny." But what Americans needed was less dreaming and more critical self-appraisal. A more mature Baldwin was beginning to make himself heard.

William Phillips, the editor of Partisan Review, recalled meeting him about the same time. "He was very articulate and he talked quite openly except for one subject—the anger inside him about being black. It took him a while to talk about being black in white society. There was some of that burning inside him. We had a number of conversations in which it came out. At that time he thought of himself as a writer, not a black writer, or rather that was what he wanted to be."

Raymond B. Rosenthal, a literary critic, editor and translator, re-membered having a drink at the San Remo and being introduced to Jimmy Baldwin. "The surprising thing to me was that he immediately confessed all his troubles. He said he was a young writer, black and homosexual, and had all these problems and couldn't get published. I found it strange and rather embarrassing. I was working as an editor at Commentary at the time so I told him, 'Come up to Commentary and I'll get you some work.' We gave him an assignment to do a piece about Harlem." But Rosenthal then discovered "the amazing thing was that although he said he couldn't get published, he had already been pub-lished in The Nation and, I think, The New Leader."

The Harlem piece for Commentary gave the young author a lot of trouble both in organizing it—deciding what to write about in the large, sprawling, complex ghetto, whose way of life wasn't familiar to most of Commentary's readers—and in selecting what to use of his own experience. He went through several drafts with the help of the editor, Robert Warshow, over a period of six months. It said a lot for Bald-win's satisfaction with the final version that although he was exhausted from so much rewriting he had high praise for Warshow. "He made me feel like a real writer in the end. He kept turning it back to me saying I had avoided something or left something out and he was right. He kept pushing me and I literally sweated it out. Anti-Semitism in Harlem was particularly difficult for me to deal with. Although I'd grown up with Jewish boys in high school, I hadn't consciously explored anti-Semitism. It was too delicate. And Robert Warshow forced me to deal with it. He was a marvelous editor. He taught me a lot at the right time. I learned you had to force from your experience the last drop, sweet or bitter, it could possibly give." Baldwin was to write for many other editors, but few he respected as much or who pushed him quite as hard as Warshow.

"The Harlem Ghetto," which appeared in the February 1948 issue of *Commentary*, was widely read and made its author enemies as well as admirers. Americans, both white and black, were not used to such frankness about the racial scene. Some of Baldwin's comments were never forgiven. Twenty years later George S. Schuyler, a black novelist and journalist, still remembered bitterly what Baldwin had written about him. Schuyler's "Olympian serenity infuriates me," Baldwin had observed, adding that he reflected "with great accuracy the state of mind and the ambitions of the professional, well-to-do Negro who has managed to find a place to stand." Baldwin wrote as if he represented the put-down poor of the Hollow and Schuyler was one of the rich representatives of Sugar Hill. He was equally forthright about the black press. The *Amsterdam Star-News* was probably the bestselling black paper—and also the worst in Baldwin's eyes. He couldn't help observing, he wrote, "Some Negro leaders and politicians are far more concerned with their careers than with the welfare of Negroes." He wrote the way blacks usually only talked among themselves. As for anti-Semitism, "just as a society must have a scapegoat, so hatred must have a symbol. Georgia has the Negro and Harlem has the Jew."

Raymond Rosenthal, who had introduced Baldwin to *Commentary*, was pleased that his judgment had been upheld by the Harlem essay. "It was a fantastic piece, a masterpiece, and immediately he became everybody's darling in that circle." Continually short of money, "Jimmy borrowed money from everyone," Rosenthal remembered, "but had a reputation for not giving it back. He borrowed fifty dollars from me. I said after a time that my wife was going in a hospital and so I would need the money back. I lived on Thirteenth Street then. The bell rang one day and Jimmy came up the stairs to my apartment, and he had the fifty dollars in notes crumpled into a knot, and he dropped it into my hand like a turd. That was the last time I saw him for years."

One wonders how Richard Wright would have reacted to the Harlem essay. Would its cutting tone have surprised him coming from the shy young writer who had come to see him not too long ago? Would he perhaps have had the first intimation of what he might expect if Jimmy Baldwin ever got around to writing about him? But Richard Wright had already left for France in 1946 and what was to be a final fourteen-year exile ending in his death. Baldwin even managed to see him before he departed. Wright had moved from Brooklyn to an apartment in the Village on Charles Street. Baldwin went there to say goodbye, but still found it hard to face him because this man had witnessed his failure, his humiliation. He remembered it as "a strange meeting, melancholy in the way a theater is melancholy when the run of the play is ended and the cast and crew are about to be dispersed." Wright was jaunty, but "Richard and I seemed really to be at the end of *our* rope," and then Baldwin added, showing he still hadn't fully accepted it, that Wright "had done what he could for me, and it had not worked out, and now he was going away." From Baldwin's attitude it seemed obvious that Wright was no longer an idol and that they would have to clash one day so that Baldwin could get over feeling embarrassed before this man who had witnessed his, as Baldwin saw it, humiliation. Richard Wright in his very different way had become another stepfather figure from whom Jimmy Baldwin apparently felt he had to free himself.

But would he and Wright ever meet again? "It seemed to me that he was sailing into the most splendid of futures, for he was going, of all places! to France, and he had been invited there by the French government." Wright was following in the footsteps of so many other American writers such as Hemingway, Scott Fitzgerald and Henry James. Jimmy Baldwin felt lonely when Wright finally left, as if he were being left behind to struggle alone against failure. But he was no longer completely unknown. The book reviews had made him talked about in the New York literary world. He met Dwight MacDonald, whom he admired for his magazine Politics and his independent, feisty opinions. MacDonald looked at him with wonder and pronounced him "very smart." One suspects Baldwin would have liked Richard Wright to be there to hear that. He had such an inferiority complex where Wright was concerned, though he tried to talk himself out of it. They were so different they could never be real friends. Their minds were different, they had little in common as writers. And what would he do if he was handed a book by Wright to review? Was *Native Son* really as good as it seemed when he first read it? Hadn't he been overimpressed because he was young and it was the first real novel about black life he could identify with?

Another artist to be influential in Baldwin's life was a young actor who became famous overnight when he starred in Tennessee Williams' *A Streetcar Named Desire* in New York in 1947—Marlon Brando. Like Baldwin, Brando had checked out the Village bohemian scene while he tried to make it as an actor. When I asked Baldwin how they first met, he was vague about the year and the place. He thought it was at the New School for Social Research, where he was taking a class on the theater with the dream of writing a long-running Broadway play. Brando was just beginning his stage career. "I think I was about twenty so it was probably about 1944," Baldwin said. "I think Marlon was hanging out at the New School, too. I had never met any white man like Marlon. He was obviously immensely talented—a real creative force—and totally unconventional and independent, a beautiful cat. Race truly meant nothing to him, just society labels—he was contemptuous of anyone who discriminated in any way. Very attractive to both women and men, he gave me the feeling that reports I was ugly had been much exaggerated. We enjoyed each other's company." The two men obviously became good friends, because later when Baldwin needed $500 at a crisis period of his life, Brando was the one he turned to. When the two men met at civil rights events in the sixties, they seemed very much at ease in each other's company. Elia Kazan told me that Baldwin and Brando got on well because they were "both flirts." But in later years they didn't see much of each other because Baldwin spent much of his time in Europe whereas Brando settled in Tahiti. Roughly the same age, Brando was already a Broadway star in *Streetcar* when Baldwin was still struggling to break through as a writer.

The more Baldwin wrote for the weeklies the less overtime he worked at the Calypso, and so he was more short of money than ever. He compared himself to George Orwell in *Down and Out in Paris and London*. He decided to try to raise money with a book, a sort of extended essay. He went round Harlem with a photographer he knew, Theodore Pelatowski, who took pictures of storefront churches, and then he wrote a text to go with them. But the book "met exactly the same fate as my first—fellowship but no sale." This time it was a Rosenwald Fellowship, and with the money he decided to begin a new novel, perhaps he could raise an advance, too, from a publisher. But he wasn't ready yet for another attempt at his Harlem family novel. He focused instead on the white bohemian world of the Village—the world he knew outside Harlem—and the gay underground. There was a great potential for violence there and he was fascinated by a current murder trial involving bisexual relationships and high-society marriages. It gave him the idea for a novel with a murder case as the climax. With the title *Ignorant Armies* he began to write enthusiastically, but then he couldn't make up his mind about the setting or exactly where his bisexual hero fitted into the plot. He seemed to be plotting two novels in one. It was only later he realized it was a first version of *Giovanni's Room* and *Another Country*.

One reason he gave up was news that had sent him into a depression when he couldn't do any writing—news about his socialist friend Eugene Worth. As he came out of the subway station at West Fourth Street in the Village one evening, a man he knew came running down the steps to catch a train. The man yelled: "Did you hear what happened to Gene?" Baldwin said: "No, what happened?" While the train doors were closing, the man just had time to shout back: "He's dead." That was how Baldwin got the news. Later he learned the details—that Eugene had committed suicide by throwing himself off the George Washington Bridge. It was late winter. Eugene had been twenty-four.

Baldwin had known he was in trouble over a white woman, with jobs, and above all from the city's ceaseless racial pressures. Eugene had been one to speak up. Claiming that New York was responsible for Eugene's death, Baldwin forty years later—it was still a heartfelt matter to him even then—tried to explain how it happened to the Paris Review: "Looking for a place to live. Looking for a job. You begin to doubt your judgment, you begin to doubt everything. You become imprecise. And that's when you're beginning to go under. You've been beaten, and it's been deliberate. The whole society has decided to make you *nothing*. And they don't even know they're doing it." Eugene's death was a blow. "We were never lovers: for what it's worth, I think I wish we had been," he wrote two years before he died, his memory of that time still painfully fresh. Eugene had once run down a list of his girlfriends, those he liked and those he *really* liked, one or two with whom he might really be in love, and then he had added to Jimmy Baldwin, "I wondered if I might be in love with you." Baldwin commented in *The Price of the Ticket:* "I wish I had heard him more clearly: an oblique confession is always a plea. But I was to hurt a great many people by being unable to imagine that anyone could possibly be in love with an ugly boy like me." When he received the news of Eugene's suicide, he "realized that I would have done anything whatever to have been able to hold him in this world." What it meant to him was conveyed in *Another Country*—the character of Rufus, the most engaging in the novel, was based on Eugene, and he, too, threw himself off the George Washington Bridge. Baldwin put himself in Eugene's place in the final moments as Rufus stood on the bridge "and then the wind took him, he felt himself going over, head down, the wind, the stars, the lights, the water, all rolled together, *all right.* He felt a shoe fly off behind him, there was nothing around him, only the wind, *all right, you motherfucking Godalmighty bastard,* I'm coming to you."

He had the feeling his own luck was "running out. I was going to go to jail. I was going to kill somebody or be killed." An enormous tension seemed to be building inside him. None of his gay friends could reach him. He walked the streets for hours trying to distract his thoughts. It was his good luck to meet a young black woman who "dug me." Baldwin fell in love with her and they lived together in the Village

59

for over a year. Both of them had jobs. He even got back to his writing, though it was hard to find the time to do it. The only chance was when she was at work. In his state of mind, he could only attempt short pieces. He wrote a short story, "Previous Condition," in one night that mirrored his own condition. A young black actor is "drowning" in the Village. "I don't want to hate anybody," he declared, "but now maybe, I can't love anybody either." Baldwin rewrote the sixteen pages three times, then sold the story to Commentary, where it was published in the October 1948 issue. He wanted to write a major essay about all that was troubling him but he couldn't concentrate. The most he could do was to put together an article entitled "Journey to Atlanta" based on a journal kept by his younger brother David. An enthusiastic musician, David, still in his teens, was a member of a quartet known as the Melodeers that had been invited to perform in Atlanta by the Progressive party, which was trying to win black and white liberal votes. The trip was a disaster and David concluded, "Ain't none of 'em gonna do a thing for *me.*" Jimmy Baldwin leaned heavily on David's journal and resorted to a preacher's rhetoric and generalizations rather than writing with the deadly precision he achieved in his best work. He hadn't been there himself and his best writing always came from direct involvement. "Journey to Atlanta" appeared in The New Leader of October 9, 1948, but when he read it he knew he had faked some of it. He had to make a change in his life.

He wondered if marriage might do it. Settle down with a wife, have children—a family. He had considered marriage twice before, but not as seriously as this time. He bought a wedding ring. But then at the very last minute, he drew back. At first he raised a writer's objections. How could he ever give the time he needed to writing and also be a good husband and father? But he knew he wasn't being honest with himself. He remembered what he had read of Oscar Wilde's marriage and particularly André Gide's. Both writers, one Irish-English, the other French, had been homosexuals who married. Their marriages had been unhappy. Both wives had suffered greatly from their husband's deception and guilt. Baldwin decided he couldn't risk a marriage like that, perhaps with a child involved as there had been in Oscar Wilde's case.

His homosexual nature was too well developed, Baldwin reflected. He had met this woman, though he was only in his early twenties, "many light-years too late."

In later years, although Baldwin often talked and wrote about friends like Beauford Delaney and even Eugene Worth for all the painful memories Eugene's name brought back, he seldom referred to this woman he had nearly married. He never told of how he broke up their relationship or what happened to the woman. He never even mentioned her name. I remember when I wrote about a black woman I had been friendly with in New Orleans, he took me into the kitchen for privacy in his crowded apartment and said quietly, "I knew a woman like that—once. I even nearly married her." He didn't say any more, but remained silent and somber-faced for a long time. He referred to her very briefly, not naming her, in "Here Be Dragons", an essay published in Playboy in 1985. The wedding ring he had bought he threw in the Hudson River near where Eugene had drowned. He realized, he said, he couldn't marry—"or shouldn't, which comes to the same thing."

He told Margaret Mead in *A Rap On Race* that how to treat a black woman was a great dilemma when you knew you couldn't protect her "unless you were prepared to work all your life in the post office, unless you were prepared to make bargains I was temperamentally unfitted to make." And even then, he said, "it wouldn't have worked. It didn't work. I could see that all around me. I could see the price some black people paid, some great black men had paid."

It meant he was alone again, desperately alone—so much so that "walking past a group of whites, I sometimes felt so angry I wanted to go 'bam.'" He felt New York was out to beat him down as it had Eugene; as he described later in *Another Country,* "the weight of this city was murderous." He seemed to be heading for a complete breakdown. Nothing seemed to help—liquor, tranquilizers, marijuana. He acknowledged later: "By this time, of course, I was mad, as mad as my dead father. If I had not gone mad, I could not have left."

A Village friend suggested he should take his problems to a psychiatrist, but even if he had had the money, that was no solution for him; the suggestion merely irritated him. Not only were there too many schools—Freud, Jung, Reich were merely the tip of the iceberg—but "anyone who thought seriously that I had any desire to be 'adjusted' to this society had to be ill." People, he said, went to a shrink to find justification for the empty lives they led and the meaningless work they did. That wasn't his problem.

He told himself he couldn't help his mother if he was in a mental hospital or in jail or was dead, which seemed to be the three possibilities if he stayed. "I no longer felt I knew who I really was, whether I was really black or really white, really male or really female, really talented or a fraud, really strong or merely stubborn. I had become a crazy oddball. I had to get my head together to survive and my only hope of doing that was to leave America." Enough was left of the money from the Rosenwald Fellowship to pay his fare somewhere overseas— but where? At first he considered Israel. It was far away from America, and he was interested in the Jews and knew that part of the world from his Bible reading. Above all Israel was a new nation of immigrants and perhaps a good place for him to emigrate to and make a fresh start. But he was also attracted by the traditional home for American writers in exile—Paris. The French capital was so much closer, so much cheaper to reach, and several young writers he had known in the Village were now living there. Richard Wright was still there . . . and some other prominent black artists, including the mythical Josephine Baker. Even Beauford Delaney, beginning to prosper after a write-up by Henry Miller and pictures reproduced in several magazines, was talking about moving to Paris. It had always attracted black American artists, who found themselves freer there.

Baldwin kept putting off his decision. He felt he shouldn't leave his family, the very idea made him feel guilty, and yet he felt he *had* to. Indecisive, confused by conflicting advice from friends, he watched his money slowly melt away. Finally he had to make up his mind before it was too late. There was only one decision he could make: he was leaving. So Paris it was, mainly because he could still afford the fare there. After buying a ticket—a one-way air ticket—he had forty dollars left. That wouldn't go far in Paris, and if he had to hustle for a living, he had a great handicap in not being able to speak French. "But I was past caring," he said later, recalling his desperate, half-crazy mood. "My whole life had become a gamble. I wasn't really choosing France, I was getting out of America. I had no idea what might happen to me in France, but I was very clear as to what would happen if I remained in New York. I would go under like Eugene."

He packed all his unfinished novels into a duffel bag and told the various editors he had worked for what he had decided. Most of them were vaguely encouraging. After all he was following a well-trod literary trail. It was too far away to send many books to be reviewed, but as an American—a black American—in Europe, the experience was bound to give him new subjects for essays. He interested Partisan Review in one essay he had in mind—an essay about protest fiction using as examples *Uncle Tom's Cabin* and Richard Wright's *Native Son*. But in later years when he discussed this desperate period, he was annoyed that he couldn't get much financial backing in advances from anyone to take to France with him. "What did they think I would live on while I was writing—air? They just wanted to be nice to me, treat me like a dancing dog, the cute little black boy, but no one on Publisher's Row wanted to gamble on me. The people who ever really bet on me and backed me, I can count them on one hand!"

Jimmy Baldwin's last day in New York—November 11, 1948—he spent with his family in Harlem. He had dreaded telling them so much that he had put it off until the last minute. How could he explain his desperation to them? They needed him, and Paris seemed so far away. Well, it couldn't treat him any worse than New York had. He had tried several times to tell his mother he intended to make it as a great writer and then he would be able to buy her whatever she wanted. And Mrs. Baldwin replied very calmly, very dryly, "It's more than a notion," the kind of dry understatement which, he said, characterized so much of black speech in America. How could he tell his mother—as he would explain years later to Nikki Giovanni, a young black writer—that he was moving to Paris because he couldn't find in America "a certain stamina, a certain corroboration that I needed." He had to go to Paris to learn Alexandre Dumas was a mulatto and Pushkin was black. But he couldn't tell this to his mother when her mind was probably on how was she possibly going to pay the rent.

When he got up to leave, Paula Maria, the youngest child, only five but with a great love for Jimmy, burst into tears and wouldn't be consoled. She sensed she wouldn't be seeing him for a long time. His mother came down with him to the stoop and stood silently, arms folded. Her expressive eyes conveyed what she felt. It was too much for Jimmy. He rushed across the street to a cab, waved and drove quickly away, trying not to look back. He was twenty-four.

4

Exile in Paris

It was Baldwin's first long flight. He downed a few scotches before boarding the plane, and midway across the Atlantic, seeing only dark storm clouds and the choppy ocean far below, he was soon in a panic, unable to sleep, anxious to land, to feel the solid earth beneath his feet again. The plane seemed to circle over Paris for hours. He expected to be "dashed to death on the vindictive tooth of the Eiffel Tower." He couldn't remember feeling "the remotest exhilaration" but was haunted by the memory of Paula Maria in tears and his mother's inscrutable, stoic silence. He had informed a few people he was coming, though he didn't expect much help from them. But when he landed he discovered he was wrong. Several were there to greet him. It was "my first lesson, perhaps, in humility; perhaps the first opening of a certain door." He was forced to recognize that his friends cared about him. It was "a bewildering, a paralyzing revelation, and I know that I was not very graceful."

They took him at once to Les Deux Magots, a popular meeting place for artists in St. Germaine des Pres, the Parisian equivalent of Greenwich Village. Sitting there was Richard Wright at a crowded table. "Hey, boy!" called Wright, very friendly, looking younger and happier than the last time Baldwin had seen him in New York. He introduced the men with him as the editors of Zero, a new magazine, and he told them Baldwin was a promising writer and they should consider his work for their first issue. Wright's encouraging, pleased, faintly conspiratorial manner suggested to Baldwin they were going to be friends at last. "I took this meeting as a good omen, and I could not possibly have been more wrong."

On this first day Baldwin was surprised to find that so much about Paris was familiar—from reading Balzac. "I'm sure that my life in France would have been very different had I not met Balzac," he told the Paris Review forty years later. "Even though I hadn't experienced it yet, I understood something about the concierge, all the French institutions and personalities. The way that country and its society works. How to find my way around in it, not get lost in it, and not feel rejected by it." He was also surprised how gray, even ugly, much of Paris looked. It was winter and it was even colder than in New York.

The first thing to do was to find a cheap hotel and get a good rest before taking on this new country. He still had most of his forty dollars left. What he would do when it was gone he had no idea. When he checked into a hotel recommended by Richard Wright, he found he had lost or left behind in New York the duffel bag containing his unfinished novels. He was very upset. It meant he would have to start over. But then he consoled himself that none of the novels was much good anyway. He had to find a new approach to his family novel and a fresh plot for the bisexual murder-trial story—perhaps he should divide it into two separate novels. But first he had to pick up enough French to get by and learn how to survive in this strange country.

Otto Friedrich, later a senior writer for Time, had recently settled in Paris to write a novel. He recalled, "We were sitting around in a cafe on the Left Bank one day in 1948 when a friend, Mason Hoffenberg, an American poet who later co-wrote Candy with Terry Southern, came over and said Jimmy Baldwin was coming to Paris from New York that night. Hoffenberg had known Jimmy in Greenwich Village. We were all penniless writers hanging out in cafes, surviving through communal living. We went around to the Hotel de Rome not far away in a quiet area where Jimmy was staying. When we got there, he had already gone to sleep. We woke him up. He was very glad to see Mason. We took him out on the town. I had friends at another hotel, the Hotel Verneuil, including my future wife, Priscilla Boughton. She had known Jimmy in New York, too. He came to see her at the Hotel Verneuil and she got him a room there. He lived there for a long time. Mary Keene also lived there. She was a motherly type and everyone tended to congregate in her room. We were Left Bank bohemians, all penniless. It was a very informal way of life and Jimmy became one of us."

Novelist Herbert Gold was also staying at the Hotel Verneuil. He had met Jimmy Baldwin in the San Remo in the Village, Jimmy said, but Gold didn't remember. "I think Jimmy came up and introduced himself to me at the Hotel Verneuil. Terry Southern was also staying there. I remember hanging out with Jimmy in the cafes. He bummed cigarettes, which you had to buy on the black market."

At first Baldwin was in a difficult mood. There were several drunken scenes in bars, breaking glasses, even getting involved in fights. Although he knew he was behaving badly, it was a necessary release of all his pent-up feelings. "For the first time I realized what a puritan I was. I judged people by my stepfather's morality that I still carried round with me. Yet people everyone despised—Arab laborers, French whores and pimps—were very nice to me when I was desperate, and it humbled me, opened me up to whole new areas of life and tamed that puritan in me." But he tried to keep his street experiences separate from his meetings with his new friends in the American colony.

"I had never really known a black before," recalled Otto Friedrich. "Most of us hadn't. It's almost impossible now to imagine how American whites thought about blacks in those days. You didn't know any if you were a middle-class northeasterner like me. There were three blacks in my college. We had no blacks in my part of Boston where I was born. You thought about it as a southern problem. Like all northern liberals, you thought the South was very bad, very prejudiced, but it was not your problem. Jimmy was the first black I knew at all. That was true of most of the people I knew in Paris. Jimmy didn't talk to us much about being black. But he changed over the years. Like most blacks he was radicalized by the civil rights movement and then he radicalized others. He may have thought about the black situation when we first met him, but he didn't discuss it with us. I suppose he must have suppressed his feelings with us, for it was one of the first things he wrote about. I didn't sense any hostility from him. I didn't know any blacks, but I was interested in their problem, so I took a fair amount of time to get to know Jimmy. He was soon part of the cafe life we all lived, getting up at noon and wandering out to meet people. It was a great period for exchanging manuscripts and news of home. If someone read things you had written, you then read theirs. I was only nineteen then, Jimmy was twenty-four, but the age difference wasn't important. We had all come to Paris to stay and try to write. The main thing Jimmy had written up to then was an essay in Commentary about the Harlem ghetto. It was good. He had also done some book reviewing. I waited to see what he would write next."

Terry Southern went with his friend Mason Hoffenberg and Baldwin to the Arab Quarter to change some money and buy some hashish. "Jimmy wasn't using any himself, he only smoked grass, but he sat there with us, very interested in the whole Arab ritual with pipes. I heard him later telling someone in a cafe about the experience."

When Baldwin became desperate financially, he often went back to the Arab Quarter on his own. "I lived mainly among *les miserables*—and in Paris *les miserables* are Algerian." He got to know their rundown hotels where they slept five or six to a room in shifts in freezing conditions. He often ate at their cheap cafes and he learned to identify with them because the French looked down on them—"they were treated like dirt"—and he envied them because they were together with a great sense of camaraderie and shared their problems and their homesickness.

Yet Baldwin must have felt in those first few weeks that he hadn't escaped from America. You could be a part of the large American colony in Paris and have almost nothing to do with the French. It was almost like being a member of an exclusive private club with many of the same privileges. When he had spent his forty dollars in the first three days, he found it easy to borrow from other Americans, most of whom had a steady income from student grants or from well-off families. Richard Wright was also generous. Baldwin was grateful, but irritated to be under obligation. He watched Wright with the French intellectu-

als in the cafes. Jean-Paul Sartre and Simone de Beauvoir admitted him
to their celebrity circle, but they had little interest in the comparatively
unknown Baldwin, who had yet to prove himself by their lights.
Baldwin told Julius Lester many years later that a lot of what happened
between him and Richard Wright occurred "because Richard was
much, much better than a lot of the company he kept. I mean, the French
existentialists. I didn't think that Simone de Beauvoir or Jean-Paul
Sartre—to say nothing of the American colony—had any right whatso-
ever to patronize that man. It revolted me and made me furious. And
it made me furious at Richard, too, because he was better than that."

This influenced him, Baldwin said, when he referred to Wright's
Native Son in the essay he was writing about protest literature for
Partisan Review. The editors of the new magazine, Zero, he had met
in Wright's company when he first arrived said they would be interested, too, in considering the essay for their first issue. This meant that
the essay would then be published on both sides of the Atlantic, but
more important it would be read by everyone who knew him and
Wright in Paris. Originally the idea for the essay had come from all
the books he had reviewed about American blacks and racial relations,
and his plan was to ridicule the white liberal stereotypes of blacks, but
now he decided to give more attention to Richard Wright than he had
intended; it would get more attention.

But he found it difficult to settle down to write in the first few
months—"I just tore up paper." He said that he had "to go through a
time of isolation in order to come to terms with who and what I was,
as distinguished from all the things I'd been told I was." Being away
from home enabled him gradually to see everything more clearly. He
told Margaret Mead in *A Rap On Race,* "It was a great revelation for
me when I found myself finally in France among all kinds of very
different people—I mean, at least different from my point of view and
different from anybody I had met in America." One day somebody
asked him about a man he'd been seen with and "I really did not
remember whether he was white or black." His whole frame of reference all the years he was growing up had been black and white, but
suddenly in Paris he felt he'd lost it, and "once that has happened to you,
it never comes back." Eventually he came to feel "that I'd come through

something, shed a dying skin and was naked again. I wasn't perhaps, but I certainly felt more at ease with myself. And then I was able to write."

He achieved the necessary "time of isolation" through a serious illness. The winter of 1948–49—his first European winter experiencing Paris' inefficient postwar heating—was particularly cold, and Baldwin, drinking more and missing meals and sleep quite often and without heavy winter clothing, picked up a cold that gradually turned into pneumonia. One of his problems was that after he became an established member of the American colony and had borrowed widely to get by without being able to pay back many of the loans, he found obtaining money even for essentials more and more difficult. Chain-smoking cigarettes had become as much a part of his life as drinking, and often he had to choose between buying cigarettes or a sandwich, usually deciding on cigarettes. Many of the Americans expected a newcomer after a breaking-in period of a few weeks to find a source of income. Some of the rejections obviously rankled even many years later because Baldwin told the Paris Review that when he arrived in Paris, "I didn't know anyone and I didn't want to know anyone. Later, when I'd encountered other Americans, I began to avoid them because they had more money than I did and I didn't want to feel like a freeloader." He said he borrowed money whenever he could, often at the last minute, and moved from one hotel to another, "not knowing what was going to happen to me." Sometimes with the rent owing, he would be locked out of his room and had to sell clothes and even his typewriter to get by. People lent him heavy sweaters and pants for the winter, but they were invariably too big for him. He remembered baggy pants he had to hold up with an enormous leather belt. He did, however, have regular drinking companions in the American colony and homes he visited often. Eileen Finletter and her first husband, Stanley Geist, for example, used to have writers and artists in to dinner. She recalled: "We didn't have a salon, just dinners, no set thing. We met Jimmy just after he arrived, I forget how, and he came over all the time. He was living hand-to-mouth in those days and always seemed to be short of money. We also had people like Saul Bellow at our dinners. Saul Bellow lived nearby—I think he was finishing *Augie March* at that time. Of course Saul was already established and Jimmy at best was a coming star. Jimmy was always talking about Richard Wright. Dostoevsky and Dickens were his great enthusiasms in those days. But he was preoccupied with his troubles. We tried to help him as much as we could."

Finally, after coughing and sneezing for days, he woke up at the Hotel Verneuil seriously ill with a high fever, unable even to get out of bed. From his experience of the ruthlessness of other Parisian hotels, he expected to be thrown out, ill or not, because he couldn't pay the rent. To his surprise and overwhelming relief, the Corsican family who ran the hotel, "for reasons I'll never understand," took care of him. The matriarch of the family, a very old Corsican woman, nursed him back to health over three months using ancient Corsican folk remedies. She climbed five flights of stairs twice a day to his room. When Terry Southern visited him, he found the invalid eating from a big bowl and inquired what was in it. "Gruel," replied Baldwin. Southern laughed. It sounded Dickensian. "I will never know what made her suppose that I would ever be able to pay the rent or why she didn't simply call the American embassy and have me shipped home," Baldwin said. "Perhaps the old lady sensed that to have done that to me then would have been tantamount to murder."

Herbert Gold, who remained in touch with Baldwin to the end of his life, recalled that Jimmy Baldwin was so grateful that he corresponded with the Corsican family when he left Paris. Baldwin told me he sometimes visited them when he returned to Paris, even though he could then afford to stay at much more luxurious places. But the means to live as he wished were a long way off then, and when he recovered from his illness he set about repaying the old woman, his nurse, by at least catching up with the rent. He borrowed what he could and tried to find jobs he might do, though he still had little French, even looking for patrons in the gay bars—the nervous, competitive, sometimes vicious bars he described later in *Giovanni's Room.* He also tried to make some money from his writing. From the disaster of *In His Father's House,* he had retained a chapter for sale as a possible short story. Now he gave it the title "The Outing"—it began: "Each summer the church gave an outing . . ."—and he made the homosexual undertones more obvious at the end ("After a moment Johnnie moved and put his head on David's shoulder. David put his arms around him. But now where there had been peace there was only panic and where there had been safety, danger, like a flower, opened.") Baldwin was to use a similar scene, greatly expanded, in *Giovanni's Room*. Through a friend he offered "The Outing" to Présence Africaine, which he knew Richard Wright read, and was embarrassed—and angry—to have it rejected. He was sure Wright would hear about this second humiliation. Baldwin was in such a difficult situation that what he might have shrugged off in better circumstances became a great blow to his pride, though it seemed as if anything remotely touching on his relationship with Richard Wright affected him deeply however he was placed. That "The Outing" was published the next year in New Story, a new magazine aimed at a young readership, didn't console him, even though Wright—along with Tennessee Williams, William Saroyan and Jean-Paul Sartre—was on the list of patrons. It was the rejection he remembered as if he were still little Frog Eyes in Harlem.

There is a clue perhaps to his attitude in a remark he made years later about the period after his illness: "I was very much alone and wanted to be." He had to be alone much of the time to do his writing, but he also had a busy social life. The remark probably referred to his deeper feelings that he kept hidden from the American colony, as Otto Friedrich suspected. Just as he sought the gay scene to satisfy that side of himself, so he also tried to meet some of the many black Americans in Paris to share the thoughts and feelings he couldn't share with the white colony. He missed the black scene of Harlem more than he had expected—the black jokes and attitudes and styles, the faces, even the faded tenements and the slick-talking hustlers. There were estimated to be some five hundred American blacks living in Paris, the vast majority veterans studying on the G.I. Bill everything from the fine arts to brain surgery. The great majority also didn't mix much with each other the way black entertainers did in Paris, but lived deliberately a much more isolated life. In an essay he wrote for The Reporter magazine, "The Negro in Paris" (which he retitled "Encounter on the Seine: Black meets Brown" when he reprinted it in *Notes of a Native Son*), Baldwin tried to explain why American blacks took this attitude. By leaving the American ghettoes, they "not merely have effected a social and physical leave-taking but also have been precipitated into cruel psychological warfare. It is altogether inevitable that past humiliations should become associated not only with one's traditional oppressors but also with one's traditional kinfolk. Thus the sight of a face from home is not invariably a source of joy, but can also quite easily become a source of embarrassment or rage."

Baldwin wrote this while he was in the middle of his bitter row with Wright that followed the publication of his essay on protest literature. Did he have in mind his own "past humiliations" and "embarrassment"? Was he waging "cruel psychological warfare" himself? In another essay, "The Exile," reprinted in *Nobody Knows My Name*, he referred to the "later, terrible warfare" between Wright and himself. It was a labyrinthine relationship hard to understand, but given Baldwin's complex subtle mind, already well-developed by that stage of his career, it is difficult to accept his surprise that Wright was offended by what he wrote. Anyone who knew Wright even slightly, how insecure and touchy he could be, would have known the effect on him.

Baldwin called his essay "Everybody's Protest Novel." He began by dismissing that favorite book of his boyhood, *Uncle Tom's Cabin,* as "a very bad novel." He used it as an example of American protest novels whose faults were forgiven because of their good intentions, "whatever violence they do to language, whatever excessive demands they make of credibility." One was told to put first things first, Baldwin claimed, "the good of society coming before niceties of style or characterization." Finally he referred to Wright's *Native Son* and described the chief character, Bigger, a young black American, as "Uncle Tom's descendant," so exactly opposite a portrait that Wright and Harriet Beecher Stowe, the author of *Uncle Tom's Cabin,* were "locked together in a deadly, timeless battle; the one uttering merciless exhortations, the other shouting curses." Bigger's tragedy was not that he was cold or black or hungry, but that he had accepted "a theology that denies him life, that he admits the possibility of his being sub-human and feels constrained, therefore, to battle for his humanity according to those brutal criteria bequeathed him at his birth." Baldwin summed up: "The failure of the protest novel lies in its rejection of life, the human being, the denial of his beauty, dread, power, in its insistence that it is his categorization alone which is real and which cannot be transcended." It is not surprising that Wright and his admirers concluded that in calling *Uncle Tom's Cabin* "a very bad novel" and in coupling *Native Son* with it, Baldwin was implying that Wright's novel was also "very bad" in its own way.

It was a short essay, but it was much talked about in literary circles on both sides of the Atlantic when it appeared in the first issue of Zero and the June, 1949, issue of Partisan Review. It established Baldwin in the American colony in Paris. People took sides over it—pro-Wright or pro-Baldwin. Otto Friedrich considered the essay "essentially an attack on Richard Wright. Wright was a father-figure he wanted to shed. By the side of Wright, Jimmy was just a kid. For him to have a piece in Zero meant he was a real writer, not just a black. Something of mine was in the second issue. That helped our relationship." Terry Southern also saw Baldwin's essay as a "scathing" attack on Wright. "I think he had a genuine resentment against Wright's Uncle Tom attitude relative to his own, and resentment against his great fame. I don't think Jimmy was too charitable toward writers who were successful. He was complimentary to writers who hadn't yet published much. He read a story of mine in the first issue of Paris Review and he wrote me a note and dropped it by my hotel saying he liked it. He had a highly critical mind and still being young, could let his jealousy get the better of him."

On the day Zero was published and before Baldwin had seen a copy, he walked into the Brasserie Lipp, one of the American colony's favorite gathering places. Richard Wright was sitting at a table and called Baldwin over. Ten years later Baldwin commented, "I will never forget that interview." Wright accused him of betraying him, and not only him but all American blacks by attacking the idea of protest literature. Baldwin said he was astonished. "It simply had not occurred to me that the essay could be interpreted in that way." He was proud of it and "sad and incomprehensible as it now sounds," he had rather expected to be patted on the head for his original point of view. Wright had thought that he had attacked *Native Son* "whereas as far as I was concerned, I had scarcely even criticized it." Wright accused him of trying to destroy his novel and his reputation, "but it had not entered my mind that either of these *could* be destroyed, and certainly not by me." Baldwin tried to defend himself, but what made the exchange "so ghastly" and "most painful" was that he realized Wright was right to be hurt and he was wrong to have hurt him. "I had used his work as a kind of springboard into my own. His work was a roadblock in my road." Yet he felt this was the greatest tribute he could have paid Wright. The older writer had been an idol, "and idols are created in order to be destroyed."

"What do you mean, *protest*!" Wright said. "*All* literature is protest. You can't name a single novel that isn't protest." Baldwin replied that all literature might be protest, but all protest wasn't literature. "Oh," said Wright, "here you come again with all that art-for-art's-sake crap." This made Baldwin furious and Wright, beginning to cool down, was amused by Baldwin's angry face and vehement finger-wagging. When Baldwin mentioned "roots"—the black past stretching back to Africa—Wright snorted, "Roots! Next thing you'll be telling me is that all colored folks have rhythm." Baldwin had to chuckle and there was a momentary lull. But the two men had several more angry arguments over the next few weeks and attempts to patch up their quarrel never really worked.

William Phillips, the editor of Partisan Review, was in Paris in the winter of 1949–50 and met both Baldwin and Wright. "Wright became slightly Frenchified as Baldwin did, though Baldwin's French as I recall wasn't very good. The atmosphere in Paris affected them. Wright never suggested writing a reply to Baldwin's essay. Baldwin borrowed some money from me, and I think he felt guilty about never paying it back and that's why he avoided me for a while."

But instead of staying off the subject of Richard Wright in his writing, Baldwin soon returned to *Native Son* in another much longer, even more critical essay. Entitled "Many Thousands Gone" and also published in Partisan Review in the November–December, 1951, issue, this new look at Wright began in a seemingly complimentary way, *Native Son* was "the most powerful and celebrated statement we have yet had of what it means to be a Negro in America." But then the tone changed: "Such a book, we felt with pride, could never have been written before—which was true. Nor could it be written today. It bears already the aspect of a landmark." Wright's work "is most clearly committed to the social struggle. Leaving aside the considerable question of what relationship precisely the artist bears to the revolutionary, the reality of man as a social being is not his only reality and that artist is strangled who is forced to deal with human beings solely in social terms; and who has, moreover, as Wright had, the necessity thrust on him of being the representative of some thirteen million people. It is a false responsibility (since writers are not congressmen) and impossible, by its nature, of fulfillment." Recording his rage, Wright had also recorded the fantasy Americans had when they spoke of blacks and they had lived with since the first slaves. "This is the significance of *Native Son* and also unhappily its overwhelming limitation." Baldwin went on to examine the novel in critical detail. "We would be discussing a very different novel if Wright's execution had been more perceptive," he commented. *Native Son* "finds itself at length so trapped by the American image of Negro life and by the American necessity to find the ray of hope that it cannot pursue its own implications." The essay ends like one of Baldwin's teenage sermons with a fine rhetorical ring about how he sees the black situation ("the battle is elsewhere . . .").

"Many Thousands Gone" is not one of his finest essays, its style conveys a sense of strain, with too many wordy generalizations about "The Negro," and given his already bitter misunderstanding with Wright, it does seem like a deliberate challenge. Some of Wright's admirers were so incensed that they suggested Baldwin must have a homosexual hang-up over Wright. They quoted Baldwin as having talked about American blacks' "profound, almost ineradicable self-hatred" and suggested he had lashed out at Wright to deal with his own "self-hatred." They accused him of having mainly white friends. But Otto Friedrich's impression that Baldwin was shedding a father-figure seems more likely. Wright himself, naturally enough, became a little paranoid about Baldwin's motives. The FBI had kept Wright under surveillance for his Communist party involvement and revolutionary racial pronouncements, and the surveillance apparently continued through the CIA when Wright went into exile. American propaganda overseas played down the racial problem at home whereas Soviet propaganda played it up, and prominent American blacks like Wright became pawns in the Cold War that had developed between the two superpowers. Wright suspected some of the American colony in Paris of being CIA informers, and in late-night drinking sessions he accused more than one of the Americans in his entourage of setting him up, of being a

Judas. But it is absurd to think that young Jimmy Baldwin, whose stern, uncompromising views could hardly have pleased the American propaganda experts any more than Wright's, could have been bought by the CIA, even though he was forever short of money. It is likely that he didn't appreciate how what he wrote could be used by Wright's enemies in the propaganda war. Or didn't he care? Wright wondered.

Michel Fabre reported in his biography, *The Unfinished Quest of Richard Wright,* for which he had the cooperation of Wright's family and friends in Paris, that after "Everybody's Protest Novel," Wright told Baldwin "he would have no more to do with him." But Baldwin, "still fascinated by his mentor" and needing "Wright's recognition of his talent in order to believe in himself," sought a reconciliation, and finding there was no hope, "he naturally turned hostile in his disappointment." Fabre commented: "Since at that time the U.S. government was resolutely hostile toward the leading black novelist living in exile, Baldwin was letting himself be used in an attempt to destroy Wright's reputation." This interpretation, naturally, angered Baldwin because part of his explanation of why he and Wright had never become real friends was that he was much smarter about politics than Wright and they could never agree. If only they had become friends back in the New York days, "we might at least have caught a glimpse of the difference between my mind and his; and if we could have argued about it then, our quarrel might not have been so painful later." Baldwin rejected the idea Wright "held himself so rigidly against me" just because of the criticism of his work. He depicted himself merely as having been honest like a true friend and went on to elaborate how touchy Wright had become in so many relationships not only with fellow black Americans like himself but with French intellectuals and Africans from the French colonies who lived in Paris—in fact, "anyone who seemed to threaten Richard's system of reality." Wright, Baldwin said, brought out his sardonic side, and he often wanted to kick him and say, "Oh, come off it, baby, ain't no white folks around now, let's tell it like it is." From being embarrassed, apologetic, confused, seeking a reconciliation, Baldwin was becoming more openly critical of Wright personally as well as professionally.

It was impossible for the two men to avoid each other in the small tight world of the American colony. When Wright helped to organize a French-American Fellowship Club Baldwin was there to hear the addresses by the guests of honor, Sartre and American journalist Louis Fischer. One of Wright's aims was to protect black Americans from job discrimination by American companies in Paris and by U.S. government agencies. Baldwin told Wright it seemed "unrealistic" to him—few of the black Americans in Paris were there to get a job—but Wright became angry and impatient. "Richard often made me feel that the word 'frivolous' had been coined to describe me," said Baldwin. Yet Wright also made him feel "so guilty" that he agreed to find out how many black Americans were working for American companies. The supporters of the Fellowship Club held a melodramatic secret meeting in an obscure district of Paris over a workingmen's bistro with "some vague notion, I think, of defeating the ever-present agents of the CIA, who certainly ought to have had better things to do, but who, quite probably, on the other hand, didn't." Michel Fabre commented in his biography of Wright: "It might seem strange that James Baldwin, who was also an active member of the Fellowship, described Wright's endeavors with as much scorn as injustice, were it not for the fact that their personal relationship had complicated their professional dealings."

After his experience with the Fellowship Club, Baldwin claimed to keep a "helplessly sardonic distance" as much as he could. He and Wright "drifted farther and farther apart—our dialogue became too frustrating and too acrid." Yet Baldwin was by no means free of Wright if that had been his intention. They would still run into each other in the cafes and have another argument, and Baldwin in his writing would continue to worry over their quarrel.

Some of the new established writers in the U.S. were continually passing through Paris in those postwar days. Young Truman Capote had just published his first novel, *Other Voices, Other Rooms,* with a photograph on the jacket that made him look like a seductive choirboy. Homosexual, aggressive, articulate with a tart wit, Capote made his presence known throughout the American colony. In later years he claimed that James Baldwin followed him around, the implication being that Baldwin had a crush on him. Baldwin expressed anger at what he considered was a patronizing attitude on Capote's part, especially when Capote took the credit for solving Baldwin's problems with his novels. According to Capote, Baldwin said he was working on two novels but wanted to make sure neither was a protest or problem novel, and he described their plots. Capote, in his own account, replied that a novel with a black homosexual in love with a Jewish woman was nothing if not a problem novel, and Baldwin allegedly saw the light at last and decided to concentrate on the other novel—his family saga set in Harlem—forever grateful to Truman. Capote also suggested he helped to get the novel published. Baldwin denied the story, which he said was "typical Truman."

He also encountered Saul Bellow, who, he thought, disliked him. Bellow was already an established novelist, but Baldwin's essays had established him in the American colony. Otto Friedrich recalled: "I was touting Jimmy as a great writer in the Latin Quarter and various Jewish writers were touting Bellow. My hero is better than your hero! They were used as rivals." Baldwin also made the acquaintance of Philip Roth ("I loved Jimmy," said Roth of those days), and later Baldwin was to feel very competitive toward him when Roth was getting bigger advances than he was. There was also Jean Genet, Sartre's protege, whose *Our Lady of the Flowers* had been recommended to an American publisher by Richard Wright. Although Genet portrayed himself as a homosexual ex-criminal and lover of tough pimps, obsessed with the police as sexual symbols, Baldwin found him to be a quiet, gentle, amusing man, "more moral than any minister I've ever met."

The Baldwin whom Otto Friedrich meanwhile had begun to know was different from the man who gave Richard Wright a hard time. Friedrich recalled: "Jimmy liked to kid around, he could be very funny, he knew a lot of jokes, he could be very winning not as a black but simply as a very nice guy. He could of course be malicious and spiteful when he wanted to be. There were a lot of people he didn't like. He had strong likes and dislikes not to do with race but how they were as people. That side of him didn't change over the years. We all judged him as Jimmy, not someone you had to be nice to because he was black, and he seemed to accept or reject us the same way." Their friendship developed to the stage of reading each other's manuscripts. "The first thing he showed me was a novel. He was then writing two novels, veering to and fro between them. *Crying Holy* was the main novel. It was essentially *Go Tell It On the Mountain.* He kept saying, 'I'm going to start a new novel called *So Long at the Fair.*' It was to be set in Greenwich Village, and it was essentially an effort to write about homosexuality. It wasn't an early version of *Another Country;* it was more *Giovanni's Room.* It had the same ideas. It was an effort to write about male love. I thought *Crying Holy* was very good and I was very impressed. I urged him to finish it. He had problems with it, however, he couldn't yet solve. It was about his father and he found it difficult to deal with. His father was black like everyone else in the world he was writing about in the novel." At one meeting Baldwin had explained to Friedrich it wasn't his real father, who hadn't been married to his mother "and if they ever lived together, it was only until Jimmy was two or three." Jimmy had explained how he was tyrannized by his step-father—"he was a figure Jimmy hated and loved." Jimmy was trying to work out his problems by writing about them and "that made it a good subject because he really felt it very deeply. Yet that was also the reason why he couldn't get it done. In a psychological sense, he couldn't deal with it. Whereas *Crying Holy* was a wholly black novel, the homosexual novel, *So Long at the Fair,* was wholly white. Eventually he showed me some of it. I didn't like it at all. I told him so. He replied I didn't understand it. He couldn't finish that one either. He was stuck on both novels. He had difficulty at that time getting anything done. A lot of people in New York kept asking him to write essays— Commentary, etc.—but they didn't pay much money. He was really very, very penniless in those days. He had no way of getting money. He scrounged, begged and borrowed. He didn't pay his debts. He cadged his drinks.

"He had hangers-on even in those days. Jimmy was very gregarious. There were friends and admirers who liked to be seen with him, people who paid the bill. I can't speak with any authority about his sex or romantic life, but he was always in love with someone and he had sex on the side with all kinds of people. He did it for fun or just to impress people. He had a very active sex life apart from his romantic one. The two happened simultaneously. He was having a love affair with someone and at the same time picked up people or got picked up by people. In the early days I knew him, the big romantic interest was a young Frenchman, a would-be actor who was a real jerk. He thought he was muscular, a Jean Gabin type, but he was mostly phony. He had no money so someone always had to pay for his drinks, and being a French type, he wouldn't drink a cheap beer like the rest of us but wanted Pernod. The would-be actor couldn't speak any English and Jimmy's French at that time was almost nonexistent so usually the actor just sat there. He was a street kid. He and Jimmy weren't living together, I think. The actor may have camped out sometimes with Jimmy, but Jimmy himself was moving around a lot. Some tourists, people he had known in Greenwich Village, came over on a trip to the South of France and he went with them. He went along for the ride.

"Paying the rent was always a problem for Jimmy. He moved to various hotels. I remember one very crummy hotel where the stolen sheets incident took place. I had returned to New York to win my future wife and I did so. I went back to Paris and took Jimmy out to dinner and he told me the story about the sheets. I said write it." He did and it appeared in Commentary as "Equal in Paris." He had been arrested as a receiver of stolen goods, and spent eight days in a Paris prison. An American friend had moved into Baldwin's hotel from another hotel and brought one of the hotel's bedsheets with him. Jimmy borrowed the sheet because his own were dirty. Two policemen came looking for the sheet and arrested Baldwin. Eventually after a grim week in various cells, being interrogated, photographed and fingerprinted, an American patent attorney he had worked for as a temporary officeboy helped him to get the case dismissed. The story of the bedsheet even moved the French court to laughter. Baldwin commented it was "the laughter of those who consider themselves to be at a safe remove from all the wretched, for whom the pain of the living is not real." He had heard that laughter in New York and now he realized it was "universal and never can be stilled."

What he did like about his prison experience was that he was treated more as an American than as a black. It was a new identity. The incident of the bedsheet was much discussed in the American colony, and the story was somewhat embroidered as it was passed on. Now forty years later, it has become legendary among the survivors of those Paris days, and there are various accounts of what happened. Terry Southern remembered seeing Baldwin led away in handcuffs. He was told Baldwin himself kept the sheet from another hotel and some of his drinking buddies got him out. Herbert Gold suggested to an interviewer that Baldwin's account might have been a way to explain why he was arrested by French police raiding a gay bar. He told me, "I felt that Jimmy was saying the French police were racist, but perhaps it had more to do with homophobia. In not saying that, he may have been protecting himself. It was before *Giovanni's Room* when he wasn't publicly announced in print as a homosexual. I know he was picked up in a gay bar and given bad treatment. But there may have been something else that happened I didn't know about. But like all good writers, Jimmy sometimes wrote lies that told the truth."

Otto Friedrich found that being Baldwin's friend meant you also had to accept his friends. "Every black in Paris treated Jimmy as though they were fellow aliens in a strange land. Some were homosexual, some were heterosexual, it didn't matter. All were in an armed alliance against the white world. I remember one guy was really awful. He was a criminal, he stole things. He didn't even pretend to be a writer or a singer like some did. I complained to Jimmy about him. I said, 'He's a real rat, you have nothing in common.' Jimmy said, 'I don't care if you don't like him. I understand him and know why he's the way he is.' That was rare in my relationship with Jimmy. He didn't usually treat you as white. I think we were really genuine friends. My wife thought she was, too. But it is also true that I never heard him say a bad word about any black under any circumstances." That incident could have inspired his later short story, "This Morning, This Evening, So Soon," which involves not only father-son relationships on several levels but an African friend who is accused of stealing by a white group. The narrator, a friend of both the African and the white group, reflects about the African, feeling himself to be caught in the middle: "I want to say, I know you steal, I know you have to steal. Perhaps you took the money out of this girl's purse in order to eat tomorrow, in order not to be thrown into the streets tonight, in order to stay out of jail . . ."

Friedrich recalled a time when Baldwin borrowed a typewriter from a mutual friend when she was away on a trip. "She said, 'Why do you think you have a right to my typewriter because you are a writer and I'm not?' It was the kind of thing that can spoil a friendship because of the social difference and the realization that the other person doesn't take you as seriously as they take themselves."

Baldwin was the best man at Friedrich's wedding. The owner of the typewriter was the other witness. "We all went out and got drunk on champagne in a cafe we all used." Friedrich said he was always amused by Baldwin's putdown remark to white folks, "I've been inside your kitchen," as if he spoke for all blacks. "He meant he knew something about them they didn't know about him. But I *had* seen *his* kitchen. When I came back to New York to court my wife, Jimmy said, 'Look up my mother.' My wife said, 'Let's take her out.' And we did.

"Mrs. Baldwin said it would give her a lot of pleasure if we would have dinner in her house. We didn't know Harlem, but arriving in 125th Street was like going into enemy territory. I had never even been to Harlem before. We got to Mrs. Baldwin's apartment door and it opened up into Mrs. Baldwin's domain. It was very hot and full of people. They were all having their Sunday night get-together. There were her children, her children's friends and neighbors and relatives, all sitting around the piano. They had been to some religious program in New Jersey and they sat there and we didn't have much to say. Mrs. Baldwin took us into the kitchen and we ate all by ourselves. Mrs. Baldwin waited on us and served us spare ribs and potato pie. She sat with us, but didn't eat. Nobody else joined us. It became very clear the others wouldn't eat until we left. Even though Mrs. Baldwin had invited us, they thought we would be more comfortable or they would be more comfortable if we ate by ourselves."

Baldwin once told me in talking about his boyhood reading that he had tried to read Henry James but hadn't got very far. James' elaborate sentences and the aristocratic European scene he described seemed completely foreign to him in Harlem. *The Portrait of a Lady* had been the novel he dipped into, and he still remembered the first sentence that had put him off: "Under certain circumstances there are few hours in life more agreeable than the hour dedicated to the ceremony known as afternoon tea." Said Baldwin: "It might have been in a foreign language for all it meant to me then." Henry James probably isn't any teenage reader's cup of tea, but Baldwin made another, more successful attempt at appreciating him in Paris.

"I was in a big Henry James phase then," Otto Friedrich told me, "and I probably preached to Jimmy about him. I don't think he knew much about James then. I'd be very surprised if anyone else introduced him to James. For Christmas 1949 he gave me as my Christmas present a copy of *The Journals of Henry James,* and he inscribed it with a quotation from *The Middle Years* he had got from me: 'Do what we can . . .' Jimmy was very big on Faulkner then and I probably learned a lot from him about Faulkner."

Eileen Finletter remembered a conversation Baldwin had with her first husband about Henry James. "He said what a terrible time he was having trying to connect with James. There seemed to be no point of reference either in the style or subject matter. James was writing about a world he couldn't care less about. My first husband advised him to 'wait awhile.' He couldn't have given him better advice. It took some maturing on Jimmy's part to identify with James as a fellow exile."

Baldwin had become a Jamesian by the time Ann Birstein, then studying in Paris, and Alfred Kazin, the critic, met him. Kazin said that "with his sexual tastes and this and that, he lived a life very much outside mine," and they didn't see much of each other until they met in New York in later years. But Birstein, who met him at a dinner at Eileen Finletter's with a group of writers, all of whom like Baldwin were "very impecunious," became very friendly with him. "I adored him. He looked so African, so aborigine, and yet he was so eloquent in English. It was as if Henry James had inhabited this odd body. We talked about everything, including Henry James, though Jimmy liked him more than I did. We talked about subjects of articles to sell and Jimmy's idea was to sell 'A Negro Looks at Henry James' to Partisan Review. Of course he was joking. Jimmy was always having hard luck in those days—lousy luck. I remember someone loaned him a chalet outside Paris and there was an immediate avalanche and he couldn't get out for three days. Once he and I were walking along the street and somehow he stumbled into a car. Nobody worried whether *he* was hurt because the car was dented . . ."

Terry Southern had the impression Baldwin "would have liked to be like Henry James. Sometimes elements of his style had a resemblance. He tried to have the same ethereal quality. There were passages with a tone quite like James. I remember he also liked Thomas Mann's *Death in Venice* a lot. It was partly the homosexual theme. He was always trying to read Proust in translation. He said he wished he could read it in the original French. He had only cafe French like everybody else."

Baldwin's interest in Henry James has already become the subject of doctoral dissertations, and before his death Baldwin lectured at several universities in the U.S. and abroad on such of James' novels as *The Ambassadors, The Princess Casamassima* and *The Portrait of a Lady* that had mystified him as a youth. Lyall H. Powers argues that the aims of James and Baldwin as writers were much the same: "to examine the problem of learning to live in a 'civilized' society whose manners, conventions, prejudices often threaten individual integrity; of coming to terms with that society's demands; and of managing to make the necessary compromises—but without giving up one's essential self."

David Adams Leeming, who interviewed Baldwin in later life for The Henry James Review, said James was his "standard" for the novelist's art. James, Baldwin decided, shared with him the one essential theme—the failure of Americans to see through to "the reality of others" that was apparent in America's race problem. Baldwin told Leeming: "As a writer I needed a box to put thoughts in—a model. I couldn't use D.H. Lawrence, for example (I was far too much like him). I had to find someone else, and James became, in a sense, my master. It was something about point of view, something about discipline. And something about the silence in which I myself was living began to help me because I was able to go back to something in myself in that silence—the silence of living in Paris—which allowed me to write." He said he could never have written *Go Tell It On the Mountain* "without that silence and without James." Balzac was helpful but French, he couldn't read Proust, he couldn't "use Dostoevsky until I had read all of him. But I was too much like him anyway." The closest thing to a model he could find "for the means to order and describe something that had happened to me in the distance—America—was James." At last he had found the way to finish his novel about his family. "James was my key."

Baldwin explained to the Paris Review why the book had been so hard to write. "I was too young when I started, seventeen; it was really about me and my father. There were things I couldn't deal with technically at first. Most of all, I couldn't deal with *me*. This is where reading Henry James helped me, with his whole idea about the center of consciousness and using a single intelligence to tell the story. He gave me the idea to make the novel happen on John's birthday." John was the chief character and very much like Frog Eyes. By making his birthday the central event—John thinks his family has forgotten until his mother surprises him—Baldwin could interweave flashbacks concerning his parents without losing the suspense of his story.

So Henry James had showed him how to finish his novel at last. Now the problem was to find the peace to do it. Writing was impossible in the grim, cheap hotels he stayed at, enormous dark, cold and hideous establishments in which Paris abounds. They made you understand the necessity for French cafes. As soon as Baldwin got out of bed, usually about noon, depending on how late he had stayed out the night before, he took a notebook and a fountain pen to the famous upstairs room of the Cafe de Flore. "A lot of *Go Tell It On the Mountain* had to be written there, between there and the Hotel Verneuil." It had been one of the existentialists' great meeting places and tourists still came looking for them. As Baldwin was sitting there one afternoon a big car with luggage piled on the roof stopped outside and a large woman opened the car door and yelled, "Is Jean-Paul Sartre here today?" A waiter answered, "No, *madame,*" and the car sped off. Baldwin was never a Sartre admirer, perhaps because Wright was, and he dismissed existentialism as a "curious and, on the whole, rather obvious doctrine." As he sat in the busy fashionable cafe trying to write through the afternoon, he drank a lot of coffee and was interrupted numerous times by friends coming in and out. The custom, according to Terry Southern, was to let anyone you knew share your table when the cafe was crowded, which it generally was. A quiet place to write was therefore almost impossible to find. You always had company. As evening approached, Baldwin switched from coffee to alcohol "but did not get much writing done." The evening, Southern said, was spent trying to get a meal at somewhere like Eileen Finletter's or at a very cheap restaurant with other friends, if someone had money. Terry Southern also recalled that he and Mason Hoffenberg were students and had student cards and restaurant coupons that enabled them to get cheap meals. "I remember we took Jimmy along sometimes. I apologized to him that it wasn't gourmet fare, but Jimmy was used to poverty meals in Harlem and was pleasingly surprised."

Actress Simone Signoret remembered seeing Baldwin often "solitary in the back of the Montana bar at the time when the Rue St. Benoit was drawing its first breath just after the war." She wondered whether the small young black man "was a trumpeter or a deserter, or perhaps both." They didn't speak but exchanged smiles, and it was years before she discovered he "had become one of America's greatest contemporary writers."

Baldwin also had a good friend, Mary S. Painter, an economist, who worked at the U.S. embassy, and he sometimes dined with her. In gratitude for those days and their continuing friendship, he dedicated *Another Country* to her in 1962. Otto Friedrich said she "wasn't part of our bohemian group, but had money and was therefore in a different class." Mrs. Sol Stein knew her as a shy woman and used to see her in offbeat restaurants dining with a "funny little black man" she learned was the writer James Baldwin only years later in New York. Baldwin had several friends like Mary Painter who helped keep him alive, but his big problem was somehow to get away from the pressures of Paris to find the peace to finish his novel. Once more he needed to escape, but this time he didn't see any way of doing it.

It was about this time that, back in New York, Dr. Kenneth B. Clark, the black psychologist and educationalist, met Elliot Cohen of Commentary. Cohen told him about a young black writer who was then living in Paris and was going to be one of America's major writers "if he survives." Cohen was afraid he might be moving "toward self-destruction" and felt "every opportunity should be seized to keep him alive and productive" so he could make the contribution Cohen believed was essential "to Americans' understanding of themselves." Cohen described the young man as "extraordinarily sensitive, intense, a man of burning passion."

Dr. Clark asked what his name was.

"James Baldwin," replied Cohen. "Don't forget it."

5

Getting Mountain *Published*

ONE OF James Baldwin's friends was a much older man who had left Germany soon after the coming of Hitler. Eventually he had reached Paris, but he was never free from the fear that the Nazis would catch up with him until the French capital was liberated toward the end of World War II. He was one of the people who had regularly taken Baldwin to dinner at Left Bank cafes, and had also tried to find jobs for him. In 1951 he learned his mother was dying in Germany and she wanted to see him for a last time. Baldwin accompanied him to the railroad station. "I never, never forgot that moment," Baldwin wrote nearly thirty years later. "I wondered if that was going to happen to me."

After that he had a recurring nightmare in which he received the news his mother was ill but he didn't have enough money to go to her. It was almost three years now since he had seen his family. His brothers all had jobs and had occasionally sent him a few dollars to change into francs when he was desperate. So had Beauford Delaney. Baldwin consoled himself that he couldn't go home until he had finished his novel. It was the only trophy he could take his mother to show his going away had been worthwhile—"All my love was in it, and the reason for my journey." But the novel was still far from finished. "It seemed, indeed, that it would *never* be finished."

All the daily pressures had once more begun to affect his health, and just when he was about to put the novel aside again, someone arrived to help him, as so often happened in his life.

Lucien Happersberger was a young Swiss artist who had left his parents' home to try to make it in Paris, the famous art center where Picasso was the postwar king. A tall, slim, quiet, good-looking youth, much younger than Baldwin, he was completely different in both appearance and personality, and yet this was to be probably the most important relationship of Baldwin's life. It lasted on and off for almost forty years and the two close friends were together at the end when Baldwin died. They met in a seedy bar run by a woman from Brittany who allowed Baldwin credit, he told me years later. The eternal elder brother, he advised the quiet white youth about how to survive in Paris. They very quickly reached an understanding because Lucien knew some English and Baldwin's French had improved. "I began to think in French," he recalled, and by "stepping out" of his native language, he said, he began to understand that better, too. He and Lucien were soon friendly enough to form an alliance and pool their resources. Baldwin told me: "We used to meet late in the day at a cafe and pool what money we'd managed to raise and then we'd eat. We shared everything. Once I remember we were down to zero so we went to a restaurant where I had credit, but the staff had gone to a funeral that day and it was closed. We didn't eat that night."

He introduced his new friend to the American colony. Terry Southern remembered meeting Lucien at a time when the young Swiss was exhibiting some of his paintings. Emile Capouya, who had a fellowship to Oxford University, arrived in Paris for a short vacation and met Jimmy and Lucien in the Latin Quarter. He hadn't seen Baldwin for nearly four years, but "he didn't look very different. I remember a great harangue about Richard Wright and his philosophy, and then he got on the phone and asked Wright to lend him some money. It reminded me that in New Jersey he used to borrow books from Tom Martin and then sell them. He was sending money home then to his mother. He talked to me about how hard it had been to leave his family, but he had to do it if he was ever to become a writer. My culture would have rejected such a decision as egotistical selfishness. I came from a tribe that said you can't act that way, you're supposed to keep things going at home. Jimmy and I discussed the two points of view. He understood what he was doing. He *had* to get away if he wasn't to have the soul pushed out of him and end up in some hospital for the criminally insane. It was certainly a big gamble on Jimmy's part, but in the end it came off. He was able to support his family and also be a writer."

Baldwin also met another young American who was later to be important in his writing career—Norman Podhoretz, then at Cambridge University, later to be editor of Commentary and to commission what was to be Baldwin's most famous work, *The Fire Next Time,* which resulted in a great row between them. "I was in Paris during the Christmas vacation," Podhoretz recalled, "and I think I met Jimmy through a mutual friend. I knew his name from his stuff in Partisan Review, I think. Anyway I admired his writing. We talked, but I didn't learn much then about his life in Paris."

These encounters must have boosted Baldwin's confidence because he showed a section of his novel he was pleased with to the editors of Zero and several other small literary magazines. The extract described a youth who was based on his stepfather's eldest son, Samuel, who had left home. In the novel he was called Roy. The extract was perfectly understandable on its own and could be read as a short story. He entitled it "Roy's Wound." One of the editors liked it a lot and Baldwin took it as a good omen that the novel's days of rejection were over. All he had to do now was to finish it, but that seemed as far off as ever.

By now Baldwin's extraordinary nervous vitality was drained and he seemed to be heading for a breakdown. Lucien became so worried about him that he decided he had to get Jimmy away from Paris so he could recover in more restful, healthier surroundings. That meant back home in Switzerland. Baldwin found himself in a remote village near Lausanne, where Lucien's mother had been born and the family still had a chalet. It proved to be a culture-shock for both the village and Baldwin. Lucien had warned him that the six hundred villagers would be intensely curious about him. Baldwin took this to mean "people of my complexion" were rare in Switzerland and also the villagers didn't see that many city people. "It did not occur to me, possibly because I am an American," recollected Baldwin, "that there could be people anywhere who had never seen a Negro." Well, the villagers hadn't and they treated him as if he were some kind of freak. The children called after him in the street and the adults were fascinated by the color and texture of his hair. When Baldwin sat in the sun, someone would put fingers in his hair or touch his hand to see if the color rubbed off. Baldwin tried to be friendly, "it being a great part of the American Negro's education" to make people "like" him, but he found the situation a great strain. He imagined what it must have been like to be the first white men arriving in an African village, but the white men went there as conquerors, whereas he was merely a visitor among a people "whose culture controls me, has even, in a sense, created me." The most illiterate among the villagers was related to Shakespeare, Michelangelo, the cathedral at Chartres in a way he was not. "Out of their hymns and dances come Beethoven and Bach. Go back a few centuries and they are in their full glory—but I am in Africa, watching the conquerors arrive."

That collective "I" was a sign of how much Baldwin under his big public smile had been angered. His treatment as a freak in the village brought back memories of childhood he thought he had buried long ago. It awoke in him his stepfather's bitter hatred he had sworn to overcome with love, it sent coursing through him that racial rage he had not really felt since he was in New York. In reflecting on the village's treatment and its effect on him, Baldwin wrote: "No black man can hope ever to be entirely liberated from this internal warfare—rage, dissembling, and contempt having inevitably accompanied his first realization of the power of white men."

He stayed only two weeks, just long enough to recuperate, then returned to Paris. But he could return to the village if he wished to work on his novel. Away from the village, he found the experience less serious—he even described as a joke how they had felt his hair and rubbed his hand. Finally he packed his bag again and returned—it was the only hope of finishing his novel. This time the villagers were less curious about his hair and skin and some were even downright friendly. Men bought him drinks and recommended he learn how to ski. But others behind his back suggested he stole wood "and there is already in the eyes of some of them that peculiar, intent, paranoic malevolence which one sometimes surprises in the eyes of American white men when, out walking with their Sunday girl, they see a Negro male approach." But this time Baldwin was determined not to let the villagers interfere with his work and spent most of his time typing in the chalet. He told the Paris Review: "After the years of carrying that book around I finally finished it in Switzerland in three months. I remember playing Bessie Smith all the time while I was in the mountains, and playing her till I fell asleep."

He had given up the title *Crying Holy* and had finally found the title he would keep. He liked the idea of calling it *Go Tell It On the Mountain* when he was finishing it on a mountain. He had no difficulty now in writing about his painful family memories. His stepfather was called Gabriel and he was satisfied he had portrayed him as he was and without hatred. His mother was Elizabeth, whom he depicted with love. He himself was John, and at the end he made his homosexuality clear even though that was still daring in a book. He thought long and hard about the dedication, then wrote simply: "For My Mother and Father"—no names. He admitted to feeling a "tremendous sense of elation." He had already been introduced to a New York agent, Helen M. Strauss of the William Morris Agency, by one of his writer acquaintances. As Helen Strauss described herself in her autobiography, *A Talent for Luck*- "I represented black writers before it was 'in': Frank Yerby, friend, scholar and great storyteller; Ralph Ellison, a marvelously talented gentleman; and Jimmy Baldwin, whose essays are masterpieces, whose plays and novels are not. Jimmy can be engaging, charming and irritating. On some occasions I could have slapped him as I would a naughty child." This remark may have been influenced by Baldwin's later moving to another agent. Otto Friedrich thought Strauss became irritated by many appeals from Paris for money and help when Jimmy was involved with the police. Lee Eisenheimer, managing editor of McCall's and Helen Strauss' assistant at the time, said: "When Helen said she could have slapped Jimmy, it was probably a reference to his failure to keep appointments. Jimmy had great trouble keeping appointments. You would set up a date and then he'd forget. But he was a very likable person." Jimmy made a parcel of his bulky manuscript and then, with Lucien, took it down the mountain to the nearest post office and mailed it off to Helen Strauss in New York. It was February 26, 1952, and, he hoped, the start of his career as a novelist.

Back in Paris, he shared the good news with fellow writers. Otto Friedrich remembered late at night in a cafe how Baldwin proudly sketched the title page of his novel on a beer-stained paper tablecloth: *Go Tell It On the Mountain, a novel, by James Baldwin.* Friedrich was delighted to learn that the piles of typed pages in Jimmy's hotel rooms— all the inserts and scribbled revisions—had at last been sorted out and sent off to Helen Strauss. Jimmy had introduced him to the New York agent, and he had become one of her clients, too, after his father, Prof. Karl Friedrich, came down from Harvard to see if she were suitable to represent his young son.

After several weeks, news came from New York. Alfred A. Knopf was interested in the novel and would like to meet with him if possible. If possible? This was the moment Baldwin had been waiting for: a summons to New York! But how could he possibly raise the fare? Not from his friends in Paris. He already owed too many of them. Just then, with perfect timing, an old friend from his New York days rescued him—Marlon Brando. Since Baldwin had last seen him, Brando had followed up his Broadway triumph in *Streetcar* by becoming a big Hollywood star with his first film, "The Men." Brando was recognized as an original, setting a new style and bringing the Method school of acting based on Stanislavsky and centered at New York's Actors' Studio into international prominence. But apparently he was little changed by fame. He was still independent in his behavior and radical in his ideas. Baldwin promptly requested that Brando loan him $500 and Brando promptly did. Baldwin lost no time in buying the cheapest available ticket on the next ship going to New York.

He welcomed the few days crossing to prepare himself for New York. He had changed in the last four years and so had New York. He felt he was more capable now of dealing with the pressures of the city. France and Switzerland had taught him how right Henry James was when he observed, "It is a complex fate to be an American." He wasn't merely an American black, he was an individual named James Baldwin.

"In America, the color of my skin had stood between myself and me; in Europe, that barrier was down." The question of who he was had at last become a personal question, and the answer was to be found inside himself. What was he *really* afraid of—returning to America or journeying any further within himself? Yet to him an "unexamined life" wasn't worth living. A friend had once warned him: "Be careful what you set your heart upon for it will surely be yours." Well, he had told his mother that he was going to be a writer, "God, Satan and Mississippi notwithstanding," and here he was with a novel about to be published. It would be years, he said, before he would realize that a writer's first breakthrough was simply "a crucial skirmish in a dangerous, unending and unpredictable battle."

Looking back over his recent experiences, he accepted that his breakdown and rage at the villagers' treatment had been partly a reaction to the change in himself. His black identity back home was a crutch as well as an affliction, the victim of the "white devils" conjured up by his stepfather. It was only in listening to Bessie Smith records while he typed the story of how his family had survived that he really became reconciled to who he was. "Once I was able to accept my role—as distinguished, I must say, from my 'place'—in the extraordinary drama which is America, I was released from the illusion that I hated America."

Brother David was at the dock to meet him. Baldwin told me he had so little money that he had to borrow from David to tip the steward who had been helpful to him on the trip over, then went uptown to see his mother and the rest of his brothers and sisters. They all seemed to have grown up, even Paula Maria, who was now nine. His mother greeted him quietly, as if he had just been away for a couple of days, but he knew her well enough, could read those eyes that were so like his own, and he sensed her feelings deep down. When he told her about the novel she seemed pleased.

To visit the offices of Alfred A. Knopf, he borrowed a suit from David. A photograph of him at the time shows a serious, intense young man with fairly short hair, a faint mustache and an almost innocent, boyish look. Unknown to him, his novel had not been completely approved, several editors had reservations. William Cole, who was the publicity director and also did editing, had read some of Baldwin's essays in Commentary and Partisan Review and recommended him to the editor in chief, Harold Strauss (no relation to agent Helen Strauss) as a promising young writer. When Helen Strauss submitted *Go Tell It On the Mountain,* Harold Strauss, who liked well-crafted, strong narratives and not sensitive "bleeding heart" novels, as he put it, summed up in his reading report: "This is definitely not my kind of book. It is embroidery rather than narrative," and he passed on the manuscript, rather messy-looking with Baldwin's last-minute insertions and also well-thumbed as if other publishers had already seen it and turned it down, to William Cole, whose reaction was much more enthusiastic. "I found the writing rich and poetic," he reported. "The dialogue is excellent. Some of the long 'Come to Jesus!' passages should be cut, and there are small points that need clarification throughout. I find the last chapter disappointing, lacking punch. This is a book (and a novelist) I would like to see us publish." Another editor, Philip Vaudrin, found the first section slow and rather boring, and he thought it needed a good deal of "working over." Vaudrin summed up: "I like much of this book, but I don't think it is publishable as it stands. Baldwin can certainly do a better job with this material than he has given us here, and for his sake as well as his publisher's he should be persuaded to do something about it." Vaudrin recommended that Knopf make "a small investment" in Baldwin "if, that is, he will undertake a revision of this present manuscript." No mention was made of homosexual undertones or an openly homosexual ending, although Emile Capouya, who read what was probably a very similar version to this one, said the novel ended with young John, the Baldwin character, revealing his homosexuality and saying, in effect, "I want a man." Capouya understood that the publisher did not like this ending and Baldwin had to take it out.

Knopf decided to offer a "small investment" of $250 for Baldwin to go away and revise the novel, and then another $750 if the revised manuscript was accepted. This was a big disappointment to Baldwin, who was unsure whether he could do still another version. Philip Vaudrin, the editor assigned to work with him if they could reach an agreement, said when Baldwin entered his office, "What about all that Come-to-Jesus stuff? Don't you think you ought to take it out?" Baldwin was bewildered. His novel, he said indignantly, was the study of a Negro evangelist and his family. They did, indeed, talk in a "Come-to-Jesus" idiom, but to "take it out" could only mean that the editor was suggesting that he destroy the book. "I gagged literally and began to sweat," Baldwin recalled, "ran to the water cooler, tried to pull myself together and returned to the office to explain the intention of my novel. I learned a great deal that afternoon; learned, to put it far too briefly, what I was up against." A talk with William Cole, who conveyed his own enthusiasm for the novel, helped. It didn't mean cutting all the church-service scenes, just trimming, focusing more sharply. Baldwin credited Cole with helping to save his life "when the editor assigned *Go Tell It On the Mountain* had me on the ropes." Cole and he became friendly, which helped. "In those days in the fifties," Cole recalled, "a white and black walking together and obviously friendly attracted a lot of attention. When we walked from Knopf's office to my apartment on West Fifty-fourth Street, people looked at us very strangely. I had a wife then and two little girls, six and eight. Jimmy was great with the girls. He became a real friend, often dropping by and drinking martinis. He was always a great talker. He didn't talk about black or homosexual problems with us, but my wife, Peggy Bennett, was a novelist published by Knopf, and she and Jimmy talked about novel writing. I remember taking him to lunch one day at a fancy Italian restaurant and I had just discovered the negroni and got it wrong and ordered a negrito and got a big laugh from Jimmy. He was always a fairly sophisticated man." Cole repeated to Baldwin what he had written in his report to Knopf— that he was "one of the few exciting young writers around."

Although Baldwin was staying with his mother in Harlem, he spent much of his time revisiting old haunts like the San Remo in Greenwich Village. He noticed a changed attitude in some of his old acquaintances in Harlem and the Village. They actually seemed envious of his new status as a published writer and of his Paris experiences. He was no longer merely a black boy from uptown, he had made it, according to some of these people, an attitude he found amusing when he was sitting with them in a suit borrowed from his brother.

The big family event during his stay in New York was David Baldwin's wedding. Jimmy and David, the oldest and youngest boys in the family, seemed to have a natural understanding, perhaps because

David had artistic aspirations, too. When Jimmy talked about his novel, David appeared to know instinctively why it had taken him so long to write and why he was having so many problems with the publisher downtown. Friends of the two brothers in the years ahead sometimes compared them to David and Jonathan in the Bible.

Baldwin found New York changed for the worse, partly, perhaps, because he saw it more with his French perspective. It was the time of McCarthyism, the period of communist witch-hunting, and many writers he knew, even those who had been dedicated left-wingers, seemed scared to talk openly about politics. If they scared so easily, Baldwin reflected, how could one expect them to do anything about the country's racial situation, the segregation practiced in education, jobs and housing? Baldwin could not readjust to life in New York—"I had been away too long." He found that Beauford Delaney was also disillusioned about the change in the country and was planning to move to Paris the next year.

Baldwin collected the money from Knopf and walked straight to the nearest steamship office and booked a passage back to France. Paris seemed curiously calm after the tensions of Manhattan. He was much more relaxed there with no real responsibilities, none of the feeling of being involved in the political situation that he had in New York. He was still an outsider in Paris—an American. But what did upset his peace of mind was the absence of Lucien, who had returned to Switzerland to see a woman he intended to marry. Baldwin feared that it meant the end of their alliance and talked emotionally about a phase of his life coming to an end.

He tried to settle down to revise his novel. He wished to get it back to Knopf as fast as possible. When he took a break, he generally drank in the bars and clubs where he would meet American entertainers. He had retained his great interest in the theater, and although he no longer thought of becoming an actor, he had in mind to write a play next. Gordon Heath, a black American actor who had made his name in a popular racial drama, *Deep Are the Roots,* back home and then moved to Paris, often sang at a club he partly owned, and Baldwin liked to hang out there. Bernard Hassell, a young black American dancer, had just

arrived in Paris when he met Jimmy Baldwin in the bar of the Montana
Hotel in St. Germain des Pres, an old haunt of Baldwin. This, too, was
to develop into one of Baldwin's lasting friendships. (Hassell was also
with him when he died.) But when Hassell first began talking to the
little black man with an actor's mannerisms he had no idea who he was.
When Baldwin introduced himself, he immediately recognized the
name. He had read the extract from the novel, "Roy's Wound," in a
literary magazine. "I was thrilled to meet him," Hassell recalled. Jimmy
seemed very lively but frail. "Jimmy's health was always fragile, but he
had the energy of three men and loved to stay up all night drinking and
discussing literature. His conversation at that period was always on his
work and the importance of others doing their work. He had great
courage and was very generous."

The first reports on *Go Tell It On the Mountain* had been in March-
April and the revised manuscript was back at Knopf by July. Philip
Vaudrin wrote that Baldwin had not carried out all the proposed
revisions, "but he has done a good deal and it is a better book all around.
He has cut some of the Come-to-Jesus scenes to which we all objected,
and he has improved the opening section greatly." As for the ending,
"I now feel that it stands up very well, that it flows quite naturally out
of what comes before. This is the one Come-to-Jesus scene that has not
been cut, and it needs only a very little work, mostly tinkering, to make
it perfectly intelligible." Vaudrin concluded: "I find this a very powerful and a very moving book—a real reading experience. In character
and tone, it seems to me perfectly justifiable to compare it with Paton's
Cry the Beloved Country, without meaning to imply that I think it would
have that kind of sale. But I think it would sell, and it would certainly
get wide and favorable review attention. Quite apart from that, Baldwin has a true talent, one that I am convinced is going to grow. He has
a remarkably acute ear, great knowledge of people, and all the perception in the world, so far as I can see." Vaudrin also made the curious
observation that "although this is a first novel, it isn't an autobiographical one." This would have come as a surprise to anyone who knew of
Baldwin's life in Harlem with his stepfather. But Vaudrin was convinced "it deals more with the lives of other people by far than it does

with anything Baldwin himself could have experienced first hand. It is this, as much as anything else, that leads one to feel that he is going to become a productive and first-rate writer."

When the revised manuscript was passed to William Cole, he merely typed a brief comment at the end of Vaudrin's lengthy report: "Baldwin has done a fine job of revision. If he'll now tidy up the last chapter a bit, we've got a fine book."

Knopf decided to take up their option on the book, give Baldwin the other $750 and publish the next year—1953. Baldwin was jubilant, but the experience made him forever skeptical about editors. Years later he told James Monroe Parker, a young artist friend of the Baldwin family, "You have to be firm with editors and not just go along with any changes they want and in time you hope they will grow used to your style. They know that basically you are a kind person, sometimes even uncertain of yourself, and some of them try to take advantage of that. It's like being in a lion's den and you keep them at bay until you can come out. I've had my struggles, baby, and not only over *Go Tell It.* I've had some struggles over endings. Sometimes they want them too neat."

A young editor at Knopf who didn't wish to be identified remembered going to lunch with Baldwin and having the same experience as William Cole. "I stood in for his editor at a meeting when he came back from France about the time *Go Tell It On the Mountain* was about to be published, I think I met him at the boat or at least I took him out to lunch. I remember we were walking up Sixth Avenue. It was a sunny day and Jimmy, who always looked very odd anyway, was still a little shell-shocked from returning to the U.S. and looked more bug-eyed than usual. He told me, 'I'm probably suffering from paranoia, but my impression is that everybody's staring at us.' Baldwin knew well that an interracial couple always attracted attention, but he probably wanted to make sure his white companion didn't miss it.

While Baldwin was waiting for his novel to be published he decided to write the play he had in mind based on his experiences with Mother Horn. A woman like her would be the chief character—Sister Marga-ret—and the drama would revolve around the life of her church and her relationship with her rebellious son. It would be a companion work to *Go Tell It On the Mountain,* coming as it did from the same period of his life. A play about a Harlem church was hardly a typical Broadway success story at that time, and since it was bound to contain any number of Come-to-Jesus references, which he had gathered from Knopf were not likely to appeal to white audiences, *The Amen Corner,* as the play was to be called, seemed "a desperate and even rather irresponsible act." Helen Strauss certainly thought so. She didn't wish to discourage him, but it was her duty "to let me know that the American theater was not exactly clamoring for plays on obscure aspects of Negro life, especially one written by a virtually unknown author whose principal effort until that time had been one novel." The agent explained that with one novel under his belt, it was the magazine market that was open to him, not the world of the theater. She urged him to write some popular feature articles or short stories. But Baldwin ignored this advice and began work on his play. He accepted that it might never be produced, but instinct told him to do it. Often in his life he was to ignore the logical recommendations of agents, editors, lawyers, accountants, producers and civil rights leaders and trust his instincts instead. He would make his decision and then rap on the nearest wood for good luck, a very superstitious man all his life. So *The Amen Corner* became something he *had* to do even though it seemed a commercially hopeless project.

He also needed to raise some money because the Knopf advance was soon gone. William Cole at Knopf remembered receiving an urgent appeal. "I had no spare money," Cole said, "but I was owed $250 by a French literary agency, and so when he wrote to me desperate for money, I told the agency to give him the $250 and he could repay me later. The agency was very uneasy about giving the money to a poorly dressed black man. I didn't even get the money back. He was not meticulous about debts. The same thing happened to a lot of people he knew."

He wrote some of the play in Paris, some in Switzerland, where he went to meet Lucien's wife and find out the state of their alliance. Lucien's first child was later named after him—Luc James—and he was the boy's godfather.

When *The Amen Corner* was finished he sent it to Helen Strauss in New York and she again expressed her misgivings and she was proved right in the sense that it was ten years before the play was professionally produced. Baldwin himself felt it was too wordy and rather cumbersome in construction, showing his theatrical inexperience, but he decided he could revise it only after seeing it performed.

Baldwin complained of being lonely and unhappy when he returned to Paris, but the arrival of Beauford Delaney soon cheered him up. He enjoyed helping the artist find a studio and introducing him to people who might buy his paintings. He also introduced him to Bernard Hassell, and Delaney painted a fine portrait of the young dancer. Hassell remembered: "Jimmy and I really got tight in 1953 after I started dancing in the Folies Bergère. When Beauford Delaney came to Paris we all became like brothers. If one was in trouble, the others were there. They were two of the most understanding and lovable people I ever met."

Another arrival in Paris was the black American novelist, Chester Himes, who was a friend of Richard Wright and who knew of Baldwin because he had reviewed Himes' book, *The Lonely Crusade,* in The New Leader. Wright had told Himes how cheaply one could live in Paris and had advised him to bring money in twenty-dollar travelers checks since they were best for the black market. He also warned Himes not to expect rooms with baths, "which was more or less an American indulgence." Wright spoke about his row with Baldwin, but Himes commented, "As all his friends knew, Dick had an excitable temperament and was given to such self-indulgent exaggeration that the buzzing of a blowfly could rage like a typhoon in his imagination."

Chester Himes was present at yet another row between Wright and Baldwin, this time at Les Deux Magots. According to Himes in his autobiography, *The Quality of Hurt,* Baldwin was waiting at a table on the terrace, "a small, intense young man of great excitability." Baldwin had phoned Wright for a loan of five thousand francs (ten dollars) and Wright "sat down in lordly fashion and started right off needling Baldwin, who defended himself with such intensity that he stammered, his body trembled, and his face quivered." Himes said Wright played the role of the fat cat, forcing Baldwin to be the "quivering mouse."

Wright accused Baldwin of showing his gratitude for all he had done for him by his scurrilous attacks. Baldwin defended himself by saying that Wright had written his story and hadn't left him, or any other American black writer, anything to write about. "I confess at this point they lost me," Himes commented. A group joined them and took sides. All the women and the majority of the men backed Baldwin, "chiefly, I think, because he looked so small and intense and vulnerable and Dick appeared so secure and condescending and cruel." Later the three of them went on to another cafe where the argument continued. "It seemed that Baldwin was wearing Dick down and I was getting quite drunk. The last I remember before I left them at it was Baldwin saying, 'The sons must slay their fathers.' At the time I thought he had taken leave of his senses, but in recent years I've come to better understand what he meant . . . On the American literary scene, the powers-that-be have never admitted but one black at a time into the arena of fame, and to gain this coveted admission, the young writer must unseat the reigning deity. It's a pity but a reality as well." Himes teased Wright by referring to Baldwin as his son.

Meanwhile in New York, *Go Tell It On the Mountain* was about to be launched. William Cole as publicity director tried to help the novel as much as he could even though there was only a small advertising budget for a first novel. He collected tributes from some well-known writers for use in promoting the book. Poet Marianne Moore, for example, praised its "unfalsified dialect" and added that the "verisimilitude is continuous; it does not lapse." When Baldwin received the usual publicity questionnaire to fill out, he decided he couldn't answer all the personal questions, so he wrote some autobiographical notes that Cole used for publicity purposes. These notes were also reprinted in Baldwin's first collection of essays, *Notes of a Native Son.* They added to a portrait of Baldwin as the man saw himself at that time. After detailing his Harlem poverty and religious background and discussing the situation of a "Negro writer," he went on: "I hazard that the King James Bible, the rhetoric of the store-front churches, something ironic and violent and perpetually understated in Negro speech—and something of Dickens' love for bravura—have something to do with me today; but I wouldn't stake my life on it." He said his aim was to be an honest man and a good writer—and to own a sixteen-millimeter camera and make experimental movies. He also replied to a newspaperman who asked for biographical details, denying his novel was about his stepfather—or his father, as he called him. "By the time a book is finished, the germ which caused it has—in the literal and the biblical sense—died." A novelist was not a portrait painter; he dealt "in distortions." He did not want any of the critics to think it was merely a book of reportage about his family; it was a truly imaginative work of literature.

When publication day came at last, Baldwin could hardly believe it after all those years. His first copy went to his mother suitably inscribed, though the book and the dedication said it all. William Cole hoped for a great critical reception, for raves across the country that might persuade Knopf to increase his advertising budget and help the novel become a bestseller. He remembered being disappointed, but there were quite a few reviews that praised the novel highly. Donald Barr in the New York *Times Sunday Book Review* described *Go Tell It On the Mountain* as "this beautiful, furious first novel." Orville Prescott in the daily New York *Times* considered it "a striking first novel" and "an odd and special book" written with "great intensity and feeling." But he suggested it would not necessarily appeal to everyone. "Somehow his story seems almost as remote as a historical novel about the Hebrew patriarchs and prophets." Commentary classed it as "the most important novel written about the American Negro." Time thought the church scenes "as compelling as anything that has turned up in a novel this year." Harrison Smith in the Chicago *Sun-Times* praised Baldwin's prose style "that is at once poetic and true." One of the more negative comments came from a Harlem resident who lived only a few blocks away from the Baldwin family—the veteran black writer Langston Hughes. As a friend of Richard Wright, he had disliked Baldwin's essays on *Native Son* and was perhaps influenced by this feeling when he judged Baldwin's novel. He had been published and then dropped by Knopf and, with the success of Ralph Ellison's *Invisible Man* and now *Go Tell It On the Mountain,* he was beginning to feel that he was being outstripped by the new generation of black writers. Baldwin, he thought, "over-writes and over-poeticizes in images way over the heads of the folks supposedly thinking them," in what was an " 'art' book about folks who aren't 'art' folks." He described the novel as "a low-down story in a velvet bag." Richard Wright himself was more magnanimous. As Michel Fabre reported in his Wright biography, Wright did not "fail to recognize and publicly proclaim the value of *Go Tell It On the Mountain,* but he always avoided its author, who, in turn, was not satisfied until he finally took Wright's place in the eyes of the American critics after Wright's death."

Baldwin wrote no more about Richard Wright for the time being—he would return to the battle when he was ready—but not yet willing to take on another literary father figure, he ignored Langston Hughes' comment about this novel though apparently he was aware of it. Besides, Langston Hughes had once been more generous, writing to Baldwin five years earlier in praise of his essay on Harlem in Commentary. Baldwin had never replied, explaining later, "I just didn't know what to say so I didn't say anything." Impolite certainly, perhaps the awkwardness of the intensely shy, and then he also may have been worried about getting involved with another literary father figure he would have to "slay." Baldwin and Hughes would have more exchanges in the future that would cause bad feeling between them, but all that mattered at the time was that he was a *published* novelist—his career had begun.

6

Giovanni's *Rejection*

THE RECEPTION of *Go Tell It On the Mountain* helped Baldwin get a Guggenheim grant, which he decided to spend on a return visit to New York to follow up on the publication of his novel and find new sources of income. He also applied to spend some time at the MacDowell artists' colony at Peterborough, New Hampshire, to work on a new novel he described as "a study in ambivalences, of people struggling in pain to find their proper balances." Philip Vaudrin backed his application with a strong statement that Knopf considered Baldwin "to be a novelist not only of extremely high promise but of already demonstrated ability" and referred the colony's admissions committee to the recent reviews of *Go Tell It On the Mountain*. He described Baldwin as "a sensitive, perceptive, and stimulating person" who would "contribute much to the life of the group, both intellectually and socially."

Vaudrin also wrote to Helen Strauss that he was pleased her client was coming home. He said it had always been his view that Jimmy Baldwin "would be better off and more productive back here, and I hope he comes home and gets to work. I have a feeling that most people

work better and with a deeper sense of reality on their home grounds."
Many people—other editors, journalists, friends—were to echo those
sentiments over the years, often to Baldwin's irritation.

He told Helen Strauss he was "homesick." The curtain had come
down on a certain aspect of his life, that aspect most closely connected
with his reasons for going to Europe in the first place, and he felt he'd
like to try his homeland for a change. But he had an almost superstitious
terror of crossing seas and continents with an unfinished novel. He had
rashly promised her some short stories, but these had turned into parts
of a new novel. Since he was not so foolish as he used to be, he wouldn't
now try to tell her when it would be done, except that he could
probably assure her that it wouldn't take anything like as long as the
Mountain took—that was because he was not as young as he used to be.
But he thought it might be a good deal longer than *Mountain.* The new
novel did not have a Negro theme nor even a Negro character. It took
place in Paris during one year—mainly in the American colony—and
was a love story between a thirtyish American divorcee and a slightly
younger, extremely unstable American actor. Baldwin was beginning to
separate *Giovanni's Room* from *Another Country,* but he still had a long
way to go. He summed up the main theme as the incredible varieties
and fashions and immense range of human desperation, human anguish,
and the paradox which dictates that the only means of escape from this
human condition was the acceptance of it, acceptance which was not at
all the same thing as subservience or surrender or defeat. There was also
a second theme involving his belief that Americans were the most
disturbed people in the western world today and that precisely the fact
that they were capable of being so disturbed was their great virtue, their
great strength, their great potential. The bare plot was ugly and involved
dope, blackmail and the guillotine. No mention, however, of homosexuality, and one wonders whether he was trying to spare Helen Strauss
at this stage, since it was a controversial, not very commercial subject,
or whether he hadn't yet worked it out for himself. He told his agent
he couldn't think of anything like his novel, but it had something of
James' *The Ambassadors* except of course it was much more violent and
explicit. Still James' Lambert Strether in groping toward a larger view

of life was perhaps the key to his own hero. There was also something in the novel of Hemingway's *The Sun Also Rises* though his own generation wasn't even so well defined as to be considered "lost," and he also wanted his texture more dense, his pain more awful, his resolution less despairing. He thought his heroine was more closely related to James' Isabel Archer in *The Portrait of a Lady* than to Hemingway's Brett. He was using as a title *A Fable for Our Children,* though he thought this wouldn't survive. He was right about that and much more would change, too, or would disappear to be used in *Another Country.* But at least, as he told Helen Strauss, he was relieved to be over his attack of second novel jitters. He asked her to say a little prayer for him.

The Guggenheim grant, the sale of paperback rights of *Mountain* to New American Library, the publication of an essay about the Swiss village in Harper's Magazine—all this meant he had a little more money than usual and with more to come, so he decided to take Lucien Happersberger with him to New York. Lucien had showed him his village, now he would show Lucien *his* village—Harlem. The first few days back home were spent introducing Lucien to his family and showing him his "turf" as a boy. He was delighted when he arrived late for a meeting at a bar on 125th Street to find his Swiss friend deep in conversation with the barman and the other customers as if he had no awareness of being the only white person there. But midtown they had a grim experience when they were stopped by police on Broadway and interrogated separately for hours. They were supposed to resemble men the police were looking for, but Baldwin was convinced they were harassed because they were a black and white together.

His old classmate, Emile Capouya, met them both on a subway train, but he was getting off and there was time only to say hello. Another old classmate, Sol Stein, saw Baldwin and Lucien in the Village, where they were living. He understood Lucien was earning money painting pictures in the Village and seemed to have some older women friends. "I don't know if Jimmy was jealous," Sol Stein told me, "but I do know he was tortured by the fact Lucien had a child and that kind of relationship." Stein, who was working as an editor, suggested Baldwin should publish a collection of his essays. Baldwin wasn't enthusiastic, saying he was "too young to publish my memoirs." He finally agreed, mainly because there was a possibility of some more money; what he had was fast disappearing. Sol Stein had interested Beacon Press in Boston in the idea, new at that time, of publishing the book as a large-size quality paperback with a simultaneous small hardcover edition to make sure reviewers would take it seriously. "I fought with Jimmy over what should be in the collection and the order," said Stein. They agreed on nine essays from those Jimmy had already published, but Stein wanted a tenth and so Baldwin agreed to write a new one.

He also worked on a project with another old classmate, Burton Bendow, who was on the staff of the International Motion Picture Service. Baldwin talked eagerly about his interest in making a film and they decided to make one together. "I borrowed from my boss a two-thousand-dollar, sixteen-millimeter camera and all the necessary lighting equipment," Bendow said. "Jimmy took me round to the church where, I think, he had his conversion. He introduced me to the pastor of the church, a handsome sour-faced woman selling to poor local children chipped ice flavored with cheap, poisonous brilliant-colored liquids—bright oranges and reds—which was Harlem's cheap form of ice cream. We were going to film some important meeting. We had worked out a little plot to alternate shots of Holy Roller enthusiasm there with cut-rate drugs that were all over Harlem at that time. We had to be very discreet because anything to do with films seemed sinful to many in the congregation. The sour-faced pastor was transformed in a white silk robe and was in her glory. There were hymns and people testified emotionally. But after all our preparations we found the camera wouldn't work, so the film was never made. It was a great disappointment." At least Jimmy Baldwin must have been forgiven for his defection twelve years before, but it was surprising that the pastor would allow even such a tiny camera crew into the church. The former Young Minister must have been very persuasive.

Baldwin and William Cole at Knopf now renewed their friendship. Baldwin had "a dumpy room on Greenwich Street in the Village," Cole remembered, and they went around the Village bars together. They also listened to jazz in the Village clubs. "I don't care for jazz, but Jimmy was very keen." Cole and his wife went up to Harlem for dinner, "and he took us to Mother Horn's revival service full of shouting and hallelujahs and marching in the aisles. Jimmy participated and sang." Temporary return of the ex–Young Minister? Cole also went to dinner with the Baldwin family. "I remember a gaffe of mine. I said, 'Where do you go for your vacation?' That didn't go down very well, they didn't go for vacations. There was lots of generous laughter at my expense."

When the Coles went to Florida for a vacation, "I told Jimmy he could use our apartment. We went away for two weeks after giving Jimmy the keys. It was a big mistake. When we came back the whole apartment was a mess. The beds were unmade, there were piles of dirty dishes, we discovered bedbugs in the children's beds and the neighbors were enraged because people had been coming in at all hours. I don't think I ever mentioned it to him." Jimmy had written in Cole's copy of *Mountain:* "You pray for me and I'll pray for you." Baldwin continued to come by occasionally for a drink, but "he usually had people with him, an entourage, especially when he got some money."

Baldwin had come back to New York "off duty" as far as the new novel was concerned, not allowing it to be "screaming in my head." But he got down to it at the McDowell artists' colony, where there were few distractions compared with Manhattan. Sol Stein, also at the McDowell colony working on his own writing, noticed a change in Jimmy—greater self-confidence, taking himself more seriously as if the reception of his novel had affected him. "One time we were both going back to New York, just the two of us," recalled Stein. "In those days, without the highways of today, it was a six-hour drive. We drove through one of the worst rainstorms since Noah—or rather, I drove. We debated whether we should go or not and decided to take a chance. We were going through some place in New England and over the crest of the hill we could see a river had broken its banks. All we could see ahead was water. We were heading for it when Jimmy said, 'This is going to be a terrible day for American literature,' which meant he could still see it in perspective! We did find the bridge and went on all right."

By then Baldwin had decided how he would separate the new novel from what was to be *Another Country*. To handle homosexuality, the "Negro problem" and a Paris setting in the same novel "would have been quite beyond my powers." He decided to limit it even more than he had outlined to Helen Strauss. The title now was *Giovanni's Room,* and he was dedicating it to Lucien with a quotation from Walt Whitman: "I am the man, I suffered, I was there." Even more important to the novel, he decided to write it in the first person from the viewpoint of an American man trapped between two loves—an American woman and an Italian man. This was a gamble to give the novel maximum intensity because Baldwin said generally he tended "to be in accord with James, who hated the first-person perspective, which the reader has no reason to trust—why should you need this *I*? . . ." He also revised the opening so that now it began: "I stand at the window of this great house in the south of France . . ."

While he was writing the novel with surprising speed—the scenes of the American colony in Paris were particularly easy to write—he had good news. His old buddy, Marlon Brando, had won an Oscar for the role of the ex-boxer Terry Malloy in "On the Waterfront," the dockyard film written by Budd Schulberg and directed by Elia Kazan. Baldwin watched on TV as Bette Davis, the lady with eyes almost as prominent as his own, presented the Oscar to Brando in Hollywood and kissed him. Brando, perhaps a little heavier, looked his old self, not taking any of it too seriously. It was a good omen for his novel, Baldwin decided. Then he received more good news—Owen Dodson, a well-known black writer and teacher, planned to direct a student production of *The Amen Corner* at Howard University, a leading black college in Washington, D.C., and he invited the author to attend. It was the first college campus Baldwin had ever seen. He enjoyed working in rehearsals trimming some of the speeches and listening to his words spoken for the first time. It was a tremendous boost to his morale and also put him more closely in touch with the new black generation. He was very pleased at the way the students received him. Not knowing much about university life, he had expected some snobbery because they were all more formally educated than he was. But the students treated him with great respect, and some had even read *Mountain* and the essays. He enjoyed the late-night arguments with them. He was aware of the difference in the ghettoes and down South since the return of black servicemen from wartime and postwar service overseas. They felt that if they could fight for the country, then it was time they had full rights as citizens. Some of their sons were at Howard University. They were full of the recent Supreme Court ruling against segregated education. The effects on the country could be revolutionary in racial relations. But the white racists down south were willing to try to resist the new law. It could mean another civil war. Baldwin had never been down South. He would have to go one day to complete *his* education.

The play was a huge success with the students, less so with some of the faculty and a reporter from *Variety,* the show-business trade paper, who seemed a little bewildered. There were no more offers to produce *The Amen Corner,* which would have to wait nearly ten more years for its first professional production—a disappointment for Baldwin, who, in his upbeat mood, had thought he was on his way to Broadway.

Between Owen Dodson's home and the Dunbar Hotel he somehow found time to write the essay Sol Stein wanted to complete the collection. He had chosen his stepfather as the subject and could handle it now the novel was behind him. That had been a great release, overcoming barriers inside him. He would write about his stepfather's bitter hatred that had finally driven him mad and that he himself was still struggling not to inherit. He ended his essay: "This fight begins, however, in the heart and it now had been laid to my charge to keep my own heart free of hatred and despair. This intimation made my heart heavy and, now that my father was irrecoverable, I wished that he had been beside me so that I could have searched his face for the answers which only the future would give me now."

He chose *Notes of a Native Son* as the title of the essay and also of the collection. He told me he had had in mind both Richard Wright's *Native Son* and Henry James' *Notes of a Son and Brother.* Harper's Magazine published the essay. Anne Freedgood, an editor at Harper's at the time, arranged for Baldwin to come by to go through the editing of his essay. She also intended to take him out to dinner to a nearby restaurant after checking that blacks were served there. Baldwin was well over an hour late and then had on old sneakers with his toes sticking out and blue jeans worn out at the knees. The restaurant wouldn't admit anyone dressed like that, she knew. She was annoyed with him for what she assumed was deliberate role-playing. She found him "very, very defensive." Harper's Magazine was looking for another editor and she had thought Jimmy Baldwin would be a good choice, but nothing came of her recommendation.

Notes of a Native Son was published late in 1955 and, Sol Stein recalled, "was an immediate success. There was a good critical response which helped to keep the book in print and eventually be accepted as a permanent part of the culture." Time's review was typical, describing Baldwin's collection as a "sheaf of personal essays, written with bitter clarity and uncommon grace." Included in the collection were the two essays taking Wright's *Native Son* apart, so inevitably the Wright admirers had reservations about the book. Langston Hughes was heard from again, this time in the New York *Times Book Review.* He much preferred the collection to *Mountain,* "where the surface excellence and poetry of his writing did not seem to me to suit the earthiness of his subject matter." The essay about his stepfather was "superb." Baldwin was "thought-provoking, tantalizing, irritating, abusing and amusing." When this "young man" could look at life purely as himself and for himself, "the color of his skin mattering not at all, when, as in his own words, he finds 'his birthright as a man no less than his birthright as a black man,' America and the world might well have a major contemporary commentator." Langston Hughes stressed that Baldwin was still immature—"That Baldwin's viewpoints are half American, half Afro-American, incompletely fused, is a hurdle which Baldwin himself realizes he still has to surmount."

To Baldwin, the review was patronizing and annoyed him almost as much as his essays had annoyed Wright. He awaited a good opportunity to reply. It came when the New York *Times Book Review,* which had published the Langston Hughes review, asked him to review Langston

Hughes' selected poems. "Every time I read Langston Hughes," wrote Baldwin, "I am amazed all over again by his genuine gifts—and depressed that he has done so little with them." The book contained a great deal "which a more disciplined poet would have thrown into the waste-basket." There were "poems which almost succeed but which do not succeed, poems which take refuge, finally, in a fake simplicity in order to avoid the very difficult simplicity of the experience!" Hughes had Negro speech, music and other forms working for him in his verse, but although he knew the "bitter truth" behind these hieroglyphics, "he has not forced them into the realm of art where their meaning would become clear and overwhelming." Hughes was "an American Negro poet and has no choice but to be acutely aware of it. He is not the first American Negro to find the war between his social and artistic responsibilities all but irreconcilable."

Arnold Rampersad in his biography of Langston Hughes describes this as a "tone of nonchalant dismissal." He compares it with Baldwin's "unrepented public attacks" on his "former friend and mentor Richard Wright." Baldwin, he commented, "apparently had felt an almost Oedipal need to slay the paternal figure in the field of black poetry." But he was also "repaying Hughes, with abundant interest," for his review of *Notes of a Native Son.* But, Rampersad added, "Behind Baldwin's review were issues somewhat deeper than his desire for revenge. Two, above all, were at stake in the exchange: Langston's status as an intellectual and, more important, his disagreement with Baldwin about the proper attitude of black writers toward race in the age of integration—or, for that matter, at any time."

It is, in fact, questionable whether Baldwin's usually complex motives could ever be simplified as mere revenge. Langston Hughes had predicted that when Baldwin was able to fuse his American and Afro-American viewpoints, "there will be a straight-from-the-shoulder writer, writing about the troubled problems of this troubled earth with an illuminating intensity." But Baldwin felt he had been "straight from the shoulder" from the beginning. He particularly disliked the schizophrenic, hypocritical attitude of many black Americans—playing a phony role with whites and being themselves only with fellow blacks.

Necessary as it might sometimes be for survival and to hold on to jobs, Baldwin felt it was a confession of weakness, an acceptance of inferiority. He was determined in his own life to be himself at all times, to "let it all hang out" whomever he was with. That was his definition of being free and independent, "a man, not a nigger," and to his credit, this explained some of the trouble he had experienced in New Jersey, the Village and even Paris. "Nobody need ever tell me to speak up," he liked to say. Basically with both Richard Wright and Langston Hughes, he saw himself as being true to the same attitude, "straight from the shoulder" in the sense Hughes meant. Playwright Lorraine Hansberry, the author of *A Raisin in the Sun,* who knew both Baldwin and Langston Hughes, once told a journalist, "Jimmy shows Langston no *respect* . . . He refers to Langston in public the way we niggers usually talk in private to each other." Baldwin took that as a tribute to his consistent attitude, his refusal to play a role, but some black writers accused him of being disloyal to a fellow black as if racial loyalty were more important than anything else in a literary world dominated by whites. Baldwin rejected that attitude, and it partly explains his unpopularity with some older blacks. Langston Hughes himself remained angry about Baldwin's treatment of his poems. In a bitter mood with the right audience, he made fun even of Baldwin's appearance, and sometimes when he received a request for a free personal appearance from some organization, he would recommend instead that "wonderful Negro writer" James Baldwin and even provide his address.

When I interviewed Langston Hughes at his home in Harlem, he said he envied some of the younger black writers who had made a lot of money out of one book, and he mentioned particularly Baldwin and Ralph Ellison. He himself, he said, had had to slave like one of the old men of letters, writing in all possible genres from essays to plays, to make a bare living. We shared a joke that he was a sort of G.K. Chesterton in burnt cork—he knew the English writer's work well. Professor Rampersad in his Hughes biography didn't think much of that comparison—"Langston's color was real, not a theatrical daubing, and this forbade him in America anything remotely like the settled identity of a British man of letters"—but in liking the comparison, Langston

Hughes probably had in mind what he had told Baldwin in his review of *Notes of a Native Son*—to look at life purely as himself, "the color of his skin mattering not at all," finding "his birthright as a man no less than his birthright as a black man." The irony is that that attitude was close to Baldwin's own about role-playing. The two writers had much more in common than either was willing to admit at that time. This was, I think, partly because they were at different stages in their literary careers, Baldwin just at the start of his, still trying to assert his individual talent and find his place in the literary world, whereas Langston Hughes was the veteran who was beginning to feel insecure in the face of the new generation.

Just how insecure was shown when he met Baldwin and Ralph Ellison together and felt the two younger black writers were condescending toward him. He immediately defined their failings as he saw them from the viewpoint of an older black writer who made his home among fellow blacks in Harlem. Baldwin, in his opinion, had shown a lack of confidence in blacks by living among whites in exile. Although he was more passionately troubled by race in his writing, his attitude partly reflected his own personal problems and homosexual tensions. As for Ralph Ellison, he looked "fat, fine and worried (about the Hungarians and such) as usual." He considered Ellison an intellectual obsessed with the latest crisis in the Cold War and not as concerned with the plight of black Americans and Africa as he should have been as a black writer. Neither Baldwin nor Ellison, he thought, was a very helpful guide for young blacks in the changing postwar period, with increasing demands for integration spurred by the Supreme Court's ruling against segregated education. Many of them were trying to become integrated as imitation whites instead of being true to their own black pride. Integration often meant an inflated intellectual idealism that wasn't realistic. The place of Baldwin and Ellison, he implied, was at home among blacks, boosting their pride and helping them to prepare for the changes ahead. Langston Hughes, in fact, had yet another public disagreement with Baldwin, and this time it was directly over Harlem. In an essay entitled "Fifth Avenue Uptown: A Letter from Harlem," published in Esquire and reprinted in *Nobody Knows My Name,* Baldwin revisited the Harlem of his childhood and took a dim view of the changes there, especially the giant, anonymous projects which were "hated almost as much as policemen." He concluded, "It is a terrible, an inexorable law that one cannot deny the humanity of another without diminishing one's own: in the face of one's victim, one sees oneself. Walk through the streets of Harlem and see what we, this nation, have become." To Langston Hughes, this was too grim, too negative and one-sided a view, and he cheerfully stressed in a TV interview that Harlem was congested—with people. "All kinds. And I'm lucky enough to call a great many of them my friends."

He had cast Baldwin as the pessimist and himself as the optimist. For him, both Baldwin and Ellison seemed more interested in addressing the white majority than the minority of their black brothers. Yet Baldwin and Ellison were not as close in their thinking as Langston Hughes' attitude suggests. Ellison was to give more and more of his time to teaching, distinguished professorships and membership on prestigious committees, publishing only essays and a couple of extracts from a second novel in progress that was often announced as being ready for publication over the next twenty years, but never appeared. He and Baldwin did not stay in touch, and Ellison in his more detached, intellectual way was reportedly in disagreement with Baldwin's much more active role in the civil rights movement. Ellison's long academic career seemed to reflect a personality that did not communicate as easily with a popular audience, black or white, as did Baldwin. In 1984 Baldwin told the Paris Review that he hadn't seen or corresponded with Ellison for many years—"I gather Ralph did not like what he considered I was doing to myself on the civil rights road." He said he'd love to meet Ellison for lunch and share a bottle of bourbon and talk about the last twenty years. "I have nothing against him in any case. And I love his great book [*Invisible Man*]. We disagreed about tactics, I suppose." They were never to have a last meeting, but Baldwin did see Langston Hughes before Hughes died in 1967, and his own thinking had changed a little in the meantime as a result of his experiences on both sides of the Atlantic.

One of the most traumatic experiences was the fate of *Giovanni's Room*. He knew from the beginning this was a much more daring novel than *Mountain*. He had been made to tone down the homosexual ending

117

of the first novel, but there was no way the theme of homosexuality could be cut out of this second novel. It was a bisexual love story and he realized as he wrote it that this time he was holding back nothing but was being "straight from the shoulder" about his life and concerns. Originally he had thought it would be much longer than *Mountain,* but writing in the first person seemed to concentrate the drama and it ended by being much shorter. In portraying various characters, he had used aspects of people he knew in the American colony in Paris. He wondered if they would recognize themselves. He depicted the bars and typical regulars in the Parisian gay underworld. He also drew from the emotional side of his own life in the French capital, even though he didn't portray anyone directly. The relationship between the American narrator and the handsome young Italian barman, Giovanni, meant a great deal to him. It was like a record of his own feelings in more than one affair. The room the two men shared, the sense of confinement as the affair broke up, of being in a prison, was something he knew intimately. A love affair of his own had ended in such a room. But the bisexual triangle was only the surface concern of the novel as far as the author was concerned. To him, the real theme was the price of lying to yourself, of not facing the truth about yourself. The American narrator was playing a macho male with a woman at the same time he was having an affair with Giovanni. He had to choose between them if he was not to be dishonest with both of them. He chose the woman to maintain his macho image, and in the end he lost both of them. The woman, as she left, told him, "Americans should never come to Europe," like a Henry James character, and Baldwin's point was that it was a situation everyone should be able to identify with, heterosexuals as well as homosexuals. But he was soon to find out that very few readers would see his novel the way he did. It would merely be a homosexual novel to most people, even publishers. In 1955, when the majority of American homosexuals found it much safer to remain in the closet, the reaction to a homosexual novel was unpredictable. Most of Baldwin's homosexual friends loved the book and considered it a real breakthrough, but others, even some of those who greatly admired his first novel and his essays, thought it sensational and more cheaply written. His old classmate, Sol Stein, recalled, "We had some words about *Giovanni's Room*. I thought the story was faked. Jimmy wanted to be a novelist more than anything else and I pressed him to be as true as he could be. He was a very great essayist, not a great novelist, certainly not in the same class. We had a kind of falling out about it. When we talked about *Giovanni's Room* I quickly saw this was not a talkable subject. To me, it was a book in drag as it were, much less good than *Go Tell It on the Mountain*."

Helen Strauss must have had misgivings when she received the manuscript and read some of it. At least, by the strictest standards of those days, it could not be dismissed as pornographic. In the classic style, the sex scenes ended when the two men reached the bedroom. "He pulled me against him, putting himself into my arms as though he were giving me himself to carry, and slowly pulled me down with him to that bed. With everything in me screaming *No!* yet the sum of me sighed *Yes.*" End of scene. She sent it on to Philip Vaudrin at Knopf. Unfortunately William Cole, Baldwin's main supporter, was away on vacation when the manuscript arrived. Vaudrin read it and passed it on to other editors for their opinion. One of them recalls that Alfred Knopf was drawn in and he, like some of the editors, found the homosexual theme "repugnant." The editor commented, "I thought it was a very good book, but I hadn't been there long and my opinion didn't carry much weight. The book was way ahead of its time. I think Alfred himself made the decision to reject the book." Baldwin said he was told the novel would ruin his reputation as a leading young black writer and he was advised to burn the manuscript. The editor has no recollection of that, but he said it was quite possible. "He was a black writer, which isn't easy, and that would have given him the identity of a black homosexual writer. Of course now no one would think twice about such a book. We've moved on."

William Cole returned from vacation to find there was nothing he could do. The decision to reject had already been made. "I was very annoyed," he said. He didn't remember, however, that Alfred Knopf was involved. He thought Philip Vaudrin and another editor had made the decision. "It was judged not the time for an out-and-out homosexual novel. There had only been Gore Vidal's." Knopf also turned down Nabokov's *Lolita* and Norman Mailer's *The Deer Park,* two other serious novels that were regarded as daring in the sexual field. Another executive at Knopf who disagreed with the decision was William Koshland, who was in charge of rights and permissions. Only a few months before he had sent Helen Strauss the remainder of the $3,000 which was Baldwin's share of the advance from New American Library for the paperback rights to *Mountain,* and he had told her how pleased he was that Baldwin had gotten a Guggenheim grant and hoped to hear "he has all kinds of plans afoot." He thought it was a mistake to turn down *Giovanni's Room.* "The second novel is always a difficult one," Koshland told me. "Look at Mailer's *Barbary Shore.* The author generally tries to do something different. The publisher should publish the second novel no matter what. They should think of his future career if they admire the writer."

No one envied Helen Strauss the task of informing the author. William Cole remembered how "very angry" Baldwin was. Even four years later Baldwin was still furious about it. "They told me to burn it!" he said indignantly. "They said it would ruin me if I tried to get it published. I had turndowns because they treated it like pornography. But I wouldn't accept such treatment!" When the first version of *Mountain* flopped, he felt humiliated, on the defensive, but not now! Knopf should feel that way, not him. He believed in his book—in himself as a writer—and he was determined to fight for it. He told me, "I took it over to England and my publisher there, Michael Joseph, said if his lawyers passed it, he'd love to publish it. And there were no problems. None at all! The book got good reviews. And once the English accepted it so well, the cowards here took it. Never talk to me about the *courage* of American publishers. You're stupid if you let their rejections worry you—and I say that as one who was stupid. Always make up your own mind. You just can't afford to let people give you your evaluation of your own book. Certainly not if you're a Negro. If I've learned one thing from life, that's it . . ."

This was Baldwin at his most dramatic remembering a traumatic event a few years before. He talked as if he had dashed to the airport and personally taken the rejected manuscript to Michael Joseph. Apparently it went through Helen Strauss' London representative. Raleigh Trevelyan, who was Baldwin's editor at Michael Joseph for many years, said that even though the novel had been rejected by Baldwin's American publisher, "such was MJ's faith in him" that the company decided to risk publishing it. Now Baldwin had to find a similarly loyal American publisher.

7

Paying Dues

SEVERAL OTHER New York publishers turned down *Giovanni's Room* before it arrived at Dial Press, a lively young publishing house on the lookout for new writers. Helen Strauss must have decided by then it was hopeless trying any more of the older, larger, prestigious, but quite conservative companies. James B. Silberman was then a young editor at Dial and he found *Giovanni's Room* in a pile of manuscripts that had come in for the president, George Joel. As Silberman had heard of Baldwin, he took the novel home to read that night. "I thought it was extraordinary, certainly compared with anything else I had read recently from the manuscript pile. My memory is that I recommended it to the president and he had some reservations about it. So he sent it to Philip Rahv at Partisan Review, who was his literary adviser. Jimmy of course had been published in Partisan Review and Rahv wrote back that the book was, indeed, extraordinary, that no doubt it should be published—and it was."

So Baldwin at last had an American publisher for *Giovanni's Room* and at the same time began a close relationship with a company (which was to be joined on the paperback side by Dell Books) that was not only to be his publisher but banker, adviser, confidant and even at times his travel agent. The editors changed frequently but the publishers— Richard Baron for Dial and Helen Meyer for Dell—remained constant, and Baldwin in time learned to trust them as much as he ever trusted a publisher.

James Silberman was his first editor at Dial. "I handled *Giovanni's Room*," Silberman said, "but there was very little editing to be done except as regards the beginning and the end. In the draft I saw, Jimmy had given away the ending at the beginning and I suggested he keep it until the end. All our exchanges were by mail because by then he was back in Paris. He came over later and it was then I met him for the first time in a restaurant with a couple of people from the William Morris Agency who represented him. I saw before me a tiny, unique-looking, odd-looking, amazing-looking black guy. My memory is that he was shy at that first meeting. I knew quite a lot about him by then, but he knew nothing about me. We were roughly the same age—he was thirty-one and I was just a little younger. We got on well. We were both really kids. We worked on three more books together."

It was typical that Baldwin had set off again for his refuge—Paris. He needed an escape from all the extra pressures and tensions that *Giovanni's Room* had brought. He learned about Dial Press' acceptance by mail. It was typical, too, that he left the William Morris Agency soon after. Helen Strauss had been a witness of his rejection, and she hadn't been as enthusiastic about *Giovanni* as he felt his agent should be. She reprimanded him like a headmistress about being late for appointments and she had shown impatience about his appeals for help and money from Paris. Perhaps he needed a man to represent him—a man who wouldn't be halfhearted about anything he wrote, however realistic, because the next novel was going to go beyond *Giovanni*. Lee Eisenheimer, Helen Strauss' assistant then, said, "I don't know what made Jimmy go off to another agent. I think *Giovanni's Room* was the last book we handled. It often happens a writer has an agent when he is unknown and then when he becomes famous, things change between them and he goes elsewhere. I don't think there was any fight, they just decided to part." Baldwin then took on Robert Mills as his agent, a tall, lean man who chain-smoked like Baldwin and also had the kind of lively social conscience that appealed to him.

Back in Paris, a growing success in his own right with a third book about to be published, Jimmy Baldwin tried yet again to make his peace with Richard Wright. He wanted a reconciliation and also Wright's acceptance of his right to his own vision and, as his equal, to disagree with him. The ill-feeling between them continued to make him a lot of enemies, and with *Giovanni* about to appear to perhaps a hostile reception, he could do with all the allies he could find among influential American writers. But he found Wright was even more opposed to anyone who threatened his own "system of reality." According to Baldwin, Wright seemed out of touch with the rapidly changing scene back home and also with Africa, although he talked authoritatively about both. Baldwin's view of Wright, however, was hotly disputed by Wright's admirers, and Wright himself found Baldwin's attitude repugnant. "This man disgusts," he wrote to a friend. "There is a kind of shameful weeping in what he writes." He also instructed his American publisher not to send proofs of his new book, *The Color Curtain,* to Baldwin or to Ralph Ellison because they were "not independent enough to give their honest reaction to a book like *The Color Curtain.*" Michel Fabre in his Wright biography stresses that Wright was not influenced by Baldwin's homosexuality because he had homosexual friends "and knew how to appreciate the sensitivity and finesse of their minds." A later biographer of Wright has even suggested Wright had a homosexual side himself.

While Baldwin was in Paris the National Institute of Arts and Letters gave him an award, and he asked William Cole to escort his mother to the awards ceremony so she could receive it for him. "On my Knopf expense account I took a taxi to pick her up," Cole recalled, "and she went on the stage at the Institute and got the award."

Baldwin took on another literary father-figure, this one white. William Faulkner, who lived most of his life in the small town of Oxford, Mississippi, with a black and white population, was the only American white novelist who wrote of blacks as well as whites with equal understanding. Although his experimental books hadn't sold well, he was awarded the Nobel Prize for Literature, partly because of his extremely high reputation in France among such influential writers as Sartre and Camus. Baldwin had been a great admirer of Faulkner when he first arrived in Paris. Emile Capouya remembered Baldwin "read Faulkner again and again. I think Faulkner gave him a license to develop his biblical prose. In *Go Tell It On the Mountain,* you know, the sermon is meant to be the equivalent of Father Mapple's sermon in Melville's *Moby Dick,* and it comes off, and he wrote that when he was a very young man. I think it began with Faulkner's influence."

Otto Friedrich recalled "he was always talking about Joe Christmas, who was partly white and partly black in Faulkner's novel, *Light in August.* Jimmy also praised the character of Dilsey, the black housekeeper who holds the decadent white family together in *The Sound and the Fury.*" He wrote very respectfully of Faulkner in his early writing, once coupling him with Ralph Ellison. But between then and 1956, his attitude had changed. He was becoming more politically minded and used Faulkner as a whipping boy in an essay entitled "Faulkner and Desegregation." There was little respect shown the author of *Light in August* and *The Sound and the Fury,* who had condemned racism long before it was fashionable or even safe to do so. Baldwin merely used *Intruder in the Dust,* a postwar Faulkner novel combining his reaction to the current racial situation with the form of a detective story, as the text for a Baldwin sermon. But then, as Lorraine Hansberry had pointed out, he hadn't shown Langston Hughes respect—or Wright. He was only treating Faulkner the way he had treated the two veteran black writers. Faulkner, with his deep love for the South, white and black, dreaded a violent confrontation and argued desperately in *Intruder in the Dust* that real progress meant going slow. Baldwin wrote scornfully that Faulkner must know the time he asked for didn't exist. "There is never time in the future in which we will work out our salvation. The challenge is in the moment, the time is always now." Why should blacks have to wait any longer for their rights? Referring to Faulkner sarcastically as "the squire of Oxford," Baldwin even quoted an interview in a British Sunday newspaper that Faulkner had already said misquoted him. The essay was not one of Baldwin's profounder efforts—in effect he was using Faulkner for propaganda purposes—and ironically it was published where the Wright articles had appeared, in Partisan Review.

I asked Otto Friedrich about Baldwin's changed attitude toward Faulkner. "Jimmy himself changed," Friedrich said. "All blacks got radicalized by the civil rights movement. You had to admit being a black, to being different from whites. It changed our relationship and the way Jimmy saw many people. I became part of the enemy race and he became a black militant to me. Some militant blacks had been caught looting, they seemed dangerous people to me, but to Jimmy they were all 'my people.' In the Paris days we talked about early Faulkner and both of us admired him. *Intruder in the Dust* was no good and Faulkner in later years set up as a conservative oracle in Mississippi."

Baldwin had now knocked three literary father-figures, two black, one white, off their pedestals. He had probably attacked Faulkner with particular relish because he had become a white liberal sage, an ideal target for raising people's consciousness about the meaning of the racial struggle. It makes one wonder about Henry James' fate at this stage of James Baldwin's life if he had been still alive rather than a safe dead classic.

The sense of competition was like electricity in the air at an exchange with another writer of his own generation. Norman Mailer, a middle-class Jew born in New Jersey who had graduated from Harvard and served in the army in World War II, was already an established bestselling author with his first novel, *The Naked and the Dead,* a big realistic war story based on his own experiences. His next novel, *Barbary Shore,* had been much more experimental and had been neither a big seller nor a critical success. His third novel, *The Deer Park,* a grim view of Hollywood as a sexual-political mirror of America, too erotically written for the fifties, had been turned down by several publishers, and when eventually published had confirmed Mailer's reputation as one of the more adventurous, rebellious and radical of the younger writers. His long essay, "The White Negro," about the hipsters of the Beat Generation, even ventured onto Baldwin's literary turf—the underground world of blacks. As short as Baldwin but much more huskily built, Mailer was strongly influenced by Ernest Hemingway in such interests as boxing and in his general macho literary attitude. Hemingway was nicknamed "Papa" in tribute to his standing as a father-figure for a great many people, and, of course, the time came when Mailer had to assert his independence. In *Advertisements for Myself* he wrote about Hemingway's "shrinking genius" much as Baldwin had put down Wright's declining prestige. The two men had much in common even though superficially they seemed to be different in every way—of different races and social classes and sexual character. In Mailer's novels, homosexuals tended to be rather unpleasant, ridiculous, perhaps even sinister. When a homosexual magazine asked him to write an article he replied he didn't know the first thing about homosexuality—"I hardly even know any homosexuals." Eventually persuaded to change his mind, he wrote an essay entitled "The Homosexual Villain" and admitted the subject stirred fear and some prejudice in him. He also criticized some homosexuals for a defiant superiority and said they would never achieve social equality and acceptance until they gave up their prejudices, too. How would Baldwin react to that side of Mailer?

They met at the home of the French philosopher, Jean Malaquais. Baldwin said later, "I wasn't comfortable with intellectuals, French or American, since they seemed to leave so much out of account." He claimed Malaquais patronized Mailer, not seeming to take Mailer seriously as a writer, and "I was a little offended by that." Malaquais' version was quite different. He had the feeling, he said, that Baldwin was "a confounded snob. He would throw names around, he was more 'elegant' than Norman, more 'European.' " Both Baldwin and Mailer were drinking a lot at this first meeting, according to Malaquais, and they were soon arguing. "It was a love-hate relationship from the start," observed Malaquais. Baldwin described himself as "a very tight, tense, lean, abnormally ambitious, abnormally intelligent, and hungry black cat." He was edgy, extremely worried about the reception of *Giovanni's Room:* "A writer who is worried about his career is also fighting for his life." Also his friendship with Lucien seemed to be on the rocks. So it was in a low, nervous mood that he met Mailer. They circled each other, Baldwin concerned that Mailer would pull rank because he was better known as a writer and was also white and comparatively wealthy, Mailer guarded perhaps because Baldwin was a challenge, being both black and homosexual. As a black, Baldwin claimed to know more than

127

Mailer "about that periphery he so helplessly maligns in 'The White Negro' than he could ever hope to know. I could not, with the best will in the world, make any sense out of 'The White Negro' and, in fact, it was hard for me to imagine that this essay had been written by the same man who wrote the novels." He was baffled by what he perceived as the passion with which Mailer appeared to be imitating so many people inferior to himself, such as "Kerouac and all the other Suzuki rhythm boys."

Yet the two men got on well enough to meet several times over the next few weeks until Mailer returned to the U.S. It helped that Mailer's then wife, Adele Morales, also liked Baldwin, because she had strong likes and dislikes among her husband's varied acquaintances. Baldwin eventually confided to them how "very apprehensive" he was about *Giovanni's Room,* hoping Mailer might write something favorable when the novel appeared. Mailer was sympathetic and recounted his own troubles over the reception of *Barbary Shore.*

Baldwin could not shake off his lonely, unhappy mood and found his growing fame in the American colony no consolation. "One of the reasons I had fought so hard after all was to wrest from the world fame and money and love. And here I was at thirty-two finding my notoriety hard to bear, since its principal effect was to make me more lonely; money, it turned out, was exactly like sex, you thought of nothing else if you didn't have it and thought of other things if you did." To try to overcome his growing depression, taking advantage of being no longer "poor and ugly and obscure," he wandered through the Parisian underworld "drinking, screwing, fighting—it's a wonder I wasn't killed." Many an American, used to an active, optimistic life, might have lost his mind, Baldwin reflected gloomily, or committed suicide or taken up good works or tried to enter politics. Instead he did what had worked for him before—he took off for another place, this time the isle of Corsica, where Napoleon had once been imprisoned and where the people who ran the Hotel Verneuil had relatives. In a house overlooking the Mediterranean, far from the literary gossip of Paris and New York, he awaited the publication of his controversial novel. Perhaps Knopf and the others would be proved right and it would "ruin" his career. One reason he enjoyed having more money was that he could send more to his family in Harlem. What would happen to *them* if he was ruined?

He need not have worried. The postwar winds of change were beginning to affect the literary world, too, more than the older, conservative publishers yet appreciated. It also helped that Baldwin had a serious reputation as an essayist, and *Go Tell It On the Mountain* had furthered this reputation. Even the most influential critics were beginning to talk about him. Alfred Kazin, who had met Baldwin in Paris, recalled that Edmund Wilson, the literary critic who had spotted Scott Fitzgerald and Hemingway very early, told him that young Baldwin was one of the best writers who had come along recently. The new novel might have a sensational, upsetting theme, but it couldn't be dismissed. The reviews, in fact, were largely favorable. It was to be expected that some of the younger, more adventurous reviewers would be more responsive to what Baldwin had to say. John Clellon Holmes, the novelist and critic who was often credited with giving the Beat Generation its name, praised *Giovanni* in a way that influenced other critics. He thought the novel was "beautifully written" and had "candor and dignity. Mr. Baldwin is very, very good." Philip Rahv considered it Baldwin's best writing so far—"It has been a long time since I have read anything as good by a younger American writer." Harper's commented that "the intensity with which he endows ideas is very nearly miraculous." Granville Hicks in the New York *Times Book Review* referred to the bisexual triangle and decided "Mr. Baldwin writes of these matters with an unusual degree of candor and yet with such dignity and intensity that he is saved from sensationalism." Mark Schorer described *Giovanni* as "beautifully written" with a "harrowing intensity" and as "nearly heroic." His career certainly wouldn't be ruined by such approving reviews, he was established even more solidly as one of the outstanding younger writers, but the novel did officially identify him as a homosexual writer, which limited his image in the literary community and might in future influence critics to interpret what he had to say as being the special viewpoint of a homosexual—a black homosexual. Some critics claimed a homosexual writer could never write successfully about love between a man and a woman, and they would treat Baldwin's future novels this way, although his experience had been bisexual and his talents in any case provided a powerful imagination and understanding of both men and women. *Giovanni* also inspired a lot of gossip about him. I remember one leading publisher telling me that Baldwin went down to the French port of Marseilles for weekends and picked up young sailors, although there was no way he could possibly have known this. The novel made him both friends and enemies he didn't yet know he had and also restricted the offers and invitations he received in public life. The membership of some prestigious committees and organizations, which might have welcomed a token well-known black writer, would now be closed to him. But Baldwin was not thinking of literary politics or his public reputation so much as survival to write his next novel, which was to carry on from where *Giovanni* had left off, not as regards the characters and storyline but as a picture of contemporary interracial, bisexual America. Among the copies of *Giovanni* he sent to people in New York was one to William Cole at Knopf inscribed: "With much affection and God bless you for your confidence—your friend."

A sign of his rising confidence was his acceptance of an offer from Encounter magazine to cover a conference of Negro-African writers and artists to be held in the Sorbonne's large Amphitheatre Descartes. It meant wrestling yet again with the elusive subject of Africa that had challenged him ever since he had first come to Paris and met the African immigrants from the French colonies. With ancestral African roots, he had assumed that he and the Africans would immediately identify with each other, only to find that the Africans were preoccupied with gaining their freedom from France and were not very interested in the problems of black Americans. When an African with a mocking laugh said of Richard Wright, "I believe he thinks he's white," Baldwin found himself defending Wright. "I did not think I was white either, or I did not *think* I thought so. But the Africans might think I did, and who could blame them? In their eyes, and in terms of my history, I could scarcely be considered the purest or most dependable of black men." Back in the U.S. his skin was considered very black and he had been despised by both blacks and whites for it "and I had despised myself," but the Africans were much darker than he was—"I was a paleface among them, and so was Richard." The more he observed the dark, enigmatic Africans the more uneasy Baldwin became. "The disturbance thus created" caused all his extreme ambivalence about color to rise again to the surface and upset him. The Africans seemed "at once simpler and more devious, more directly erotic and at the same time more subtle, and they were proud. If they had ever despised themselves for their color, it did not show, as far as I could tell." Feeling shut out, Baldwin said he "envied" them and "feared" them—"feared that they had good reason to despise me." Which led him to compare his reaction with that of his old standard—Richard Wright.

Wright did not really know much about "the present dimensions and complexity of the Negro problem" back home nor did he really want to know, Baldwin claimed, because "his real impulse toward American Negroes, individually, was to despise them." As for the Africans, at least the younger ones, they knew he did not know them and did not want to know them, "and they despised *him.*" Baldwin added: "For who has not hated his black brother? Simply *because* he is black, *because* he is brother. And who has not dreamed of violence?" He had in mind the recurring nightmare of rage, of hatred he had written about in the essay on his stepfather who had been driven mad by it—a nightmare of an apocalypse of bloodshed washing away generations of horror, releasing one forever from the individual horror carried everywhere in the heart. "Which of us has overcome his past?" Certainly not *you!* was the angry reply of the Wright admirers who hotly denied his interpretation of Wright's relations with both American blacks and Africans. As Michel Fabre saw it in his Wright biography, "Baldwin was then in the clutches of personal problems caused by his search for an identity and his complicated relationship with his adopted father," and he stressed that Baldwin's version of events was contradicted by Wright and others. Fabre in effect was claiming that Baldwin had not yet overcome the hang-ups of Frog Eyes and was taking them out yet again on Wright, but this did not allow for the long way Baldwin had come since his youth and his genuine disagreement with Wright over protest literature and his very different reading of the Africans. Baldwin was not to feel more at ease with Africans until he saw them in their own countries, but at least he was more at ease with himself. At this stage of his life, in 1956, he obviously had some way to go yet before he fully accepted himself, and he was "straight from the shoulder" enough to admit it—"Which of us has overcome his past?"

Richard Wright was one of the main speakers at the conference of Negro-African writers and artists. When Baldwin met Wright there, the older writer was still courteous enough to introduce him to the five black delegates from the U.S. John Davis, the chief delegate, was asked later during the conference why he considered himself a Negro when he didn't look black. Baldwin tried to explain he was legally considered a Negro in the U.S. because some of his ancestors had been black and Davis himself claimed he was also a Negro by choice and by depth of experience. But the question of choice could "scarcely be coherent" to the Africans, and Davis' kind of American experience—or even Baldwin's—remained "a closed book" to them. For Baldwin, the position of the American delegates merely seemed to stress how far apart they—and he—were from the Africans.

The conference started badly from the American delegation's viewpoint. Loud sarcastic laughter from the Africans greeted the news that W.E.B. Du Bois couldn't attend because, as a message from him explained, "the U.S. Government will not give me a passport." The South African delegation had also been prevented from attending by its government, and some of the African delegates linked the two cases. Du Bois' message ended with a boost for a socialist Africa following in the footsteps of Russia and China. Baldwin's own experience of socialists and communists in the Village with Eugene Worth had permanently disillusioned him, and he dismissed Du Bois' remarks as "extremely ill-considered," which further angered the Wright group and revived rumors that he was allowing himself—deliberately or from political innocence—to be used by CIA informers.

His best answer to such gossip was his extremely respectful attitude toward the African speakers, some of whom were far more militant than Du Bois. He was fascinated by poet Leopold Senghor's attempt to describe the very different African attitude toward art and artists, reflecting "a way of life which I could only very dimly and perhaps somewhat wistfully imagine." He was much impressed by the idea that a work of art "is itself a part of that energy which is life." It was in a debate about culture that followed that Baldwin concluded there *was* something which all black men held in common—"their precarious, their unutterably painful relation to the white world" and their need to remake their world in their own image. Senghor astonished him by referring to Richard Wright's *Black Boy* as an African autobiography even though it described growing up in America, and Baldwin commented, "Granted that there was something African in *Black Boy,* as there was undoubtedly something African in all American Negroes, the great question of what this was, and how it had survived, remained wide open." The more Baldwin listened to the Africans' speeches the more American he felt.

Next came Aimé Cesaire, then George Lamming from the West Indies and then Richard Wright, who had been acting as liaison between the American delegates and the Africans. Wright surprised Baldwin, too, by describing the effects of European colonialism as "liberating" in some ways. Baldwin dealt with Wright much more "straight from the shoulder" than he had with the enigmatic Africans, calling him "tactless" and reporting his remarks about colonialism sardonically. Wright's admirers no doubt took it as yet more evidence of his hostility.

At the end of the conference Richard Wright made another speech that Baldwin found even more romantically idealistic. Wright argued that American blacks were in the technological vanguard, in command of a great diversity of techniques, and this could prove of inestimable value to the developing African nations. Baldwin was skeptical. American blacks hadn't much power, and anyway too much was happening at home for anyone to have much time for Africa. Richard was out of touch.

The conference didn't make Baldwin feel any closer to the Africans, but their militancy and their adsorption in the problems of home with little interest in anywhere else affected him. The conference had officially kept out of politics in discussing culture, but political attitudes, although unstated, were obvious in all the speeches. Du Bois' message of regret had been one of the few to be politically explicit. But in between the official sessions there were some heated political arguments

133

over drinks. Baldwin found that regarding the Cold War between the U.S. and Soviet Russia, the superpowers competing for the leadership of the postwar world, few of the Africans took the American side, considering the U.S. among the colonialists, whereas many of them, like the European intellectuals, were still believers in communism as a solution, which irritated Baldwin. He had to admit the Africans were much more politically educated, much more doctrinaire than American blacks, for whom religion often took the place of politics. But arguing with them only made Baldwin more interested in what was happening across the Atlantic.

Several major confrontations had taken place in the South following the Supreme Court's ruling against segregated education. President Eisenhower had been forced to send in the army and the National Guard, putting obscure southern towns in the headlines. But most interesting to Baldwin was a mass movement that had begun in Montgomery, Alabama, with one woman's protest against the segregation of the local public transport system. Mrs. Rosa Parks, a tailor's assistant returning home from a tiring day's work, had refused to give up her seat in a bus to a white man and had set off a boycott of the buses by blacks. Their leader was a young Baptist minister from Atlanta, Georgia, named Martin Luther King, Jr. Black and white liberal sympathizers from across the South and from up North as well had volunteered their services, and the spirit of the boycott movement was catching on in other places. Now there was talk of trying to desegregate the lunch counters and restaurants in the South. Dr. King was becoming a national figure. Baldwin felt he wanted to meet the young minister and discover how much support his movement really had. Was it possible America was changing and was ready to accept an integrated society at last? It was time to go home to find the answers—and to pay his dues.

8

Down South

WHEN DR. KENNETH Clark heard that James Baldwin was back in New York, he arranged to meet him through mutual friends at Commentary. He hadn't forgotten what he had been told about the young black writer's hard struggle to survive so he invited him to dinner with him and his wife at their home in Hastings-on-Hudson, a small, almost entirely white-populated town about forty minutes by train from New York City. A short man about Baldwin's size, Kenneth Clark was quiet and scholarly, quite unlike the emotional, largely self-educated Baldwin. But the two men got on well from the start. "We both felt as if we had known each other for a long time," recalled Dr. Clark. "Jim was an extraordinarily intense, passionate, friendly person and a wonderful conversationalist. As I listened to him, I was spellbound. His view of American racial injustice went beyond what I had read in his essays." Baldwin was beginning to reflect the militancy of the Africans—and the growing civil rights movement in the South.

Kenneth Clark was a good person from whom to learn much of the background. He knew all the principals, including Martin Luther King, Jr. He had done much of the research to back up Thurgood Marshall's argument before the Supreme Court that "separate but equal" education, legally approved for the previous fifty-eight years, was unconstitutional. He had also appeared before the court as an expert witness. He invited Baldwin to dinner several times and they had a number of intense discussions about the changing racial situation.

When Dr. Clark met Langston Hughes he told him about meeting James Baldwin, unaware of the bad feeling between the two black writers. "I remember I said that Jim had spent some time in our home at Hastings, and Langston said, 'Kenneth, you have never invited me.' I was surprised. One of the reasons we had had Jim was that it was a period in which he was nomadic. One wanted to help him. He was surviving through his advocacy—his writing. He always remained a marvelous preacher. What a talker!"

Baldwin introduced Dr. Clark to his family, particularly his brother David with whom he now spent much of his time. He got David a job with Sol Stein, who was running the Midcentury Book Society. He and Sol Stein had also collaborated on a television play based on his essay, "Equal in Paris," about the stolen hotel bedsheet. The Theater Guild was interested "if we made the leading character white instead of black, which would have destroyed its meaning. We never did anything with the play," Stein said. It must have given Baldwin some bitter amusement that they wanted to make him white.

Dial Press had a collection of essays under contract and wanted to take advantage of all the publicity about the racial situation down South. Encouraged by his editor, James Silberman, Baldwin began to gather and arrange the essays that had already been published in magazines since the first collection appeared. He realized he didn't have enough strong topical essays. Both Harper's and Partisan Review wanted him to go south, but the prospect scared him. The South had been the subject of nightmares ever since he could remember. His stepfather had described lynchings in vivid detail. The violence was now being directed at black children trying to attend previously all-white schools. Some of the black demonstrators in the bus boycott had been beaten up. Martin Luther King had been jailed several times. The idea of becoming part of that violent scene was certainly frightening, but he decided he couldn't put it off any longer.

He went first to Charlotte, North Carolina, and watched the first attempts there at integrated education. Police had to hold back a white mob as four black children showed up at four white schools, one to each school. Out of a population of fifty thousand blacks there had been only forty-five applications. Baldwin interviewed some of the children and remembered particularly one boy—"pride and silence were his weapons." He felt a rush of racial pride in the children and their parents that affected him in a way he didn't quite understand—almost as if he had acquired some of the militant pride of the Africans.

From there Baldwin flew to Atlanta. As the plane hovered over the city's dogwood trees he was impressed by the color of the earth—blood red. He couldn't suppress the thought "that this earth had acquired its color from the blood that had dripped down from the trees. My mind was filled with the image of a black man, younger than I, perhaps, or my own age, hanging from a tree, while white men watched him and cut his sex from him with a knife. My father must have seen such sights ..." Everywhere he looked that day seemed to be already familiar—the landscape, the people's speech and their ways. He felt that he was seeing the remains of his ancestors that proclaimed his "inescapable identity"— and that his ancestors were both black and white. He was only one generation removed from the South and couldn't lose his fear. The trees, the silence, the liquid heat, the great distances along dark lonely country roads, all seemed designed for violence, so sensual, so languid, so private. It all stirred up his imagination, as did riding on his first segregated bus. And he was haunted by the eyes of old black men that seemed to reflect their lives, in which they had never owned anything, not even their wife or child, that could not be taken away by the power of white people. Not that he didn't meet some blacks who put him down because he was from the North. One black educator made him admit he'd never been to college and that northern blacks lived herded together like pigs in a pen whereas southern blacks formed "a community." Baldwin commented wryly "my humiliation was complete with his discovery that I couldn't even drive a car." The black middle-class tended to avoid the problems of segregated buses by owning cars, and this educator, Baldwin observed, was less than wholehearted about integration, partly because he might lose his job. As when Baldwin wrote about Harlem, he was "straight from the shoulder" about his fellow blacks as well as whites.

Finally he met Martin Luther King, who was on a visit to Atlanta from his home in Montgomery. King had shut himself away in a hotel to finish a book about the civil rights movement and was seeing no one officially. Baldwin persuaded a mutual friend to try to introduce him, and King agreed to see him. When the hotel door swung open, Baldwin was unsure what to expect. He didn't have a high opinion of either ministers or celebrities. But King proved to be a restrained, by no means outgoing man, and he met Baldwin with an inquiring and genuine smile. Baldwin found him "immediately and tremendously winning." He was the first black leader in Baldwin's experience who spoke the same way to blacks and whites, as "straight from the shoulder" as Baldwin himself. King told him, "Segregation is dead," and Baldwin replied the question was "just how long, how violent and how expensive the funeral is going to be."

Later that day he met King at a party. The young civil rights leader drank something nonalcoholic and didn't stay long. He seemed very slight and vulnerable "to be taking on such tremendous odds."

Baldwin traveled to Montgomery, where he heard King preach in his own church, Dexter Avenue Baptist Church, at the main Sunday service. Sitting in the congregation, Baldwin sensed a feeling "which quite transcended anything I have ever felt in a church before." He had heard all kinds of preachers and was no mean preacher himself, but he considered King "a great speaker." He thought King's secret lay in his intimate knowledge of his audience, black or white, and in the forthrightness with which he spoke of those things that hurt and baffled them. He was also willing to criticize them in spite of the dangers they all faced, calling them to moral attention. "There are many things wrong in the white world. But there are many things wrong in the black world, too," Dr. King said, and began to list what they were. The whole congregation sat forward to listen as he urged them not to pretend to accept segregation. "The next time the white man asks you what you think of segregation, you tell him, 'Mr. Charlie, I think it's wrong and I wish you'd do something about it by nine o'clock tomorrow morning!'" A wave of good-humored laughter filled the church, Baldwin joining in. After the service, he attended a dinner in the church basement where he met Mrs. King, a slim woman he thought "really quite beautiful with a wonderful laugh." He watched young Martin, as he began to think of him, circulate among the church members and visitors, explaining to one of them that bigotry was a disease and bigots could only be saved by love. In liberating oneself, one was also liberating them—all sentiments that Baldwin thoroughly agreed with. Someone also showed him the damage done to the church by bombs. It made what was happening seem like another civil war, justifying his nightmarish attitude toward the South, and increasing his admiration for King's cool manner even though he must have known he was "menaced," a target at any time. What made Baldwin's personal relationship with the civil rights leader easier was his comparative youth. King was five years younger than Baldwin and therefore there was no danger of him becoming another father figure.

Little Rock, Tuskegee . . . the places multiplied as he traveled farther to see the Movement in action—"I don't know how long I was on the road." By the time he returned to New York his bulging cheap canvas suitcase, which he lugged over one shoulder, burst in the middle of Grand Central Station, scattering confidential Movement documents that he had to chase and collect. He crammed them back into the remains of the suitcase, which he tied together with the belt from his trousers.

He got as far as a friend's cold-water apartment in the Village and collapsed, feverishly reliving the nightmares of his trip around the South. He had phoned Gloria from the station but hadn't told her where he was going. After he didn't show up in five days his family and friends went round all his Village haunts searching for him—as Rufus' sister, Ida, was to do in *Another Country*. Eventually a friend met him on the street and he realized how much he had worried everybody and went to his sister's house. He knew he had been irresponsible in vanishing, and yet it had been like a hangover from the South he first had to recover from.

From this time on Baldwin felt committed to the civil rights movement. The bomb damage to King's church and the meetings with King had swept away his artist's reservations about working with a political

139

group. Other writers and critics would later suggest his involvement affected the independence of his writing, but at the end of his life Baldwin concluded, "I had to go through the civil rights movement and I don't regret it at all. And those people trusted me. There was something very beautiful about that period, something life-giving for me to be there, to march, to be a part of a sit-in, to see it through my own eyes." The camaraderie of the civil rights movement and the sense of a cause beyond mere personal ambitions helped him enormously at a difficult period of his life, Baldwin told me. He compared it to the time he had been "saved" and become a Young Minister enjoying the security of a church group. And there were other similarities. He was soon making almost as many speeches in the South and up North raising funds for the civil rights movement before church groups, interracial organizations, colleges and schools as he had preached sermons in Harlem, and if racial concerns were substituted for religious themes, there was little difference between his speeches and his teenage sermons. He soon recovered his old fire and fervency and found he could improvise as eloquently as ever and hold almost any kind of audience. Dr. Kenneth Clark recalled, "He gave many, many talks to students and other groups. He impressed me as resembling an Old Testament prophet. For a while I was afraid that his total involvement in meetings with large and small groups would interfere with his writing. I saw him fluctuating between hope and despair. At times he would call and ask if we could meet so that he could spew out his anguish. He was concerned about the future of America. He saw a lack of concern or an inability in this nation to deal ethically with the problem of race."

Baldwin didn't see Martin Luther King again for a long time, but he met the other leaders of what was now becoming a movement that involved all shades of black opinion. An illusion of many white liberals was that blacks were unified behind King, but in reality there were as many different groups and leaders as among white Americans, ranging from the conservative National Association for the Advancement of Colored People to the aggressive, exclusivist Black Muslims. It was only when Baldwin met with different black leaders that he appreciated the extent to which the Supreme Court's school-desegregation decision had revived black hopes everywhere of at last attaining first-class citizenship.

But the different leaders and groups were by no means in agreement about the strategies to employ against violent white opposition typified by the revival of the Ku Klux Klan.

Baldwin also soon became aware that some of the older black leaders viewed him with disapproval. They saw him merely as a writer with no political experience and they were concerned that his homosexual reputation might hurt the Movement. *Giovanni's Room* was as shocking to these black leaders as to many whites. Over the years of his involvement, Baldwin felt more at ease with the younger, more militant activists of the Congress of Racial Equality and later the Student Nonviolent Coordinating Committee than with the older officials of the NAACP and even the group of advisers around Martin Luther King, except for Bayard Rustin.

Rustin, then in his mid-forties, was one of the great characters of the civil rights movement. A tall elegant man with flowing hair like a romantic poet's, he was a lifelong pacifist who had spent twenty-eight months in prison for resisting the draft during World War II. He worked for the Fellowship of Reconciliation, an old pacifist organization that had helped establish CORE and pioneer nonviolent direct action in the North. Early in 1956 Rustin had rushed south to Montgomery to volunteer his services to King and advise him on the organizational techniques of nonviolence. King was already being attacked as a communist and was under FBI surveillance, and Rustin warned him that his own history might be used against the Movement. As a student he had joined the Young Communist League only to quit when it tried to restrict his integration efforts. He had also had a brush with the law over his homosexuality, which had been well publicized. King wasn't worried. "Look," he said, "we need everybody who can come to help us." Rustin quickly became one of King's most trusted advisers.

He was among the first to recognize Baldwin's value as a popular speaker who could woo all kinds of audiences and also attract the media. He and Baldwin, in fact, had many similar qualities. Rustin was a sophisticated intellectual who enjoyed late-night philosophical conversations over drinks as much as Baldwin, and he was also expert at leading group choruses at mass meetings the way Baldwin enjoyed swaying a crowd with his words. They not only had their homosexuality in

141

common, but like Baldwin, Rustin was illegitimate. In later life when he had a New York apartment on West Twenty-eighth Street, Rustin liked to reminisce about how he and Jimmy Baldwin used to joke each other about being "bastard black queers," though they allowed no one else to call them that. Rustin also remained grateful for the way Baldwin spoke up for him when Adam Clayton Powell, the flamboyant black Harlem minister and congressman, worked against him with the support of many who disapproved of him, including Roy Wilkins of the NAACP, or were jealous of his close relationship with King. Anxious not to lose any support, King listened to Congressman Powell and Bayard Rustin went back up north. Baldwin at once rushed loyally and loudly to Rustin's defense. He wrote in Harper's that King had lost much moral credit, especially in the eyes of the young, for allowing Powell to force the resignation of his "extremely able organizer and lieutenant." He praised Rustin's "long and honorable record as a fighter for Negro rights" and called him "one of the most penetrating and able men around." Other people in the Movement also came to Rustin's aid and he was soon back in favor, staying closely in touch with King although they had many disagreements over strategy. From then on Rustin tried as much as possible to work behind the scenes to save King any embarrassment, and because he was under surveillance by the FBI.

Harry Belafonte, the singer and actor who was a King confidant for years, worked with Baldwin on several big Movement events and never found his homosexual reputation a problem. "One advantage was that he never made a secret of it," explained Belafonte. "His own utterances and dignity were so great and of course there were other homosexuals in the Movement. It was the least important consideration about a person. Jimmy seemed to be invulnerable on the issue, at least publicly. He was very vulnerable personally. I have met few people quite as tortured as Jimmy. I mean personally. In public he didn't show it. He was quite outspoken, he didn't hide his feelings about most things. People were more afraid of his radical reputation than his homosexuality. Some people were concerned about being put too far out on a political limb in his company. But neither his homosexuality nor his radicalism ever disturbed Dr. King or the SNCC leadership he worked with. The Movement was too sensitive about oppression to begin to carry on a campaign against anyone."

Roy Innis, the director of the Congress of Racial Equality, first met Baldwin as a young member of CORE. "Rustin had been forced out as chief-of-staff for King based on certain allegations of left-wing commitment," said Innis, "but it was really more because of his homosexuality. Nobody said you couldn't be one. I met a lot in the Movement. It was no big deal in the Movement except as you related to the public—the media and Congress. I don't know how much it hit Jimmy, but it must have had some kind of effect. King did feel obliged to tone down the public involvement of Rustin and consequently I would have to assume something happened to Jimmy Baldwin, too. Jimmy was in the intellectual phase of the Movement, not the front line like Bayard Rustin, and CORE used him to get publicity or to get a crowd. People would show up if Baldwin was coming. So would the press and people of rank. They might not like what he said, but they would listen."

It was astonishing that Baldwin could manage to become so involved in the civil rights movement and fit in so many varied, draining activities as well as very actively pursuing his writing career and playing the role of dutiful son and brother to his large family. Flying between New York and the South, he often had little sleep or food and lived on Johnnie Walker scotch and cigarettes. He discovered that writers he knew like Norman Mailer had formed a playwrights' unit at the Actors' Studio on West Forty-fourth Street, the home of the Method he had first heard about from Marlon Brando and the successor to the old Group Theater of the thirties where Clifford Odets and Elia Kazan had started their careers. A writer had prepared an adaptation of *Giovanni's Room* for a performance before the members. But Baldwin found it too sentimental, so he wrote his own. *Giovanni* had a simple dramatic structure in the form of a flashback, more like a movie than a play, and since some Hollywood actors attended classes at the Studio when they were in New York, he hoped the performance might lead to selling the film rights. The success of the book seemed to have blinded him to Hollywood's extreme conservatism in matters of sex. When the news was passed round the Village that he was casting *Giovanni,* every young homosexual actor approached him for the role of the young Italian barman last seen tragically being led away to the guillotine. "I had would-be Giovannis sitting on my doorstep or coming out of the faucet," Baldwin said. He couldn't have a drink in the Village bars without someone coming up and suggesting he would be ideal for Giovanni. "I even got propositioned," said Baldwin, "as if that would make sure they were chosen. But they hadn't read my book properly. Giovanni was a *man,* whatever he did in bed. Their conception was always too self-conscious, too gay—too obvious or effeminate. I despaired of ever finding anyone who could do it as written."

When he was invited to a Village party to meet a potential Giovanni, he went without any expectations. He was introduced to a sturdy, dark-eyed young Turkish actor named Engin Cezzar who had been educated at Yale and looked and behaved as if he could do it. Baldwin took him next day to the Actors Studio and he got the part. Baldwin was excited by his performance, but the adaptation was by no means generally popular. Some of the big Hollywood and Broadway names there seemed to hate it. But a young black woman at the back of the small workshop audience disagreed with them. She had liked the play, she had liked it a lot, she said firmly. "I was enormously grateful to her, she seemed to speak for me," Baldwin said. Afterward he went over to introduce himself. "She talked to me with a gentleness and generosity never to be forgotten." He had the impression of a small, shy, determined person. Within a year she would have a hit play of her own on Broadway about a black family. The play was *A Raisin in the Sun* and her name was Lorraine Hansberry—"Sweet Lorraine" as Baldwin called her. As for *Giovanni's Room,* there were no Hollywood or Broadway offers. For a short time Baldwin tried to interest some star name in the other male role—David, the narrator, who cannot face his homosexuality and betrays Giovanni—but nobody would consider it. Eventually Engin Cezzar decided not to wait any longer but to return to Turkey, inviting Baldwin to visit him and his wife in Istanbul.

Another writer Baldwin met who was to become a friend was James Jones, the ex-army man who had written the huge bestselling novel, *From Here to Eternity.* Jones was also a friend of Mailer, although their relationship was complicated by, among other things, the fact that

Mailer's then wife, Adele Morales, did not much like Jones and made no particular secret of it. "I didn't get along with Jones, so we didn't see him," she said. Baldwin and Jones became friendly at once, establishing a much easier relationship than either had with Mailer. Jones had recently married Gloria Mosolino from Pottsville, Pennsylvania, which John O'Hara had written about in his novels and short stories (a character in O'Hara's first novel, *Appointment in Samarra,* was said to be based on one of her relatives). After taking acting lessons she had worked as a stand-in for Marilyn Monroe in the film "The Seven-Year Itch." Baldwin liked her as much as Jones, whom he admired for his directness and lack of phony liberalism. He even listened when Jones urged him to "forget all that nigger shit" if he wanted to write a real novel. Would he consider *Giovanni's Room* "homosexual shit"? They managed to argue vehemently without lasting ill-feeling. "People like you are very important to people like me," Baldwin told him, "and in this sad bad world, very important *period."*

It sounds like a slightly drunken conversation, and there must have been many of those, considering the amount of liquor both men were consuming at that time. In any case, Baldwin felt none of the competitive tension he had felt with Mailer. Gloria Jones considered Baldwin "the most brilliant man" she had ever met, after her husband. "He had such wisdom and knowledge and such ability to be intimate, to share his thoughts, to be so understanding." She remembered big drinking sessions with him and her husband and other American writer friends such as William Styron and Irwin Shaw and Budd Schulberg. "In New York we did a lot of integrating bars with Jimmy. There was never any trouble over Jimmy, but I remember once there was an objection to Styron's shoes." The Joneses were going abroad for a few years following in Baldwin's footsteps to Paris, and they all arranged to carry on their drinking sessions when Baldwin was next in the French capital. . . .

When a party was held in the Village to celebrate the "End of the Beats" or "The Funeral of Hip," Baldwin and Mailer were among the speakers. Maria Irene Fornes, off-Broadway dramatist and director, recalled: "They were burying Hip, prematurely perhaps, and Jimmy was saying to Norman, 'I'm a Greek, you're a Roman,' meaning that he was a private person and Norman wasn't, and that the essence of Hip was in private life, not in a movement." But she said you could feel there was tension between the two "because Norman got more attention."

One night when Baldwin was drinking at the Riviera in the Village a young black writer recognized him and introduced himself. His name was John A. Williams and he was writing a first novel based on Charlie Parker, the great black musician. "I expressed a desire to talk with him about writing," Williams said. " 'Why do you want to write?' he said. Ah, shit, I thought. I was working on *Nightsong* [the Charlie Parker novel] at the time. Later we had the same agent, Bob Mills, and he got a quote from Jimmy for the jacket of *Nightsong.* "

Working on the production of *Giovanni's Room* had brought back all Baldwin's old interest in the theater. He learned the Dramatists League had a program for educating its younger members about the actual production of a play, and since his success had brought him some influential contacts he was able to arrange to be assigned as Elia Kazan's assistant on two new plays heading for Broadway—Archibald Mac-Leish's *JB* and Tennessee Williams' *Sweet Bird of Youth*. The idea, according to Kazan, was that Baldwin "would watch the progress of the production and be better prepared to write his own plays." Kazan was as small and slight as Baldwin, a dozen years older, and a Greek immigrant with still much of a poor American immigrant's tough competitiveness and sense of what went in the marketplace. He had lost many of his theater friends by cooperating with the congressional "witch-hunters" at the time of McCarthy, an act that seemed to reflect an immigrant's insecurity and wish to prove himself officially all-American. He had worked successfully with many of the big contemporary names in both the Broadway theater and in Hollywood, including Marlon Brando, Tennessee Williams and Arthur Miller, but he still appeared insecure, to feel the necessity to prove himself. When he wrote about Marilyn Monroe, for example, his account included the information that he had been to bed with her.

Kazan's decision to direct *JB* was difficult to understand, except in terms of MacLeish's reputation as a member of the Washington establishment since the Roosevelt days and a leading American intellectual. Not only did Kazan have little interest in poetry, and *JB* was in verse, but he confessed the merits of *JB* "eluded me." Baldwin had an even lower opinion of the play and told me that he found MacLeish rather patronizing and paternal, and that he had no intention of accepting *that,* his feelings about father-figures—especially white ones (shades of Faulkner!)—being what they were. So the director and his new assistant sat through rehearsals, helping to bring to life a poetic drama based on the biblical story of Job that they disliked. Kazan remembered that Baldwin "sat at my side all through, pad and pencil ready, and he full of charm." But if Kazan was uninterested in the play's content "and writhed under the weight of the lines, Jimmy was poisonous." Kazan thought MacLeish was "awfully cordial" to Baldwin, who was "successfully slippery in avoiding telling Archie what was going on in his mind." According to Kazan, "it was a case of two different cultures, Harvard and Harlem."

Kazan remembered how restless Baldwin became during the rehearsals. "He couldn't sit still because of his dislike of the play. His feeling against Archie wasn't really personal, but artistic. He just didn't like the way the guy wrote. It looked like poetry on the page, but it wasn't poetry. He was so highly esteemed I think that irritated Jimmy more. He wouldn't accept him as the leading intellectual he claimed to be."

Sweet Bird of Youth was a happier experience for Baldwin, if not Kazan. Kazan told me, "Jimmy liked and admired Tennessee Williams a lot. Tennessee was a wonderful man, you couldn't help liking him. He was really a terrific fellow, full of fun when he got away from work, and he was also very good at working." Williams was a white southerner, a homosexual and essentially a poet in outlook. At this time his homosexuality had only been expressed indirectly in his plays, though he made no secret of it in his personal life. Nor did the racial scene in the South play any real role in his writing. There were no major black characters, though the corruption and ignorance and violence of many white southerners was vividly depicted. He and Jimmy Baldwin had some late-night drinking sessions that could have rivaled those with James Jones. But Williams was in a very nervous, self-doubting state, not helped, one would guess, by Kazan's requests for rewrites. Kazan's opinion was that "I don't think anybody could really like *Sweet Bird of Youth* because it breaks in two—the second act has nothing much to do with the first. But that kind of thing didn't worry Jimmy very much. Jimmy didn't have a very firm sense of dramatic construction, so what faults Tennessee's play had didn't necessarily invalidate it for him. He liked Tennessee in a simple visceral way, friend to friend. They were very compatible, whereas Archie MacLeish was enough of a paternal figure to put Jimmy on edge. He reminded me of the guys who used to teach college. But Tennessee didn't sit in judgment with anybody. I don't think Tennessee and Jimmy saw much of each other over the years. Tennessee really didn't see anyone regularly except the homosexual group. Jimmy stayed in touch with me, so we met four or five times a year. We became close friends that way. I went to his mother's house a few times and got to know his brother David."

In 1959 when *Sweet Bird of Youth* opened, Broadway productions still went on the road to other cities for a few weeks for glorified dress rehearsals before arriving in New York, a system since replaced by previews in New York to save the expense of travel. Baldwin got to know the actors better when he traveled with them, particularly Rip Torn, who was appearing in *Sweet Bird*. Torn had grown up in East Texas and was interested in the civil rights movement. He and Baldwin had many late-night discussions about the South. "I don't remember talking to Jimmy much before we opened in Philadelphia," Torn said. "I was very preoccupied during rehearsals. After the first read-through and rehearsal, Tennessee Williams left with a 'forget it, baby' attitude. Jimmy talked to me about my role as a white southerner and was curious about how I had arrived at my characterization, where it came from in my own life. East Texas is very southern. My people were farmers and ranchers and I'm a rural person." His father had known George Washington Carver, the famous black chemist and educator at Tuskegee, the black college in Alabama, "and ate at Dr. Carver's house. They were mainly concerned with changing the economy of the South. Jimmy and I talked about our different starting-out places, but at least we were on the same boat. Jimmy was circumspect, he didn't have much experience in the theater. He was very careful not to overstep the trust Kazan had given him. I don't remember which of Jimmy's books I had read then, but I had been struck by the voice he had. He was a very vital person—small, but he didn't appear to be that way because he was very erect. But I didn't see a great deal of him during the preparation of *Sweet Bird.* I had had a checkered past with Kazan and I was much more focused on opening night and the work. But my playing a southerner and our talks about the South made Jimmy think of me for a play he had in mind probably even then. Writers are like that." (The play that Rip Torn referred to was *Blues for Mister Charlie,* which he was to act in five years later.) "After *Sweet Bird,* we kept in touch and met from time to time. We had a number of friends in common, white and black, and I became friendly with his brother David, who was also an actor."

Another play on the way to Broadway, *A Raisin in the Sun,* also opened in Philadelphia, and Baldwin once more met Lorraine Hansberry. He found this attractive, lively woman had grown up thinking of herself as comical, round and "as plain as her brother was angrily handsome." Baldwin talked to her about little Frog Eyes. They shared a great many fears—of heights, bridges, elevators, planes. She was so afraid of hospitals she seldom visited even close friends there; luckily she couldn't see into the near future that she was soon destined to die in one. She was also so committed to the civil rights movement that when she was seriously ill she decided, "When I get my health back I shall go into the South to find out what kind of revolutionary I am." The South had become a testing ground for a great many Americans, white and black. She had taken the title of her play from a poem by Langston Hughes in which he described a dream deferred as perhaps drying up like a raisin in the sun. She and Baldwin had many heated arguments about the older black poet and also about Richard Wright, she believing Baldwin was too critical of them in public and that white racists might use his words against them. He argued that he had to say what he thought, there had been too many lies of the diplomatic and public-relations kind already. What did she think he was saying in *Giovanni's Room*? What was she saying in *Raisin* through her black family?

After the curtains came down on their plays, they often sat up for hours over drinks "sometimes seeming for anyone who didn't know us," Baldwin said, "to be having a knock-down-, drag-out battle." One of the few subjects they agreed wholeheartedly on was Norman Mailer's

"The White Negro." She admired Mailer as a serious writer, as Baldwin did, but she agreed with him that this particular essay was a classic example of white liberals who assumed they had more knowledge of black life than they really had. Comparing white beatniks and hipsters with blacks, indeed! What delighted Baldwin about her play was that he had never before seen so many black people in a theater audience because never before had "so much of the truth of black people's lives been seen on the stage." When Lorraine Hansberry was mobbed outside the stage door Baldwin loaned her a pen to sign autographs, and it led him to reflect on what a special case black artists were. "One is not merely an artist and one is not judged merely as an artist: the black people crowding around Lorraine, whether or not they considered her an artist, assuredly considered her a witness." *A witness:* it was an expression he would use more and more in the years ahead to describe his own work.

Baldwin also got to know the star of *Raisin*—Sidney Poitier, who was the first black actor to become a major Hollywood star, a sign of the changing times even though his movies weren't shown in parts of the South. Baldwin hadn't liked *Blackboard Jungle,* the film in which Poitier made his name as a New York student dealing with a tough class—"I know much more than *that* about the public school system of New York"—but he had considered Poitier's performance "beautiful, vivid and truthful." Now Poitier was in a play that Baldwin felt was more relevant to his talent, although Baldwin doubted it would have been produced if Poitier hadn't agreed to appear in it. Poitier had a "fantastic presence" on stage; it was easy to explain his great appeal to blacks in an audience, but why had he been the black actor to be so widely accepted by whites? It was "something of a puzzle," Baldwin said. Poitier was extraordinarily attractive and winning and virile, "but that could just as easily have worked against him." Baldwin thought Poitier's great appeal had to do with "a quality of pain and danger and some fundamental impulse to decency that both titillates and reassures the white audience." As a black artist, Poitier was up against the country's furtive sexuality that made him a sexual symbol, but no one dared use him as any of the Hollywood white he-men were used. "Black men are still used in the popular culture as though they had no sexual equipment at all," Baldwin said. It was a topic he and Sidney Poitier discussed at great length during their stay in Philadelphia.

While Baldwin was working on *Sweet Bird of Youth,* he also learned that he had been awarded a Ford Foundation grant, and with Kazan and Tennessee Williams he had a big celebration in a bar. He needed money until he could publish another book, and the grant would help him buy time to work on two books—the new essay collection and the novel.

He also received an invitation to spend a weekend in Connecticut from Norman Mailer, whom he hadn't seen for a long time. He would have welcomed spending a weekend with Mailer and his wife, but other people were going to be there and he felt too drained for a social gathering. He kept putting off taking a train and eventually he and Mailer talked on the phone. "I guess you just don't like the Connecticut gentry," Mailer said, according to Baldwin. They talked about meeting another time. Apparently it wasn't an easy relationship for either of them. Baldwin later heard about Mailer being involved in fights in Village bars and wondered why he bothered—"It seemed simpler, as I was always telling myself, just to stay out of Village bars." Many of the people who claimed to be seeing Mailer regularly struck Baldwin as being far beneath the writer, "but this is also true, alas, of much of my own entourage. The people who are in one's life or merely continually in one's presence reveal a great deal about one's needs and terrors. Also, one's hopes."

9

Going to Meet the Man

JAMES BALDWIN was already well-known in literary circles and to many people in the civil rights movement, and it was obviously not going to be long before he became a celebrity—a star—recognized everywhere by the general public. One book that caught the changing mood of the country could do it.

It was then—the summer of 1959—that I first met him, and I recorded my impressions because I was working as a newspaper reporter. It was a good time to meet him while he could still enjoy some privacy in public, before he had to cope with all the new pressures of fame. I was introduced to him by Tennessee Williams. Soon after *Sweet Bird of Youth* opened on Broadway I interviewed Williams in his disheveled fifth-floor apartment on East Sixty-fifth Street, listening to him tell of his anguish over *Sweet Bird* in his southern drawl, almost everything punctuated by a highly infectious chuckle that belied the misery of many of his words ("I have never before been so depressed or found it so hard to work . . .") He was a small, round, untidy man with a big mustache, the opposite of his spruce, athletic secretary and roommate, Frankie Merlo, the love of his life, who was soon to die of cancer.

As I was leaving, Williams suddenly said at the door, "Why don't you interview James Baldwin?" At first I didn't recognize the name, and then I remembered a novel I had picked up by chance at an English railway bookstall—*Giovanni's Room*. I still had a vivid memory of the book as a moving story about homosexuality and self-deception amid exiles in Paris, a Jamesian theme but written by a more down-to-earth Henry James. When I mentioned this to Tennessee Williams he said, "I'll give you his phone number." I phoned next day expecting an affected show-business voice—the hero of *Giovanni's Room* was a spoiled white American and I assumed that the author was very much like him, a talented white American with a private income who was really writing his memoirs. The nervous, intense voice that invited me down to his apartment in Horatio Street in the Village came as a surprise.

Baldwin's apartment was two flights up in a rather drab building, and with only a few people there it seemed overcrowded. I was surprised to see several blacks because it was very unusual to find interracial groups in white homes in New York, even in the with-it Village. In fact, in Baldwin's apartment that day there was only one white, a middle-aged man with a high nervous giggle, and so I went over to him to present myself. But when I addressed him as "Mr. Baldwin," he looked vaguely at me as if he hadn't even heard and had a quick drink from a tall glass he was holding. "You want Jimmy," a tall young black man said. "He's in the kitchen."

A small black man appeared with a glass of scotch whisky in each hand. His head was formidable with big, incredibly expressive eyes and a wide mouth that flashed frequent gap-toothed grins. His slight, erect body hardly matched that large head and was like a frail wire connected to a big bulb that continually lit up: you noticed only the intense look of his dark face and especially the eyes, which were peacefully friendly now but which I was to see flash like fire when he was passionately involved in an argument.

"Hi," he said, shaking hands, "I'm Jimmy Baldwin." He gave me one of the scotches and introduced me around. The tall young black who had spoken to me was Tony Maynard, remarkable for a mane of curly black hair and a pantherlike grace, who was acting as Baldwin's assistant and later was to be involved in a murder case that dragged on for seven years before he proved his innocence. Another young black man, smaller and quieter, was an artist named Lorenzo Hail. The white man I had stupidly taken for Baldwin was a professor, and everyone made light of the fact, including the professor.

Baldwin was wearing an open-necked, short-sleeved shirt and dark pants; he didn't give the impression of bothering much about his clothes. A bust of him by Lorenzo Hail was on a table; it was a good likeness and expressed something of his unusual vitality, his nervous energy. Hail said he planned soon to go to Europe. It had worked for Jimmy so why not for him? He had gentle manners and a dreamer's eyes; at present he worked in a local post office but wanted to give all his time to art "like Jimmy." Baldwin heard him: "What do you mean—like me?" The large eyes flashed, but with a humorous glint. "I haven't written a line for days, have been too busy making speeches." When I tried to begin the interview, he said cheerfully, "Look, if you don't know anyone in New York, why don't you join us tonight? I've got to go to my publisher's first and then we're going by a friend's house."

Baldwin prepared then for a trip uptown to his publisher's. His only suit, dark and rather worn, came out of the closet. A clean shirt followed but it took some time to find a tie. Soon he looked transformed, quite businesslike, though the combined efforts of Tony Maynard and Lorenzo Hail couldn't quite keep his tie straight, and he was off "to meet the Man," as he put it.

(I spent the time until our next meeting reading his other books. *Go Tell It On the Mountain* seemed like the other side of *Giovanni's Room,* describing the black condition whereas *Giovanni* had suggested how it had come about by the self-deception of the privileged. *Notes of a Native Son,* set in the U.S. and Europe, was concerned with the discovery of what it meant to be black in white society. Taken together, the books suggested that Baldwin, for all his friendliness, had great anger inside him. Knowing him might be like keeping the company of a volcano.)

His visit to his publisher's must have been satisfactory because he was in a very good mood that evening. At the friend's apartment on Eighteenth Street, a young Puerto Rican asked him to look at his poetry.

Baldwin gave the romantic verses long and careful attention, but I sensed he liked the handsome young man rather better than his poetry, though he said something encouraging. Over a drink I asked him if he had any sense of African roots, and he told me, "I was an interloper from Africa, but the jungle wasn't my home. I therefore have had to take over white history and make it my own, make it work for me, a part of me on *my* terms. You understand what I mean?" I wasn't sure. I also found the generalized "I" as if he were speaking for the whole black race a little off-putting. His eyes were wide and flashing fire now, his right hand gesturing. About a dozen people were listening intently. "I sometimes don't understand white people"—his voice rose, was the volcano about to erupt and Baldwin catch fire?—"but I'm working on it, and I've always understood them a lot more than they've ever understood *me.*" He touched my hand impulsively. "Don't take what I say personally."

The professor arrived, even more drunk than he had been earlier, and the party was on again. Suddenly Baldwin said to me, "Anger is a waste of time, but it's inevitable. It's not open to any arguments whatever."

"In your essay on your father, you say hatred never fails to destroy the person who hates."

"That's right."

"You also say that we not only have to accept the world as it is but must also never stop trying to change it for the better."

"That's what I believe," he said. "Even more than when I wrote it. That's what the civil rights movement is all about."

The professor came over to accuse him of being too serious. "You're sitting there pontificating like Henry James, Jimmy."

Baldwin flashed me a wide-open grin; he gave the impression of a great capacity for enjoying himself, the deceptive other side of the volcano.

"Let's rejoin the party."

I was going to Detroit, and when Baldwin told me he and Tony Maynard planned to spend a week "away from it all" in the Michigan woods, we arranged to meet. They never showed up. When I returned to New York I phoned Baldwin, concerned something might have happened to him. He was there. No, nothing had happened; he'd just had to stay in the city to take care of business. I went around some of the Village bars with him that night—all kinds of drinking places from workingmen's Irish bars to sleek show-business hangouts, from his old refuge, the San Remo on Macdougal Street, to the Riviera on Sheridan Square. People came over to speak to him in most of the bars. We ended in the early morning in a basement bar near his apartment. The young barman received Baldwin like a prince and asked him to autograph a copy of *Giovanni's Room* that he produced from under the bar. Several drinkers in the bar stopped talking to watch Baldwin; here he was already famous. Baldwin took advantage of his status to ask the barman to cash a check for him. It was a sign of power that obviously pleased him, as if it were a herald of the fame on the horizon.

He told me he hadn't lost hope that *Giovanni's Room* would be made into a movie. "Times are slowly changing," he said, his big eyes glowing. "In this bar a lot of people identify now with *Giovanni;* they feel as oppressed as blacks. But a breakthrough is coming, a willingness to listen. Great changes are on the way. It's difficult now to remember how difficult it was to get *Giovanni* accepted." He told me about the rejections. "But wait until you read my next novel. Maybe I've gone too far this time." He sounded worried. "I'm going to call it *Another Country.*"

"Is it nearly finished?"

"Not yet. I need something to give the narrative a lift. I'm still working on it every chance I get."

When he was at his most intense, the boy preacher's mannerisms reappeared, and he used his face and hands like an actor to help his words. I was always surprised when I read of him described as ugly. His face was so lively, his eyes and his mouth so expressive that the impression he always left was incredibly vivid. His appearance wasn't ugly but eccentric, much more interesting than a conventionally "good-looking" person. But I suspected sometimes that Baldwin would have given all his talents to have the humdrum muscular good looks of the average beachboy. A face, as Aldous Huxley once put it, like a battering ram. That might have been a dream in a weak moment. But never to be white, at least not now; he had outgrown that. The anger was too deep and genuine. He told me that night, "I do *not* hate white people. I haven't got enough emotional energy. There are some people I hate, some are white, some are black." Occasionally, to back the feeling of his words, he liked to touch the person he was speaking to, a sort of laying on of hands to convey emotion physically so you would have no doubt he meant what he said. He gripped my hand then as he said, "The only time you'll hear nonviolence admired is when black men preach and practice it. Whites admire violence in themselves." He stared at me as if waiting for my disagreement. "Remember, to hate, to be violent, is demeaning. It means you're afraid of the other side of the coin—to love and be loved."

I walked him partway back home—the latest of his temporary homes—through a wilderness of gray backstreets, the edge of a lonely warehouse district, the edge of poverty. When fame and riches came, the first thing he would change would be where he lived. It'd be nice to have a big apartment in a pleasant area, he said, and eat in expensive restaurants—nice, too, to take his family out of Harlem. He invited me to go uptown next day to meet his mother. I must have been feeling all the liquor because I found myself arguing with him about William Faulkner. He wouldn't concede an inch. If he had once admired Faulkner, there was no sign of it. I mentioned Dilsey, the old black woman who held the decadent white family together in *The Sound and the Fury*. "Dilsey is my mother!" he said fiercely. "Why should she spend her life saving some sick no-good white people?" Next day when I met Mrs. Baldwin, she didn't remind me of Faulkner's Dilsey but of her eldest son. She had the same slight physique, the same eyes, the same humor round the mouth, and a similar pleasant well-modulated voice, but she was much lighter in color and much calmer, at least on the surface. It was sometimes difficult to read her reaction, whereas Baldwin himself always appeared to be very open about his feelings. I heard him tell her he was shortly taking a trip and she asked, "Where to this time?" She was used to his always being on the move. "Sweden," he told her.

Ingmar Bergman, the Swedish film director, had become very fashionable in American intellectual circles, and his highly personal movies and religious background—he, too, had grown up as a minister's son—fascinated Baldwin. Bergman was one white artist he definitely identified with. What Bergman saw when he looked at the world "did not seem very different from what *I* saw." An essay about Bergman would be useful for the new collection and also perhaps one day he and Bergman could collaborate on a film. He persuaded Esquire magazine to send him to Sweden.

The Filmstaden, the headquarters of the Svensk Film-industri, one of the oldest movie companies in the world, was situated in Rasunda, a suburb of Stockholm. When Baldwin saw the landscape he realized immediately where so much of the Swedish director's films came from—"the landscape of Bergman's mind was simply the landscape in which he had grown up." It was the same sensation his readers might have if they saw Harlem. Bergman himself was a tall, lean man of forty-one, five years older than Baldwin, and was wearing a heavy sweater like a college student and was pleasantly informal. He had a good-natured, self-possessed directness much like Baldwin's own manner, together with "the evangelical distance of someone possessed by a vision." They walked over to the movie company's canteen and had a cup of tea. Baldwin had a very bad cold verging on flu, and as he coughed and sneezed, Bergman asked could he help. "You haven't to be shy," he said. "I know what it is like to be ill and alone in a strange city." He refused to discuss his famous religious film, "The Seventh Seal." "I had to do it," he said, adding he had to be free of questions about God and the Devil, life and death, good and evil. "It's the same for you when you write a book? You just do it because you must and then, when you have done it, you are relieved, no?"

Baldwin envied him for being able to love his country so directly and stay there and work, and yet realized it was foolish to feel that way. It was "like envying him his language." Everything in a life "depends on how that life accepts its limits." They talked about Bergman's more recent film, "The Magician," which Baldwin suggested was a long, elaborate metaphor for the condition of the artist. Bergman described the artist just the way Baldwin saw his own life. The artist "is always on the very edge of disaster," said the Swedish director, "he is always on the very edge of great things. Always. Isn't it so? It is his element, like water is the element of the fish."

Baldwin came away thinking there was something in the "weird, mad, northern Protestantism" that Ingmar Bergman came from that reminded him of "the visions of the black preachers of my childhood." Since he was so struck by their similarities, he tried to imagine a film he would make that would be as important to his own life as "The Seventh Seal" was to Bergman's. It would have to play on the theme of eternal rebellion. Inevitably the film would begin with black slaves boarding the good ship *Jesus* owned by white slavemasters. One slave would rebel—a witch doctor or a chief or a prince or a singer—and he would die in protecting a black woman. She would bear his child, who would lead a slave insurrection and be hanged. During Reconstruction days his child would be murdered leaving Congress. Yet other rebel successors would be a black soldier returning from World War I and a jazz musician in the Depression. But who would the rebel be now? A junkie? What would the title be for "this grim and vengeful fantasy?" Perhaps what divided him and Ingmar Bergman—the black and white Protestants—was "the nature of my still unwieldy, unaccepted bitterness." Perhaps today's rebel in his film should be himself, tell his own half-finished story, because, he reflected, "all art is a kind of confession, more or less oblique. All artists, if they are to survive, are forced at last to tell the whole story, to vomit the anguish up."

Ingmar Bergman had become reconciled to his past in a way that Baldwin hadn't yet managed. Bergman and his pastor father hadn't got on well when Bergman was young, but now the battle between them was over and they often had friendly meetings. Baldwin had said how much he envied him, and Bergman smiled and replied, "Oh, it is always like that—when such a battle is over, fathers and sons can be friends." It made the acceptance of an artist's "arduous, delicate, and disciplined self-exposure" easier for Bergman. But such a reconciliation had so far eluded Baldwin. He couldn't have friendly meetings with the father he had never known or his stepfather who was dead. He still identified with the youngsters in New York "searching desperately for the limits which would tell them who they were, and create for them a challenge to which could rise." Was the civil rights movement such a challenge—or *Another Country*?

Baldwin had written an essay on Norman Mailer for Esquire, but Mailer was in trouble because he had stabbed his wife after a party and "I refused to turn it in before showing it to his sister, Barbara," said Baldwin. "I left the typescript with her and said, 'I want to show it to you before anyone else. I don't want to betray Norman.' " The essay was subsequently published in Esquire entitled "The Black Boy Looks at the White Boy."

He was faced with another painful part of his own past when the news arrived from Paris that Richard Wright had died of a heart attack at the age of fifty-two. They had never achieved a reconciliation. In Wright's last lecture three weeks before he died he had referred bitterly to the quarrel he claimed Baldwin and other young black writers like Richard Gibson had sought with him. He had also left an unpublished novel, *Island of Hallucinations,* in which writers like Baldwin and Gibson were easily recognizable in composite portraits. One character Baldwin took to be a satirical picture of himself was homosexual with a face scarred by smallpox and who was the son of a fanatic follower of Father Divine, the black evangelist, and who once threw a bottle of ink at an editor who refused him a job as a reporter because of his color. As Michel Fabre comments in his Wright biography: "Nowhere else, with the exception perhaps of his journal in 1947, does Wright express so openly his often extremely unflattering opinions of people he knew. This can certainly be interpreted as revenge, the striking down on paper of the puppets and phantasms that troubled him." Baldwin had been angry when he first heard about this, but Wright's death changed his attitude. He thought back to their first meeting in Brooklyn and Wright's kindness to him, and he felt regretful and even slightly guilty that their relationship had soured so much. He decided to achieve his own reconciliation on paper in a long essay he called "Alas, Poor Richard."

"The man I fought so hard and who meant so much to me is gone," he wrote. He found good things to say about Wright's last short-story collection, *Eight Men,* which ranged from "The Man Who Saw the

Flood," first published in 1937, to "Man of All Work," a new story that
Baldwin called "a masterpiece." The story suggested to him that Wright
"was acquiring a new tone, and a less uncertain esthetic distance, and
a new depth." He even agreed with a reader of *Native Son* who suggested the novel meant more now than when it was first published
because we didn't read it now as a militant racial manifesto. But when
he began explaining the row between Wright and himself, he became
more defensive, conceding little, depicting Wright as a tragic, even a
pathetic figure trapped in a no-man's land between black and white and
bewildered by the "conundrum" of Africa. But he seemed to be writing
more about himself than about Wright when he commented: "What an
African, facing an American Negro sees, I really do not yet know; and
it is too early to tell with what scars and complexes the African has come
up from the fire." He summed up that Richard Wright was "among
the most illustrious victims" of the war in the breast between blackness
and whiteness. But this did not help him much when the essay was
published. He was again attacked by Wright's admirers, who saw it not
as a conciliatory approach but as yet another critical onslaught.

And even that was not to be the end of the famous row. For the rest
of Baldwin's life interviewers would ask him about it. Eventually he
found himself in Wright's position, attacked by younger black writers.
He had seen this coming in "Alas, Poor Richard" and had warned
himself: "Be careful. Time is passing for you, too, and this may be
happening to you one day." He wondered how he would take the kind
of treatment he had given Wright "when my time comes." When his
time did come and he was attacked by Eldridge Cleaver, LeRoi Jones
and others, he seemed to mellow toward Wright. He told me he thought
he had been "too harsh, with too little charity," and had made "a
mistake." Just three years before he died he insisted to Julius Lester,
another black writer of the younger generation, that he was not "attacking" Wright but "was trying to clarify something for myself." He also
told the Paris Review that their "early hostile period" had been "ridicu-
lously blown out of proportion." He added, "When I thought I was
dealing with Richard, I was in fact thinking of Harriet Beecher Stowe
and *Uncle Tom's Cabin.*" He had the utmost respect for Wright, "especially in light of his posthumous work, which I believe is his greatest

161

novel, *Lawd Today*." It was the closest to a reconciliation he would ever get, but it still didn't satisfy Wright's admirers, who remained bitter about it even after Baldwin's death.

Baldwin was becoming increasingly worried by the growing divisions within the civil rights movement, frequently finding himself the man in the middle—between the cautious, older black leaders and the younger black students impatient for faster progress. Out of their impatience had come the Student Nonviolent Coordinating Committee and the Freedom Riders, who descended on segregated strongholds across the South with the panache of old-time cavaliers. Michael Thelwell, a young student at Howard University, was taking part in demonstrations in the nation's capital when he was invited to meet James Baldwin. About all he knew about Baldwin was that he was a writer. He was told Jimmy Baldwin was "a very curious and interesting man" with a personal life "so complicated, always chaotic, skirting the edge of crisis," an extraordinary writer and a brilliant speaker. He was to give a talk in Washington's affluent district of Georgetown and had asked to meet "some of the Movement kids." Thelwell found himself part of a group that decided to check out Baldwin. The meeting was held in the home of a wealthy ex-socialist. Baldwin was already speaking when they shyly entered and saw before them a small, very black man with huge eyes standing in the center of a packed living room surrounded by well-off whites. The group of young blacks were nervous and ill-at-ease, but Baldwin flashed them a friendly, protective smile.

"Hi," he said, "I'm James Baldwin and I'm so very glad you came."

He spoke brilliantly, always gracious with questioners, but quite uncompromising, never defensive nor apologetic. His theme was that it wasn't a question of whether whites would accept blacks but whether blacks could forgive whites. Thelwell commented that even the radical young blacks of his group were very favorably impressed—"He made believers of us." It was the beginning of a unique relationship, Thelwell felt, between Baldwin and "our whole generation of black Americans."

Baldwin's audience was growing.

10

Discovering Istanbul

HE NEEDED a break. He persuaded Dial Press that he had to visit Paris to complete his essays on Richard Wright and Norman Mailer, which were to be in the new collection, so he was advanced some more money. In the French capital he spent most of his time with several old friends, including Lucien, who was hoping to start commuting between Switzerland and New York when possible. James and Gloria Jones had settled down in a house overlooking the Seine River with a view of Notre-Dame cathedral through huge windows. Baldwin took them to Beauford Delaney's studio in Clarmart. Jones promptly bought several paintings, and Delaney entertained them with a dinner of southern American stew and French wine. When Tennessee Williams passed through Paris, Baldwin took him to see Delaney's paintings, too, and the playwright and the painter, both southerners, exchanged reminiscences about their very different childhoods in segregated society. To Baldwin's disappointment, Tennessee Williams didn't buy any paintings.

The Joneses' home on the Ile St. Louis had become a great meeting place for visiting Americans, ranging from fellow writers and Hollywood movie producers like Darryl F. Zanuck to international racehorse owners and vacationing congressmen. "This was the place where the lonely could find friends," said Irwin Shaw, the famed novelist and short-story writer, best known for his novel *The Young Lions,* which was filmed with Baldwin's old buddy, Marlon Brando, playing a blond German. Baldwin dropped in frequently at the Joneses' and found there was always a noisy argument about politics or literature occupying the guests. Jones used a wooden Renaissance pulpit with prayer stools found in a flea market as a bar, and there was a house rule that if you couldn't make yourself heard in an argument, you could announce, "I invoke the pulpit!" and you then had the right to stand at the pulpit-bar and speak uninterrupted for three minutes. Willie Morris in his memoir of James Jones recalled that Jimmy Baldwin "would get drunk and stand behind the pulpit-bar and show everyone how he used to preach, and give a hellfire sermon on the evils of drink."

Another writer who was often Jones' drinking companion was William Styron, who had made his name with his first novel, *Lie Down in Darkness.* He was from the South and therefore was of particular interest to Baldwin, who had in mind a novel or a play set in the contemporary South. Styron gave Willie Morris an account of what he called "the monumental drunk of 1960." Jones and he decided "to get good and drunk, no fooling around." Jimmy Baldwin accompanied them. They set a hot pace at several Paris nightclubs and finally, Styron recalled, "even Jimmy Baldwin faded—a very good man with the bottle. He folded around four or five A.M., to give him credit, maybe a little later. The collapse of Jimmy Baldwin should've given us pause for thought, but didn't . . ." Jones and Styron drank on. Toward the end of his life when his health, never robust, began to be affected, Baldwin became rather defensive about his drinking. He told one interviewer, "I don't know any writers who don't drink. Everybody I've been close to drinks. But you don't drink while you're working." American literary history seems to bear him out. Of seven American Nobel laureates in literature, at least four were more or less alcoholics for much of their lives.

Gloria Jones remembered that "In Paris we saw loads of each other— my Jim and me and Jimmy Baldwin. There was a civil rights march by Americans to express support for the movement back home, and Jimmy carried our daughter Kaylie on his shoulder. I remember during the

Algerian troubles in 1960, we were in our Mercedes with Jimmy and his great friend, Lucien, and Tennessee Williams, who had a beautiful German with him. The police stopped us with guns. I remember the German asked Tennessee, 'What are we doing with these people?' and so Tennessee took him away. Jimmy enjoyed our pulpit, doing his number that he used to do in church as a boy preacher. My Jim and Jimmy sometimes got into loud arguments when they were drinking, calling each other 'motherfucker.' My Jim saw that I was kept out of that. Jimmy would point his finger and say, 'You white people have done this or that.' And my Jim would reply, 'Don't call me a white motherfucker. You owe me two hundred dollars.' Jimmy would burst into crazy laughing and throw the money at him. Jimmy didn't dance or wouldn't but stamped and sang."

Back home Norman Mailer had published a collection of his essays, _Advertisements for Myself,_ and had added an analysis of his contemporaries entitled "Evaluations—Quick and Expensive Comments on the Talent in the Room." Baldwin remembered sitting with James Jones and William Styron reading aloud "in a kind of drunken, masochistic fascination" what Mailer had written about each of them. None of them was treated in a friendly way, though Baldwin decided he came off best because what Mailer said about him was "less venomous." Mailer wrote that Baldwin was "too charming a writer to be major." The best of his paragraphs were "sprayed with perfume" and he seemed "incapable of saying 'F——— you' to the reader." _Giovanni's Room_ was "a bad book but mostly a brave one." He did allow that _Notes of a Native Son_ had "a sense of moral nuance which is one of the few modern guides to the sophistication of the ethos" and added that "since his life has been as fantastic and varied as the life of any of my fellow racketeers, and he has kept his sensitivity, one itches at times to take a hammer to his detachment, smash the perfumed dome of his ego, and reduce him to what must be one of the most tortured and magical nerves of our time. If he ever climbs the mountain, and really tells it, we will have the testament, and not a noble toilet water. Until then he is doomed to be minor."

It made what Baldwin had written about Richard Wright seem quite mild. Baldwin was infuriated by the "condescension" and was tempted to send him a cable with the message: "F———— you." But he decided that was what Mailer wanted. He would remain cool and wait until he met Mailer again, the way Wright had treated him.

They came face-to-face at the Actors Studio in New York a few weeks later. An adaptation of Mailer's novel, *The Deer Park,* was being performed, but Baldwin deliberately arrived too late to see it. He just wanted to confront its author. It was typical of the slight, frail Baldwin not to duck a challenge. "I really did not know how I was going to react to Norman and didn't want to betray myself by clobbering his play." He found Mailer surrounded by a crowd discussing the play with him. Baldwin stood on the edge of the crowd, patiently waiting for his chance. Their eyes met over someone's shoulder and Mailer smiled. "We've got something to talk about," Baldwin told him. "I figured that," replied Mailer, hunching his shoulders like a boxer, according to Baldwin.

They sat opposite each other in a bar. "Why did you write those things about me?" Baldwin demanded. "Well, I'll tell you about that," Mailer replied in what Baldwin said was a tough-guy Texan accent. "I sort of figured you had it coming to you."

"Why?"

"Well, I think there's some truth in it."

"Well, if you felt that way, why didn't you ever say so—to me?"

"Well, I figured if this was going to break up our friendship, something else would come along to break it up just as fast." Mailer added, "You're the only one I kind of regret hitting so hard. I think I— probably—wouldn't say it quite that way now."

Baldwin commented: "With this, I had to be content." It presumably counted as some kind of reconciliation because Baldwin later spent some time with Mailer and his wife in Provincetown on Cape Cod. Adele Morales Mailer recalled that Baldwin and Mailer had a terrible fight over "The White Negro," but "he was very nice to me, never rude. And he used to listen to me, for a change." Mrs. Mailer was dancing in the chorus at the Provincetown Playhouse in a musical, *The Pirates of Provincetown,* and Baldwin went to the opening "and was very complimentary. I had the feeling that he was a loner. He and I went out to Long Nook Beach with a couple of other people, and there was something very moving about Jimmy, this little figure, short and very thin, in a bathing suit. I felt a deep unhappiness in him. Lonely, so lonely. It was like seeing this spidery little black figure against an enormous white dune. I don't think he felt he belonged, he felt uncomfortable and out of place. I don't know if it had to do with his homosexuality, I don't know what his hang-ups were. He wasn't coming on like the preacher boy, he was quiet and not terribly sure of himself, very articulate but shy. I doubt that Norman realized this."

The way Baldwin described it, he loathed Provincetown, "the scene was crazy—touristy, cheap, filled with bellicose cops." He found Mailer increasingly interested in the source and manipulation of power in American society, which he considered a white man's attitude because someone black grew up feeling the effects of that power and had to know all about it from an early age just to survive. He was furious when he learned that Mailer seriously intended to run for mayor of New York. He described his reaction: "You son of a bitch, you're copping out. You're one of the very few writers around who might really become a great writer, who might help to excavate the buried consciousness of this country; and you want to settle for being the lousy Mayor of New York." Mailer was his friend, but perhaps, he said, he didn't really understand him at all. It was remarkable, however, that when the difference in their styles and attitudes was allowed for, what Baldwin and Mailer said about each other was very similar. Each saw in the other the talent of a potential major writer, but agreed that that promise was not being fulfilled, perhaps because of their attitudes or way of life. Certainly each writer seemed to feel a challenge from the other more deeply personal than the mere competition of the literary marketplace.

Baldwin had decided to call his new collection of essays *Nobody Knows My Name.* He liked the play on the obscurity he had come from and on his illegitimacy. "The question of color takes up much space in these pages," he wrote in an introduction, "but the question of color, especially in this country, operates to hide the graver questions of the self." His own experiences proved to him that the connection between American whites and blacks was far deeper and more passionate than anybody liked to think. But "one can only face in others what one can face in oneself"—that was becoming a favorite Baldwin theme. He compared the new book to a private logbook written over the preceding six years, which he saw now as being on the whole "rather sad and aimless" years though they had led eventually to his growing success.

Richard Baron, who became the publisher of Dial Press, remembered meeting Baldwin at that time in the office of James Silberman, his editor. "It was the first of many meetings. He was dressed very neatly. He and Jim Silberman had had lunch in a nice hotel nearby. My first impression was of his unusual physical appearance. His face was very expressive. We talked about business matters. He talked about his needs. The book in the works then was *Nobody Knows My Name* and he was also working on a much larger book."

So unbusinesslike was Baldwin that it was extremely difficult for him to adapt from a struggling, hustling existence to having something like a regular income. The more money he received the quicker it seemed to go. He was generous not only with his family but with the growing number of friends and acquaintances who seemed to form a permanent entourage as he moved about the city. He enjoyed buying even his casual intimates expensive presents and eating in luxurious restaurants, invariably picking up the check unless he was with a publisher. To help him with his growing "needs," he not only had a literary agent but a lawyer to represent his interests, though where the dividing line was between them was sometimes difficult to tell. His representatives seemed to last only a comparatively short time and then he usually made a change, hoping some newcomer he had met or who had been recommended would improve his financial situation, with the result that his business affairs were often rather chaotic.

Judge Theodore Kupferman was in private practice in 1960 when he became Baldwin's lawyer. "A patent-lawyer friend of his recommended me. I had some background in the entertainment field with the legal department of Warner's, NBC and Cinerama. I also represented James Dean. Jimmy had several problems. That was probably the reason why he was referred to me. He had contracts with Dial Press. Every time he wrote something, they got an option on the next book and they were contending they had five or six options altogether. We took the position that they had only one option when we discussed it with Dick Baron at Dial. I had no great feeling about Jimmy. It was a professional relationship. I knew of course he was a homosexual. Another writer who knew I was representing him told me he was known as 'Martin Luther Queen.' But race and homosexuality were no barriers. My wife was a stewardess and many of her friends were male stewards in flying who were both black and homosexual. As long as I agreed with what Jimmy was doing, everything was fine. Mine was a business relationship and I did the best I could. His contract with Dial limited him to $15,000 a year, though he must have earned hundreds of thousands at one time when he had several bestsellers. He couldn't live on $15,000 so he was borrowing against the rest and we were worried that the tax people would take the position that the $15,000 limit was a tax dodge. So I said he shouldn't borrow against it, but I tried to get advances on the new books so he would have that money as well and it wouldn't be part of the old deal. He wasn't doing his own taxes. They had an accountant at Dial. But it was ridiculous for Jimmy to have all that money piled up with his publishers and not be able to get to it. He was always in need of money. People used to say he was late for appointments or didn't keep them, but I had no real problems with him that way. When he came to my office he was alone, but when I saw him elsewhere, he always had people with him."

Richard Baron said, "Each of his contracts had an option so he was almost indentured. He had a limit-of-income clause in his contracts which meant he could only receive so much in any one year for the sake of taxes. He later earned very big money, but with this limitation he couldn't get enough to live on in the style he wanted. We were able to raise the limit when he arranged to give us another book. We kept him with plenty of money. Taxes boxed him in so he felt he was enslaved to us and there was a period of hostility. But he always cooperated with us on the books. He had no real problems with us. We genuinely liked him."

Baldwin hoped *Nobody Knows My Name* followed by *Another Country* would solve his financial problems. Silberman worked with him on the selection of the essays. Baldwin couldn't make up his mind whether to end with "Alas, Poor Richard" or his Mailer essay, "The Black Boy

Looks at the White Boy." Finally he decided to put the Mailer last. That way the book would end with the words "Where there is no vision, the people perish." He liked that. He dedicated the book: "For my brothers, George, Wilmer and David." Silberman recalled that Baldwin showed him different parts of *Another Country*. "For all his gregariousness, Jimmy worked privately. I read sections a couple of times, maybe three times, but not until it was in reasonably final form. Not many suggestions were necessary. No big switching around, nothing like that. Like all really good writers, he did his own work. Jimmy acquired a reputation later for being difficult to deal with, but that wasn't my experience with him. I once said to him, 'I understand that the times when you aren't writing are also part of the creative process with you and the delay is not procrastination and not willful.' It was the way he came to what he was going to write. Like most writers there was as much thinking time as writing time. Most writers can do that simultaneously, but with Jimmy it was a separate process. He would get it fully understood and then write it. I don't know if he composed any of it in his head, but some of his creating was done in the time when he appeared to be doing nothing. When something finally arrived on paper, it was really in final shape. His voice was always there, so was the organization."

Baldwin had typed and retyped about five hundred pages of the novel, *Another Country*, and he knew something wasn't working but wasn't sure what. At first he had thought of setting it in Paris like *Giovanni's Room* and making it another story of American exiles or "ambassadors," as Henry James had put it. But that wasn't right. It was an American story. *Another Country* was the United States as it might be seen from outside with all the warts. The two main characters were a young Italian-American writer named Daniel at first and then renamed Vivaldo, who was based on a man Baldwin had had an affair with in the Village, and a young black woman named Ida, who was based on a lot of women he had known, including his sisters and the woman he had once lived with in the Village. There was also a third important character, a bisexual white American actor named Eric who returned to New York from Paris—he reflected much of Baldwin's experience in the theater over the previous two years. But the narrative didn't work yet. Why was Ida so difficult with her lover, would readers understand? Then Baldwin realized what he had to do. Ida's brother, Rufus, who had committed suicide, had to be introduced. And he knew suddenly how Rufus would kill himself—like his friend Eugene. It was as if only then would he really accept the fact that Eugene was dead, something he hadn't really faced to the point of writing about it all these years. It would also explain Ida's state of mind—he was Ida! She was trying to live with the pain of her brother's death, that was why she lashed out at Vivaldo. When readers had met the brother and followed the events leading up to his fatal plunge off the George Washington Bridge, they would understand Ida and the entire action would then make sense.

He described the suicide scene in *Another Country* as "the hardest thing I ever wrote." He always knew Rufus had to die very early on, "because that was the key to the book. But I kept putting it off. It had to do, of course, with reliving the suicide of my friend who jumped off the bridge. Also, it was very dangerous to do from the technical point of view because this central character dies in the first hundred pages, with a couple of hundred pages still to go. The point up to the suicide is like a long prologue, and it is the only light on Ida. You never go into her mind, but I had to make you see what is happening to this girl by making you feel the blow of her brother's death—the key to her relationship with everybody. She tries to make everybody pay for it. You cannot do that, life is not like that, you only destroy yourself."

It took him a long time to find the right opening, doing a lot of "painful" rewriting. He finally knew he had it when he couldn't do any more to it, though it wasn't exactly the way he wanted it—writing never was. This was the final version: "He was facing Seventh Avenue, at Times Square. It was past midnight and he had been sitting in the movies, in the top row of the balcony, since two o'clock in the afternoon . . ." Baldwin drew on his own Forty-second Street experiences seeing cheap movies as a teenager. "Twice he had been awakened by the violent accents of the Italian film, once the usher had awakened him, and twice he had been awakened by caterpillar fingers between his thighs . . ."

That was it, the start of Rufus' last hours. Now all he had to do was find the time to tell the rest of Rufus'—Eugene's—story. He had little money left and he couldn't expect any more from Dial Press until the reception of *Nobody Knows My Name,* he hoped, proved his market value. At this time he compared himself to Hyacinth Robinson, the hero of Henry James' *The Princess Casamassima,* who was trapped between the worlds of politics and art. Every time Baldwin went off raising funds for the civil rights movement he figured it cost him a chapter of *Another Country.* He had to settle down to finish the novel or he would lose it. He was doing what was quite common with him when he had something difficult to accomplish, and that was to create a dramatic situation with himself at the center, forcing himself to deal with it. As his friend actor Billy Dee Williams told me, "Jimmy looked at things in very dramatic terms. People like him are a romantic breed—like the cavaliers and musketeers in Paris in the romantic period."

To earn some quick money he accepted an invitation to join an Esquire magazine symposium on "The Role of the Writer in America." He included his address, which he delivered at San Francisco State College, in *Nobody Knows My Name* as "Notes for a Hypothetical Novel." In showing how he could turn his own life into a novel, he put over many of his ideas on the current racial scene. He found that as usual he made instant enthusiastic contact with the large student audience, and he told them: "This country is going to be transformed. It will not be transformed by an act of God, but by all of us, by you and me."

Two other writers taking part in the symposium were Philip Roth, whom he had met in the early days in Paris, and John Cheever, whom he didn't know and whose work he had tended to avoid, thinking he was concerned exclusively with affluent white commuters in upstate New York who didn't interest him. To his surprise and delight, he discovered that John Cheever, a small slight man like himself with a boyish grin, was very friendly and a great drinking companion. They drank their way through a lot of scotch while they talked about everything from literature to religion and even the civil rights movement. Before Baldwin left San Francisco, he bought a couple of Cheever's books in paperback and discovered Cheever was not only a fine prose writer but plumbed the spiritual depths of the commuters' way of life. He was fond of quoting a line from a Cheever short story entitled "The

Country Husband": "It is a night where kings in golden suits ride elephants over the mountains." Several times in interviews he went out of his way to speak approvingly of Cheever. He told Julius Lester, for example, that many white writers were remote for him, not relevant to his experience, and he gave the contrasting examples of John Updike and John Cheever "whose subject matter is roughly the same." He said Cheever "brought something to that subject that engages me" while John Updike's people "do not engage me." Somehow those lost suburbanites in Cheever's fiction, he said, were very moving. There was a depth of anguish and he engaged your compassion. His people were "not remote."

Cheever returned the compliments. When I interviewed him at the Plaza Hotel in New York shortly before he died, he was officially off all liquor but was still the merry talker Baldwin admired. I mentioned Baldwin and he was immediately enthusiastic. "What a style! What intensity! What religious feeling! And no hostile racial feeling. The man has mastered his rage and his bitterness. He's a marvel!" Later he said, "I found I had much more in common with James Baldwin personally than I had ever imagined." He knew then what they shared regarding homosexuality, but this was not to be revealed until after his death when his daughter, Susan Cheever, described her father's secret life in a memoir. But no doubt to both writers that would not have been the most important matter they had in common. It was more, one suspects, the intensity and compassion they shared.

The news had now spread that Jimmy Baldwin had "financial problems," and a mutual friend asked William Styron and his wife, Rose, if they could give Baldwin a place to stay at their place in Connecticut. The Styrons promptly invited him to move into a cottage they used as a guest house. Styron not only liked Jimmy Baldwin as a drinking companion, but he was working on a novel himself about the slave insurrection led by the black revolutionary Nat Turner and thought Baldwin might provide him with valuable insights. There was even a rumor that the fiery, intense Baldwin was his model for Nat Turner. Baldwin stayed with the Styrons on and off for the next few months.

Whereas he was the grandson of a slave, Styron was the grandson of a slave owner, and they had long conversations about their family histories. Styron enjoyed Baldwin's "vivid images" of slave times passed down by his grandfather, and Baldwin told him that he often thought "the degradation of his grandfather's life was the animating force behind his father's apocalyptic, often incoherent rage." By contrast Styron's impression of slavery was "quaint and rather benign," gained at the bedside of his grandmother, then close to ninety, who had owned two little slave girls when she was young. Both Baldwin and Styron were writing novels about the tangled relations of blacks and whites in America, and this helped to make them friends when they took time off from their typewriters.

Baldwin recalled: "His hours and mine are very different. I was going to bed at dawn, Bill was just coming up to his study to go to work; his hours going on as mine went off. We saw each other at suppertime." Baldwin remembered their hours together as happy times. They rarely spoke about their work. "We sang songs, drank a little too much, and on occasion chatted with the people who were dropping in to see us. We had a certain common inheritance in terms of the music."

Styron, with his shrewdness about the literary marketplace, could see that Baldwin's fame was "gradually gaining momentum." Absorbed as Baldwin was in writing *Another Country* in Styron's cottage, he regularly took off to give talks for the Movement or to deliver well-paid lectures on the club and college circuit. He welcomed the lecture fees, but what he had to say often scared his affluent audiences and he found himself facing bewildered or even hostile questioners. Although a southerner, Styron had never known a black man on intimate terms before, and Baldwin knew few southerners well, black or white. In countless sessions over drinks they got to know each other. Styron felt that he was "in the company of as marvelous an intelligence as I was ever likely to encounter." Chain-smoking Marlboros, Baldwin described the various kinds of prejudice he had experienced, slowly educating Styron about what it meant to be black in America and clarifying much in his own mind. Baldwin spoke "unselfpityingly but with quiet rage." Styron, aware of his own gaps, was uncertain about impersonating a black man in his novel—he was trying to write it in the first person—but

Baldwin, who had already written a novel from the viewpoint of a white man, gave him strong encouragement, as if daring him to pull off the same trick in reverse. Sometimes white liberal friends joined their sessions and some of them regarded Baldwin's pronouncements as too extreme. "Yes, baby," Baldwin would say, "I mean *burn*. We will *burn your cities down.*" Some of Baldwin's entourage in the city learned of his whereabouts, and when they arrived there was no possibility of doing any work. But a welcome visitor was Lucien, whom Styron got to know and liked.

Such was Baldwin's "manic gusto" that when he finally left, restless but with *Another Country* still unfinished, there was a sense of a vacuum, a silence, in the house, Styron told me. He compared Baldwin at his peak to the "beautiful fervor of Camus or Kafka," and he appreciated that Baldwin had revealed to him "the core of his soul's savage distress."

The reviews of *Nobody Knows My Name* were on the whole enthusiastic. It was clear that for the mainstream media Baldwin had arrived. Time published a photograph of him standing in front of an abandoned building in Harlem, dressed in a natty dark blazer, white shirt and tie, and under the heading "Intelligent Cat" the magazine said of the new book: "Although he sometimes lowrates the country that he claims to love, his anger at the wrongs done his people is relatively restrained, hence doubly effective." Time even seemed to take Baldwin's side against Richard Wright, finding "Alas, Poor Richard" a "sad but enlightening account" of their unhappy friendship, and noting that unlike Wright, Baldwin knew that neither of them would have found Paris "a city of refuge" if they "had not been armed with American passports."

The New York *Times* praised Baldwin for writing about bigotry "as if it had never been written about before" and for believing in "the light of the spirit" and not giving way to "our time's stylish despair." The book was "brilliant" and "masterly." Newspaper reviews across the country reflected the same respectful approval. The Chicago *Tribune* called it "a bright and alive book, full of grief, love and anger." The Kansas City *Star* hailed it as "a vastly important book," and the Dallas *Times-*

Herald described him as "the most effective spokesman between the races in America." A fresh wave of critical praise came from the literary weeklies. Saturday Review referred to the book's "conviction" and "boldness" and, more significant in terms of Baldwin's future standing, the Atlantic Monthly decided he was "the voice of a new generation" and "a major literary talent." *Nobody Knows My Name* was also honored with a Certificate of Recognition from the National Conference of Christians and Jews, and was selected by the Notable Books Council of the American Library Association as one of the outstanding books of 1961. It was soon on the national bestseller lists and stayed there for many weeks, all of which strengthened his bargaining position with Dial Press.

Helping with the publicity for *Nobody Knows My Name* kept him busy. There were more requests for interviews this time, for television and radio appearances, and inevitably he lived an even fuller social life. With his face in the media, the pressures grew in all directions. It was sometimes hard for him to find any time alone. As one publishing executive who knew him at this time said, "He couldn't shake off the lovers and sycophants to get his work done and finish *Another Country*. They all demanded a lot of his time. He had to keep them supplied with liquor and parties." I met with Baldwin at this time to discuss my experiences down South, reporting on the start of school integration in New Orleans—more mobs like those he had seen in Charlotte—and one of his entourage inquired who I was and why he was spending so much time talking with me. I heard Baldwin reply angrily, "He's the only person here who hasn't asked me for something." The pressures were beginning to get to him. Dial Press, anxious to follow up the success of the new book, came to the rescue. Richard Baron recalled: "He told me he really wanted to get away to write so I took him to my place in the country in Bedford and gave him a wing as his hideaway. I kept his presence there quiet. But it didn't take very long before all the entourage showed up there. Yet he needed that. He didn't really want to be by himself."

Baron had the impression Baldwin finished *Another Country* "in three months in Bedford," but Baldwin himself claimed to write the last pages in Istanbul. Once more, apparently, he created a dramatic situation to force himself to accomplish what he knew he had to do. "I couldn't find the peace of mind—the space free of other people—to write anywhere in America," he said. "People always seemed to know where I was hiding with my typewriter and they were always dropping by at all times of the day and night. Consequently I was drinking far too much and getting hardly any sleep. I was too exhausted to write." He reached the same conclusion he had at similar dramatic stages in his life: "I *had* to get away." By "away" he meant out of the country. But Paris was becoming as distracting as New York, he said. He knew too many people there. He would *never* get the time to finish *Another Country*. But he wanted his youngest sister, Paula Maria, then eighteen, to get out of New York and see something of Europe. He introduced her to friends like James and Gloria Jones and showed her some of his favorite parts of Paris before he departed for another foreign refuge—Turkey. Engin Cezzar, the young Turkish actor who had been in *Giovanni's Room* at the Actors Studio, had become a leading player in his own country's theater and had continued to invite Baldwin to visit him and his wife, Gülriz. So Baldwin booked a plane ticket, recalling a dozen years earlier when he had bought a one-way ticket to Paris. He was escaping again to a foreign country where he didn't know the language or the people. But this time he was going as an established writer—with a return ticket.

He liked Istanbul at once. The ancient city on the Bosphorus seemed to combine the Europe he knew with the Orient and the Arab world that were both strange to him. In an apartment on one of Istanbul's many hills, overlooking the continental ferryboats linking Europe and Asia, Baldwin settled down to establish a new refuge that he would return to many times over the next ten years, but above all to finish *Another Country*. On the day he typed the last sentence of his novel describing a young Frenchman's arrival in New York—"Then even his luggage belonged to him again, and he strode through the barriers, more high-hearted than he had ever been as a child, into that city which the people from heaven had made their home"—Baldwin added: "Istanbul, Dec. 10, 1961." That night he went out to a party at Robert College to celebrate. In the kitchen he met a young American lecturer named David Adams Leeming, and they quickly discovered they shared a great interest

177

in Henry James. Leeming even wrote a doctoral dissertation on James under Leon Edel, the James authority. He later recalled: "That evening we spent a great deal of time talking not about *Another Country* but about Henry James. On the surface *Another Country* was light years away from James' novels, yet James was obviously central to Jimmy's writing and also therefore his life."

Leeming asked Baldwin why a writer who wrote about people who were for the most part free of the need to be political or to worry about black as opposed to white interested him so much. Baldwin replied that James was the only American writer for him who seemed to have some sense of the American dilemma. To Baldwin, Henry James in his fiction, but above all in *The Ambassadors, The Portrait of a Lady* and *The Princess Casamassima,* described a certain American inability to perceive the reality of others, just as so many white Americans today failed to perceive the reality of blacks. So that Hyacinth Robinson, for example, in *The Princess Casamassima,* was never a real person to the Princess, merely "an opportunity for her to discharge a certain kind of rage, anguish and bitterness." They talked for hours about how James depicted Americans and how his vision applied to today, and in so doing they started what was to be a long friendship. Baldwin lectured several times on novels by Henry James, notably *The Ambassadors, The Portrait of a Lady* and *The American,* for Leeming's classes at Robert College. In both their conversations and in his lectures, Baldwin gave Leeming the impression "his relationship with James was of a very special sort, perhaps of the sort that existed between James and Balzac," when James was a young novelist admiring and learning from an older master. James was Baldwin's "standard—the writer he thought of when he thought of the heights to which the novelist's art might aspire." At the start of *Another Country* he added a quotation from James: "They strike one, above all, as giving no account of themselves in any terms already consecrated by human use; to this inarticulate state they probably form, collectively, the most unprecedented of monuments; abysmal the mystery of what they think, what they feel, what they want, what they suppose themselves to be saying." As Leeming had said, *Another Country* was very different from James on the surface—the shocking, sensational, emotional, sexual, biracial, thoroughly contemporary surface—but Baldwin's intention in using that James quotation was to stress that his Americans were much like James' in the dilemma they faced in their lives. In essence, Baldwin was telling the story of a black woman who forced a white man to see her as she was, to "perceive her reality." Even technically, in trying to solve his problem of losing the main character so early in the narrative, Baldwin had looked to Henry James for help. Yet when a friend asked him what the new novel was like, Baldwin made no mention of James, but replied, "It makes *Giovanni* seem conservative—almost square."

He packed the bulky manuscript in his bag and prepared to return to New York to give it to Dial Press for publication as soon as possible. He wondered what kind of reception he would face. Already, as the plane rose above Istanbul—his friend Engin Cezzar had given him an ancient Turkish silver ring to ward off evil and bring him back—he was creating another dramatic situation: *Another Country* versus the critics.

11

At the White House

THE EISENHOWER administration had intervened reluctantly in civil rights cases, so movement strategists were pleased when the eight-year Eisenhower reign in the White House was over. The new president, John F. Kennedy, was much younger than Eisenhower, a liberal Democrat and Irish Catholic of Baldwin's generation from Boston. He appointed his younger brother, Robert Kennedy, as his attorney general, the government official most concerned with civil rights. But Bayard Rustin told James Baldwin that he had no high hopes of the new administration because John Kennedy had won by so few votes, which would dissuade him from making big changes, and he owed much of his victory to the white South and would need southern votes in Congress.

Neither John nor Robert Kennedy, the sons of an Irish-American multimillionaire, knew much personally about the racial scene and took the rather easy, cautious line that the federal government had been too coercive in similar changing times in the Reconstruction period, and that they must not make the same mistake. But the racial situation had grown beyond the control of Washington and continued to escalate rapidly as black demands were met by increasing violence. And the more the Kennedy brothers were involved, the more interested they became in the civil rights movement and its leaders like Martin Luther King and its media stars like James Baldwin.

The radical students at Howard University who had gone to Georgetown to hear Baldwin now invited him to Howard to discuss the black writer's responsibility. The students had helped to form SNCC in 1960, a reflection of the growing generation gap in the movement. Some of the older black leaders had reached the stage of being apprehensive about where the radical young students might take the movement. Michael Thelwell, who became chairman of SNCC's Washington branch, remembered the meeting with Baldwin as being "highly charged." The discussion, which raged all night, ended in a small student apartment as dawn was coming up over the capital. Thelwell recalled Baldwin saying slowly and thoughtfully, "As a black writer I must in some way, some very real way, represent you, my young brothers and sisters." They hadn't bestowed the responsibility and he didn't choose it, but . . . "All I can say is that I will never betray that . . . never betray you." The students applauded. The link between them was even stronger.

Baldwin told interviewers much the same. When he was asked if his Movement work interfered with his writing, he replied that whatever talent he had "would simply have to survive whatever life brought." He couldn't sit somewhere "honing my talent to a fine edge after I had been to all those places in the South and seen those boys and girls, men and women, black and white, longing for change. It was impossible for me to drop them a visit and then leave." When he was described as a spokesman, he denied it. "I have always thought it would be rather presumptuous." He was a witness—"In the church in which I was raised, you were supposed to bear witness to the truth." He was asked if he would describe any white writers as witnesses. Yes, Dostoevsky, Dickens, Proust and of course Henry James. One contemporary white writer had amazed him—Warren Miller in a novel entitled *The Cool World.* In a review in the New York *Times Book Review* he wrote that after reading the novel he couldn't be sure whether Miller was black or white. "I *was* certain, however, that I had just read one of the finest novels about Harlem that had ever come my way." It described the life of a street gang and prompted Baldwin to reflect that "there is something suspicious about the way we cling to the concept of race, on both sides of the obsolescent racial fence." White men panic or wallow in their guilt, and usually call themselves liberals. Black men drown in their bitterness or wallow in their rage, and usually call themselves militant. "Both camps have managed to evade the really hideous complexity of our situation on the social and personal level." *The Cool World* described the effect on a Harlem youth who has "long since ceased believing a word we say—about honor, ideals, equality, hope." Frog Eyes growing up then might well be like him, a member of a violent street gang and involved in drugs. Increasingly Baldwin looked to the civil rights movement for hope, for a way out.

He was worried about the growing criticism of King's effectiveness as a leader. When he heard him preach at Ebenezer Baptist Church in Atlanta, King didn't look any older, but there was a new note of anguish in his voice. It must be remembered, King said, that the white racists were not ruled by hatred but by terror, and therefore if community was ever to be achieved, they must not be hated whatever they did. One must "overcome evil with good." He had been charged in a Montgomery court of perjury, tax evasion and misuse of public funds, and had been acquitted. But speaking "more candidly than I [Baldwin] had ever heard him," King described his personal torment at being publicly accused and at having to go through such a trial, and he had been tempted to cancel a speaking trip to Chicago but forced himself to go. Afterward he spoke to Baldwin of a recent visit to India—he was a student of Gandhi and admired Nehru—and discussed the South, where, he said, "perhaps four or five percent of the people are to be found on either end of the racial scale," actively for or against desegregation—"the rest are passive adherents." The next day King was to preside at a meeting of black ministers from all over the South and hear their problems about being under pressure from the radical students—from SNCC, the Freedom Riders and the growing sit-ins. King would be under pressure from both sides. Baldwin wondered if he could still manage to lead such a varied movement. "For everything is changing, from our notion of politics to our notion of ourselves, and we are certain, as we begin history's strangest metamorphosis, to undergo the torment of being forced to surrender far more than we ever realized we had accepted."

King had been critical of Eisenhower and, as if to show the Kennedy administration's different attitude—it was also further proof of his growing fame—Baldwin received an invitation to a dinner of American Nobel Prize winners at the White House. One of the Nobel laureates, William Faulkner, turned down the invitation, telling a reporter it was "too far to go to eat with strangers," but actually he disliked Kennedy's approval of the appointment of several racist judges in the South, which was paying off some debts from the election. Baldwin, however, enthusiastically accepted. Arthur M. Schlesinger, Jr., the historian of the Kennedy administration, described James Baldwin as "a small, darting man of brilliant articulateness as well as, when he wished, of great charm." In Schlesinger's *A Thousand Days,* he gives an account of Baldwin that is revealing because, presumably, it is the picture the Kennedy administration was given of him. Baldwin's own life, wrote Schlesinger, "had not perhaps been so entirely desperate, externally at least, as his writings sometimes suggested. White society had discerned his gifts early enough to make him in his teens editor of the literary magazine at a high school for bright children in New York City (a predecessor was Paddy Chayefsky, an associate, Richard Avedon) and to turn him into a best-selling author while not very much older. But this was all irrelevant; indeed, Baldwin's own opportunities made him the more sensitive to the fate of his brothers who had never had a chance. He drew into himself the agony he saw around him and charged it with the force of an electric and passionate personality."

After the Nobel dinner, Schlesinger took some of the guests, including Baldwin, back to his house. Baldwin "suddenly turned on Joseph Rauh, presumably because Rauh was a white leader in the civil rights fight. It was evident that Baldwin could not abide white liberals." He seemed to regard them "as worse than southern bigots, who at least were honest enough to admit that they, like all white men (by definition), hated the Negro." Schlesinger added: "Now he baited Rauh as if to goad him by sarcasm and insult into confessing that his concern for civil rights was a cover for prejudice. Rauh equably fielded Baldwin's taunts and kept asking him what he would have the government do. Baldwin, who showed little interest in public policy, finally muttered something about bringing Negroes into the FBI."

Since Baldwin had a number of white liberal friends, Schlesinger's remark that he couldn't "abide" them seems an exaggeration if he meant white liberals of real conviction, but perhaps not if he meant whites who proclaimed themselves liberal because it was fashionable. Baldwin himself defined a liberal of this kind as "someone who thinks he knows more about your experience than you do." His behavior was probably influenced by the setting, and he may have tried to create a debate to make an impression on the policymakers there. It was, after all, as close as he had come to the nation's center of power. It perhaps becomes clearer what he was up to when seen in relation to his meeting with Robert Kennedy the following year when he treated Kennedy much the way he had treated Rauh. Alfred Kazin and his wife had Baldwin over for an evening, and when he talked about his White House invitation he was "very lively and full of jokes."

Baldwin had also been selected to be in the American delegation at the international literary conference on the Mediterranean island of Majorca, where the Prix Formentor, a new literary prize that had received a lot of attention because it was worth over $10,000, was to be awarded. Literary prizes then generally amounted to no more than a medal and the price of dinner, so there was some hot international competition over this one. An international group of publishers was behind the prize—the winning author's book would be published simultaneously in about a dozen languages. Delegations of judges came from a number of countries, all expenses paid. That Baldwin had been invited was yet more proof of his growing reputation. But by the start of the first session, with all the delegations pushing particular candidates, Baldwin still hadn't arrived. Some of the other American delegates recalled his reputation for being late. The second day came and went without Baldwin. The organizers sent a car to the airport for him, but he wasn't on the plane. The American delegation was now anxious; a strong personality on their side was badly needed. The Italians, led by Alberto Moravia, the novelist who was also a superb diplomat, were assuming a dominant role, and maybe Baldwin, who was both black and could

speak French as forcefully now as he could speak English—two aces—
could redress the balance.

The American delegation's influence had been weakened because not
all the members had read the books nominated, especially those from
Europe and Asia that were untranslated. After Henry Miller retired with
influenza, Harvey Breit became chief spokesman, and he often admitted,
quite openly and honestly, his ignorance of some of the writers being
considered. It caused a few of the more cynical Europeans to shrug their
shoulders at this latest example of American innocence. It was giving
the more wily Italians and the suave British, who were led by novelist
Angus Wilson, smiling and friendly and very shrewd, their answer to
Moravia, too easy an advantage in battling for the prize. Only a strong
contribution from the missing Baldwin (as strong as those renunciations
of the Devil when he was a teenage preacher) could turn the tables now.
He kept promising to arrive . . .

Then suddenly he was there, making a dramatic entrance close to the
end. He was sorry to be late, but—and his mouth widened in a happy,
gap-toothed grin—he'd been detained at the White House, dining with
President Kennedy and the Nobel Prize winners. From Harlem to the
White House! It was even better than the old white American from log
cabin to the White House. Not bad for a nigger, huh? Baldwin's pleased
expression seemed to say as the other delegates applauded him. He
looked sleeker, better dressed, even a little heavier as if he was eating
better. The politicians, the lobbyists, the literary strategists faced each
other in a final confrontation over the $10,000 prize. The American
delegation put Baldwin forward. He made an impassioned, finger-
wagging speech in favor of Katherine Anne Porter, but his eloquence,
the strength of his personality were no match for the days and nights
of old-fashioned persuasion. The cynical, sophisticated Europeans
clapped for Baldwin, nodded and smiled, but they had already made up
their minds—or had them made up for them. Moravia's candidate—
Dacia Maraini—was the winner.

Barney Rosset of Grove Press, a New York publisher noted for
radical and avant-garde literature, found Baldwin "extremely warm—I
liked him, I think, more than I had expected. He got really involved

in whatever he was doing or with anyone around him. He had tremendous insight that was immediately apparent when he met people." Rosset introduced him to a young woman, half-black, half-Jewish, who had dreams of becoming an actress "but hadn't really done anything." Baldwin was obviously impressed and he told her she was going to be the lead in a play he had in mind and even produced a half-written script to show her. Rosset said: "Really? Are you serious?" and Baldwin replied, "Absolutely." Rosset then asked, "Why not give her a contract?" and Baldwin immediately gave her one written out on a napkin. Rosset said, "I think she became terrified and ran away. She didn't have the voice or the projection to be an actress." But what then was Baldwin up to? Was he just carried away by all the liquor he was drinking at the conference?

One of the British publishers there wooed Baldwin, wanting him to drop Michael Joseph, his then British publisher, and sign a contract for *Another Country* with him. Baldwin sat in a hotel bar, a glass of scotch at his elbow forever being refilled, listening to extravagant compliments and big offers. It was like a cat-and-mouse act, though Baldwin was not as innocent and starry-eyed as he pretended for the British publisher's benefit. He was playing a game of his own that he was thoroughly enjoying. It must have been a pleasant change to be courted so enthusiastically after the years of rejections, the Village and Paris struggles, and then the small advances. News of the wooing soon reached London and there was great alarm at Michael Joseph at the prospect of losing Baldwin. Eventually the Michael Joseph executives caught up with him, did their own wooing and persuaded him to stay with them for *Another Country*. "He was thereafter always very loyal," recalled Raleigh Trevelyan, his editor there.

Before Baldwin left Majorca on an early morning flight he exchanged greetings with Angus Wilson and congratulated Moravia on his triumph. "No wonder," Baldwin commented, "that American writers still run off to Europe. In this decadent continent there is a strange kind of peace we're too young to know. Europe has lived long enough to learn the inexorable limits of life—that it all ends in tragedy. And we have that youthful quality that Europe has lost—a sense of life's possibilities, that you can change things for the better if you have the determination.

The two really should go hand-in-hand if we are to progress. But I can only find them by straddling both continents. And that is why I shall have to go home shortly . . . and yet when I get there, I immediately plan when I'm coming back here. We need to wed the vision of the Old World and the New into one society, a society realizing the intangible dreams of people." He looked at the beautiful Mediterranean early morning sky. "That is what is happening at home now—people are trying to put their dreams into reality. It will be wonderful if they succeed, but a nightmare if they don't." The level of violence was certainly rising, suggesting a possible nightmare.

I was in London working for the *Guardian* when I received a phone call from Baldwin, who was passing through on the way to Paris. The familiar intense voice told me to lose no time in coming over to his hotel. When I arrived, a fifth of Johnnie Walker was already open and Baldwin was being interviewed by Donald Hinds, a local correspondent for a West Indian newspaper. Although he was now used to being interviewed, Baldwin responded freshly to the questions and also asked some questions back about the treatment of West Indians in England. The answers he received were depressing; he didn't escape by leaving home.

He was accompanied by a friend, a young painter from New York. Baldwin obviously saw him as his young self and was trying to give him the same experience of Europe he had had, but without the grim struggle for existence. Baldwin also had invited a young Indian who worked for his publisher, Michael Joseph, and during noisy arguments produced by mixing Americans, Europeans and Asians, spurred on by liberal doses of Johnnie Walker, Baldwin volunteered to show the Indian and the English what they had been missing all those years— American soul food. We all then moved on to the young Indian's flat, and while Baldwin took over the kitchen, the rest of us sat around talking and drinking like a bunch of students. "Remember, I helped my mother bring up a large family," Baldwin told us midway through his preparations as if allaying fears of what was to come out of the kitchen. "What I don't know about cooking, baby, ain't worth knowing." And what finally emerged on the table justified all his boasting—and he even volunteered to do all the washing-up afterward.

Next day, while the young painter went off to select some presents to take home to New York, I bought Baldwin a slap-up lunch in return for the soul food banquet at an olde worlde restaurant off Baker Street. An ancient waiter served us with grave courtesy; for some reason this treatment moved Baldwin deeply. He said the waiter spoke to him like an equal human being; for once a waiter was not making him feel like a nigger. But surely he had been in many restaurants, especially over the past year or so, where the waiters had been similarly professional and polite. Perhaps it was his mood that day; perhaps it was because Baker Street brought back memories. "I came over from Paris once with . . . Oh, I suppose you'd call them hustlers, maybe even gangsters. I was dependent on them. I had nothing. Now . . ." Now his luck had changed—he rapped on the wooden table—and perhaps that was what made his mood so responsive and grateful. He insisted on adding to the adequate tip I had left the old waiter. "I'll remember this restaurant . . ."

When we returned to Baldwin's hotel the young painter had already arrived loaded with his gifts. Baldwin had been invited to see a preview of a new film, "Lawrence of Arabia," directed by David Lean and starring Peter O'Toole, so they went off to that. Over a drink later Baldwin was still upset about the film. "It's nothing but an update of Rudyard Kipling's *Gunga Din,*" he said. "The British Empire on the brink." He then told the young painter he had decided to give him a trip to Greece so he could do some painting there before he returned to New York. A Mediterranean adventure sounded like a fine idea, but when he learned Baldwin wouldn't be going with him, the young painter wasn't keen to make the trip. The prospect of being alone in a foreign country obviously scared him. Baldwin pooh-poohed his fears. You had to take opportunities when they were offered, he said, because they seldom came a second time. You also had to do things on your own—then you learned to be independent. "If it's easy, don't do it," Baldwin said. He tried to draw me in as an ally but I kept out of it. I was sympathetic to the young painter—he was far from New York and I knew how he must feel, even in England where at least he could make himself understood. He was at the stage Baldwin had been when he first went to Paris. Baldwin had made himself sternly independent, had become a self-reliant cosmopolitan, but the process had taken years and the price had been high in terms of endurance. The young painter had probably seen enough for one trip, his first away from home. They went on to Paris, and I heard later that Baldwin introduced the young painter to Beauford Delaney and asked him to point out the benefits of going to Greece.

Another Country was published in June, 1962, with a huge party at one of Baldwin's favorite hangouts in Harlem, Small's Paradise. As almost all the main characters in the novel were vigorously bisexual and he was unsparing in plumbing the relationship between sex and race in the U.S., he had worked himself up into a thoroughly nervous state about the critical reception. It was *Giovanni's Room* again but potentially much worse. Baldwin arrived early at Small's, and one of the first guests to appear was Sidney Poitier. He had already read the novel and liked it, and was aware, Baldwin said, "how frightened I was." Poitier walked him slowly around the block outside "and talked to me and helped me get myself together." And then he walked Baldwin back to Small's and left, and Baldwin realized the famous actor had come only for that—"he hadn't come for the party at all." But many others had by then. There was a huge guest list and a great many gate-crashers. For many there, it was their first visit to Harlem. Virginia Baron, who was in charge of publicity at Dial Press, said the party was Baldwin's own idea and turned out wonderfully, remembered even twenty-five years later with guest lists preserved as mementos. "Of all the celebrity authors I've dealt with," she said, "Jimmy was the one I was most fond of. I went on publicity tours with him and he was a delight. There was no phony baloney with him. He loved caviar and elegant places and was quite open about it. He was like a kid. He was always ready to say yes to anything, but whether it worked out was something else. He was always late. I remember once we were trying to get a taxi and none would stop, so Jimmy said, 'Listen, baby, you're going to do much better without me,' and he went over to the other side of the street and the very next cab stopped for me. I remember another party at his little apartment in Horatio Street in the Village. It was so crowded that people were practically hanging out of the window. It seemed a strange place to find a great writer."

Many of the reviewers of *Another Country* disagreed with that assessment of him. The novel received a very mixed reception ranging from high enthusiasm to angry dismissals and charges of "obscenity" down South. Mark Schorer found it "a shattering experience" and pronounced it "one of the most powerful of contemporary American novels." Paul Goodman's opinion was the opposite. He described it as "mediocre. It is unworthy of its author's lovely abilities." Charles Poore in the New York *Times* considered it "a sad story, brilliantly and fiercely told." Life magazine was more guarded in calling it "a ferocious, abrasive drama of a wild, jazzy bohemian other world where races, sexes and values are hopelessly and tragically entangled." Under the heading "Magic Realism in Prose"—which also included reviews of books by two of Baldwin's fellow writers in the early Paris days, Philip Roth and Herbert Gold—the National Review praised Baldwin's "capacity for understanding divergent types of people" and "the clarity, the high finish, and jolting fidelity to nature," and borrowed a term from art criticism to call his novel "magic realism." Time, describing Baldwin as "one of the brashest, brightest, most promising young writers in America," concluded that *Another Country* was "a failure—doubly disappointing not only because it does not live up to advance hopes, but also because it so clearly has tried to be an important book." Baldwin's writing skill, "adequate in simpler novels, is not up to maneuvering so complex a collection of people." He "apparently" didn't know that homosexual lovemaking could be as boring in literature as the heterosexual kind. Time suggested he made the same mistake that he accused Richard Wright of in *Native Son* in his essay "Everybody's Protest Novel." Norman Mailer even did a new assessment of him. Mailer found much of *Another Country* "abominably written," adding that possibly Saul Bellow, white and Jewish, succeeded in his novel about an imaginary Africa, *Henderson the Rain King,* "in telling us more about the depths of the black man's psyche" than Baldwin did. One of Mailer's former wives, Lady Jeanne Campbell, granddaughter of Lord Beaverbrook, the

British newspaper owner and politician, suggested Baldwin made Mailer nervous. She remembered one occasion when Baldwin was supposed to be visiting with one of his sisters and Mailer was very jumpy and made sure everything was just right before their arrival.

But whatever the critics said, *Another Country* was soon on the national bestseller lists. It was condemned as "obscene" in New Orleans soon afterward, which only helped to increase the book's sales. Many younger people seemed to identify with the way of life that Baldwin described, or read his novel as a revelation. Michael Thelwell met Baldwin by chance in New York. "He was getting into a cab and we shook hands. I had read *Another Country* and I was totally mesmerized by it. I asked him how it was doing. He had a puzzled expression. He said the reviews had been good everywhere except in New York, even in the Deep South. Then he was gone." Baldwin told the New York *Times Book Review* that he was surprised by the large sales of his novel, and he supposed it meant many more people than were willing to admit it led lives not at all unlike his characters. He hoped some readers responded the same way they might to two artists "I unreservedly admire"—musicians Miles Davis and Ray Charles. "I really do not, at the very bottom of my own mind, compare myself to other writers. I think I really helplessly model myself on jazz musicians and try to write the way they sound. I am not an intellectual, not in the dreary sense that word is used today, and do not want to be: I am aiming at what Henry James called 'perception at the pitch of passion.'"

He felt that many of the critics had been overinfluenced by the sexual scenes of the novel and the interracial relationships, which were still very rare in American literature, as in American life. Whether it was the central relationship between white Vivaldo and black Ida or the accompanying bisexual affairs involving most of the other leading characters, all were intended by Baldwin to illustrate how difficult he felt real love was in contemporary American society. Facing each other without lies and perceiving the relationship realistically were much more important than which sexes were involved or how love was expressed, in Baldwin's opinion. The novel's main character, Rufus, for example, had killed himself because he had failed to control his racial rage, his hatred, and had destroyed the white southern woman he loved. The whole racial situation, according to the novel, was basically a failure of love. Some critics thought the characters were merely Baldwin's puppets conveying his message, just as he had seen Wright's characters in *Native Son*. His most intense feeling was undoubtedly put into Rufus, whose portrait became an elegy for his dead friend Eugene. Several of the other characters lacked the same kind of intensity and obviously meant more to Baldwin than they could to a reader. But with Ida, Rufus' sister, he recaptured the same intensity. "Ida has been talking to me for years," he said once when discussing the characters. In her grief Ida is overcome by the same rage as Rufus and takes it out on Vivaldo much as Rufus did on his girl, but Ida survives because Vivaldo faces the truth about her and accepts it. Love triumphs across racial lines—a happy ending!

Some critics, however, considered the style disappointingly sentimental and even sloppy after the eloquent precision of his essays. But whether it worked or not, a change in style was intended. Baldwin had used a different style in each of his novels—his novels of witness, as they might be called. In *Go Tell It On the Mountain* he had used an elegant, introspective third-person narrative, laced with reflections and flashbacks, as he served as witness to the Harlem religious scene that he could assume few of his readers would know much about. In *Giovanni's Room* it was bisexual Paris through the eyes of a white American lying to himself about his feelings. Baldwin chose a first-person narrative with a much bolder, direct, dramatic style that suggested everything had been heightened too much and much had been left out. For *Another Country* he went back to the third-person narrative but used an emotional, involved, extroverted style as if the characters were almost speaking for themselves. Here, for example, is the last glimpse of Ida and Vivaldo together: "Her long fingers stroked his back, and he began slowly, with a horrible, strangling sound, to weep, for she was stroking his innocence out of him." Like Miles Davis with his trumpet or Ray Charles singing and playing the piano, Baldwin seemed to be making a statement as a witness to a way of life. You couldn't separate the essays and the novels, they were too closely related. He was playing a witness in both and what he was witness to decided which form he chose. But the Walt Whitman quotation he used in *Giovanni's Room* could describe all his work, fiction and nonfiction: "I am the man, I suffered, I was there." How well he wrote might vary depending on his state of mind and the complexity of the subject, but his intention was always the same—to write from his deepest. Henry James had written about the need to live to the full, to "have" one's life. The writers who had followed James, such as D.H. Lawrence, Hemingway and Faulkner, wrote about *how* to live to the full. Now Baldwin was carrying it a stage further into the racial field by describing the perils of hatred and guilt, the heart destroyed by not being able to love.

One critic had seen Jean Genet as a major influence on Baldwin, and he certainly welcomed a production of Genet's play, *The Blacks,* in the Village. Maya Angelou, a black writer of the generation after Baldwin, recalled: "Although Jimmy was known as an accomplished playwright, few people knew that he was a frustrated actor as well. I had a role in Jean Genet's play, *The Blacks,* and since Jimmy knew Genet personally and the play in the original French, nothing could keep him from advising me on my performance." Baldwin and Lorraine Hansberry also had a public disagreement with Norman Mailer over *The Blacks.* In a long essay on the play, Mailer dismissed many of the black leaders for being "as colorless as our white leaders and all too many of the Negroes one knows have a dull militancy compared to the curve and art of personality their counterparts had even ten years ago." This struck Baldwin as being in the same key as the myth of black sexuality, and Lorraine Hansberry called Mailer one of the "new paternalists." Mailer replied that they had a fundamental disagreement; whereas he believed there were qualities, essences, innate differences of being between white and black, she thought the only difference was pigmentation of the skin, that all else was environment. He challenged her and Baldwin to a three-cornered debate in Carnegie Hall. He also proposed that a touring company take *The Blacks* into the racist strongholds of the Deep South with a white and black cast, and with some tough Village cats as bodyguards. Mailer ran into Baldwin a few nights later in the White Horse Tavern in a gathering of Village artists and intellectuals. Baldwin was furious. "You're not responsible," he told Mailer. It was easy to picture Baldwin's eyes widening fiercely and his finger wagging as Mailer waited for his turn. "We had another brotherly quarrel," Mailer summed up afterward. They seemed to have a permanently uneasy relationship. "He still sees us as goddamn romantic black symbols," Baldwin said. "We still haven't been granted ordinary human status, the right to go to the bathroom. Until Norman sees us with no more romanticism than he views Jewish storekeepers, he'll never understand or be on to what's happening, *really* happening beneath the surface of this country." The more successful they both became, the more they seemed to be growing apart.

On magazine assignments, they both covered a world heavyweight boxing match between the champion, Floyd Patterson, and the leading contender, Sonny Liston. Patterson and Liston were both black, but the resemblance stopped there. Although Patterson had been wild in his youth, he had reformed and was now regarded as an exemplary citizen. Nobody could say that of Sonny Liston. He had a criminal history, was rumored to have organized-crime connections and talked rough and tough, though when he relaxed he had an engaging frankness and deadpan humor. Their fight was soon regarded as a racial battle between the best and worst elements on the black side, between Patterson the Conformist and Liston the Outlaw, or Good and Evil—at least as many white Americans saw it. Patterson was so strongly supported by white American boxing fans, in fact, that there was some danger of his being considered an Uncle Tom by young streetwise blacks. Baldwin had none of Mailer's devotion to professional boxing. He was as uneasy in a gym as he was on a beach. He had no interest in athletics, in sports, in that kind of competition. His interest in Patterson and Liston—apart from the check from Nugget magazine—was in their blackness, in their common experience. He wanted Patterson to win and even bet on him, but the fight itself probably appalled him deep down—the prospect of two black men, brothers, knocking the hell out of each other for the amusement and profit of a crowd largely white.

Baldwin's magazine story showed his uneasiness, his lack of interest; it wasn't written with his usual verve and confidence, and he never republished it in subsequent collections, nor did he cover any more big fights, unlike Mailer. The fight was held at Comiskey Park in Chicago. Baldwin identified with Patterson because he found him to be "still relentlessly, painfully shy—he lives gallantly with his scars, but not all of them have healed." Watching him jump rope in a gym, he compared him to a "boy saint helplessly dancing and seen through the steaming windows of a store front church." Patterson brought back memories of Frog Eyes. The champion hadn't read anything of Baldwin's or even heard his name, but he said with conviction, "I've seen you someplace before," and then remembered it was in a TV debate on the race problem. As for Liston, Baldwin found him tough but not hard, and Liston told him, "I wouldn't be no bad example if I was up there." He also said—and Baldwin quoted it later in reference to the civil rights movement—"We got to learn to stop fighting among our own." Baldwin left feeling "terribly ambivalent, as many Negroes do these days, since we are all trying to decide, in one way or another, which attitude, in our terrible American dilemma, is the most effective: the disciplined sweetness of Floyd, or the outspoken intransigence of Liston." The two fighters in Baldwin's mind had become like representatives of the two poles of the civil rights movement.

He arrived at the fight feeling very depressed, which he blamed partly on fatigue—"it had been a pretty grueling time"—partly on betting much more than he should have ($750) on Patterson, and partly on a row he had had with Mailer at a party the night before. He called it "a pretty definitive fight with someone with whom I had hoped to be friends." Harold Conrad, the boxing promoter and journalist, who was in charge of the press at the fight, was the host at the party in a penthouse. "Everyone got into beefs," he recalled. "I needed a referee. Norman had Baldwin in tears. He was rough on him. I don't know what it was about, but I had to go placate Jimmy, and then I became a kind of father-figure for him." This didn't seem like the Baldwin who had survived so many tough times and had already confronted Mailer more than once. Perhaps Conrad was being overly influenced by Baldwin's homosexual reputation. "Everyone was drunk," Conrad told me. "Mailer was sorry afterwards about what he had said—I don't remember what it was—but he respected Jim. But Jim was a very sensitive guy and I think he had a crush on Norman. He was in love with Norman, and Norman had been very salty to him—'Fuck you,' that kind of attitude. Jim usually covered up his homosexual tendencies pretty well, but they came out when he was drinking. He had strange feelings about the fight business. He didn't like it, found it too brutal. He wanted Patterson to win, saw him as some kind of noble white knight, whereas he wasn't like that at all. But you couldn't tell Jim about the fighters. I knew him pretty well at that time. I remember him turning up drunk in my suite with a white truck driver. He was showing off. They made a very strange odd couple." Mailer's version of the party row was that "we each insulted the other's good intentions and turned away."

Baldwin sat at ringside between Mailer and Ben Hecht, the co-author of *The Front Page*. Baldwin and Mailer were becoming for some people the literary equivalent of Patterson and Liston. When would their big fight take place? journalists joked. Mailer admitted there had been "a chill" between them for the past year—"not a feud, but bad feeling." Although they tried to be friendly at ringside, the "unsettled differences" were still there. Neither turned out to be a good judge of the fighters—Liston easily demolished their man Patterson. In fact, Patterson, who was really not heavy enough to be a heavyweight, had been beaten so quickly that Baldwin had responded with a startled, "What happened?" He and Mailer attempted to bury their quarrel by commiserating with each other over their lost bets. Baldwin said, "My Lord, I lost $750 tonight." That was a long way from Paris and Village days. Mailer had lost only $28 so presumably he didn't feel so bad. Baldwin swore he would give up gambling—at least on fights.

Baldwin concluded that he and Mailer "do not get along for a very peculiar combination of reasons, probably involved with his ego, possibly involved with mine." Frank Corsaro, a theater director who had been at De Witt Clinton with Baldwin and knew Mailer at the Actors Studio, spoke of "an enormous rivalry on both sides."

12

The Fire Next Time

BALDWIN HAD been making notes for a long personal essay ranging from his teenage conversion to the civil rights movement. He was thinking of calling it "Down at the Cross" (from the hymn "Down at the Cross Where My Savior Died"). Norman Podhoretz, now editor of Commentary, solved the form of the wide-ranging essay linking past and present by suggesting that he write about the Nation of Islam or the Black Muslims, as the members of the much-publicized black separatist religion, the latest sensation on the racial front, were called. These black militants wanting no contact with the white world were at the opposite extreme from Martin Luther King and his dream of integration and brotherhood. They reminded Baldwin of his stepfather's bitter condemnation of "white devils" and of many of the congregation and ministers in the church where he had preached who believed in the same kind of separation. "They segregate us, we segregate them"—it was essentially an eye-for-an-eye philosophy and one that Baldwin had always rejected.

But the Black Muslims had begun to scare white Americans because they had recently become very prominent in the media through the efforts of their chief lieutenant and heir apparent, Malcolm X, a brilliant public speaker who also was clever at dealing with reporters. The extent to which the Black Muslims had aroused white fears was seen when Malcolm X converted the new world heavyweight champion, the fast-talking, witty Cassius Clay, who had knocked out Patterson's conqueror, Sonny Liston. The new champion changed his name to Muhammad Ali and was seen everywhere with Malcolm X at his side, and immediately not only a great many white boxing fans but even many white sports writers turned against him. The Black Muslims were certainly a topical subject that was almost impossible for white writers to deal with adequately because the top Muslim leadership dismissed the writers as literary "white devils" and wouldn't be interviewed by them. Baldwin's black skin and their approval of some of his more fiery statements would no doubt gain him admittance. But it would be a challenge to his own beliefs. He thought about it for several days and then agreed to accept the challenge. As Norman Podhoretz recalled, "I commissioned him to do an article about the Black Muslims. It was my idea and he agreed to do it."

The Honorable Elijah Muhammad, the leader of the Black Muslims, invited him to dinner at his home in Chicago, a stately mansion on the South Side, which was mainly a black ghetto. Baldwin got lost on the way across the city and was half-an-hour late, and although he had cigarettes in his pocket, he could not smoke or drink liquor once he entered the mansion. The Black Muslim who admitted him didn't mention his lateness and was gravely polite, but Baldwin felt an immediate nervous tension as soon as he stood inside—the tension between love and power he had found in Harlem religious groups, between pain and rage, reminding him of "the curious, the grinding way I remained extended between these poles." The legend was that as a boy Elijah Muhammad had witnessed his father lynched, and the blood had dripped down on him. Baldwin wondered if he would be as angry and bitter as his stepfather. But the man who joined him was small and slender with a thin face, large warm eyes and an attractive smile. His smile took Baldwin back twenty-four years to Mother Horn asking, "Whose little boy are you?" Elijah Muhammad told him, "I've got a lot to say to *you,* but we'll wait until we sit *down.*" He made Baldwin think of his stepfather as he might have been "if we had been friends." Baldwin was seated on Elijah's left, and the Muslim leader said he had seen Baldwin on television and it had seemed to him that Baldwin was not yet brainwashed and was trying to become himself. Baldwin replied yes, he was trying to become himself, but he knew that Elijah's meaning and his were not the same. He said, "I left the church twenty years ago and I haven't joined anything since." It was Baldwin's way of saying that he didn't intend to join the Black Muslims either and become James X.

"And what are you now?" asked Elijah.

"I? Now? Nothing." But this was obviously not enough to satisfy Elijah. "I'm a writer. I like doing things alone." Elijah smiled, but didn't comment. "I don't anyway think about it a great deal," Baldwin added nervously.

Elijah said to the other Muslims at the table, "I think he ought to think about it *all* the deal," and everyone agreed.

Baldwin felt he was back as a child in his stepfather's house. He boldly told Elijah that he didn't care if white and black people married, and that he had many white friends. He would have no choice, if it came to it, but to perish with them, for, as he added to himself, "I love a few people and they love me and some of them are white, and isn't love more important than color?"

Elijah indicated with great pity that he might think he had white friends and they might be trying to be decent, but their time was up. Baldwin was unsure what to reply. He knew two or three white people he could trust with his life and he knew a few others—white—who "were struggling as hard as they knew how, and with great effort and sweat and risk to make the world more human." But how could he say this to any effect because these whites would merely be dismissed as exceptions. The condition of the South Side of Chicago alone, the decaying ghetto, proved the justice of the Muslims' indictment. Didn't history show that the exceptions who had tried to change the world had all failed? Had power always been more real for people than love? Baldwin said he suddenly felt at that Muslim table like white people who tried to prove to their families and friends that blacks were not subhuman. Elijah said no people in history had ever been respected who had not owned their land. It was only the black in America who remained disinherited and despised. The Black Muslims no longer wished for a grudging, tardy recognition from whites. This point of view, reflected Baldwin, was "abundantly justified by American Negro history." But how were blacks to form a separate nation? If he were a Muslim, Baldwin thought, he wouldn't hesitate to use the current social and spiritual discontent in the country to try to achieve their aims, for at the very worst he would merely have contributed to the destruction of a house he hated.

When Baldwin left the dinner he stood in the large living room saying goodnight "with everything curiously and heavily unresolved." He felt he had failed a test in their eyes and in his own, or that he had ignored a warning. Elijah and he shook hands, and the Muslim leader asked Baldwin where he was going "because when we invite someone here, we take the responsibility of protecting him from the white devils until he gets wherever it is he's going." Baldwin intended to have a drink with several white devils on the other side of Chicago, but he hesitated to give the address because it would identify it as where whites lived. But he did give it, and Elijah walked with him to the front steps, and Baldwin felt a rush of emotion, wishing to be able to love and honor this man "as a witness, an ally and a father." He felt that he knew something of Elijah's pain and his fury and, yes, even his beauty. Yet "because of what he conceived of his responsibility and what I took to be mine," they would always be strangers, and possibly, one day, enemies.

A gleaming blue car arrived, he and Elijah shook hands once more and said goodnight once more, and then Elijah walked back into his mansion and shut the door, and Baldwin got into the car. On the way he asked the Muslim driver how the Muslims intended to get their own land. The driver spoke of the Muslim temples being built in various parts of the country, of the Muslims' strong following, and of the money available to the black population—possibly as much as twenty billion dollars. "That alone shows you how strong we are," said the driver. Baldwin argued that this money depended on being part of the American economy. He reflected that blacks had to accept they had been formed by the United States and did not belong to any other—not to Africa and certainly not to Islam. Blacks could have no future unless they accepted their past and that meant learning how to use it, not drowning in it. It meant "the transcendence of the realities of color, of nations and of altars."

And so the Black Muslim driver left him in "enemy territory" to reflect that it was extremely unlikely blacks would ever rise to power in the U.S. because they were only about a ninth of the population, unlike Africans who were in the great majority in their continent. Yet blacks and whites deeply needed each other if the U.S. were really to become a nation and they were to achieve their identity, their maturity, as men and women. To create one nation in this multiracial society was proving "a hideously difficult task"; there was certainly no need now to create two nations, one black and one white. But "a bill is coming in that I fear America is not prepared to pay," Baldwin told himself gloomily. The outcome depended on the efforts of the "relatively conscious whites and the relatively conscious blacks, who must, like lovers, insist on or create the consciousness of the others." They must not falter in their duty, and although they were a mere handful, they might be able to end the racial nightmare and achieve a real country and change the history of the world. If they didn't now dare everything, it might mean the fulfillment of the old prophecy: "God gave Noah the rainbow sign. No more water, the fire next time!"

Baldwin then walked buoyantly to join his white devil friends for a much-needed drink. He knew he had made one of the most important decisions of his life, comparable to when he gave up being a preacher or decided to go to Paris. He had decided in effect he would remain with the integration wing of the civil rights movement symbolized by Martin Luther King, and reject the growing radical younger group who wanted to go their own way, of whom the Black Muslims were the most extreme. He had turned down the idea of an exclusive black brotherhood in favor of a human brotherhood with whites. He realized it meant "I should be caught in the middle, since I cannot make alliances on the basis of color."

It was certainly a courageous decision because, like most people in the middle, he found himself shot at by both sides in the years ahead, and there were times when he wavered and wondered if he had made the right decision. But then the memory of his stepfather's rage and ultimate madness came back to haunt him. *It now had been laid to my charge to keep my own heart free of hatred and despair.* He knew he really had had no choice that evening in Chicago in the Black Muslim mansion, attractive as the paternalism was. There was only one decision he could make and he had made it and now he would have to try to live with it.

He received another magazine offer that seemed well-timed but even more challenging than Podhoretz's as it turned out. William Shawn, the veteran editor of The New Yorker, wanted him to go to Africa to write a series of articles. It was an exciting prospect at this particular time when young black Americans, in asserting their pride, were making much of their African roots with Afro hairstyles and imitation African dashikis and other clothes. Jimmy Baldwin goes back to the land of his forefathers to look for his roots! That would be the basis of the New Yorker articles. He would be a witness to what Africa was really like today. But he also had in mind the story that had occurred to him when he met Ingmar Bergman in Sweden—of a black rebel through the ages starting in Africa with the first slaves being shipped to America. Perhaps it could be his next novel and he could do some research for it on the African trip. Yet what held him back, made him indecisive over the New Yorker offer was his experiences with Africans in Paris, their impenetrable detachment and ambivalence, their strange foreign eroticism and scornful militancy. About all he had succeeded in writing about them so far were a few observations in essays and the short story "This Morning, This Evening, So Soon," which had one African character whose way of life the other characters could only guess at. In the story Baldwin had tried to convey his own awkwardness in dealing with such an African who had been based on a man he had known in Paris. Would he understand the Africans any better in their homelands or would it be like visiting whole countries of Black Muslims who didn't even share your language? In the end he made a typical Baldwin decision—he followed his instincts and his instinct was to go, not to miss what might be an important development in his life.

He met at the New Yorker office on West Forty-third Street with William Shawn, a quiet, very professional, gentlemanly editor with elaborate, almost Victorian good manners that greatly impressed Baldwin. They talked about the kind of personal-reaction piece he wanted to write and then he left it to his agent, Robert Mills, to work out the best financial terms with generous expenses. He put the long Black Muslim essay on one side until his return and packed his bags. He told Robert Mills, "My bones know somehow something of what waits for me in Africa. That is one of the reasons I have dawdled so long—I'm afraid. And of course I'm playing it my own way, edging myself into it." Once he had been to Africa, he would no longer be able to dream his fantasies about the Dark Continent. Colonial oppression was slowly coming to an end "and one flinches from the responsibility, which we all now face, of judging black people solely as people."

As always with a long journey, he couldn't face the loneliness of traveling by himself and decided to take his sister, Gloria, with him. She had been married for a time to an American airman and had gone abroad with him to live at a U.S. air force base in the north of England. She had worked for a magazine in New York and also had recently started to help her eldest brother as a secretary. She was a poised, commonsense woman who would help him to remain realistic about Africa and Africans. He was wary of being put down by Africans the way they had put him down in Paris, but both they and he played different roles—the Africans secure at home instead of immigrants in foreign Paris, he a distinguished visitor instead of a poor, struggling American black writer. The people seemed more like the men and women he knew in Harlem than the Africans in Paris—at least in spirit if not in culture. He and Gloria traveled down the west coast of Africa, from Senegal to Ghana. It took them over two months. What pleased him most was when they were mistaken for Africans. But he had no sense of coming back to his roots. His main impression was of how little he knew—"I have so much to learn! I want to go back—and back again!" He knew at once he couldn't write any articles, not even one, at least not yet. But he had spent The New Yorker's money on the trip. He *owed* them an article.

Norman Podhoretz at Commentary received a phone call from him. "Jimmy said he had written the article I had commissioned on the Black Muslims. He then said he had sold it to The New Yorker. I was extremely angry. We met and talked it out. I knew him well enough by then not to be surprised, but it was a very unprofessional thing to do. It was wrong both professionally and in terms of our personal relations. He explained that he was to have done an article for The New Yorker on Africa, but he wasn't able to do it so he gave them my article. I wasn't surprised he was irresponsible. I seem to remember that he had some outstanding advances with Commentary for articles he didn't deliver. I'm pretty sure that was the case. He was not a man you could really rely on. If he made an arrangement to be somewhere, he might not show up." He and Podhoretz were not friendly in the later years, but the Commentary editor said it had nothing to do with their row over the article. "There was no single incident, just a growing estrangement. Our political differences became broader and deeper."

William Shawn at The New Yorker raised no problems about getting the Black Muslim essay instead of several about Africa. He called the 20,000–word essay "Letter from a Region in My Mind" and published it in the November 17, 1962, issue of the magazine. It caused a sensation. The magazine was quickly sold out and the issue became a collector's item. The New Yorker reached a very affluent literary and intellectual readership, and Baldwin found himself a celebrity. Time reported that the essay showed Baldwin to be "the most bitterly eloquent voice of the American Negro," adding, "yet it also shows him as one who speaks less for the Negro than to the white—and it is in that sense that he is most compelling." The same issue of Time selected Pope John as "Man of the Year" ("To the world at large, John has given what neither science nor diplomacy can provide: a sense of its unity as the human family . . ."). Baldwin conveyed a similar sense of human unity in his essay, but stressed the price for disregarding it.

Requests for interviews poured in, so did invitations to meetings and parties. Society hostesses wanted him at their social gatherings as the latest star. When he lectured them about the evil that whites had done to blacks, they seemed to enjoy it. "I met another bunch of masochists," he told me once. It wasn't long before his face began to appear more and more on television and on the covers of magazines. Time put him on its cover, but the accompanying story was not in the magazine's "Books" section but in "National Affairs." Baldwin had made it not as a mere writer but as an activist, a black spokesman. With a photograph showing him in a smart suit addressing students at the University of California, Time described him as "a nervous, slight, almost fragile figure, filled with frets and fears. He is effeminate in manner, drinks considerably, smokes cigarettes in chains, and he often loses his audience with overblown arguments. Nevertheless, in the U.S. today there is not another writer, white or black, who expresses with such poignancy and abrasiveness the dark realities of the racial ferment in North and South."

The same issue of Time also had a lead story about the racial conflict in Birmingham, Alabama, the symbol of segregation, which Martin Luther King was assaulting in his determined, nonviolent way. The magazine described King as "the Negroes' inspirational but sometimes inept leader." Time's story and its statistics—eighteen racial bombings, so many that blacks called the city Bombingham, and fifty cross burnings in the previous six years—didn't convey the extent of segregation. Schools, restaurants, drinking fountains, toilets were all still segregated, and Public Safety Commissioner Eugene ("Bull") Connor headed an army of club-swinging cops to make sure they remained so. A temporarily depressed King once told me that he felt as if he was trying to cut his way through a brick wall with his fingernails.

When next I met Baldwin I congratulated him on his Time cover—he shrugged it off—and I asked him about his experiences in hopping from city to city to talk to college and high school students, a schedule of speaking engagements that a presidential candidate could hardly have beaten. While we were talking, an official of CORE came with a draft of some statement and they retired into Baldwin's study for Baldwin to revise it. I now noticed a slight change in Baldwin when he argued. He would use more often that collective "I" in the dramatic style of a preacher with finger wagging, his voice rising, his eyes flashing, as he told some white American: "I dammed a lot of rivers, I laid a lot of track, I hoed a lot of cotton, I cleaned a lot of dishes. You wouldn't have had this country if it hadn't been for me . . ." Success had given him more authority when he talked to strangers. There was also a more marked impatience in him, provoked by the reports of brutality against blacks filling the newspapers and TV screens.

I was in his company once when a white friend of his brought along a couple of his white friends to be introduced to the famous man. They seemed to be a middle-class couple of unremarkable complacency, not Baldwin's kind of people, but I had seen him easily accept such people when they were accompanied by friends. But something about this couple irritated him or perhaps he was simply tired and they became the target of his general anger and frustration and frayed nerves. Whatever the reason, Baldwin started to attack their few remarks about what was happening in the country. He became a collective black "I" while they suddenly became a collective white "You," responsible for all the sins of White America. Bull Connor was their brother, their responsibility. The couple tried feebly to reply, to accept no responsibility, but Baldwin wouldn't let them escape. He kept leveling accusations at them, his anger unappeasable, prosecuting and judging the couple who became bewildered and finally remained silent. I supposed Baldwin was releasing an enormous tension the way soldiers will go on the town and smash glasses and fight with bouncers. Elijah Muhammad would have thought there was still hope for him. The anger slowly receded and he sat back, brooding. No one spoke, watching him. Suddenly his whole face lit up: the storm had passed. "I guess I did overdo it," he said.

He had thought of putting the Black Muslim essay in his next collection as the leading item, but James Silberman phoned to say, "We'll publish it on its own and as quickly as we can possibly do it. Jimmy hadn't thought of that." The book was called *The Fire Next Time,* and a brief letter to his nephew James, entitled "My Dungeon Shook" and originally published in The Progressive, was added at the beginning to make the book a little longer. It caused an even bigger sensation than the original New Yorker publication and was soon heading the non-fiction bestseller lists. "With *The Fire Next Time,*" said Silberman, "the critics began to view him as an essayist not a novelist. It was very influential. It altered people's views of his literary talent. Jimmy had been practicing his whole life to write *The Fire Next Time.* It was a very sophisticated black man's warning to the white world." Virginia Baron at Dial Press remembered the book was produced in record time, about two weeks. There was an argument in those preinflation times whether it should be priced at $2.50 or $2.95—would people pay so much for such a short book? Paperback rights, she said, sold for the then-huge sum of $65,000. "Whites loved to hear him blast whites."

Don Fine, then editor-in-chief of Dell Books, who had published the paperback edition of *Another Country* as well as *Nobody Knows My Name,* contracted for the paperback rights to *The Fire Next Time.* "There's a lot of self-serving mythology that grows up around famous writers like Baldwin," he said, "put out by peripheral people like publishers and editors. It's how those once- and twice-removed from the genuine creative force—the writer—make themselves feel important to the process, if only by association. Baldwin saw through that, I think, very clearly, which was one reason he had few qualms about using such people to the hilt. Without him and other writers, he might reasonably figure, they really had nothing to work with. For myself, I thought *The Fire Next Time* was an almost overelegant, altogether polished exposition of black-white relations that white Americans could embrace without discomfort, and which really was considerably less fiery than its biblical title. For my money, as a publisher and literarily, Baldwin's novels, too often denigrated then and now, however flawed, were far more expressive of the depths of his feelings and represented the best of his artistic work. I had my most satisfying and revealing talks with Baldwin about Henry James' influence on his aesthetics—he saved his preacher's 'I' and 'You' stuff for public postures, thank God."

Donna Schrader, who had joined Dial the previous year, handled the publicity. "My experience with him on publicity tours," she said, "was that we had to cancel some things because he gave so much of himself. Anyone who wanted to talk to him was given a chance. He got so tired. He really gave of himself too much. He didn't hold back. He wasn't hiding anything. If he wanted to talk, he did—about anything. I traveled alone with him a couple of times. Another time he brought two friends, including a young friend from the West Indies, and he paid for them."

A review from San Francisco was the first to be published about *The Fire Next Time.* A two-column headline called it "a classic." Donna Schrader rushed into Silberman's office and laid it on his desk. Everyone at Dial was thrilled. "It was the first indication from outside of the success the book would have." Dial also obtained rights to *Go Tell It On the Mountain* from Knopf for hardcover and paperback editions so they could claim to be the publishers of all of James Baldwin's novels and further improve their relationship with him. *The Fire Next Time* stayed for forty-one weeks in the top five on the non-fiction bestseller lists and won the George Polk Memorial Award for outstanding magazine reporting. Dial and Dell also hired lawyers to defend *Another Country* against the threatened ban in New Orleans on grounds of obscenity.

Robert Mills had lectured Baldwin about his treatment of Commentary and had drawn up a humorous list of outstanding tasks, including "fifty commitments you've made that I don't know about." Baldwin wasn't amused. Mills and he also discussed the possibility of Baldwin being awarded a Nobel Prize, probably arising from the dinner of Nobel Prize winners he had attended. John A. Williams, who was also represented by Mills, recalled a dinner with the agent at which "Bob was high on Jimmy winning some prize. He placed a call to Paris, where Jimmy was, and they talked and sounded very high on the possibilities. I sort of had the feeling Jimmy shared his expectations." Although Baldwin spent some time with Robert Mills' family, Judge Kupferman had the impression he wasn't satisfied with his agent, and it wasn't long before Mills was out—"he didn't fuss about giving up the relationship," the judge remembered—and Kupferman found himself acting as Baldwin's literary agent as well as his lawyer.

When James Meredith attempted by his enrollment to integrate the University of Mississippi an army of some twenty thousand troops was sent in by President Kennedy and his brother Robert to protect him as the only black student at the previously all-white college. "Ole Miss" was situated in the little town of Oxford, where William Faulkner had lived most of his life, and although he had been dead for several months, the scene might have been written by him. Lynching was openly threatened, local rednecks drove into Oxford loaded with weapons, and little old ladies talked in the manner of the old dames knitting at the guillotine during the French Revolution.

Baldwin decided he must go down to meet James Meredith and give him what support he could. Actor Rip Torn saw him off at the airport in New York with his brother David and a black schoolteacher friend named Sam Floyd. "It was very brave, I thought," said Torn, "because he was going to a place where the worst of his fears could be fulfilled. He was taking a late night flight. But they told him the plane had been sold out and he didn't have a reserved seat. I knew it wasn't true so I called the clerk and told him he should consider very carefully that it was very important for the future of our country that Jimmy make this trip. The clerk soon came back and said, 'We have a seat for you, Mr. Baldwin.' " He met James Meredith during a break at Ole Miss in the nearby town of Jackson and was delighted to find he was bearing up well in the circumstances. "He takes it well," Baldwin said. "He has no rancor. He can laugh at these people and that can't be easy. I wasn't surprised he decided to stick it out."

Meredith found Baldwin a very quiet man, which was probably a sign of Baldwin's admiration—he let Meredith do the talking. Baldwin himself said, "I was scared." He also met Medgar Evers, the NAACP's chief representative in Mississippi, who was to become a friend. "He had the calm of someone who knows they're going to die before their time—like Martin Luther King." Baldwin accompanied him in investigating a murder in rural Mississippi. "People talked to us behind locked doors, lights out," Baldwin recalled. "I said very little in order not to give away my New York accent. That makes you a suspicious character. They wonder what you're up to down there."

Calling him "a celebrity overnight," a Life reporter followed him around the Deep South recording his public speeches from New Orleans—his stepfather's hometown—to North Carolina. The civil rights movement wanted to make use of his celebrity, too. Asked about the Black Muslims, he said they served "one extremely useful function: they scare white people. Otherwise they are just another racist organization and the only place they can go is to disaster." He walked round New Orleans looking for connections with his stepfather. Some of the churches must have been like those his stepfather preached in before he went north. Baldwin felt he was standing in his stepfather's footsteps when he preached in a New Orleans church.

There was a revealing incident at the time concerning his attitude toward money. He overslept in New Orleans when he was supposed to fly to Greensboro, North Carolina, to speak for CORE. Reading a poetry manuscript that a student had given him to criticize, he rushed in a rented car to the airport only to find the plane had left. He knew the meeting he was to address had been arranged weeks before and people were coming from far outside Greensboro. The only way he could get there in time was to charter a plane. He asked someone to check how much it would cost—$680 was the answer, more than a round-trip ticket to Europe. "I said I'd be in Greensboro tonight and I will be," declared Baldwin, and soon he was clambering into a small two-engine plane, looking scared. "My lawyers aren't going to be too delighted with this little extravagance, but what else is there to do?" he said. "What's money for?"

Back in New York he still lived in a modest two-and-a-half-room apartment on the edge of the Village, but Life noted that "in today's literary circles it is a sign of considerable chic to know James Baldwin well enough to refer to him as Jimmy." When leaving one of the innumerable parties he attended if only for a brief time, he invariably took a group back to his apartment for more drinks and generally his phone was still ringing at three A.M. against a background of his favorite records, usually Ray Charles or Mahalia Jackson. When friends left at last he often hugged them as if they were leaving him to his loneliness, and gave them the New York show-business farewell, *"Ciao,* baby." Considering his hectic celebrity social life it was amazing he did any business. New York publishers were in hot pursuit of him now, and he enjoyed the attention. Dial Press was especially worried about Random House, a big successful company which had resources well beyond theirs. Richard Baron was in Nassau when he heard Random House had made an offer, and he flew back immediately. James Silberman arranged a meeting with Baldwin. Baron told him, "Jimmy, I'll give you a contract for four books in fiction and four in non-fiction with more money on each book than Random House has offered." Baron explained later, "It would be an eight-book contract and his needs would be provided for."

Baldwin decided to stay with Dial, partly because being a star at a small publisher like Dial would probably be better over the years than just being one of many stars at Random House. It was the start of a much closer relationship with Dial and with Dell, his paperback publisher, who soon bought Dial, which meant Baldwin then had in effect one publisher for both hardback and paperback editions. Dial-Dell was to become much more than merely his publisher, providing help with income-tax problems and even flying his entire family for a vacation in Puerto Rico. As his editor at Dial changed several times over the years, Richard Baron as publisher of Dial and Mrs. Helen Meyer, the publisher of Dell, became his main confidants at the company. Baron said, "He was obviously a genius. He had an eye and an ear that were just unbelievable, plus an ability to write magnificently."

At a dinner Baron and his wife gave for Baldwin at their home outside New York City, the guests included cartoonist Jules Feiffer, Village Voice political writer Nat Hentoff—and Norman Mailer with his fourth wife, Beverly, and his oldest daughter. Baldwin was late and was the last to arrive. A limousine was sent to collect him. He was in a strange, high-strung mood waiting in his apartment, drinking Johnnie Walker Red quickly, nervously and grinning broadly at any feeble joke. His mother took a look at the rate he was consuming scotch, sighed, but didn't say anything, soon disappearing back upstairs to her own apartment. But before she went he suddenly held her by the waist—they were almost exactly the same height—and he kissed her, as if drawing strength from her. One had to wonder if his mood was caused by the prospect of seeing Norman Mailer—his behavior resembled the way champion boxers often act in their dressing rooms before a big fight.

He was somber but more calm in the backseat of the limousine, where his brother David joined him like a bodyguard. Baron and his wife came out to greet Baldwin, fussing around him, laughing—they seemed nervous, too. David Baldwin was beside him as he walked into the house, everyone listening to Baldwin's quick intense tones and ready laughter. Then suddenly another voice cut across Baldwin's, a familiar

wary voice: "Hello, Jimmy." Baldwin and Mailer stared at each other—
it was always surprising how small they both were, though Mailer still
was much more thickset. They went on and on staring, not speaking
beyond the first hellos. The atmosphere was electric with tension. Then
without warning David Baldwin stepped between them, smiling, holding out a big hand for Mailer to shake. That broke the tension. Baldwin
and Mailer patted each other's shoulders, nodded, smiled, but instead of
chatting together, catching up with each other's news, they quickly
separated and disappeared inside their respective groups on opposite sides
of the large living room like two Napoleons surrounded by their
marshals. The host and hostess stood looking apprehensively from one
group to the other, probably wondering if a generous supply of pre-
dinner drinks would blend the groups or merely send up the tempera-
ture.

Baldwin, his teeth flashing in the show-business grin of Louis Armstrong, gave the appearance of being entirely at his ease. He and brother
David indulged in a little subtle horseplay between them, with some
slapped palms and other flamboyant black gestures that might awaken
a White Negro's envy in the watching Mailer. Suddenly he ambled over
to Baldwin, who immediately began to introduce him to people as if
he were an unknown guest who didn't know anyone. It was a trick
worthy of a Zen master. The host and hostess quickly announced dinner
was ready and, taking the safest way out, seated Baldwin and Mailer at
different tables. It was a surprisingly quiet, peaceful dinner, and at the
end everyone, as if weary from the tension, decided to have an early
night and were not pressed to stay. Waving off the limousine, Baron
and his wife looked relieved. Baldwin was crunched up in a corner, his
face hidden. At last he spoke to brother David. "Norman and I don't
seem to have much to say to each other these days," he murmured, and
then relapsed into silence again.

On another occasion when he was flying off somewhere he had Dial
Press drive him and a large group of friends to the airport and also
arrange a party in a V.I.P. lounge while he was waiting to board the
plane. He kept talking about the huge advances and special treatment
that white writers like Mailer and Philip Roth received, and the Dial

Press staff did their best to compete and keep their new celebrity happy. Helen Meyer, who was the chief executive officer, president and chairman of the board at Dell, said, "I was very impressed the first time I met him. He wasn't shy. Jimmy's only trouble really was to settle down and write, to get the peace to write. He had so many friends and so many people were always coming to see him. They took an awful lot of his time. There was no one like him. But he had his own personal problems. He thought he was ugly. He had a terrible childhood. He was wonderful to his mother. He just loved her so much and his brother David. He was very generous to them and gave them wonderful vacations. If he had a dollar, they would get ninety cents. He was a very generous man, too, with his time as well as financially. When we at Dell first got into the act by taking over Dial, he was very nervous about being with a large company like Dell as against Dial, which was very tiny. So we had to convince him that if there was going to be any change, it would be for the better for him, not the worse. Dell was financially well set. We really did him a favor by buying Dial, but Jimmy being there of course wasn't the only reason we bought Dial. He always needed money and he came to me whenever he ran out of money. We got along very well. He took his family for vacations on the islands and we would pick up the check. Several times he met new friends and wanted them to go to France or wherever they were to join him. In such matters he called me and asked if I would buy an air ticket for them and I arranged it."

One of Baldwin's British paperback publishers, the late Anthony Godwin of Penguin Books, fared less well when he met Baldwin in New York. Godwin was an enterprising man in love with good writing. He was hardly taller or more robust looking than Baldwin himself, and he was keenly interested in the racial struggle in the U.S., seeing it through English eyes as essentially a class struggle. He went to Baldwin's apartment for a drink with me and it was obviously the wrong day. The atmosphere was already stormy. A black friend of Baldwin's recounted a humiliating experience in the Village, which led another black friend to detail some of his bad times at the hands of prejudiced whites. They laid it on for the visiting Englishman, but Baldwin merely sat nodding his head as if he were the Amen Corner. Godwin, misreading the intensity of the feelings behind the words, attempted to lighten the conversation. He knew blacks had had a hard time in America, he said, but then so had the Chinese . . . He wasn't allowed to finish. "The Chinese?" Baldwin cried at him. "The Chinese came here voluntarily. We niggers were forced here in slave ships. I had to work in the galleys to get here."

"*You*, Mr. Baldwin?" Godwin said in an ironic tone, not understanding Baldwin's strong sense of identification.

That did it. Baldwin swept into a long litany of oppression and ended the lesson by insisting that Godwin listen to a record of Nina Simone singing "Mississippi Goddam" from start to finish. It seemed an unbearably long record to me with Baldwin's solemn, angry face staring at Godwin's red one. Feeling responsible for Godwin and wishing to divert Baldwin's wrath, I said, "Look, you're treating us both as just a couple of white men."

"Well," he said, "that's just what you are."

By that time some European film producer had arrived to take Baldwin to dinner, and we all went down in the elevator in gloomy silence and parted with hardly a word. Godwin made straight for the nearest bar and had a strong drink. "I don't understand why Baldwin was so *upset*," he said. I tried to explain but apparently without success. Years later he said: "I made some idiotic remark comparing the Chinese to the blacks, though I can't remember what it was which upset James Baldwin and put me in the doghouse."

When I next met Baldwin he didn't refer to the row with Godwin and was as friendly as ever. The incident might never have happened; this was another day, another mood. It was at the home of Robert Lewis, a well-known Broadway director and teacher who had been closely involved with the old Group Theater and the Actors Studio. The only other guest was actor Roddy McDowell. The conversation was mainly light show-business gossip, and Baldwin showed great interest in all the stories that Lewis told of Broadway and McDowell recounted of Hollywood; this was another side of him. When I rose to leave he did, too. He seemed to want to make a friendly gesture—perhaps the Godwin meeting was on his mind, after all. Outside he automatically looked for a cab, but I persuaded him, as it was such a pleasant night, to walk back to his apartment on West Eighteenth Street. We strolled about thirty blocks down Third Avenue and then across town—Lewis lived on the East Side and Baldwin on the West. "This is the first time I've walked through the city for years," he said as if surprised at his own temerity, staring with wonderment at the passing people and stores and snack bars almost like a tourist. He was so used to taking cabs, he said, that on foot in this violent city he felt strangely defenseless before the onrush of experience in the streets. He was probably surprised to make it across the city without being mugged or at least accosted; he hadn't even been recognized unless someone spotted him but kept quiet. Near his apartment we met Lucien coming home. He spoke briefly to me and then hurried inside, ignoring Baldwin. "We've had a row," Baldwin said, looking embarrassed.

A foreign correspondent at the United Nations asked me to bring Baldwin along to a party she was giving. I mentioned it jokingly to Baldwin and to my surprise, he said, "I'll try it. I haven't been to a party for some time." James Purdy, a novelist who had known him in his early Village days, was among the guests. Both Baldwin and Purdy were already at the party when I got there. Baldwin was the center of a group of affluent white women who were at him with questions about race. His replies were accompanied by a good deal of finger-wagging. Purdy, with the dignified, reticent look of a world-weary bishop, was standing in a corner surveying the other guests as if they were raw material for a novel. I tried to draw him and Baldwin together. "James!" said Baldwin, embracing Purdy rather flamboyantly. "How nice to see you!" And then, without even waiting for Purdy's reply, he turned again to face the audience of women and finish what he was saying. That was the end of communication between the two writers and Purdy soon left. Baldwin eventually wearied of his audience and came over and said in a stage whisper that was probably audible all around the room: "Get me out of here!" On the way down to get a cab he said, "They really don't understand, even now. What more do they want?" He headed for a bar frequented by Broadway theater people on Eighth Avenue. When I returned to the party one of the women who had cornered Baldwin as if it were a public meeting remarked that he seemed "very bitter."

Another time he went to a party in the Village given by a woman who worked for a publisher. The other guests included some writers and teachers and television journalists. They hailed "Jimmy" and immediately began to quiz him. A TV reporter asked if he didn't feel out of touch sometimes because, in between his civil rights activities, he lived abroad so much. Baldwin said that he didn't need to be in the U.S. all the time—he knew what was going on. It was obviously a sensitive point with him. He sat straight-backed and wide-eyed, as if he had the feeling that the TV reporter was getting at him. After signing a copy of *The Fire Next Time* for his hostess' young son he left to meet his mother at the Village Gate to hear Nina Simone sing. One of the other guests remarked, "It just shows that no dialogue is possible between blacks and middle-class Jews."

Africa had come closer to Baldwin because his sister Gloria had married an African, Frank Karefa-Smart, who worked at the United Nations. At a party the newlyweds gave for relations and friends on both sides, Baldwin sat sedately in an armchair watching the Americans and Africans dancing together, then said impatiently, "I feel like Henry James," and rushed to join the dancing, making up in enthusiasm what he lacked in skill. James Meredith once said the best he could say for Baldwin's dancing was "he is game." Meredith never got over the "strange sight" of seeing him attempting the Twist at a Mississippi house party.

At another Afro-American party in New York given by his affluent African in-laws, the African connection seemed to make him feel more secure: "When things go to hell here," he said gloomily, "I'll have somewhere to take my family." He was always worrying about his family—which included a growing number of nephews and nieces—and his plan was to buy a house for his mother with the help of Dial Press and get her out of Harlem. He already had Lucien working on it; he had given Lucien the job of being his manager—in buying houses and renting apartments in New York, a white face was particularly useful. He made a big dramatic scene before his African in-laws of sending a white friend outside to stop a cab for him. The affluent Africans were slightly mystified. They wondered why he didn't simply ask the white doorman. You could never tell whether Baldwin was simply letting off steam or whether he was making a subtle point you had missed. He told a friend in warning about this side of himself: "Please don't mind or be embarrassed by any of my more hysterical outbursts. I'm like that on the top sometimes, but I've very sound at bottom."

13

Educating Robert Kennedy

ATTORNEY GENERAL Robert Kennedy was deeply concerned now about the worsening racial situation. The Oxford, Mississippi, crisis over James Meredith and Ole Miss, had shocked him, and he began to realize what the Kennedy administration was up against. But he didn't yet grasp the profound feelings on the black side and why black leaders were disappointed with the Kennedys.

William Goldsmith, a political scientist, described in *The Growth of Presidential Power* sitting with Martin Luther King and James Baldwin in a Boston railway station shortly after the Oxford crisis and listening to their "despairing reactions . . . It was not only the clumsiness and hesitancy with which the whole business was handled that depressed them, but the lack of moral conviction in the President's remarks as he spoke patronizingly of war heroes and football stars to the rioting students and yahoos in Oxford." The behind-the-scenes dealing with the Mississippi governor, King thought, "made Negroes feel like pawns in a white man's political game." A few months later in March, 1963, King described 1962 as "the year that civil rights was displaced as the dominant issue in domestic politics," but in fairness, he said, "this administration has outstripped all previous ones in the breadth of its civil rights activities. Yet the Movement, instead of breaking out into the open plains of progress, remains constricted and confined. A sweeping revolutionary force is pressed into a narrow tunnel." It was becoming increasingly difficult for King to persuade younger blacks to be patient, that nonviolence was the only way.

Sensing there was much he didn't yet understand, Robert Kennedy decided to try to extend his contacts with black intellectuals. He was aware of Baldwin's growing fame and the success of *The Fire Next Time.* They had met the year before at the White House Nobel Prize dinner, and they had agreed then that they wanted to talk some more. "Achievers fascinated him," wrote Arthur Schlesinger, Jr., of Robert Kennedy, "whether James Baldwin or General MacArthur or Richard Daley, whether scholars or astronauts or film stars." Since the troubles in Birmingham, Kennedy had become convinced the next great battlefield for racial justice lay in the cities. He saw Baldwin, born in New York's black ghetto, as an expert on blacks in the cities. He invited him to breakfast at his home at Hickory Hill, Virginia, outside Washington. The attorney general said he had kept getting messages that James Baldwin wanted to meet him, though he couldn't remember precisely from whom the messages came—Schlesinger? Dick Gregory, the black satirist?—and Baldwin denied sending any messages, though he was pleased enough to meet with Kennedy again.

Baldwin's plane was late so he didn't arrive until nine A.M., and Kennedy had to leave half-an-hour later to catch a plane himself. The two men, who were about the same height, must have looked a complete contrast as they faced each other across the breakfast table—Baldwin, black, nervous, fiery, idealistic and with a homosexual reputation; Kennedy, white, pragmatic, assertive, a macho Catholic Irish-American, a rich man's son used to deference from other people. "We had a very nice meeting," Kennedy said later. "I was really quite impressed by him," said Baldwin. "He seemed honest and earnest and truthful." Burke Marshall, assistant attorney general in charge of the Civil Rights Division, who was also present, said they "had a rather good conversation about the cities." But since the meeting was so brief, Kennedy proposed another the next day in New York. "I said I'd meet him for a drink,"

Kennedy recalled. "If he had some friends, maybe we could meet, and we could talk some more. So he said 'Fine.' " Burke Marshall had a more cut-and-dried lawyer's view that Baldwin was going to bring along some people who understood the problems of urban centers in the North "and would have some suggestions as to what role the federal government could take. That, as I understood it, was a rather clear topic of conversation."

The attorney general had met Baldwin twice and presumably had been briefed at the Justice Department (and by the FBI?) about him. Baldwin was a witness to a way of life that Kennedy knew little about. But he was by no means an expert on urban problems, and at such short notice few well-known black authorities would be available. Baldwin could have conveyed to the attorney general a knowledge of black life and aspirations he needed to be able to understand if he was to grasp the country's true racial situation. But given Kennedy's and Marshall's rather stereotyped approach and the kind of people Baldwin took along, the meeting was doomed to failure from the start.

Dr. Kenneth Clark called the gathering on May 24, 1963, "the most dramatic meeting I have ever attended," but Kennedy and Marshall tended to play down the significance of what happened. When Marshall was asked to describe the meeting he said: "It's not really worth the time." But two very different men who knew Robert Kennedy, Arthur Schlesinger and Harry Belafonte, who was at the meeting, thought it helped Kennedy to become the more enlightened man he was when he ran for president himself in 1968. Most of the others who were there would probably have agreed with Kenneth Clark's assessment. The essential problem about the meeting, which soon became a heated confrontation, was that although Kennedy wanted to learn more about the black scene, he was used to having information and opinions presented in a way that respected his superior authority. But from a man like Baldwin he could expect only the same "straight-from-the-shoulder" treatment that Baldwin had accorded Richard Wright and Langston Hughes and others. Baldwin went to the meeting with high hopes that he might influence Bobby Kennedy, and through him President Kennedy, and to do so he was prepared if necessary to tell Kennedy,

"Oh, come off it, baby. Let's tell it like it is." In fact, that was what happened.

Kenneth Clark remembered that "Jim phoned me and told me he had already had a meeting with Kennedy and had expressed his concerns and apparently they wanted some corroboration and so there was to be another meeting in New York and he asked me if I would go. Martin Luther King also called me and said he was going to be unable to attend but he wanted me to represent him. Martin had wanted to be there. The other individuals Jim invited were not ordinarily recognized as civil rights leaders: Harry Belafonte, Lena Horne, Lorraine Hansberry, Clarence Jones, Jerome Smith, Rip Torn. I met his brother David, who was also part of the group he was taking. The meeting was a reflection of a deep amount of emotional feeling on the part of those who were there to try to communicate to Bobby Kennedy how deeply concerned American blacks were about the continuation of racism in America— segregation, suppression, prejudice."

Rip Torn said the group also included Edwin C. Berry, director of the Chicago Urban League, and a friend of Baldwin acting as his secretary, a friend of David Baldwin and a television producer, Henry Morgenthau III. "Jimmy said he was taking me to test me," Rip Torn remembered. "He said he was just playing a hunch. He wanted me there as a witness. I spoke out very strongly." They met, he said, at a hotel near Central Park and then went to the Kennedy family apartment at 24 Central Park South. "I didn't stay for the entire meeting because I was appearing in *Strange Interlude* and had to go to the theater," Torn said. "The point was we were there really for Jerome Smith, a twenty-five-year-old Freedom Rider and believer in nonviolence who had been beaten, jailed and so badly injured he needed medication to get by. We were hoping to convey to Kennedy that not even the supporters of Gandhian nonviolence were going to continue being victims, and there were other people arising out there who wanted to retaliate and would rather stand and die. Jerome was hoping to tell Kennedy of his feelings, and Kennedy said he couldn't understand him because of his dialect. I told the attorney general we were there because of Jerome and you have to understand him. I said

I could understand *him* with his Boston dialect. I had been a Kennedy supporter, but Kennedy tried to outstare me, a stare contest. The meeting was a big disappointment."

According to Arthur Schlesinger in *Robert Kennedy and his Times,* "Clark and Berry arrived with statistics and proposals. They never had a chance. Jerome Smith, as Baldwin put it later, 'set the tone of the meeting because he stammers when he's upset and he stammered when he talked to Bobby and said that he was nauseated by the necessity of being in that room. I knew what he meant. It was not personal at all . . . Bobby took it personally and turned away from him. That was a mistake because he turned toward us. We were the reasonable, responsible, mature representatives of the black community. Lorraine Hansberry said, 'You've got a great many very, very accomplished people in this room, Mr. Attorney General. But the only man who should be listened to is that man over there.' "

Kenneth Clark recalled that "Robert Kennedy stated that he and his brother were sympathetic to the aspirations of blacks and that blacks, in turn, should understand this and be more responsive. This opened up the discussion, led by Smith, who recently had been physically assaulted by whites in the South. Still showing the swelling and bruises of that attack, he stated with moving intensity that under no circumstances could he conceive of himself as fighting for democracy in the American army when America did not protect him from racial injustices and physical cruelty. Smith's genuine emotion set the tone of the meeting. Robert Kennedy and Burke Marshall seemed stunned. Kennedy tried to get Smith to temper the vehemence of his protest. Not only did he not succeed, but all the members of Baldwin's group joined in support of Smith. They tried to explain to Kennedy what Smith was saying and why he was saying it. Kennedy, for his part, insisted that blacks should understand that he and his brother were sensitive to the plight and aspirations of Negroes. The impasse was unfortunately made all the more difficult when Kennedy pointed out that other Americans also had to endure periods of oppression. In support of this he noted that his grandfather was an Irish immigrant. Baldwin responded: 'You do not understand at all. Your grandfather came as an immigrant from Ireland and your brother is president of the United States. Generations before your family came as immigrants, my ancestors came to this country in chains, as slaves. We are still required to supplicate and beg you for justice and decency."

Kenneth Clark remembered that "at Baldwin's outburst Robert Kennedy's face turned purple but he remained silent. The meeting could not be put back on the track of amicable discourse. Jim Baldwin and his associates insisted repeatedly that what was required was for the president of the United States and the United States government as a whole to use their full power and force to obtain unqualified justice for Negro citizens. Specifically, they suggested that President Kennedy walk arm-in-arm with some black children to take them to newly integrated schools. Robert Kennedy concluded that this was unrealistic and transparent game-playing. After more than three hours the meeting ended. It had achieved some catharsis, but seemingly little understanding."

Arthur Schlesinger's account is slightly different: "Baldwin asked him (Smith) whether he would fight for his country. He said 'Never! Never! Never!' This shocked Kennedy, for whom patriotism was an absolute. 'We were shocked that he was shocked,' said Kenneth Clark. Kennedy 'got redder and redder and redder, and in a sense accused Jerome of treason, you know, or something of that sort. Well, that made everybody move in to protect Jerome and to confirm his feelings. And it became really an attack!' " Lorraine Hansberry, reported Schlesinger, said to Kennedy, "Look, if *you* can't understand what this young man is saying, then we are without any hope at all, because you and your brother are representatives of the best that a white America can offer; and if *you* are insensitive to this, then there's no alternative except our going in the streets . . . and chaos." By her own account she also told Kennedy there had been a change in the struggle for Negro freedom and none of them was "remotely interested in the all-insulting concept of the 'exceptional Negro.' We are not remotely interested in any tea at the White House." Blacks were *one* people "and that as far as *we* are concerned, we are represented by the Negroes in the streets of Birmingham!"

According to Schlesinger, "Kennedy tried to turn the conversation to statistics and legislation. 'In that moment, with the situation in Birmingham the way it was,' said Lena Horne, 'none of us wanted to hear figures and percentages and all that stuff. Nobody even cared about expressions of good will.' " Schlesinger reported that "they denounced the FBI. Kennedy, who privately agreed, passed the question to Burke Marshall, who said that 'special men'—that is, lawyers from the Civil Rights Division—went into areas where the Bureau seemed delinquent. This answer, said Clark, 'produced almost hysterical laughter.' Birmingham came up. When Kennedy explained how closely he had worked with Dr. King, they jeered 'that's not true.' "

Schlesinger quoted Baldwin as saying, "Bobby didn't understand what we were trying to tell him . . . didn't understand our urgency." Kennedy commented, "They seemed possessed. They reacted as a unit. It was impossible to make contact with any of them." Schlesinger quoted Clark as describing Kennedy as becoming "more silent and tense, and he sat immobile in the chair. He no longer continued to defend himself. He just sat, and you could see the tension and the pressure building in him."

The meeting ended "out of sheer exhaustion." As the group prepared to leave, Clarence B. Jones, King's lawyer, was reported by Schlesinger as drawing Kennedy aside and telling him, "I just want to say that Dr. King deeply appreciates the way you handled the Birmingham affair." Kennedy replied, "You watched these people attack me over Birmingham for forty minutes and you didn't say a word. There is no point in your saying this to me now." Jones corrected Kennedy in a letter to the New York *Times* in which he stated that contrary to stories "which have emanated out of Washington" that he remained silent, the implication being as a moderate he was intimidated from speaking, "I participated in four specific areas of discussion with the Attorney General, two of which were initiated by my questions and comments." These included the appointment of segregationist judges in the South and the role of the FBI. He concluded that the fact "the chief legal officer" of the country was "shocked over the sentiments expressed" at the meeting was "reflective of how the Administration underestimates the explosive ingredients inherent in the continued existence of racial discrimination and segregation."

There was also an incident involving Harry Belafonte, who had sometimes acted as a go–between for King and Kennedy, explaining the views of the one to the other. According to Schlesinger's account, Belafonte "had tried to smooth things over earlier by mentioning to the group the hospitality he had enjoyed at Hickory Hill; after a time, he had fallen into uncomfortable silence. Now he said to Kennedy, 'Of course you have done more for civil rights than anyone else.' Kennedy said, 'Why do you say this to me? Why didn't you say this to the others?' Belafonte said, 'I couldn't say this to the others. It would affect my position with these people, and I have a chance to influence them along a reasonable way . . . If I sided with you on these matters, then I would become suspect."

Belafonte disagreed with this account in discussing the meeting with me. He described his role at the time as a go-between or "conduit" for Movement leaders so they could go through "quiet diplomacy" and talk "through" someone like himself. He could convey the ideas of King to SNCC leaders and even to the Kennedys outside the Movement. Part of his position depended on the fact that he had never abused the trust. He had kept the meetings and information out of the press, and that further enhanced his credibility in persuading individuals to cooperate. "Many times I talked to Bobby Kennedy and let him know what we were doing and our hope for the protection of the federal government and not just state law, the worst of all. Why Bobby Kennedy convened this meeting was a mystery to many of us. But hindsight tends to endow that experience with the idea that perhaps it should be viewed with less suspicion than it was at the time. He had been into a whole kind of self-examination and was arriving at a new place in his morality and humanism. We were mystified by his intentions in meeting public people like Lena Horne, Dr. Kenneth Clark and Jimmy Baldwin, whose views were often very different from Dr. King and other Movement leaders such as Jim Forman. We listened to a very naïve unfolding of their account of events and everyone was shocked by the naïvete and by what was being said. I had met Bobby Kennedy many times and exchanged confidences, but I wasn't going to relate such private matters in front of these people who had no reason to be exposed to matters of strategy in the Movement.

"So in Schlesinger's account when I was reported as having been asked why wasn't I more forthcoming at the meeting, that's the answer.

I also wasn't a PR for the Kennedy family or the civil rights movement, and I wasn't going to talk about private discussions of high strategy. That was a meeting of a number of artists and visible people for a remedial and oversimplified dialogue with the attorney general of America, who held the lives of millions of people in his hands. Dr. King and Malcolm X and Jim Forman and Bob Moses and all those people weren't there, so what did he hope to hear from a group of celebrities sitting in a room? It was contrary to a statesmanlike approach at such an important time in American history. The impression given by Schlesinger is that a benevolent white leader had come to a meeting of blacks and he had been slapped down. That was a total oversimplification. Jimmy Baldwin asked us to come, but we didn't know what the agenda was. We expected to hear the attorney general discuss some program—look, here's what we are going to do—and that he'd try to elicit some response in a kind of open forum. But it was nothing like that. However, I'd look at Bobby Kennedy at that stage now as being in search of his soul. But his moderate attitude brought all the passion to the fore. It was quite jarring to him, but I thought very cathartic. The greatest innocent in the room, the person who had an agenda more honorable than believed, was Bobby Kennedy. I'm not a romantic, but I believe he wanted to broaden his own basis of knowledge. But in the room he faced black passion and frustration and the need for action. I knew Jimmy Baldwin from the early days. I forget when we first met. Then during the civil rights movement he and I got thrown together quite a lot, including meetings at my house for hours on end interpreting and discussing. We also discussed artistic projects to do together—films and TV and plays. We had lots of hopes. He let me use his name in support of many causes."

On returning to Washington, Kennedy told Schlesinger: "They don't know what the laws are—they don't know what the facts are—they don't know what we've been doing or what we're trying to do. You can't talk to them the way you can talk to Martin Luther King or Roy Wilkins. They didn't want to talk that way. It was all emotion, hysteria—they stood up and orated—they cursed—some of them wept and left the room." Over the next few months Kennedy tried to work out why the meeting had gone so wrong. He was interested in policy, he decided, whereas the blacks, except for Clark and Berry, were interested in "witness." Guilt, Kennedy thought, was also a factor. "There was a complex about the fact that they had not been involved personally themselves, they were not suffering like Negroes were suffering." He was presumably thinking of the celebrities there, such as Lorraine Hansberry, Lena Horne and Baldwin, and he compared them to certain white people, children of wealthy parents, "who've got some social problem about where they stand in life . . . and therefore become extreme and difficult emotionally." Well over a year later he was still angrily talking about the guilt factor—"The way to show that they hadn't forgotten where they came from was to berate me and berate the United States government . . . They didn't really know, with a few exceptions, any of the facts. James Baldwin couldn't discuss any legislation, for instance, on housing or any of these matters. He didn't know anything about them." Kennedy added, "But it obtained a lot of publicity for him, see. So he played it—James Baldwin—put him in the center of things and gave him a position of leadership. Then he put out all these statements and was interviewed about it."

Arthur Schlesinger told me Kennedy made these comments when he was still trying to recover from his brother's assassination, which took place six months after the Baldwin meeting, and that it became clear later that although Kennedy resented the experience, "it pierced him all the same. His tormentors made no sense; but in a way they made all sense. It was another stage in education."

Baldwin left the Kennedy meeting with Kenneth Clark, who was to interview him about his life for TV, an interview scheduled weeks earlier. They were already an hour and a half late for the taping, but Baldwin was too emotionally upset to go straight into the interview. In a cab, he told Kenneth Clark he wasn't sure he would be able to go through with the interview. He stated repeatedly, "Kenneth, all I need is a drink. Can't we stop at the nearest bar? I must decompress." His state of mind was easy to imagine. In *The Fire Next Time* he had committed himself to an alliance of "the relatively conscious whites and the relatively conscious blacks." Bobby Kennedy was one of the leaders of "the relatively conscious whites" and yet he did not understand the black situation. In the TV interview that finally took place, Baldwin made

227

only oblique references to the Kennedy meeting, quoting what Lorraine Hansberry had said "this afternoon" about black pride but not explaining where, mentioning a talk with Jerome Smith "this afternoon," and commenting it was "a great shock to me" to discover—where he didn't say—that the attorney general didn't know Baldwin would have trouble convincing his nephew to go to Cuba to liberate Cubans when he wasn't liberated himself. Undoubtedly some remarks like the following were inspired by the feelings he had brought away from the meeting: "I think one has got to find some way of putting the present administration of this country on the spot." He said Malcolm X and the Black Muslims, the only true grass-roots movement, could reach many of the younger black students more easily than he could. When Kenneth Clark asked him about the future, he didn't sound too optimistic—it depended on the whites facing what was wrong.

Kenneth Clark spent the rest of the evening with Baldwin and some of his friends. "His despair and anguish were dominant. I was therefore not at all surprised when he returned to Europe, from which distance he observed the civil rights confrontations that followed." Malcolm X told Kenneth Clark: "As long as they have interviews with the attorney general and take Negroes to pose as leaders, all of whom are married either to white men or white women, you'll always have a race problem. When Baldwin took that crew with him to see Kennedy, he took the wrong crew. And as long as they take the wrong crew to talk to that man, you're not going to get anywhere near any solution to this problem in this country."

Baldwin told a New York *Times* interviewer, M.S. Handler, that there was drift and danger in the country, but "despair is a sin. I believe that. It is easy to be bleak about the human race, but there are people who have proved to me that we can be better than we are." Asked if he was religious, Baldwin replied that "every artist is fundamentally religious," but he hadn't been to church for twenty years, having "abandoned Christianity as an organized religion. The church is the worst place to learn about Christianity. I have rejected it because the Christians have rejected Christianity. It is too pious, too hypocritical." He was also distressed by contemporary American literature and attributed its "sterility" to a flight from the realities of contemporary life.

"Writers are running away from social commitments. In some strange way I don't understand they seem to have the idea that one can be an artist and be safe, too. That is the American idea of success." The interviewer described him as dressed in khaki trousers and a sports shirt, his feet bare. His two-and-a-half-room apartment in the Village was considered "a dismal setting for a man depicted by Edmund Wilson as one of the great creative artists of this country." Baldwin's plans for a bigger apartment and a house for his mother were still in the works, masterminded by Lucien.

Baldwin had a reunion with his old classmate, photographer Richard Avedon, when a magazine commissioned Avedon to take pictures of him. They got on well and Baldwin agreed to write the text for a collection of Avedon photographs. Getting the time to do it was the problem, and finally they held a conference to work out the form of the book in Puerto Rico. They discussed a theme—the alienation of people, what keeps them apart. Baldwin decided it should be called *Nothing Personal.* They next arranged to meet in Europe. Dial Press flew all the Baldwin family down to San Juan to celebrate his thirty-ninth birthday. Taking his mother and his brothers and sisters on a wonderful vacation was another of his dreams come true. While they were all there they read a play he was working on, several members of the family, including his mother, taking some of the roles. He himself impersonated several of the characters and had a great time, all his acting dreams returning, but he still had a lot of work to do on it.

Then he was off to Paris to recuperate among friends like James and Gloria Jones, but not for long. The deadline for *Nothing Personal* was looming and finally he had to shut himself away and write in a nonstop stretch through day and night. *Nothing Personal,* of course, turned out to be intensely personal, a four-part essay largely going back over some obsessive themes and incidents. "I have slept on rooftops and in basements and subways, have been cold and hungry all my life; have felt that no fire would ever warm me, and no arms would ever hold me . . . Generations do not cease to be born, and we are responsible to them because we are the only witnesses they have." Again that word

229

witness. He ended with his preoccupation about loneliness: "The moment we cease to hold each other, the moment we break faith with one another, the sea engulfs us and the light goes out." Many of the critics found the essay self-indulgent and a big disappointment after *The Fire Next Time.* A celebrity writer was expected to produce a "major" work each time out.

Martin Luther King planned to hold a mass march on Washington to put pressure on the administration and the country, and Baldwin intended to return home for that. Meanwhile in Paris he helped to organize a meeting and a petition to express support from the American colony for the Washington march. At an overflow service at the American Church on the Left Bank he said: "Segregation is not now, nor has it ever been, a regional matter. We in particular have an interest in turning America into the free country it has always claimed to be." Among the first people to sign the petition were Anthony Quinn, the American actor who was making a film in Paris, and Hazel Scott, the well-known pianist. After a silent march from the American Church, the petition backing the Washington march was handed in at the U.S. Embassy.

When Baldwin flew back to America he found the organization of the march had created a conflict within the Movement. King's idea was a massive procession of witness, whereas some of the younger black leaders wanted a much more militant demonstration. J. Edgar Hoover had been putting pressure on Robert Kennedy to force King to drop the communists that the FBI claimed were on King's staff, and this had affected Bayard Rustin's position as an organizer of the march. Baldwin was sure Kennedy was behind Adam Clayton Powell's and Roy Wilkins' opposition to Rustin. All that saved Rustin, according to Baldwin, was the insistence of A. Philip Randolph, the influential veteran black labor leader, that Rustin was their most experienced crowd-organizer and must work on putting the march together.

President Kennedy officially approved the holding of the march, which prevented a lot of troublesome opposition from racist members of Congress. Robert Kennedy said the Communist party tried to take over the march but was prevented with the cooperation of the organizers. Soon hundreds of thousands of blacks and whites were arriving from all over the country by plane, train, bus, rented coach, car and hitchhiking. Much bitter feeling, however, remained behind the scenes, and the Kennedys kept their distance in public, not making an appearance at the march although the president watched most of it on television and met the leaders afterward in the privacy of the White House. John Lewis of SNCC had prepared a militant speech, but when the Catholic archbishop of Washington, Patrick A. Boyle, threatened not to take part in the march if Lewis delivered his speech, the young SNCC leader was persuaded to let it be toned down. In public at least, the march was more or less the way King had envisioned it, and the numbers alone were impressive as the masses of people spread out through the center of the capital, but the haunting climax was undoubtedly King's own moving description of black aspirations—"I have a dream . . ." Robert Kennedy said, "Boy, he made a helluva speech." The much-publicized occasion was at least a major public-relations triumph for the nonviolent, integration wing of the civil rights movement. "The day was important in itself," said Baldwin, "and what we do with this day is even more important."

On the personal side, Baldwin was pleased to find Marlon Brando among the show-business stars who were there, and for the first time the two friends met as fellow celebrities; in fact, at that predominantly black scene, Baldwin no doubt could have upstaged Brando if he had so wished. He had no further contact with Robert Kennedy while he was in Washington, however, and the two men never met again for an exchange of ideas. Probably the closest they came was when they both attended Martin Luther King's funeral five years later. Baldwin claimed that he was put under heavy FBI surveillance after the Kennedy meeting and blamed the attorney general for it. But Baldwin had been spotted by the FBI at least as early as 1960 when an FBI document noted the names of those on the Fair Play for Cuba Committee, including Sartre, I.F. Stone, Norman Mailer—and Baldwin. An FBI memorandum noted that J. Edgar Hoover requested "summaries" on those taking part. But it was not until after the Kennedy meeting that Baldwin became convinced his phone was tapped and he was being watched in other ways.

Perhaps his apartment was bugged, maybe casual strangers who latched on to his entourage were FBI informers, he suggested . . .

One evening at Baldwin's apartment the guests included an eccentric, middle-aged white man who claimed to be a Baptist minister. Baldwin asked his friends if anyone had brought the man. No one had. "I've tried talking theology to him," Baldwin said, "but got nowhere. I think he's an FBI agent." It seemed unlikely unless Graham Greene was running the FBI instead of J. Edgar Hoover. But when Baldwin died I applied to the FBI for any files they might have on him. I was informed there were 609 pages "pertaining to deceased author James Baldwin" at FBI headquarters in Washington, with 105 pages of cross-references, 1,000 pages at the New York field office, another 20 at the Los Angeles office and 16 in San Francisco, making a total of 1,750 pages. If all these pages are "determined to be releasable"—which could take a long time, apparently—perhaps there will be some reference to that Baptist minister. Rip Torn showed me an FBI report that he had obtained under the Freedom of Information Act that stated "James Baldwin and others castigated the Attorney General and the Department of Justice." Torn was sure his own FBI surveillance began after that meeting. Baldwin's surveillance was something that worried him for years—and his lovers, too—and helped to persuade him to make a permanent home in the south of France.

The Washington march was on August 28, the aftermath kept him busy, and then on September 15 came the bombing of a Birmingham Sunday school, killing four black children. Baldwin, who had a special feeling for children, perhaps because he realized now he would never have any of his own, was deeply shocked. Wearing a black armband, he held a somber press conference with Bayard Rustin and declared: "We are all responsible for Birmingham. President Kennedy *and* his brother and *both* political parties." Offered a container of coffee after a series of newspaper and television interviews, he said, "I need scotch."

He took a break on Fire Island at the summer home of Lee Strasberg, the head of the Actors Studio, and went back to finishing the play that his family had read in Puerto Rico. His mother accompanied him to do the cooking and she became used to his writing through the night and sleeping until noon. A very religious woman, she was worried about his religious attitude but was pleased he at least played spirituals on his record player. She hadn't yet got used to the change in him—that the very shy little boy she had protected from her husband had grown up able to sway large crowds, though he confided to her that behind his public act he was really still very shy. Sometimes watching all the pressures on him—his late hours, his drinking, the people around him all the time—she said quietly, "I wish Jimmy could get married and settle down."

By this time James Silberman had left Dial Press to join Random House, and Baldwin's new editor, Christopher Lehmann-Haupt, came with Richard and Victoria Baron to visit him. They had a long relaxed day and even went a walk on the beach with "the usual banter about race prejudice," Lehmann-Haupt recalled. "I remember Baldwin's mother was shy and devoted to him. I think we talked about our favorite writers and I asked him what he thought of certain writers, but I don't remember the conversation in detail . . . I admired the rhetoric of *The Fire Next Time* but found him extremely disappointing as a novelist. I never worked on a book with him because I soon left Dial to review books for the New York *Times.*"

When Baldwin returned home from Fire Island he took a cab rather than the subway that his mother wanted to take, explaining to her that people recognized him on the subways, asked for autographs or to borrow money and talked about their troubles, "and I have enough of my own." The third act of the play was one of them.

In early October he was in Selma, Alabama, with brother David to help James Forman, the SNCC executive secretary, launch a voter-registration drive. Baldwin stood outside the courthouse observing several hundred black applicants waiting in line and risking losing jobs or other reprisals. There were attempts to intimidate them as they waited, and Baldwin became more and more emotional. With his flair for drama, he imagined himself being killed by white racists, but his rising fear only made him more vocal, more eager to stay. It was as if he needed a constant state of tension, of conflict, of confrontation—even danger. His presence meant big media coverage of the event, and he made sure photographers and reporters recorded what the black applicants had to endure. After the Kennedy meeting, which he had accidentally or on purpose leaked to the media, and the Washington march, he had become an even bigger celebrity and media star. Everything he did was news, and he made use of this to publicize the Movement.

But being in the front line down South, the strain soon began to tell on him. Local whites enraged him as "mindless" and "like parrots." The police with their guns and helmets were frightening until you realized they were "terrified" themselves. He detested the belligerent sheriff, Big Jim Clark, and his deputies. His feelings rose to such a pitch that he bought a bottle of whiskey and retired to a local SNCC office to cool off. His fear was being "swallowed up by rage." He felt as if he were on the edge of giving up all self-control and letting hatred sweep him away. He steeled himself. Everyone waited for an angry confrontation between the tiny fiery Baldwin and Sheriff Big Jim, but the deputies kept the angry Baldwin at a distance. He stayed in Selma as long as possible, but he could only take the South for so long. No wonder, he thought as he had before, that his stepfather had left to go north.

Now came the assassination of President Kennedy—Baldwin called it "a tremendous loss." He didn't exactly consider Kennedy a friend of blacks, but he was a man of the twentieth century, which was rare in American politics. "You could argue with him. He could hear. He began to see. There was no reason for him, a Boston millionaire's son, to know more about blacks than anybody else. But he could listen. Imagine fighting with Eisenhower about it. You would have to be out of your mind to try. But with Kennedy you could." He hadn't seen Robert Kennedy since "that stormy day," but "if some of the things we were trying to say that day had been heard—I would go to my grave with this conviction—the president would not be dead. A country which can blow off the president's head can do anything, and if we don't do something about it right away, we may turn out to be a worse disaster for the fate of nations than Germany." He was told that when Martin Luther King heard the news about Kennedy, he said to his wife, Coretta, "I don't think I'm going to live to reach forty." Baldwin said vehemently, "I can't deal with that. They wouldn't dare. No, anybody but Martin."

He was interviewed frequently about Kennedy's assassination and about his successor, Texan Lyndon Johnson. When an interviewer suggested the new president's statements "showed great hope," Baldwin replied that he himself was "a very tight, disaffected Harlem cat and I have heard a lot of public statements." He was then asked to define "tight," and he explained it meant "when you walk out of your door in the morning you are not sure whether you will get back in it at night. You have got to face whatever you have to face all day long. And hope you get home. Every day, twenty-four hours of every day."

In December he was traveling again, much further afield this time. He was back in Africa, part of an American group attending the celebration for Kenya's independence in Nairobi. With him were Sidney Poitier, Harry Belafonte and Thurgood Marshall, who was to be the first black on the Supreme Court and who had acted as adviser to the African delegation at the first Kenya constitutional talks in London earlier that year. Baldwin noted that Kenya, about the size of Texas, had roughly eight million Africans and sixty thousand Europeans. How much simpler the racial problem back home would be, he thought, if American blacks were similarly in such a majority! But he still wasn't ready to write about Africa, either in fiction or non-fiction. When he did, he had to be well-informed, to understand truly and not leave himself open to any African mockery as Richard Wright had done—*he thinks he's white.* Africa was still too remote, too complex—too mysterious. He didn't want to write just an I-was-there article; he wanted to relate, to identify, to be a meaningful observer. That kind of intimate understanding was still, he felt, beyond him.

14

Baldwin on Broadway

ELIA KAZAN gave James Baldwin the idea for *Blues for Mister Charlie.* When they were working together on *JB* and *Sweet Bird of Youth* Kazan suggested he should write a play based on the much-publicized case of Emmett Till, a black youth who was murdered in Mississippi in 1955 for allegedly whistling at a white woman. The accused killer was acquitted. "I suggested a basic structure for the play," Kazan said. "Jimmy liked it and began to work."

Two years later, in 1961, he had enough written so that when he had dinner with an English dramatist, Laurence Dobie, in London he staged several scenes in Dobie's model theater. Baldwin was puzzled why the Emmett Till case "pressed on my mind so hard." He had no wish to write another play—"there were enough people around already telling me that I couldn't write novels"—but he began to realize that his fear of the theater "masked a much deeper fear," a fear that he "would never be able to draw a valid portrait of the murderer." Such people in life baffled and terrified him and, "with one part of my mind at least," he hated them and would be willing to kill them. Yet, "with another part of my mind" he knew the murderer was a human being to be under-stood—"I am aware that no man is a villain in his own eyes."

The play became a challenge to control his hatred of Emmett Till's killer, of that kind of southern racist, sufficiently to create him as a believable character. For it was not only Emmett Till's killer; he had in mind, too, the killer of his friend, Medgar Evers, who had been shot to death in June, 1963, by a white man in front of his home in Jackson, Mississippi, while his wife and children watched. When Medgar Evers was killed, Baldwin said, "something entered into me which I cannot describe, but it was then that I resolved that nothing under heaven would prevent me from getting this play done. We are walking in terrible darkness here, and this is one man's attempt to bear witness to the reality and the power of light." When *Blues for Mister Charlie* was published by Dial Press as a book at the same time it was produced on Broadway, Baldwin dedicated it "To the Memory of Medgar Evers and his wife and his children and to the memory of the dead children of Birmingham."

The staging of *Blues for Mister Charlie,* however, involved almost as much behind-the-scenes drama as the Robert Kennedy meeting. The start of the trouble was the launching of a new repertory theater as part of New York's Lincoln Center. Lee Strasberg and the Actors Studio had expected to be invited to join the new theater. Not only were they excluded, but Elia Kazan, an old rival of Strasberg, had been selected to be in charge. Lincoln Center and the Actors Studio thus became competitors. Kazan assumed that since he had given Baldwin the idea for *Blues for Mister Charlie,* he would be able to present it at Lincoln Center. "I was eager, as I prepared to launch our repertory theater's program," Kazan said, "to have a play about blacks, written by a black. The whole Lincoln Center institution and its program was altogether too lily-white, and still is. Jimmy and I reached an understanding," and then Kazan went off to Greece to make a film assuming all was well. "I didn't feel I had to hold Jimmy's hand as he wrote the Emmett Till play. But acquiring a play from a playwright is like a love affair: If you allow a vacuum to persist, someone else will get in. Rip Torn did."

Rip Torn told me, "Elia Kazan felt the Actors Studio had outlived its usefulness, but I wanted to put new life into it and form our own theater. Molly Kazan [Elia Kazan's wife] was critical of Jimmy's play. She said at the start: 'He doesn't have a play, only a title,' and I repeated this to him and it pissed him off." Baldwin was also informed that there were no blacks on the board at Lincoln Center, and Elia Kazan had to admit that was true—"It was a super-white group, all businessmen dabbling in the arts." So when Kazan returned from Greece he found, he said, that Rip Torn had "influenced Jimmy to give the play I'd suggested to the Actors Studio theater group. I was mad as hell but didn't ask Jimmy for an explanation. He casually offered two: first, that I was too much like his father and he wanted to be on his own, not under my influence; second, that Lincoln Center had no blacks on its board. The second reason was my own for wanting that play; the first I could do nothing about. Rip taking that play away from me was an entrepreneurial triumph for the Actors Studio Theater and for Lee [Strasberg]; it was sweet revenge. I swallowed my anger, decided to still be Jimmy's friend."

Baldwin told Rip Torn he wasn't giving his play to Lincoln Center because he didn't want to be "the nigger in the window." He told me that he felt the rightness of his decision had been confirmed when he saw Kazan's production of Arthur Miller's *After the Fall* at Lincoln Center. Kazan and Miller, once good friends, had been estranged since Kazan had cooperated with the congressional committee, and this represented a reunion. The play also included a character very much like Miller's former wife, Marilyn Monroe, who had died of an overdose of drugs nearly two years before. Baldwin thought the play as self-indulgent a "white fantasy" as *JB* had been and the Monroe character "absurdly patronizing," and he had walked out of the play in the middle. He fancied Kazan had a "blind spot" regarding certain "paternal white plays." He also considered that Kazan had influenced Tennessee Williams too much to change and rewrite, "and I didn't want to go through that with him." When I mentioned Baldwin's attitude toward *After the Fall* to Kazan he replied, "Almost everybody in the intellectual group in New York had a poor view of the play. I thought the only good part was about Marilyn Monroe."

Frank Corsaro was chosen to direct the play for the Actors Studio, and Rip Torn had the major role of the racist killer. Corsaro had been at De Witt Clinton High School in the class behind Baldwin's, "but he was someone you noticed." They met for the first time at the Actors Studio. Corsaro recalled Norman Mailer being there, too. "Jimmy was a combination of coquette, preacher boy and arrant wit all in one—in other words, a cunt. And when he and Norman were together it was like the two of them were wrestling for position, but always with a smile on Norman's face. They never went at it openly, but I knew Baldwin hated him with a passion. Norman didn't express hatred for Jimmy, just a kind of ironic sense of the occasion, because Norman occupies a much bigger space in Baldwin's world than Baldwin does in Norman's. But the same thing affected both of them. It's a disease of our time: the image, the media, becomes your raison d'être."

Rip Torn said: "When we were deciding to do *Blues,* there was a very crucial vote. There was really a tremendous battle over whether we should do it or not. Some thought it would be an end of funding [for the Actors Studio] from the Ford Foundation. Arthur Penn said even if we don't go forward, this theater is all we have and maybe the only thing we will be remembered for. Lee Strasberg had been sick, nursing his bronchial attacks. Every time there was a crisis, Lee always went to bed. When we were going to vote on *Blues* he had to rush away to the airport to catch a plane. But he phoned from the airport and his wife Paula said Lee is voting that you do the play. I could hear his voice on the phone in the background. The trouble was Jimmy and Frank Corsaro didn't get along. Frank's a wonderful director, but he felt a certain reserve about *Blues.* I think he knew he didn't want the rough language. I always urged Jimmy to write his vision even if we didn't agree with it."

Corsaro recalled: "The play was a genuine effort on Jimmy's part to balance the racial budget in the middle of a hotbed of emotion. He was trying to write not an agitprop piece but a play that balanced the struggle between the two sides. All of our endeavors were toward helping him to achieve that. The first version I saw was too extreme, almost flagrantly anti-white, although there were intimations of something more. We got together with Baldwin, and because on the other side of his paranoia Baldwin was astute enough to see the value of our suggestions, he agreed to rewrite it. I lived on West Twentieth Street, and he was nearby. Every night I went around to meetings at Baldwin's, where he always had a group of acolytes and fellow travelers. He enjoyed that adulation and attention enormously, and who wouldn't? He was always so full of energy and we talked about race and what was happening, but primarily about the play. I tried to encourage and help him continue the development of the play along the lines we had discussed, maintaining a sane view of the whole racial issue and trying to make it balanced. The difficulty and often the annoyance of dealing with him was that his attention was often taken away by other persons and I would have to cool my heels waiting until he was ready to get back to work. But he did get some work done on the revisions that was gratifying.

"The great shocker," said Corsaro, "was when, out of the blue, one night at a meeting at Strasberg's home Baldwin arrived with an aide-de-camp and flatly announced it was no longer feasible or tenable to write the play in the way discussed that was going to balance the judgment and equalize the fight, and it had to be an anti-white play, as he put it. I don't recall the name of the person Baldwin brought with him, but it was clearly someone Baldwin paid some attention to in such matters. He was simply a supportive figure and we were shocked by Jimmy's announcement because we thought we were onto something very valuable. What was the remedy for this difference of opinion? When questioned, he wouldn't discuss it. He was quite adamant and made it clear if I maintained my stance, I couldn't continue as the director. I wasn't interested in doing any hellfire-and-brimstone play. Some very harsh words were said and an effort made to equalize the situation, but he seemed not willing to listen, almost as if he had been indoctrinated by the militant leaders of the day. It seemed he wasn't speaking as himself, but was speaking *for*— as a spokesman. The result was I banned myself from the play. I asked Strasberg whether the Studio was going to go ahead with the play although we had so many reservations about it, and he felt we had to go along because James Baldwin was James Baldwin and somehow the Studio would benefit merely by producing

James Baldwin at the time *Go Tell It on The Mountain* was published in 1953, when he was twenty-nine. *(Photograph credit: William Rossa Cole)*

In Paris in 1963 *(above)* with Kaylie, daughter of James Jones, the author of *From Here to Eternity*. At the home he bought for his mother on West 71st Street *(right)* in late 1975, with James Monroe Parker, an artist friend of the Baldwin family.

JAMES BALDWIN, author of JUST ABOVE MY HEAD. The novel, a Featured
Alternate of The Literary Guild, will be published by The Dial Press on
September 20, 1979 ($12.95). Photo by Max Petrus

Posing in an exotic suit *(right)* for Dial Press' publicity campaign for the last novel. *(Photograph credit: Jerry Bauer)* The picture above also appeared on the back of the novel's jacket. *(Photograph credit: Max Petrus)*

JAMES BALDWIN, author of JUST ABOVE MY HEAD.
Published by The Dial Press, September 20, 1979
($12.95). Photo Credit: Jerry Bauer.

Professor Baldwin lectur-
ing students *(left and below)* at the University of
Massachusetts in 1984,
three years before he died.
*(Photograph credits: University
of Massachusetts Photographic
Services)*

The expressive hands, thoughtful intent, and that ageless, gap-toothed grin. *(Photograph credits: University of Massachusetts Photographic Services)*

James Baldwin, author of THE EVIDENCE OF
THINGS NOT SEEN, published by Henry Holt
and Company, October, 1985. @J. Phil Samuell.

The publisher has changed and so has Baldwin—in the six years since his
last novel he turned gray but didn't lose his Biblical prophet-look. This
was how his last original book was publicized, two years before he died.
(Photograph credit: J. Phil Samuell)

it. But it was a mistake because the play was a betrayal of Baldwin's own original purposes. Obviously there was enough venom in Jimmy against the white man to make him write what he did. But the play became much more melodramatic than it needed to be. It lacked the kind of compassion he showed in all his essays. His acute sense of observation about interracial relationships was twisted out of shape in the play. He was a man who walked his own thin line between extreme self-hatred and adulation. He lost his cool very rapidly, for all his sagacity. He remained to me a poor orphan child emotionally, and I think that kept me related to him up to a point, but my experience with him over his play was a bad one."

Lee Strasberg then brought in Burgess Meredith to replace Frank Corsaro as director and tried to develop a relationship with Baldwin himself even though he was an aloof man. "Jimmy and Lee were very different temperamentally," said Rip Torn, "but Jimmy was very fam-ily-oriented and Lee always had a kitchen scene at home. We always ended up talking in the kitchen. Jimmy liked that. Strasberg worked a lot with Jimmy and I think he was very valuable in what he said to Jimmy. I suggested the staging should be more Shakespearean and Jimmy did write some wonderful arias, soliloquies, for the main charac-ters. Strasberg, however, didn't want David Baldwin in the play. I fought for David. He's a good actor, an exceptional man with great charm on and off the stage. He's very skilled and disciplined. Jimmy's answer was: 'I wrote the play!' He kept saying that when he got angry. He knew what and who he wanted. I brought the cast in originally and fought for Jimmy's vision against other people who wanted to contain it or change it. I expected to direct the play, but Jimmy wanted me to play Lyle, the racist murderer, instead of directing it. I knew men like Lyle. Southerners can be warm, but they can change and seem like another person. Jimmy told me he had written my role with love and I said if that is love, I wouldn't like to see one written with hate. But he was a poet."

Cheryl Crawford, an experienced Broadway producer and one of the original directors of the Actors Studio, had been in favor of a workshop production first to give Baldwin a chance to polish the play for Broadway, but she was voted down. She then objected to "some of the raw language, particularly 'motherfucker.'"

"But that's every other word," protested Burgess Meredith.

"We'll get killed by the critics," replied Crawford.

"It's not my problem. Talk to the author."

"That word simply has to be deleted."

"So talk to Baldwin."

Rip Torn remembered attending one reading of the play without the "raw language" at the request of Cheryl Crawford, and Baldwin glared at him as if he were responsible. "It was like salad without the dressing," said Rip Torn, "and Jimmy said, 'They've ruined my play.' I replied it's not formed like marble, it's just one reading." The "raw language" was put back in. Cheryl Crawford had another complaint—"the time necessary to condense the play (it originally ran for five hours) made it difficult to set a date for opening and to build up any advance sale. To make it possible for a subway audience to come, a top price of $4.80 a ticket was set. We didn't expect to attract the carriage trade." She also worried about the progress of rehearsals—"Rip Torn, who played one of the leading parts, and Burgess Meredith did not agree on how the part should be played. I was called in several times to try to smooth things over."

Rip Torn said, "I was fired three times from *Blues*. I was marched around as if to an execution. Burgess fired me. Jimmy came in and heard his version. They wanted me to change my performance and make the character more craven. Who are you trying to preach to? I asked. The converted? The agony of the character of Lyle as Baldwin said is the center of the play. He wasn't craven, he had great potential. I hoped to persuade Jimmy to hear my side, but his mind was made up. It's not my nature to run after Jimmy or Strasberg or whoever."

Elia Kazan in his autobiography, *A Life*, described how Baldwin twenty years later told him that he had been dissatisfied with the rehearsals and, according to Kazan, he partly blamed Rip Torn, who, Baldwin reportedly told him, not only thought he was directing the play but thought he'd written it. Since Lee Strasberg and Cheryl Crawford couldn't or wouldn't fire him, Baldwin said he did so. One day as he approached the theater, he said, he saw Rip Torn walking toward the stage door. "Remember," commented Kazan, "the story of what followed is Jimmy's; Rip may not remember it this way." (Rip Torn, in fact, denied the accuracy of the story.) "Jimmy says he stopped Rip and asked him where he was going. Rip answered, 'To rehearsal.' Jimmy reminded Rip that he was no longer in the cast, but Rip continued on toward the stage door." Baldwin "needed little firing up," added Kazan. "He acknowledged that Rip was bigger and very likely stronger, so he wouldn't fight him, but if Rip went into the theater, Jimmy would kill him. Rip hesitated, then seeing that Jimmy literally meant what he'd said, he turned around and didn't go through the stage door. Jimmy did. He was asking himself who the hell had invited Rip to come back to the cast after Jimmy had fired him? It had to be Lee Strasberg, the theater's artistic director.

"Now Jimmy was in a fury," according to his account to Kazan. "When he bolted through the stage door he knew that, inspired by alcohol and justified anger, he might do something excessive, so in order not to choke Lee, who was on stage, or physically attack Cheryl, who was in the audience, he climbed thirty feet to the top of a tall electrician's 'A' ladder, and there, swaying, as the cast watched with what I'd been told was considerable admiration, he unloaded his rage. The actors, Jimmy said, were not too happy with how rehearsals were going either; they were ready to applaud him." So there Baldwin remained, thirty feet in the air on the single ladder length that came out of the top of the 'A', swaying from the violence of his emotion, and shouting down at Strasberg that he thought him incompetent "to the point of sabotage" and so on. Finally finished, high up on the swaying ladder, Baldwin waited for Strasberg's reply. Everybody waited. Strasberg's lips tightened, he looked furious, but in Kazan's account, "from the seat at the side of the stage where Lee had been watching the rehearsal came a silence to impress Jehovah, a calm that was, of itself, a threat—which was Lee's way. When he finally started to respond, it was too late. Jimmy had scrambled down the ladder and streaked out the stage door like a bolt of black lightning, and from there to his favorite bar."

Although Rip Torn had no recollection of the confrontation outside the stage door—"Jimmy couldn't fire me, he didn't have the authority"—there were many accounts of the ladder incident, which was gossiped about for weeks among Broadway theater people. Cheryl Crawford remembered it this way in her autobiography, *One Naked Individual: My Fifty Years in the Theater:* "On the bare stage with the whole company present, Baldwin climbed to the top of a tall stage ladder to shout a long diatribe about the ineptitude of the Studio's work. All of us, including Strasberg, looked up, silently waiting for him to tire. He finally did, but he stayed above us on his perch, while Strasberg answered him." David Garfield in *A Player's Place: The Story of the Actors Studio* reports there were "several stormy sessions, including one afternoon when Baldwin mounted a ladder to give the members of the company and the theater's leaders a lengthy stream of vilification over the Studio's incompetence."

Baldwin made a bar near the ANTA Theater where *Blues* was being rehearsed into his rebel headquarters, and there was always a large group around him, including the Baldwin supporters among Studio members. He was in such a constant high state of emotion that Rip Torn wondered if he was taking more than his usual scotch. "I thought Jimmy must be inspired with alcohol *and* amphetamines," he told me, and then quickly added: "I may have been wrong. I saw him popping pills but they may have been medication for his nerves. I just don't know. He was often very excited, but that was his nature, and the play was a very emotional occasion for him. Jimmy was a very nice person." Baldwin always talked to me as if he wouldn't dream of touching drugs except for medical reasons. In his early Village days he occasionally smoked marijuana but much preferred scotch. At times he took some form of tranquilizer when he felt close to what he termed a "nervous breakdown."

What may have encouraged Rip Torn's suspicion he might be taking amphetamines was his almost hysterical insistence that *Blues* was not only being misstaged and misacted, but mismanaged at the box office. At the time Torn attributed Baldwin's charges to an overheated imagination, a touch of paranoia that could have come from drugs. "Jimmy reckoned someone was stealing. We were full every night but we weren't making money. I felt Jimmy was duped. But later some people who were around then were indicted for something else, I believe. I apologized to Jimmy later for not taking him more seriously and he said he shouldn't have tried to fire me." As Elia Kazan commented, "Rip did return to the cast and did open in the play. How this was permitted by the dissatisfied author he didn't say, but it probably happened like many things in the theater, by waiting the trouble out."

Blues, coming after a hectic year, had exhausted Baldwin. Set in Plaguetown, USA—the raging plague was race with the power to destroy every human relationship—the play was "the tragedy of the whites," and in writing it, revising it, cutting it and polishing it he had tried to control his own feelings about the South. He wrote and rewrote Lyle's soliloquy: "I've done a lot of wrong things in my life and I ain't never going to be perfect . . ." Had he acted as a witness—or as a prosecutor? Had Frank Corsaro been right when he said it was a polemic? Whites tended to be critical, blacks to say, "Right on!" He was dressed in expensive, colorful clothes—Broadway clothes, someone said —but he looked a weary, lonely figure in spite of all the people around him. His intimate, trusted circle had been broken up and he missed it. Brother David was in the cast and busy with rehearsals. Sister Gloria was busy with her new African husband, though she still helped him as a part-time secretary. Lucien had become very friendly with the leading lady of *Blues,* Diana Sands, and Baldwin saw less and less of him. He appointed Jerome Smith, the young Freedom Rider who had been so "straight from the shoulder" with Robert Kennedy, as a special consultant on the play and often had at his elbow Robert Cordier, who had directed plays and films in Paris, and was the musical coordinator. But he missed the full-time backup of David, Gloria and Lucien, who had an intuitive understanding of his needs and feelings.

To add to the pressures on him, he'd apparently also had some trouble with the State Department. According to Kazan, Baldwin told him he had to go to Washington during the rehearsals "to demand to know why he'd been refused a visa to go to Europe." He contacted Hubert Humphrey, then vice-president, about it. A television documentary had been made comparing Baldwin's and Humphrey's lives. Christopher Lehmann-Haupt, when he was Baldwin's editor at Dial, said Richard Baron had considered the idea of getting Baldwin to make a book out of the documentary. When they talked to Baldwin about it, said Lehmann-Haupt, "it was quickly clear that he didn't want to write the book." But work on the documentary had introduced him to Humphrey so he took his troubles with the State Department to the vice-president. According to Baldwin's account via Kazan, Humphrey told him he'd been refused a visa "because every time you go to Europe you besmirch America." Baldwin answered, "When I read that a black meeting place in Alabama has been bombed, tell me what to say, Mr. Humphrey." Kazan added: "Jimmy got his visa and, returning to New York, had a couple of drinks on the train to celebrate, then went immediately to the theater where his play was being rehearsed."

The only problem with this story is that, according to the State Department, it doesn't make sense because Baldwin could have traveled to Europe on his passport, and if he needed a visa for some country, then it was up to that country, not the State Department, to decide to grant one or refuse him. When I asked if his passport had ever been confiscated like Paul Robeson's, a State Department spokeswoman told me that was a private matter, but I could apply for an answer under the Freedom of Information Act. I was informed that that office in the State Department already had over three thousand requests covered by the act and so there was no telling when they could get around to answering my question.

Baldwin continued to claim the State Department harassed him. In an interview in Italy in 1965 he said the State Department tried to stop *Blues* from being presented in Europe. "Some officials in Washington actually believe *The Fire Next Time* caused Watts," he said, referring to the riot in the Los Angeles ghetto. "The State Department thinks I'm unpatriotic, that I besmirch my government abroad." He also noted that some American embassies in Europe showed him no friendliness and that several of his books had been kept out of U.S. Information Service libraries overseas. He stated his attitude later in an open letter defending Stokely Carmichael, a young black militant: "The Government has the duty to warn me of the dangers I may encounter if I travel to hostile territory—though they never said anything about the probable results of my leaving Harlem to go downtown and never said anything about my travels to Alabama—but it does not have the right to use my passport as a political weapon against me, as a means of bringing me to heel. These are terror tactics."

* * *

Because it was James Baldwin with the added news interest of his Broadway debut, there was a lot of preopening-night publicity about *Blues*. The New York *Herald-Tribune* published a photograph of him sitting at the side of Burgess Meredith during a rehearsal. He had a hand to his mouth in a tense, emotional gesture, and was wearing large dark glasses. The *Herald-Tribune* pointed out that *Blues* was being presented in the same theater as was *JB* five years before when Baldwin had sat in rehearsals beside Elia Kazan. But this time he was the author, and although authors are generally neither seen nor heard at rehearsals, Baldwin sometimes behaved as if he were also the producer and the director. One reason he had so easily accepted another white director after Corsaro withdrew was that Burgess Meredith had little experience of the black southern society depicted so he could always pull rank with Jerome Smith's backup if there was any conflict with the director. Baldwin told the *Herald-Tribune* that he had started writing *Blues* before the murder of Medgar Evers, but "the thing that triggered it, I guess, was Medgar. I knew him well. He was a lovely man. I knew his wife and children." Baldwin pointed out that the top ticket price of $4.80 was "revolutionary in the theater." He liked to observe how many blacks were among those lining up to buy tickets at the box office. *Blues* might bring a record number of blacks to Broadway, more even than his friend Lorraine Hansberry's *A Raisin in the Sun,* though *Raisin* had had the added attraction of Sidney Poitier.

Time magazine concentrated on Diana Sands, "a very promising actress" who had the good luck to emerge when there were more parts for black actors and actresses. She was "a handsome girl with high cheekbones, liquid eyes, and a voice like the woodwind section of an orchestra." One of the highpoints of *Blues* was her "raging soliloquy" after her lover had been murdered by Lyle, still played by Rip Torn. She was consumed by passionate hatred, cursing God's "icy snow-white heaven." Although Time didn't mention it, the young actress also had a zany sense of humor. At a party in the Village before the opening she was to be seen declaiming from the Manhattan telephone directory as if it were Shakespeare. Lucien Happersberger was there paying her a lot of attention. A nervous, anguished Baldwin wandered through the party unable to settle anywhere, chain-smoking and drinking scotch. "I just want the best for Lucien," he told me. An artist friend of his from the Paris days, who had been a drug addict, took him outside on a balcony to ask him for some money. Baldwin inquired later if I thought the man was still on drugs. He seemed so remote, his eyes so unnaturally bright, that I guessed he was. Baldwin seemed very disappointed. "Every time I came back to my hotel in Paris," he said, "I used to find him waiting for me. I never knew whether to give him money or not." Later still his thoughts returned to the play. "Do you know many whites have no idea what 'Mister Charlie' means? I tell them it's a black term for a white man and they look startled or even shocked. What will they make of the play?"

Rip Torn recalled that when *Blues for Mister Charlie* opened on April 23, 1964, Kenneth Tynan, the British drama critic who also wrote for The New Yorker, said: "You could feel the shock waves across the Atlantic." It certainly was a sensation on Broadway. Describing himself as "a wreck," Baldwin was relieved when old friend Mary Painter, to whom he had dedicated *Another Country,* arrived to be by his side on opening night. He took a bow on stage at the end, looking very slight and defenseless, until a wave of applause came to reassure him. There was an opening-night party at Delmonico's. Baldwin danced with Diana Sands and ABC filmed them for a late-night TV program. Jimmy Baldwin rushed over to Ted Kupferman, who was still acting as his lawyer-agent, and said, "You have got to stop them from showing that film." Kupferman recalled: "I knew if I tried to stop ABC it would only make them keener to use it, so I said, 'Great, it will cost you $5,000,' and then they decided not to." Asked why Baldwin took that attitude, Kupferman said he didn't know—"perhaps he didn't want to ruin his reputation as a homosexual."

Baldwin waited up to read the New York *Times* review, which could make or break his play. The critic, Howard Taubman, summed up: "The Actors Studio Theater, which has been stumbling in darkness all season, finally has arrived at something worth doing. Although Mr. Baldwin has not yet mastered all the problems and challenges of the theater, *Blues for Mister Charlie* brings eloquence and conviction to one of the momentous themes of our era." He wrote that the play was not "tidy," its structure was loose, and it made "valid points as if they were clichés." But it throbbed with fierce energy and passion like "a thunderous battle cry," a summons to arms "in this generation's burning cause—the establishment in this country of the Negro's full manhood, with all the perquisites of that simple and lofty station." Baldwin's play sang the blues "for the white man's moral crisis as much as for the Negro's frustration and agony." The fundamental forces that led to the murder of the young black man in the play were what concerned Baldwin. "Even more he seeks to express the outraged thoughts and emotions that blazed within seemingly placid Negroes for so many deceptive years." Baldwin reached "his most searing moment of preachment" when the father of the murdered young man, who was a black minister played by Percy Rodriguez, speaks a eulogy over his son's coffin. Struggling with his hatred and despair in a manner that Baldwin very much identified with, the father spoke with the "wrath of the prophet," crying "What shall we tell our children?" and he answered himself: "Learn to walk again like men. Like men! Amen!"

The New York *Times* critic also praised a crucial scene between the son, played by Al Freeman, Jr., and Rip Torn's Lyle—"both men play their roles admirably, and they charge this scene with electricity." Diana Sands delivered her "impassioned incantation" with "shattering emotion." A key scene was between the black-minister father and "the only decent white man," played "with a touching decency and humility" by Pat Hingle—the minister warned his white friend that the truth must be faced for the white man's sake, not the black's.

The review was enthusiastic enough to ensure a run, but undoubtedly many of the Broadway regulars wanting escapist entertainment would stay away. But what concerned Baldwin was one comment of the New York *Times* critic: "Mr. Baldwin knows how the Negroes think and feel, but his inflexible, Negro-hating southerners are stereotypes. Southerners may talk and behave as he suggests, but in the theater they are caricatures" except for "the only decent white man's" recollection of a tender relationship with a young black woman, which is "Mr. Baldwin at the top of his form." After all his creative struggle and anguish, had he ended with white "stereotypes" and "caricatures," or could the white critic not accept a portrayal of white racists as they were? Would it have been better to struggle with his own hatred and despair over white southerners in the form of a novel? He could have conveyed more of their ancestral slave-owning roots, their upbringing, their thoughts and the cruel day-to-day routine of an officially segregated society which New York critics probably knew nothing about. While he waited for other reviews, he was taut, irritable. He had lost several pounds he couldn't spare from his lean figure. One night in his favorite Village restaurant, El Faro, his hangout when he had lived on Horatio Street, a macho young white man was too aggressive. "Ride into the sunset!" Baldwin snapped.

He had noted that blacks in the opening night audience had responded much more than whites. The murdered black man simply wasn't sympathetic enough to many whites, an attitude reflected in some of the reviews. Baldwin said angrily, "This was a southern black youth who had been north and learned different ways. He came back south no longer willing to submerge his own personality in the system of segregation. He was brash and even insolent with whites who treated him as an inferior 'boy' who should know his place, you know. In a perfect gentle world, he had no right to behave and talk the way he did to assert his own right to be himself. But did Lyle have the right to kill him? Let the critics answer me that because that's the basic question of the play." Baldwin also defended himself against making southern whites worse than they were, targets of his hatred. "I've written nothing as horrible and subhuman and grotesque and outrageous as things I've actually witnessed down South."

Cheryl Crawford said of the play's reception, "The reviewers praised the performances of Rip Torn, Pat Hingle, Diana Sands and Al Freeman, Jr.; in fact, they praised the entire company and 'the fierce energy and passion' of the play, but criticized its lack of structure and the simplistic characterizations of the southern whites." David Garfield in *A Player's Place: The Story of the Actors Studio* reported much the same: "There was a generally enthusiastic reception although there were reservations about the play's sprawling structure and its stereotypes of southern rednecks but high praise for the 'fierce energy and passion' of the play and for its relevance and authenticity as a shout of protest." The two men who had expected to direct the play but had been dropped, Elia Kazan and Frank Corsaro, expressed disappointment. Kazan commented: "The play was quite well received by the New York critics, always with respect, at times with kind concern. I don't believe that the script—which, I've been told, was five hours long to begin with—was even properly prepared for rehearsals." He said he would have persuaded Baldwin to do much more rewriting and polishing. Corsaro still found the play "a distorted view" and, he added, "that was why the reviews were so mixed and the play lasted only a short time."

Time magazine reported that *Blues* was "a hard play for a white man to take. Brutally and sometimes eloquently, it tells every white man how much every Negro hates him, and enough of them have stayed away from the ANTA Theater to put *Mister Charlie* in imminent danger of folding." Cheryl Crawford said: "Although the play was well attended—eventually the audience came to be composed of about eighty percent blacks—there were twenty-seven actors in the cast, and with the low ticket prices we lost money every week." A provisional closing notice was put up stating that *Blues* would close after its forty-fourth performance. Baldwin's dream of a Broadway hit that could be the basis of a trust fund for his family was not to be fulfilled. He responded almost as if it were a conspiracy by white racists to close *Blues* and he turned trying to save the play into a personal crusade. "BALDWIN FIGHTS FOR PLAY'S LIFE" headlined the New York *Times.* The vicar of a nearby Protestant Episcopal Church headed a group that paid for an advertisement in New York papers that said that if *Blues* "can be saved, more than it will be saved." Show business stars, including Paul Newman, Sammy Davis, Jr., and Ossie Davis, appealed for support on radio and television. Handbills were distributed all over the city and sound trucks took the message to all the boroughs. Roy Wilkins, the executive director of the NAACP, wrote a letter on NAACP stationery appealing to NAACP members to see the play.

"I haven't got the carriage trade," Baldwin told reporters. "They think it's a play about civil rights. The play is about a state of mind and the relationship of people to each other, helplessly corrupted and destroyed by this insanity you call color. I must work to keep the play alive because I don't like to go down without a fight." A week's break-even figure was $23,000, but no week's takings had come close to that. With Lucien's help—he now had the title of international manager—Baldwin had moved into a cavernous seven-room apartment on West End Avenue that became the headquarters of the Save *Blues* campaign. Baldwin claimed two experienced producers were standing by to take over if necessary and an off-Broadway theater was available if needed. But a temporary rescue for *Blues* came from an unexpected source. Two daughters of New York's multimillionaire governor Nelson Rockefeller went to see the play with their husbands, and the result was that both presented checks for $5,000 to the Actors Studio to keep *Blues* open. The $10,000 would provide a two-week reprieve. One sister was "particularly impressed with the way Baldwin attempts to deal with both sides" and the other sister, who was married to a minister who was a dedicated civil rights supporter, praised *Blues* for "the distinction of being both an excellent work of art and a play with the deepest social implications." Other donations were promised, including $500 from Sammy Davis, Jr., and ticket sales rose rapidly. Baldwin had fallen back to saying, "I'm not concerned with the success or failure of the play. I just want to shock the people and make them think." But now he revived his dream of a long run—perhaps the two-week reprieve would be long enough for *Blues* to catch on.

He took off for Europe convinced that he had done his best, but that he could stand no more. Cheryl Crawford said all the efforts kept the play running longer, "but by the end of the summer the theater had been booked for another production and we could not raise the $8,000 required to move. We had played to a consistent loss for four months. I cabled Baldwin, who was then in Beirut, that we had to close. He cabled back vehemently and at length, protesting that whatever it cost to move 'the most underproduced show in recent Broadway history' a few blocks was not too much; that the show had proved it had an audience. He absolutely rejected our reasons for closing and threatened to take us to court. He finished with: 'The only cause which I will accept is your declaration of bankruptcy. Home in a few days. Best regards.' " Cheryl Crawford added: "We closed. Nothing happened. The erupting volcano was a smokepot."

But that was not the end of *Blues.* The Actors Studio received an invitation from Peter Daubeny, an English producer, to take part in a World Theater Festival at the Aldwych Theatre in London. Famous companies from many countries were coming there to present two weeks of repertory. The Actors Studio decided to take its productions of *Blues* and Chekhov's *The Three Sisters,* but a number of actors were unavailable. "Since Rip Torn disagreed violently with Burgess Meredith's rerehearsing of *Blues* and with Baldwin's changes and cuts made for the English censor," said Cheryl Crawford, "Ralph Waite took over his part. Diana Sands, who had been so brilliant in the play, was in a success and unable to leave." Crawford remembered the London opening of *Blues* as "a disaster." There wasn't enough time or equipment to light the production properly, and the play was performed "in ghostly, gloomy half-light." During the second act, members of the fascist British National Party began shouting, "Filth! Why don't you go back to Africa?" To make matters worse, she said, "the London critics panned the hell out of it."

Elia Kazan said Baldwin told him that on opening night he waited for London's verdict in a pub near the Aldwych Theatre. "Runners brought him the audience's reaction. Everyone complained about the lighting; the play was being performed in a murky twilight. Half the audience, according to Jimmy's friends, liked the play, the other half was outraged. There were angry shouts from the balcony, including 'Go back to Africa!' from an extreme right-wing group. The write-ups the next morning could not have been much worse." The New York *Times* reported: "Some critics praised Mr. Baldwin's prose but the majority said his drama of racial conflict was so full of hatred that it overrode the message. The *Times of London* said that the author was 'exchanging creative writing for demagogic oratory.' " The London *Times* critic added that "What one had hoped was that if there was any company in the world equipped to dig through Mr. Baldwin's rhetoric to a core of true human feeling, it was the Actors Studio of New York. Nothing of the sort took place in last night's performance and it was with astonishment that one realized that the company, far from deepening the play, were broadening and coarsening it." Kazan commented: "The battle for the play's worth was lost not that night in London, of course, but long before, in the script preparation, the recasting, the chaotic rehearsals and the technical supervision."

Kazan had asked Baldwin about the ladder incident when he had denounced the Studio. "Did Lee ever forgive you for what you did? You humiliated him in front of his cast and you knew that incident would be, for a time, the talk of Broadway, not to Lee's credit but to yours. Did Lee ever hit back at you?" Baldwin replied: "He never said anything about it. Forgot all about it." But Kazan didn't believe it—"I knew Lee better, and I knew that Lee did not forgive him." Strasberg tried to get his revenge in London. Kazan called it an act "that no one involved forgave." In the face of the bad London reviews, Strasberg called a press conference and told the assembled British reporters and drama critics that they must not judge the Actors Studio from the performance of *Blues,* that this production was not representative of the work at the Studio, that they must wait to see his production of *The Three Sisters.* Strasberg said the "unclarity was partly our fault, partly the author's," and he added that Baldwin was also partly to blame that the play "does not sufficiently convey the human conflict."

"This desperate statement," said Kazan, "was a betrayal of a performance, a company and an author." The night of the opening of *The Three Sisters,* Baldwin was drinking in the same pub near the theater with British actor Michael Redgrave and Groucho Marx. An actress who had appeared in *Blues* brought the news: "They booed it." Under the headline "STRASBERG BLAMED IN LONDON FAILURE," the New York *Times* reported that all the London critics had "sharply criticized" what they saw as "an overdirected production" of *The Three Sisters.* Strasberg's wife, Paula, said that when her husband read the London reviews he burst into tears.

Baldwin had not been so involved with the London reception, but the *Blues* experience as a whole had been strangely like that with Kennedy. It had further shaken his belief in the ability of white Americans to face the truth and to change. He was confident he had been accurate in *Blues* and most of *them* had not wanted to hear it. A young black dramatist named LeRoi Jones thought *Blues* marked the point at which White America gave up on Baldwin. Michael Thelwell, a senior in college then and the author of three promising short stories, was being courted by an agent and a publisher to write a novel. The agent said, "This country is ready for a new Negro writer. That fellow Baldwin is finished. Did you see *Blues for Mister Charlie*? Really!" That, said Thelwell, was "profoundly eye-opening to a young Negro who might otherwise have had his head turned." They were the same kind of people who had also told Baldwin, "Come on, Jimmy, you still can't be angry. You've made it, you're big-time now." Of course, like Mark Twain, "pronouncements of [Baldwin's] demise were greatly exaggerated and quite premature," commented Thelwell wryly.

But the times were changing rapidly. Never again, at least in Baldwin's lifetime, would America be so preoccupied with the racial scene as it was in the early sixties. Even then, in 1964, the country's attention was beginning to switch to the growing Vietnam War, which was to become an obsession in the late sixties, obscuring the nation's other problems and dividing Americans, white and black alike. Inevitably James Baldwin's life was affected.

15

The Price of Fame

AUGUST 2, 1964, was James Baldwin's fortieth birthday and he took it very hard, even insisting that he felt much older than forty. The present was affected by everything in your past, he said, and at forty you were more aware of your past than ever before. "I think a person is in sight of his or her death around the age of forty. You see it coming." He hadn't felt that way at thirty, but at forty you were "struck by the fact of your mortality, that it is unlikely you'll live another forty years. So time alters you, actually becoming either an enemy or a friend." He quoted what Henry James had remarked on facing forty: "It's a horrible fact."

The attempts of friends and family to laugh him out of his gloom with a birthday party were unsuccessful. His low mood persisted and, fearful as always about his health, he went for a medical checkup and was told he was exhausted and to cut down drastically on his drinking and smoking. Apart from his draining theatrical experiences, part of his low spirits was probably due to the illness of his friend, Lorraine Hansberry. He had learned she was dying of cancer at thirty-four—she would never even make forty!—and she was someone he had learned to like a lot. They had had many arguments, particularly over history, in her Village apartment. "Just when I was certain that she was about to throw me out, as being altogether too rowdy a type," Baldwin recalled, "she would stand up, her hands on her hips (for these down-home sessions she always wore slacks) and pick up my empty glass as though she intended to throw it at me. Then she would walk into the kitchen, saying with a haughty toss of her head, 'Really, Jimmy, you ain't *right,* child!" He remembered often staggering down her stairs as the sun came up, "usually in the middle of a paragraph and always in the middle of a laugh." He visited her in the hospital. She tried to speak, but she couldn't. "She did not seem frightened or sad, only exasperated that her body no longer obeyed her." She smiled and waved. He remembered the last time he had seen her on her feet. She was dressed all in black with a wide black hat and he complimented her on her radiant looks. He didn't know it then, but she was already dying. She smiled at him. "It helps to develop a serious illness, Jimmy!" and she waved and disappeared. When so gifted an artist died so soon, he said, "one is filled for a long time with a sense of injustice as futile as it is powerful."

Part of Baldwin's birthday gloom was also due to his sense that his youth had receded even farther away and that the much younger men who attracted him were already beginning to treat him as an elder brother or even a father-figure, and he didn't like it. He had been in that kind of relationship with older homosexuals in his Village and Paris days and he didn't care to see the roles reversing. Many of Baldwin's most intimate companions or lovers didn't wish to be interviewed. One middle-aged man who had been twenty when he first became intimately involved with Baldwin said he couldn't possibly share his "secret life with Jimmy." Several did talk providing they weren't identified. They were black, Hispanic, white American and European and they didn't have much in common except Baldwin and a bad memory. Others explained that they didn't trust American society's inconsistent attitude toward homosexual relations and thought they were safer remaining silent. One of the most interesting accounts was by a man who had turned Baldwin down. As he didn't wish to be identified, I checked that he was a reliable witness before interviewing him. He had met James

Baldwin at a publishing party where he had become half-drunk on martinis. When he was leaving he found Baldwin was leaving, too, and suggested they go to a bar for another drink. Several drinks later Baldwin asked him to walk him home. He invited him in for a last drink, and while they were sitting on a couch drinking, Baldwin made a sudden pass at him. "He began to undo my trousers and . . . you know . . . Well, I liked him a lot, but he didn't attract me that way and I pushed him off. He was annoyed so I left. I was struck by how lonely this famous man seemed. In a curious way he reminded me of a woman I had once known; she was plain and she went out of her way to please as if to make up for her looks. I met Baldwin again at a Village party a few months later and I expected him to cut me, pretend he didn't know me, but he came over very friendly and made another pass. It wasn't that I was so attractive, but that he'd been turned down. It hurt his pride, his image of himself. I suppose there was still a little boy inside him trying to prove he wasn't ugly. I made sure I didn't go home with him this time. But it made me feel bad because I liked him a lot as a person and admired him as a writer."

He had found the huge, many-roomed apartment on West End Avenue too lonely unless he was there with a crowd, but Lucien Happersberger had helped him to find a house on West Seventy-first Street. His mother would have one floor, sister Paula another, and he would have the ground-floor apartment, where he hung on one of the walls a big painting by Beauford Delaney of a black kid playing with snowballs.

Raymond Rosenthal met him in the Village, and Baldwin told him happily, "Hi, Ray, I've just bought a house for my mother." Rosenthal accompanied him to a bookstore on Eighth Street that also sold records. Baldwin was looking for some of Duke Ellington's. Old schoolmate Burton Bendow also met him by chance in the Village. "He was with a white couple and they were looking for the Bleecker Tavern. I showed them where it was. A lot of people recognized Jimmy. He had a set polite grin on his face. I could see he was playing a great author dispensing largess. But he was just as friendly as ever to me. He asked if I'd seen Emile Capouya and then he was mobbed in the bar."

Emile Capouya had just been interviewed for a job by Richard Baron at Dial Press, possibly on Baldwin's suggestion, according to Capouya. "I went and talked to Baron, but nothing came of it. But Jimmy's then-agent, Bob Mills, said Jimmy wanted to speak to me and I had to call a certain number—in Cuba! I called the number and Jimmy said, 'Listen, baby, I understand you are talking to Dick Baron. I want to let you know I'm not going to be with that guy much longer.' I told him not to worry, it was just a job. I thought he was warning me he wouldn't grace that place with his presence. He was perfectly good-natured as always. He had a bad reputation for being unreliable with publishers, but he couldn't write to schedule. It wasn't his disorderly life, but he worked and reworked his writing until it was the way he wanted it. The last thing you can usually tell a publisher is that inspiration hasn't struck yet."

During the run of *Blues for Mister Charlie* Baldwin met Billy Dee Williams, who was appearing in *Hallelujah, Baby.* "He saw the show and came back afterwards and we started talking," recalled Billy Dee Williams. "Jimmy was like a gift. He looked at things in very dramatic terms. He was the kind of guy who would get drunk, pissed drunk, and he'd say, 'I don't care for that person.' If he was feeling negative things going on, he wouldn't hesitate to let everyone know. He became very special to me because I learned a great deal from Jimmy. He really understood the poetry of life, the living experience. I'm not that easily impressed. Before you can teach me, you have to give me the feeling you're a master. When I say that, I mean you have to have something really important, with perhaps a little craziness in your ordinary behavior. Jimmy had that. At the time I met Jimmy in the sixties, he was part of a nucleus, one of those characters who were somehow meant to change our lives. At that time people were trying to raise their consciousness in a number of spiritual ways. Jimmy was part of that spiritual, volatile period to me. It wasn't like now, which is very different, so much more hostile.

"Jimmy had great male and female qualities. He could show the bitchiness of the female, but he was more man to me than most men

I have ever met. He had a weird tendency—I understood it because I have it myself—to make dates with three or four different people at the same time, though he couldn't meet them all. He always tried to accommodate people. He couldn't say no. He was always getting into trouble over this. He was very generous. It's part of the greatness of an artist—being a maverick, being difficult sometimes, trying to hold on to a certain kind of freedom. Jimmy reminded me of Molière—the romance, the fun, the comedy. He had a great sense of humor.

"I just wanted to be around him to learn from him. I saved up some money after *Hallelujah, Baby* and accompanied him and his brothers, David and Lover [Wilmer], to Paris and England. I needed to get out of the country. I was sick and tired of racism, and I wanted to go somewhere where nobody was talking about those differences. Jimmy had a favorite saying, 'We're all Sambos of the world.' Those eyes of his! His tendency was to get into trouble a lot. He opened his mouth a lot and, bingo, he was right in the middle of trouble. That whole period reminded me of Molière exposing hypocrisy like him. Jimmy was like my grandmother, who was dramatic like him. He reminded me so much of her. He listened as well as talked, his big eyes darting round watching everything. He took me on that Paris trip to meet Beauford Delaney. Beauford had a garret, small and full of paintings. He gave me 'The Bird,' showing Charlie Parker. I also met Simone Signoret with Jimmy in California. A tough, strong woman. I had read about people like her in Paris—socialists, communists, always talking, arguing about things. I also met Marlon Brando through Jimmy. Another great moment. We're both Aries. I spent two hours in his study talking to him. Those days now all seem like a dream, but talking about Jimmy brings them back."

Playing both secretary and wife was exhausting for sister Gloria, who had shared all the ups and downs of *Blues* as well as handling his huge mail and the many phone calls, invitations, inquiries and problems arising from missed appointments. David Leeming, the young lecturer Baldwin had met in Istanbul, was in New York and so he was recruited to help out with the growing secretarial chores. While Baldwin was away lecturing, there arrived at the new home on West Seventy-first

Street a photograph of the famous portrait of Henry James painted by John Singer Sargent on the occasion of James' seventieth birthday. The photograph had been signed by both James and Sargent, and was sent to Baldwin by Michael James, a grandson of Henry James' brother, William James, who had been impressed by a civil rights speech he had heard Baldwin give in Chicago. Leeming wrote to try to convey how appreciative Baldwin would be, and, in fact, when Baldwin returned he hung the photograph directly above his writing desk for inspiration. As Leeming recalled, "the picture became a kind of direct link between him and a writer who, as far as Baldwin was concerned, came closer to sharing his concerns than any other."

But bad news had come from Paris about Beauford Delaney. He had had a nervous collapse, and when he recovered, Baldwin helped him to get established in a new studio at Rue Vercingetorix and to have an exhibition in December, 1964, at the Galerie Lambert. Delaney's new Paris paintings were a mixture of representative and abstract styles, often with somber melancholy colors but with occasional flashes of the old bright brilliance. "Perhaps I am so struck by the light in Beauford's paintings because he comes from darkness—as I do, as, in fact, we all do," Baldwin wrote in his introduction for the exhibition's catalog. He did not know, he added, "nor will any of us ever really know, what kind of strength it was that enabled him to make so dogged and splendid a journey." He had eventually reached Paris—"I have the impression that he walked and swam." He considered that Beauford's paintings had undergone "a most striking metamorphosis into freedom," and he was now "a great painter—among the very greatest." He could not do more for his old artist friend, and he hoped it would help to boost Beauford out of his recurring melancholy, but he feared his old friend would never be the same as he remembered him. It was another reminder in the year of his fortieth birthday that time was flying nonstop and the American scene, the civil rights movement, the people one loved, were changing even as one watched.

That was certainly true of Malcolm X—he had experienced a radical change in public. His prominence in the media had caused jealousy within the Black Muslims, some of his public statements had been

261

corrected by Elijah Muhammad. There was an attempt to reduce his importance, to discipline him, and eventually Malcolm X broke with the Muslims and formed his own group. He had always intrigued Baldwin, who respected his brilliance and courage even though he couldn't accept his extremist views. Before he met Malcolm, he was "a little afraid of him as was everyone else," and his first sight of him was when he was giving a lecture in New York, and he saw Malcolm in the front row. "I very nearly panicked." Baldwin added: "It must be remembered that in those great days I was considered to be an 'integrationist'—this was never quite my own idea of myself—and Malcolm was considered to be a 'racist in reverse.' " He appeared with Malcolm on radio and television programs and learned that, under his aggressive rhetoric, "he was one of the gentlest people I have ever met." Baldwin said of himself at that time that, without entirely realizing it, he was in some way "the Great Black Hope of the Great White Father," adding "I was *not* a racist—so I thought; Malcolm *was* a racist, so *he* thought. In fact, we were simply trapped in the same situation," as Martin Luther King was later to discover—King, who "in those days did not talk to Malcolm and was a little nervous with me." What made Malcolm "unfamiliar and dangerous was not his hatred for white people but his love for blacks, his apprehension of the horror of the black condition, and the reasons for it, and his determination so to work on their hearts and minds that they would be enabled to see their condition and change it themselves."

Malcolm, too, showed Baldwin respect, using King as his main target. "Any Negro who teaches other Negroes to turn the other cheek," he said of King, "is disarming that Negro." He continued: *"White* people follow King. *White* people pay King. *White* people subsidize King. *White* people support King. But the masses of black people don't support Martin Luther King . . ." King in reply wished Malcolm wouldn't talk so much about violence because it "can reap nothing but grief." After a pilgrimage to Mecca and a conversion to orthodox Islam, Malcolm began to move much closer to King's views, dropping his attacks on the evil of the "white devils," though not against American racism. He said he was glad to be free of "the sickness and madness," and it was a time for martyrs. "And if I'm to be one," said Malcolm, "it will be in the cause of brotherhood. That's the only thing that can save this country. I've learned it the hard way."

James Baldwin considered he had learned it "the hard way," too. When he compared their lives, especially their boyhoods in the streets, he identified with Malcolm more than with any of the other black leaders, even Martin Luther King. It seemed to Baldwin that Malcolm had now reached the same conclusion he had—brotherhood above all, whatever the cost—They had arrived at the same racial position even if they had traveled there by quite different routes. Malcolm was soon expressing his respect for King's point of view. He told Kenneth Clark he believed white racism and black racism were practically the same. He wanted to talk to King face-to-face. He also informed Clark that his former associates in the Muslim movement were hostile toward him and he was aware that it was only a matter of time before they would seek to destroy him. His home had already been bombed, but in spite of the danger to his life he still wanted to pursue his new approach to finding a more rational strategy for achieving racial justice. He asked Kenneth Clark to arrange for him to speak with Martin Luther King and James Baldwin. Clark phoned King and Baldwin, and both welcomed the idea. A meeting was arranged for the following Tuesday. Baldwin looked forward enthusiastically to a union of Martin and Malcolm, and determined to do all he could to bring it about. But it was not to be. On the Sunday before the meeting, Malcolm attended a gathering in Harlem and was shot and killed by black assassins.

The news reached Baldwin in London, where he was staying briefly at the Hilton Hotel as the guest of his British publisher, Michael Joseph. His sister-secretary, Gloria, was with him. That Sunday they were free of official invitations and had decided to treat themselves to a really fancy, friendly, relaxed dinner. "All dressed up," they had just ordered practically "everything" on the elaborate menu and were chatting away when the headwaiter arrived to say there was a phone call for Mr. Baldwin. Gloria went to take it and came back "very strange," Baldwin noticed. She sat down, but didn't speak, and Baldwin was afraid to question her. At last she murmured, "Well, I've got to tell you because the press is on its way over here. They've just killed Malcolm X."

Baldwin was in a very emotional state when the reporters arrived. He tried to tell them that "whatever hand pulled the trigger did not buy the bullet. That bullet was forged in the crucible of the West, that death was dictated by the most successful conspiracy in the history of the world, and its name is white supremacy." The British press, commented Baldwin angrily in *No Name in the Street,* "said that I accused innocent people of this murder." Since then, there has been a great deal of speculation about the effect of the killing of the Kennedy brothers, but very little about what the loss of Malcolm meant. Many people were quite relieved that he was gone because they were afraid of him, but Baldwin believed that it probably would result in the breakup of the civil rights movement. With Malcolm as an ally, King might have held most of the younger black generation. The young militants and rebels, who had already halfbroken with King, would go their own way now. King had already alienated some of his more conservative black allies as well as many white liberal supporters by insisting on linking the movement's resistance to racism with opposition to the Vietnam War. This had made President Johnson and his administration far less friendly and increased the harassment by the FBI. King had needed Malcolm, they had needed each other to unify the movement, and now King was on his own. "I must do what I can," Baldwin told friends, and he was soon taking part in a King demonstration in Montgomery, Alabama, and joining in the Movement's ritual chant.

"What do you want?" King cried.

"Freedom!"

"When do you want it?"

"Now!"

Interviewed in Italy, Baldwin talked about Malcolm: "When he returned from Mecca, he was a different man, a far greater man." He said his own mail had got "so horrible" he had turned it over to the FBI. "Maybe they were writing some of it. I went around a week with a bodyguard." He denied being a black leader—"It is impossible to be a writer and a public spokesman. I am a writer." He said of his writing, "I want to get strength within traditional forms, to make elegant sentences do dirty work." He even mentioned Richard Wright—one great difference between them "is what I would call my eroticism." And he mentioned his pleasure at learning that Ingmar Bergman's theater in Sweden had had a great success in staging *Blues for Mister Charlie.* "They played it straight with all Swedes. No black face. They understood the play is about tribes, not races, about how we treat one another."

Christopher Lehmann-Haupt, his editor at Dial, had now left to join the New York *Times Book Review* and wanted Baldwin to review Malcolm X's autobiography that had been written with Alex Haley before Malcolm was killed. "Baldwin said he would," Lehmann-Haupt recalled. "I knew I was taking a risk because Baldwin was regarded as unreliable. You heard all these stories of his promising to do something and then he never did. He wasn't great at turning up at meetings or keeping commitments, I understood, but as it concerned Malcolm X, I felt he would have to honor it. Well, he never did. We never got a review from him and then it was too late to ask someone else. So of course we didn't cover the book. We caught hell about that."

Baldwin wasn't ready yet to write about Malcolm. When he did he probably would try to reach as big an audience as possible in a novel or a play or even a film. But he was continually on the move in America and Europe for much of 1965—when Gloria felt he needed a break she sent him off to fulfill one of the invitations from his foreign publishers—and Lehmann-Haupt wasn't the only book editor to be disappointed. *The Guardian* in Britain asked him to review a book about the civil rights movement by a friend of his. Baldwin read the book, liked it and readily agreed, but no review had arrived by the week of the deadline. Traced to Rome, Baldwin again promised to send a review but none ever arrived. As if to make amends, when the New York *Herald-Tribune* asked him to name the three best books of the year, he chose Malcolm's autobiography, his friend's civil rights book and Claude Brown's *Manchild in the Promised Land.*

E.L. Doctorow, who was to write novels himself, including the much-praised *Ragtime,* was now Baldwin's editor at Dial Press. "I was not a little wary," recalled Doctorow, "because famous writers tend to put everyone on their guard, but Baldwin treated me like a colleague during our meetings and didn't tax me with my youth or my relative inexperience. I edited his collection of short stories, *Going to Meet the Man,* and his novel, *Tell Me How Long the Train's Been Gone,* and I saw his plays, *Blues for Mister Charlie* and *The Amen Corner,* through publication. That occupied about five-and-a-half years. Then I left Dial to do my own work. So my memories of Jimmy were primarily of the sixties when all hell was breaking loose in the best sense of the term. Black people got their hands on the ball and suggested the game wasn't going to be one-sided ever again. Memory settles on a few images.

"Dial Press was a small publishing house so when James Baldwin called to have lunch, everything stopped. The entire staff was affected by his presence into an impromptu festivity as with visiting royalty. When we went to a restaurant, I found myself sitting at a large table among many of his friends and perhaps the day wouldn't end until we'd gone on to dinner. Jimmy would sit there with a glass of Johnnie Walker in one hand and a cigarette in the other. It seemed as if we never discussed any of the editorial things we had met to discuss. It would all finish at his house on Seventy-first Street. David and Gloria might be there and friends from Paris and New York. Jimmy liked company and he maintained an entourage just as Norman Mailer did on the other side of town. Perhaps their generation of writers felt they were born to battle and needed supporters, whereas my generation tend to be loners and regard success as the gravest of dangers. Jimmy did, too, but he needed it, as he would have admitted."

Baldwin spoke at several Harlem schools that year. At Frederick Douglass Junior High School where he had been a student twenty-five years before, one of those voting for him as "alumnus of the year" was his nephew, James, to whom he had addressed the essay, "My Dungeon Shook," that was included in *The Fire Next Time.* Sister Paula accompanied him there. When he went to Benjamin Franklin High School, Doctorow was with him and remembered how "he told the children what his life had been like when he was a student. The place was transformed. The students were spellbound and absolutely quiet as he spoke extemporaneously and worked his way through sentences and found the form of what he wanted to say right in front of them." He brought what Doctorow called "a typical Baldwin message" about the question of who each of us is and its enormous moral consequences. The students listened wide-eyed as he told them that beyond color was the question of self and the tragedy was that the one had to be fought through before the other could be undertaken. An almost inconceivable historical fact was the use of skin color to create fear, power, abasement—death. Baldwin "knew this in his bones," Doctorow said. He had an ability "not to make you question but to make you see, as Joseph Conrad said."

When Doctorow worked with him on selecting his short stories for the collection and reading early chapters of the new novel, Baldwin "used to savor the titles of the books." Doctorow said he would find the title first "and then build the book on the feelings the title evoked in him. He would call me and we would meet. He would look at me reading what he had written to observe instantly my reaction, but he would say nothing in that baritone voice scratched up by liquor and tobacco. Giving a look from that small face he insisted was ugly but was really quite beautiful, he would say, 'Tell me how long the train's been gone—and that's the title.' " To Doctorow, he seemed to live on music—jazz, the folk music of Black America. He tried to dramatize his apocalyptic vision of America and tell how long the train had been gone, when did it happen and why. Doctorow also recalled that Baldwin talked to him about the idea for a novel about Black American history that had occurred to him after interviewing Ingmar Bergman. "He planned to write a big epic of slavery beginning in Africa with a huge cast of characters and he knew only the title: *House Nigger*. He never did write part of it." David Leeming said some work was done on the novel. It seemed quite similar to Alex Haley's *Roots*, which Haley was then writing, and as Baldwin and Haley met several times, it is possible Baldwin dropped the idea when he learned about *Roots*. "That could be true," Leeming said. "I remember Alex Haley visiting Jimmy in Turkey when he could have been working on it. He could have stopped working on it then." He also talked in the mid-sixties about being part way through a novel entitled *When the Rest of Heaven Was Blue,* concerning two families, one black, the other white, from the Civil War to World War II. Was this part of *House Nigger*? There was also talk of a play, *The 121st Day of Sodom,* that he said Ingmar Bergman was interested in staging in Stockholm.

He decided to call his short-story collection *Going to Meet the Man,* and to dedicate it to Beauford Delaney to give his ailing friend a further boost. *Going to Meet the Man* drew on stories written as far back as 1948 and included an extract from the first version of *Go Tell It On the Mountain.* The change in characters and locations in the stories showed how his life had changed, though the style was obviously formed early and didn't change much. The reviews were generally respectful, several a little disappointed that Baldwin hadn't broken any new ground. The *Saturday Review's* "Stories beautifully made to frame genuine experience . . . They sing with truth dug out of pain" was a typical comment. Probably the most important stories to Baldwin himself were "This Morning, This Evening, So Soon" with its paternal and racial (including African) relationships, and "Sonny's Blues," in which he delved into relations between brothers, which he was to explore further in his last novel, *Just Above My Head.* He said of the reviews, "The ones some called the best the others thought were the worst. The general opinion seems to be I was a nice sweet cat with talent when I was twenty but now I'm bitter and it's had a terrible effect on my work."

Although Baldwin was the only celebrity among them, all the established black writers found themselves in fashion. But unlike Baldwin's generation, older writers like Langston Hughes remembered when it had all happened before and then had passed. "I've been twice lucky in enjoying a Negro renaissance," Langston Hughes told me. "Negro literature was in vogue in the twenties when I was getting my start as a poet and now here it is again. But with this difference. The twenties were hung up on art. It was Negro art that people looked for. The present vogue is a by-product of the conflict over civil rights. The twenties vogue grew out of the success of artists like Ethel Waters, Duke Ellington and Louis Armstrong. The present one arises from the spirit of protest. James Baldwin and LeRoi Jones, writers as protesters, have been in the center of it."

The bad feeling between Baldwin and Langston Hughes persisted. They met unexpectedly in a New York restaurant-bar called The Ginger Man near Baldwin's home that had been taken up by affluent West Siders. Baldwin was accompanied by brother David and a young white friend who had drunk too much and was noisy about it. David Baldwin took the young man outside to walk him around and try to sober him up. But he returned just as drunk, staggering to the table, and it was obviously time he went home. Baldwin, who was usually relaxed and philosophical about such occasions, was strangely embarrassed, and when he was asked what was troubling him, he said Langston Hughes was sitting at a nearby table. It was as though his father had caught him in bad company; it at least reflected great respect for the older writer's opinion. When he left, Baldwin went over to Langston Hughes, and the two men, one black, one brown, one so slightly built, the other much plumper, shook hands and exchanged a few polite remarks. They both seemed extra courteous, in the way of people uneasy with each other. Both extraordinary men, both eloquent witnesses for the black experience in their totally different ways, they really had nothing to say to each other that night.

Several versions of a WPA history of *The Negro in New York,* written in the thirties by a group of black writers headed by the late Roi Ottley, were lying unpublished in the Schomburg Collection at the library on West 135th Street. It was a genuine Harlem document that had been there for over twenty years and was important enough to be published even in its unfinished state. The New York Public Library decided to publish it in collaboration with a small publisher, Oceana Publications. Baldwin volunteered to write an introduction for nothing. Then he went off to Istanbul, leaving everybody worried that he might not deliver on time. A long introduction arrived well before the deadline. "The book can be startling only to the brainwashed," he wrote. An editor at Oceana Publications worried that a scathing remark of Baldwin's about Ronald Reagan, then governor of California, might be libelous, and he immediately sent back a revision from Turkey. In this instance he seemed a very easy, obliging author to deal with.

There had been many flirtations between Baldwin and Hollywood, but none yet had led to an actual movie. A group of filmmakers presented scenes from a screenplay based on the short story, "This Morning, This

269

Evening, So Soon," to try to interest backers, but nothing came of it. Baldwin's militant reputation made the conservative, insecure film studios tend to shy away from him. Which was part of the cost of his civil rights activities—the loss of what might have been if he had kept his mouth shut and maintained a low profile. It was a price he was apparently willing to pay. The urge to make movies himself was still with him, as a friend discovered who walked through the Village with him. Along the way Baldwin, who had been drinking scotch all lunchtime, kept stopping and studying the old brownstone houses, and then put his hands to his face as if he were looking through a camera at them. "I'd forgotten," he said, "how photogenic certain areas of New York are— just as much as parts of Paris." He had recently seen the French film, *La Guerre Est Finie,* about a revolutionary twenty years later. The friend suggested a similar movie about American black militants twenty years later. "Not now," Baldwin said. "In the seventies." The friend quoted Robert Frost's poem about not daring to be radical when young for fear of being conservative when old. Baldwin didn't smile; he looked suddenly grim. "I wonder if we'll be like that," he said, and then shrugged and looked again at the photogenic brownstones.

It wasn't only Hollywood that flirted with Baldwin's movie ambitions; individual film people with white liberal sentiments, eager to do something for the cause, often discussed possible movies with civil rights leaders, and sometimes Baldwin was drawn in as a potential scriptwriter, though such proposals seldom got past the first intense, ambitious exchanges. Marlon Brando, nagged into liberal causes by the old rebel still inside him for all his fame and wealth, told Baldwin he wanted to do something big and effective for the civil rights movement. He suggested a movie with himself playing a violent, prejudiced southern sheriff.

There was a meeting to discuss it at Baldwin's apartment on West Seventy-first Street. Those taking part included James Forman and Stokely Carmichael, two of the youngest, most militant leaders. They eyed Brando skeptically as he sat there, dressed in a quiet sports jacket, talking very seriously about his proposal. Baldwin was a fussy host obviously wanting the two young Freedom Riders to like his old friend. But they were clearly going to make up their own minds, these two veterans from the front line, and they asked some hard questions, testing

Brando as he faced them impassively beneath Beauford Delaney's painting of a snowballing black kid. Stokely Carmichael was well-known
for his flair for the dramatic, for pushing slogans like "Black Power"
and "Black Is Beautiful" and links with the new independent African
countries, but that day in Baldwin's apartment he didn't try to compete
with Brando or Baldwin. He sat quietly listening, nodding, his long legs
stretched out, chuckling when Brando did his southern sheriff act. His
presence was felt all the time, however, and when he rose casually to
get a glass of water, all eyes followed him across the room. Brando,
recognizing his power, suggested that Stokely might play himself in the
movie. Stokely thought about it but didn't commit himself, at least he
didn't laugh at the prospect of being a movie star as he might have done
down South among the SNCC people to whom nothing and nobody
were sacred. He showed Marlon Brando the respect of taking him
seriously, partly for Brando's sake, partly for Baldwin's. Brando did
seem deadly serious—talking about schedules, when he would be free
to make the film, that sort of humdrum but convincing detail, though
with actors one didn't know well one could never be sure when they
were performing and when they were not. Baldwin watched Brando
with an encouraging smile, raising no questions, no doubts. Only time
would tell whether the movie would ever be made (it wasn't).

Everyone at the meeting attended a SNCC reunion outside New
York at the home of Gordon Parks, the black photographer, writer and
movie director. Stokely Carmichael and Marlon Brando, free of the
restraints of their more formal business meeting about the movie,
showed themselves to be carefree dancers. They both danced every dance
with an eager boyishness so different from their manner at the meeting.
It was good to see Brando drop his big star's guarded reserve, his face
a mask, and become the way he must have been when Baldwin first
knew him in the Village. Baldwin was also in a happy, festive mood,
making up in enthusiasm as usual for what he lacked in ballroom skill.
Everyone told his or her favorite story about southern cops. The host,
with a mane of graying hair and melancholy baggy eyes contemplated
the busy dance floor as if mentally photographing the scene. "They
deserve a good party," he said, and anyone who had seen the SNCC
people down South replying to racist intimidation with the panache of

cavaliers had to agree with him. Brando, who seemed to dominate on the screen, was quite short like many big stars, broader but not much taller than Baldwin, though as you watched him, even on the dance floor, he seemed to grow in stature. But the SNCC veterans there made no fuss over him. Baldwin was more of a star to them.

Another Hollywood actor came by Baldwin's apartment for a talk about a movie—Warren Beatty, fresh from his success in "Bonnie and Clyde." He discussed a possible movie about an interracial romance, presumably with script by Baldwin and with Beatty as the white half of the romance. Baldwin seemed too keen to please, laughing too readily at the young actor's wisecracks. A jacket of Baldwin's latest book, *Going to Meet the Man,* lay on a table with a picture of Baldwin in the kind of tight macho clothes that Brando wore in some of his early movies. It was as though Baldwin had selected the most unliterary picture he could find of himself. Often he talked about himself as if he were a jazz musician or a blues singer, the kind of artist who meant something to young blacks in the Harlem streets. The photograph also suggested dreams of being handsome, muscular, athletic, filling out the kind of formfitting clothes that the slickest dudes on the street wore, the wardrobe of a sex symbol in the movies. How ironic if this feeling lay behind his overly respectful treatment of handsome young Warren Beatty.

For many white Americans, including some of Baldwin's fellow writers, the Vietnam War had come almost as a relief: here was a civil rights movement in which no black could pull rank! However liberal whites felt about the black struggle, however much they agreed with its aims and even demonstrated side by side with blacks, most white Americans could not identify at the deepest personal level because they were not discriminated against themselves. Baldwin claimed this was the explanation of Robert Kennedy's attitude at their famous meeting. But the Vietnam War was different—white Americans or their grown-up sons were likely to be directly involved. It was astonishing what a difference this made. Baldwin noticed that much of the support for the Movement had switched to the Vietnam protests. King's controversial linking of the two now seemed like a shrewd move, but it continued to lose him a lot of friends among the white establishment who had considered him a safe figure. Baldwin left no doubt of his attitude. "We have no right to be in Vietnam," he said. "They do not want to be 'liberated.'"

Some big public debate between Baldwin and Norman Mailer had been expected, but instead Baldwin and William Buckley, Jr., the witty, articulate, conservative editor of the right-wing National Review, confronted each other at Cambridge University before more than seven hundred British students crowded into a high-ceilinged debating chamber, with five hundred more in a bar, a library and other college rooms watching over closed-circuit TV. Baldwin and Buckley, roughly the same age and from extremes of American society, debated the motion, "The American Dream is at the expense of the American Negro." The white South's violent resistance to integration had been well reported in the British media, and the Cambridge students obviously identified so closely with Baldwin that Buckley must have felt discouraged from the start.

"I find myself, not for the first time," began James Baldwin, "in the position of a kind of Jeremiah." He spoke intensely without notes at the top of his preacher's form—"I picked the cotton. I carried it to market. I built the railways . . ."—forecasting doom in his best biblical style unless white Americans accepted the fact that his ancestors were both black and white and that "we need each other" on equal terms, yet he spoke with a born actor's sense of his audience, maintaining a confident good humor that made Buckley that day appear pedantic and on the defensive. Buckley's sarcasm suggesting Baldwin was treated throughout America with "unctuous servitude" and with the "kind of satisfaction that a posturing hero gets for his flagellations of our civilization" didn't match Baldwin's powerful rhetoric before the young British audience. "I challenge you," said Buckley, "to name another civilization where the problem of a minority creates as much dramatic concern as in the United States." The aye votes in favor of Baldwin's argument totaled 544, the nays supporting Buckley numbered 184. Jack Gould, reviewing the TV film of the debate for the New York *Times,* noted "the beaming smile on Mr. Baldwin's face after his intense and moving speech was accorded the rare honor of a standing ovation by the students. By contrast, Mr Buckley's involved rebuttal was burdened with wild histrionic excesses that quite understandably appeared to tax his audience's store of reserve."

Baldwin and Buckley crossed swords again on American TV, and Buckley reopened the debate in his syndicated column, "On the Right." He criticized the Cambridge University motion as not making sense and then added that "the gentlemen of Cambridge simply wanted to censure America, and happily found the opportunity to do so when Mr. Baldwin raised his eloquent voice to denounce those of his fellow citizens born with the misfortune of white skins, than which there is no graver contemporary offense in the view of the young Anglo-Saxon aristocrats who dominate the life of Cambridge University today as they have over the past five hundred years." Buckley returned to the attack in his column after appearing on a TV program with Baldwin, whose reputation was "in part owing to his fine writing, in part to the implacability of his theme (Hate the System)." Baldwin's attack on the capitalist system and his association with such socialist magazines as Dissent made Buckley question Baldwin's claim to be "neither a socialist nor a Marxist" and suggested the voices of black moderates, such as Thurgood Marshall and Roy Wilkins of the NAACP, should disassociate themselves "from the swollen irrationalities of such as Mr. Baldwin." The trouble was they dare not do so for fear they suggested "a lack of militancy." How long was it to be, wondered Buckley, before Baldwin and "his coterie of America-haters" were ghettoized in the corners of fanaticism where they belonged? The moment was overdue for someone who spoke authentically for the Negroes "to tell Mr. Baldwin that his morose nihilism is a greater threat by far to prospects for the Negroes in America than anything that George Wallace [governor of Alabama] ever said or did."

When Black Power advocates such as Stokely Carmichael and Floyd McKissick began to challenge moderates such as Roy Wilkins and Vice-President Hubert Humphrey with his liberal civil rights record, Buckley wrote that the "cataract of contempt for America" had been "foreshadowed by James Baldwin" in The Fire Next Time. Baldwin dismissed this as "CIA rhetoric" and described Buckley as a "right-wing James Bond who doesn't know anything about American black life. He is merely a witness for affluent conservative white America." End of debate.

Theodore Kupferman had been elected to Congress in 1966 in a special election when John Lindsay became mayor of New York and his congressional district was therefore vacant. In talking with voters Kupferman grew more aware of the change in American public opinion toward civil rights. James Baldwin was still his client, but he hadn't seen much of him recently so he arranged a meeting with him and gave Baldwin what he thought was some good advice. "I told Jimmy his next book should be different, that his rage period should be over and he should surprise everybody and do a book about a black who made it. I told him this because in my opinion from my recent experience the whole system was changing and it was possible for a qualified black not to be restricted in any way." Baldwin listened but obviously didn't like what he heard. "He disliked my idea. He was annoyed with me for suggesting it. That plus the fact I wasn't going to be available much decided him. He said he wanted to make a change. We had a friendly parting and he told me to turn over everything to Robert Lantz, which I did."

Robert Lantz was famous for his Broadway and Hollywood contacts and his big deals. Baldwin hoped through him to get the Hollywood offers that had so far eluded him. Lantz, who had known most of the Hollywood charmers of his time, said, "Jimmy was mercurial. It was precisely his passion that made him so and he was the most seductive human being I have ever known. I don't mean that in a sexual sense. He could charm anybody. He was slightly larger than life. I remember he had some very warm and excitable evenings at Lillian Hellman's apartment in New York when they had extensive arguments. Once when he was in France there were reports that he had given an interview in the French press making anti-Semitic remarks. I sent him a cable asking him if he had given such an interview because it sounded very unlike Jimmy. I told him if he had made such remarks I was sending Lillian Hellman to meet him when he returned. He cabled back: 'Are you out of your mind?' "

Lantz recalled a meeting between Baldwin, Hellman and Mike Nichols. They were all "enraged" about Arthur Miller's *After the Fall*. "They agreed they would meet at Lillian's house on Eighty-second Street and jointly tape a discussion between them that then would be transcribed and edited by them and published to voice their rage. They met as arranged and had set up a very good and big tape recorder and then discovered none of the three geniuses knew how to work it. They had to get my son out of school to fix it for them. His teacher wouldn't believe him when he said he had to go and see James Baldwin, Lillian Hellman and Mike Nichols. Lillian sent him a copy of her collected plays in thanks. But the tape itself was bad, gibberish, you can't follow it.

"Jimmy," Lantz said, "was basically not an intellectual, but the passion, the fire and the emotion were really incredible. I always tried to persuade him not to go on the Bill Buckley show because he gets under your skin, only someone who can stay cool should go on, and Jimmy was never cool and amused about the world's problems, he was always aroused. I remember we were once in the Russian Tea Room. Some big success had just happened for Jimmy. We talked about the fact of his enormous fame and success and reputation, then he looked at me and said, 'When we leave the Russian Tea Room together, I, this very famous figure we have just been discussing, won't be able to get a taxi'—and he couldn't. They wouldn't stop. That is not a situation that a sensitive man like that can live with, no matter what. I always understood that rage in a man who was basically gentle and kind and even romantic. People who want to seduce you are not hostile. But the conflict in him, which gave great color and power to his work, was ever present. We have made progress from our white point of view, but not from the point of view of people who are black. I told Jimmy very often I understood because I had lived in Berlin when Hitler came to power. It wasn't the best thing to be there and be Jewish. Not everybody at first looked at you and said you were Jewish, they sometimes couldn't tell, but everybody knows you are black. We often talked about the most urgent thing was education, particularly political education. Look at Jesse Jackson. In the last four years he has certainly learned an enormous amount about how to handle the Establishment. Where are the politicians who can learn that? Jimmy thought there should be a school for diplomats. Blacks need the training. Ten to fifteen years ago the situation was even harder. But the change in Jesse Jackson shows it's startling how much people can learn.

"I adored Jimmy and I think he was fond of my wife and me. In the time I knew him, he always had constant money problems. He was often late on delivery. No matter how much he earned he always seemed short. Even on a rack of torture I would have nothing unkind to say about Jimmy. There are some people you would be tempted to say less than friendly things about, but not Jimmy. People could irritate him, even make him furious. But no one turned him to hatred. Disparaging and cross perhaps, but not hostile. Passion like his has gone out of circulation. A low profile is popular now, but that wasn't Jimmy's way. I never got involved even remotely with Jimmy's private activities. His predilections must have added problems to his life. There was the problem of aging and of celebrity. Jimmy wasn't deceptive in any shape or form. Once he broke through, he got a huge audience, but he tried always to be honest."

The Amen Corner, represented by Lantz, at last received a Broadway production—at the Ethel Barrymore Theater on West Forty-fourth Street, staged by Frank Silvera and with Beah Richards as Sister Margaret. The play was twelve years old, part of his distant past now, and Baldwin couldn't get as involved as he did with *Blues.* It was also noncontroversial in the sense that it wasn't about interracial relations but wholly concerned with the black congregation of a Harlem church. Howard Taubman in the New York *Times* found some affecting scenes and performances compensated for the play's "sketchiness and slowness." He found Baldwin's approach "tentative and tenuous" in putting over his thesis that "for too many poverty-stricken Negroes, religion is an evasion of living," and he concluded that Baldwin in this early play was "only beginning to measure himself against the theater's challenge." He added that "even in the much later *Blues for Mister Charlie,* Mr Baldwin had not mastered the dramatic form." Richard Watts, Jr., in the New York *Post* stated "where the growth of anger in the playwright gave *Blues for Mister Charlie* its snarling power, it was at the cost of the warm compassion that is luminous in *The Amen Corner.*" The Broadway production of *The Amen Corner* closed after eighty-four performances and then toured Western Europe, where it was much better received.

There were more violent disturbances in the South and in the northern cities, including Harlem, and on each occasion Baldwin was sought out by reporters for a comment. They were trying to make him into a political spokesman. It seemed to be useless for him to insist that he was merely a witness of the life of black people and their activities. He was also aware of the shrinking of his trusted circle. Lucien Happersberger had married Diana Sands and gossip columnists had been busy suggesting he was annoyed by the marriage and hadn't even sent the couple a wedding gift. Baldwin told me he regretted Lucien couldn't give as much time to helping him with his complex affairs, but he wished the couple well. Diana Sands, however, like Lorraine Hansberry, was fated to die young, long before Baldwin, in fact. Feeling that he had been left alone, Baldwin once more had to get away. "New York wasn't working out for him," as David Leeming put it. "His life was too complicated there." So he was soon on a plane again with a ticket for Istanbul and the unfinished manuscript of *Tell Me How Long the Train's Been Gone.*

It was ironic that Judge Kupferman annoyed Baldwin by suggesting he should write about a black making it, because in one sense his new novel was about just that. Baldwin had wanted to write about what success meant in the United States, what he called "the star or celebrity game." He considered writing a long essay bearing witness about his own experience in going from complete obscurity to great fame, but he anticipated too many problems—personal inhibitions, threats of libel, too many explanations. He decided a novel would be better. Then he could choose an example that was more dramatic than a writer—a famous black actor. At once there was gossip in New York that he was writing a novel about his friend, Sidney Poitier. In an article about Poitier in Look magazine he therefore stated: "There's speculation that the central figure of my new novel, who is a black actor, is based on Sidney. Nothing could be further from the truth, but people naturally think that, because when they look around them, Sidney's the only black actor they see. Well, that fact says a great deal more about this country than it says about black actors, or Sidney, or me."

He was having difficulty with the novel. In Italy over a year before he had told interviewers that it was "almost finished." He said it had broken off from a longer work—like *Giovanni's Room*—and he thought at first it was going to be a short story. He planned it in three parts, which would describe the "decay" of the famous actor (perhaps he was really writing the opposite of what Judge Kupferman had recommended—the unmaking of his black hero), the actor's white mistress and "ruined" older brother, and a young black activist who "more or less takes over the book." The novel was to begin with the actor's having a heart attack. The first part would be called "The House Nigger"—his old title for the novel starting in Africa that now he would never write. The new novel began: "The heart attack was strange—fear is strange. I knew I had been working too hard . . ." It might have been James Baldwin talking to a friend. He worried that he hadn't found the right voice for his witness. It had to be less literary than his other first-person novel, *Giovanni's Room*. It had to be more direct, more conversational like an actor. In flashbacking over the actor's past, he would use some of his experience with *Blues*. He would portray Lee Strasberg but call him "Saul." He also wanted the novel to be topical and reflect the change in the civil rights movement between the generations of King and Stokely Carmichael. The actor, who was bisexual, would have an affair with a young black militant named Black Christopher. But how militant should he be? Some of the younger militants were preaching an eye-for-an-eye philosophy and completely rejecting King's commitment to nonviolence. "Guns," said Christopher. "We need guns." How far should Black Christopher go? Where should the actor stand?

He phoned me from Istanbul that he was "going through the unspeakable end-of-the-novel jitters." He was "running late, of course, have a tremendous amount of work to finish in a very short time." Once the novel was completed he planned to leave for Italy to see his publisher there and then appear on a TV program in Amsterdam. Bertrand Russell, the Nobel Prize-winning British philosopher, had invited him to take part in an international war tribunal concerning U.S. involvement in Vietnam, but, he told me, "matters are somewhat complicated" because he had decided he "would now like, I think, to withdraw—briefly, their motives are not my motives—but I can't possibly do anything about that until I hear from Stokely [Carmichael]. I've written him giving him my opinion in some detail; but I don't yet know what he's going to do; and I don't think I should leave him there alone." He added that he was "exceedingly tired." When I met him later, he told me that brother David in Istanbul was getting on very well, "he's picking up the language, which *I've* not done, and is teaching new versions of the belly dance, and it's quite a delight to watch him." Referring to his novel, he said he was now alone with the actor whom he had named Leo Proudhammer, and for whom he felt "believe me, no affection whatever. But I got the mother out of the hospital, and he is now rapidly—I hope—achieving his melancholy destiny." He couldn't do much traveling because it would mean "leaving convalescent Leo in the wintry streets too long." His struggle with this latest novel had also made him reflect on the hard art of fiction; he reread some of Henry James' prefaces to his novels to refresh his thoughts. He decided, "I don't know what makes a novelist—some quickness of sympathy, perhaps, which telegraphs to him the treacherously relevant detail, a story, an ultimate morality—which is not to be confused, of course, with morals, the fewer a novelist has, the better—which gives him his voice and bathes, illuminates his people." He wrote the last words of the novel in San Francisco: ". . . and then I did a new play, and so found myself, presently, standing in the wings again, waiting for my cue." It was autobiographical to some extent. Even Black Christopher caused arguments as to which of Baldwin's lovers he was based on.

Baldwin told me he had trouble with Dial Press over the militant ending, but neither Baron nor Doctorow remembered it. "Doctorow and I spent time with Jimmy over the novel," Baron said, "but the only problem was finding Jimmy with time to work. We went to his apartment. As you may know, to make an appointment with Jimmy meant worrying whether it would work out to time. Even when he arrived, he invariably had company with him. What was to have been an editing session turned into something different. He would be involved with a lot of people in his bedroom while we would be waiting to work on the manuscript in the living room. Jimmy was not typical of celebrity authors. He had great stage presence and knew how to handle people, but he had so many people around him at that time it definitely became hard to work on the book."

E.L. Doctorow said he didn't recall "any serious disagreements between Jimmy and me. In fact, he was habitually careless about the final form of a book once he'd submitted the manuscript. He'd mail it from Morocco or Paris or wherever he was and ignore follow-up correspondence. One of the books, I forget which, he didn't bother to read in galleys. I think I proposed the order of stories for the collection and he agreed to it. As for the novel, I will have to reread it to refresh my memory. Perhaps he argued with Richard Baron, the publisher, who tended to communicate his own editorial views to Dial authors, but I don't remember his arguing with me."

Although Baldwin had strained to find an ending that reflected the new black generation, several reviewers dismissed his vision as out of date. Time magazine claimed there were two Baldwins—the racial rhetorician who remained painfully relevant, and a private man loaded down with personal problems that he must defeat—or be defeated by. The new novel was further evidence that "as a fictioneer Baldwin is in great danger of becoming drearily irrelevant." Time concluded that " '30s protest realism seems to be Baldwin's out-of-step, out-of-date fictional method. But the highly specialized theme of a contemporary black bisexual requires far more savage honesty and a far more ruthless sense of the absurd if it is to achieve any literary validity."

The New York *Times Book Review* gave the novel to a young novelist who had written a well-received novel, *The Fortunate Pilgrim,* which had disappeared with poor sales, but who was in the middle of a long novel about the Mafia that would be a huge bestseller the following year under the title *The Godfather*—Mario Puzo. "Tragedy calls out for a great artist, revolution for a true prophet," wrote Puzo. "Six years ago James Baldwin predicted the black revolution that is now changing our society." His new novel was "his attempt to re-create, as an artist this time, the tragic condition of the Negro in America." Baldwin, according to the author of *The Godfather,* "has not been successful; this is a simpleminded, one-dimensional novel with mostly cardboard characters, a polemical rather than narrative tone, weak invention, and poor selection of incident." Puzo noted that among the characters was an alienated, bitterly religious father "who appears often with slight variations in Baldwin's fiction." After praising Baldwin's essays, Puzo went on: "It is possible that Baldwin believes this is not tactically the time for art, that polemical fiction can help the Negro cause more, that art is too strong, too gamy a dish for a prophet to offer now. And so he gives us propagandistic fiction, a readable book with a positive social value. If this is what he wants, he has been successful. But perhaps it is now time for Baldwin to forget the black revolution and start worrying about himself as an artist, who is the ultimate revolutionary." The huge success of *The Godfather* would soon give Puzo problems of his own as an artist.

Commentary didn't agree with Puzo, claiming that the novel was "a masterpiece by one of the best living writers in America." The magazine's critic, John Thompson, wrote that it was a book "filled with powerful protest, with hatred even, but it is not what Baldwin called, years ago, an example of 'Everybody's Protest Novel.' Baldwin has changed a lot since those days, no doubt he knows a great deal more about the difficulties of doing what he seemed to be advising Richard Wright to do rather than to protest—to accept, to understand, so that he might not, like the author of *Uncle Tom's Cabin,* be forced 'to depend on the description of brutality'—unmotivated, senseless—and to leave unanswered and unnoticed the only important question: What it was, after all, that moved her people to such deeds." Baldwin was "concerned with what moves his people. He is able to show us what moves them, on the very deepest levels."

James Baldwin had now reached the stage of being an established veteran leading writer heading for middle age whose work divided critics, white and black, into those who saw him as a witness of the life he knew in both his fiction and non-fiction, and those who measured him in the role of a spokesman, which they thought made his novels increasingly into the protest fiction he had once condemned. Sometimes critics also seemed to be influenced by their reaction to Baldwin's bisexual themes and what they had heard about his colorful life, which often wasn't very accurate. But it wasn't his own new novel that involved him in the most heated controversy. His friend, William Styron, at last published his novel, *The Confessions of Nat Turner*—a long, elegant narrative trying to recapture the black revolutionary's thoughts and feelings. There was both high praise from many literary critics, predominantly white, and a loud angry outcry from some black critics and historians, who complained that Styron had made Nat Turner into a white man more like himself. This put James Baldwin in an awkward position between his friend and fellow blacks he respected, but he said firmly Styron's novel—a white man's account of a black uprising—was the start of a literature of integration, and he refused to budge from this position. Nearly twenty years later he told Julius Lester that the country's attitude toward blacks was reflected in its literature, but Styron was "a kind of exception, if only in the effort. I'm thinking of course of his *Confessions of Nat Turner,* which has been so violently attacked and so praised and overpraised. It's a book I admire very much. But, you see, I read that book as the *Confessions of Bill Styron*—and I'm not trying to put the book down when I say that. I respect the book very much."

He showed a similar loyalty when Elia Kazan published a novel, *America, America,* about his hard immigrant start. "Gadge, baby, you're a nigger, too," he wrote for the book jacket ("Gadge" being Kazan's nickname in show-business circles). This was a little too much like a cozy exchange between show-business stars, and some reporters of the cultural scene made skeptical remarks suggesting fame was slowly turning the brilliant, fiery Baldwin into a more conventional celebrity. But Baldwin's immense success had put him in a vulnerable position whatever he did, and the more the civil rights movement lost popular white support, the more vulnerable Baldwin would become. He was even the subject of a full-length biography by journalist Fern Marja Eckman, *The Furious Passage of James Baldwin,* which further documented his colorful, eccentric celebrity life. In Eckman's acknowledgments in her book, she thanked Baldwin "for his unstinting cooperation on those occasions when he kept his appointments with me." She often had to pursue him to try to research his complex past. Most of their talks, she wrote, took place in Baldwin's New York residence, "first in a friend's apartment, then in his own," but several were held "under less formal circumstances in schools, a backyard, the lobby of the building in which he lived, the Overseas Press Club, a car, two bars and a station wagon."

There were tributes to the power of his writing when his books were attacked along with Ernest Hemingway's and J.D. Salinger's as not being fit for high school libraries in Vestal in upstate New York, and there were also protests in Chicago when a father angrily complained that his grown-up daughter was being made to read *Another Country* in a literature course. Loud allegations of "obscenity" continued to be made against the same novel in New Orleans. But no one apparently took Baldwin's influence more seriously than the British Home Office, which arranged for him to be detained at London Airport and closely questioned for over an hour by immigration officials. Apparently the cause was that Baldwin had originally been listed as a member of the controversial Bertrand Russell "war crimes" tribunal that put the U.S. on trial for its Vietnam policy, but he had not attended the hearings of the tribunal in Stockholm and had written an "open letter" distancing himself from it. In the open letter he admitted having "reservations" concerning the tribunal, adding "in spite of my somewhat difficult reputation, I have never had any interest in attacking America from abroad. I know too much, if I may say so, concerning the complex European motives, of which envy and fury are not the least." But he made the point that if the U.S. could not fully "liberate" its own black population, how could it "liberate" any other country? "The American endeavor in Vietnam is totally indefensible and totally doomed, and I wish to go on record as having no part of it. When the black population of America has a future, so will America have a future—not till then." A Home Office spokesman in London told reporters that Baldwin was detained because Britain had a policy of not admitting aliens for "the purposes of the so-called Russell tribunal" and that when immigration officials had "satisfied themselves" he was not coming to Britain for a related purpose, he was let in. Baldwin commented he had come to see his British publishers, but he was scathing about this treatment in a country that prided itself on freedom of speech. He wished he were more sympathetic toward the Russell tribunal because there was obviously an international effort to suppress its condemnation of U.S. Vietnam policy. He also noted that British reporters mentioned the treatment of himself as the latest in a series of "frontier" incidents that raised the question of whether British immigration officers abused their authority and subjected visitors and immigrants, particularly blacks, to needlessly harsh interrogation and delay. One wondered how Baldwin's personal critics, who claimed that fame had changed him, interpreted his continued willingness to speak out in public against anything he saw as injustice, even if it hurt his own reputation, and his comfort.

16

The Turning Point

ELIA KAZAN invited James Baldwin and Alex Haley, who had worked with Malcolm X on his autobiography, to a meeting at Kazan's weekend retreat on Long Island. Kazan proposed they do a play about Malcolm based on the autobiography. The two black writers expressed interest. "We had a long talk and worked out some kind of structure for the play," recalled Elia Kazan. But the project was soon abandoned when Columbia Pictures announced a big-budget movie based on the same book. James Baldwin, however, could still be involved because he received an offer to write the screenplay.

He more and more identified with Malcolm, who had come from the ghetto streets, he was fond of pointing out, unlike Martin Luther King, who was middle-class Baptist. "I crossed swords with Malcolm, worked with him," Baldwin said, "and held him in that great esteem which is not easily distinguishable, if it is distinguishable at all, from love." The idea of making Malcolm a popular figure, the hero of a popular movie, greatly appealed to him, but would Columbia Pictures, would any of the major Hollywood studios, really be willing to make a true film about a black rebel like Malcolm? Adapting the sprawling autobiography into a film presented enough formidable problems without any conflict with Columbia or the producer.

Baldwin agonized alone over his decision in a Geneva hotel—afterward he couldn't explain why he had gone to Switzerland unless it was to avoid Paris, where he could never be alone—and he read and reread Malcolm's book, and then flew on to London, where he had rented a house to share with sister Paula and brother David. He enjoyed the comparative peace of London, though he was recognized almost everywhere he went, and he stayed in much of the time, sharing the cooking with Paula and David. Being with his family always calmed him and boosted his morale, and he finally decided to respond positively to the Hollywood challenge. He cabled Robert Lantz to accept the offer.

He didn't care for Hollywood as a place to live, but he would probably have to be there several months. He started out by staying at the plush Beverly Hills Hotel in the center of the movie capital's social life, and then he moved away to the quieter surroundings of a rented house in Palm Springs. He made it clear from the start that he wanted Billy Dee Williams to play Malcolm, but Columbia Pictures favored a bigger commercial name. As Billy Dee Williams recalled after Baldwin's death, "With his Malcolm X film, he wanted to show Malcolm's life as it developed from the early period, through his teens, on to when he died. Jimmy wanted me to play Malcolm, but at that particular time James Earl Jones was very popular after 'The Great White Hope,' and Columbia were more interested in him playing Malcolm. But he could only have played the older Malcolm, he couldn't have played the full range Jimmy had in mind. There were all sorts of problems for Jimmy over the film. He wasn't used to dealing with people on that level—I mean, the Hollywood movie people. I don't know if you can deal with them under normal circumstances. I don't believe movie executives really understand a person like Jimmy Baldwin. He was too much a romantic for them and aggressive, like Malcolm. They were both good men, a gift really, responsive to our dreams and hopes."

In the midst of settling down in Hollywood, consultations with Columbia Pictures and starting work on his screenplay, Baldwin also had to deal with a complex, dangerous situation involving Tony Maynard, the old friend who had been with him when I first met Baldwin.

They had since had some kind of falling-out over the strategy for a rent strike in Harlem, as complicated as rows between friends generally are, and, said Baldwin, Tony no longer acted as his bodyguard and chauffeur, and they had "gone our separate ways." But now he was in trouble, big trouble, accused of killing a Marine in the Village, and on the point of being extradited from Hamburg, Germany, to stand trial in New York. He sent Baldwin an S.O.S. via William Styron, who had met Maynard when Baldwin was staying in his guest cottage. Baldwin immediately shelved his screenplay and flew to Hamburg. With the help of his German publisher he managed to get into the prison to see Tony Maynard. He was concerned Tony might have been broken by his prison experiences, might have "turned his face to the wall" and be beyond all help. Tony looked very thin, wasted, his eyes wet and blazing, but he grinned and Baldwin saw with relief that he wasn't broken, he could still fight for his life.

"Upon my soul," Maynard said, "I didn't do it."

Baldwin was glad he'd said it, though he didn't have to.

"Upon my soul," he replied, "we'll get you out."

It was to take a long time. While he was in Hollywood working on the screenplay he was continually making quick flights to New York for consultations with lawyers and with Maynard and his sister Valerie, a sculptor, who was close to her brother. Justice can take its time, often an interminable time. If Tony Maynard was found not guilty, nobody would be able to give him back the part of his life he had spent proving it. Eventually the labyrinthine case reached court and ended in a hung jury, which meant Maynard would have to go through it all again—and Baldwin, too. The next time he was sent to prison, officially guilty, but there were still weak links in the police evidence, which were eventually proved unacceptable. The more one examined this evidence, the weaker it seemed, and in time Tony Maynard and his lawyer were back in court trying to convince a judge that they should go to trial again. The memories of policemen and other witnesses, whose evidence was under fire, had to go back far into the past, and the phrase, "to the best of my recollection," was continually used in their replies to questions. Getting Tony Maynard out of prison became a seemingly endless saga for

Baldwin but he didn't give up for a moment, and eventually the charges against Maynard were dropped.

By then the Malcolm X screenplay was part of the past and Baldwin was involved in new dramas. But he had shown the same determination on the screenplay as on the Tony Maynard case. Failure had come at last during what could well be considered a major turning point in his life. While he was writing the screenplay, Martin Luther King had attended a fundraising meeting in Hollywood presided over by Marlon Brando. Baldwin hadn't seen King for a long time and found him "five years wearier and five years sadder," showing the increased pressures on him within the civil rights movement from the latest militant group, the Black Panthers, and without from the white establishment which objected to his uncompromising opposition to the Vietnam War and his new effort to form a united front between poor blacks and under-privileged whites. A special effort to bring a campaign similar to those in the South to a northern city like Chicago had seemingly failed. Baldwin thought "the impetus" behind the civil rights movement was gone, whites were more and more obsessed with Vietnam, they had lost interest in the racial scene at home. King's weariness, obvious also in his assistant, Andrew Young, seemed to reflect the movement's lack of success. Baldwin told them about his Malcolm X project and they looked "a trifle dubious" but wished him well. King made a speech, very low-key, very humble, stressing he was only one of many workers of the Southern Christian Leadership Conference, as his organization with headquarters in Atlanta was called. Baldwin thought he made everybody in the Hollywood audience feel that what they were doing was "impor-tant." He didn't flatter them, he challenged them to live up to their moral obligations. At the end the audience was "still, thoughtful, grate-ful: perhaps, in the most serious sense of that weary phrase," wrote Baldwin, "profoundly honored." Baldwin compared the King of that night with the more confident King of five years before at the time of the march on Washington. "Five years later it seemed clear that we had merely postponed, and not at all to our advantage, the hour of dreadful reckoning." The level of rage and frustration had certainly risen even more. Martin Luther King would never feel hatred, the rage in the blood, Baldwin reflected, but after a long talk with him, he sensed Martin had to struggle more now against despair, the dark night of the soul. It was the last real talk he had with King, though he met him briefly weeks later at a fundraising event on the other side of the country, at Carnegie Hall in New York. King looked even "wearier."

Baldwin was tempted to abandon the screenplay and stay in New York and concentrate all his energies on freeing Tony Maynard and on selecting the right lawyers—some New York lawyers, he said, seemed to have stepped right out of Dickens' *Bleak House.* "But I knew, of course, that I couldn't do that; in a way they were the same battle: yet, I couldn't help wondering if I were destined to lose them both."

To add to the mounting pressures on him, some of the new generation of militants had not been content to criticize Martin Luther King but had turned on him, too. SNCC, once the most radical of the frontline groups, seemed almost staid and conservative compared with the Black Panthers with their uniforms and weapons and aggressive macho bravado. They scared most whites as much as the Black Muslims and Malcolm X had once done, and the FBI and local police forces had begun to follow them around and allegedly harass them. Several times Baldwin had spoken up in their defense as an influence for peace and stability in the ghettoes as long as they weren't forced like rats into a corner. What a shock it must have been to Baldwin when the Panthers' laureate, the minister of information for the Black Panther Party for Self-Defense, attacked him in a book in the most personal terms and praised—of all his fellow writers—Norman Mailer! Eldridge Cleaver, who described himself as an Afro-American born in Little Rock, Arkansas, praised Mailer's "The White Negro" as "prophetic and penetrating in its understanding of the psychology involved in the accelerating confrontation of black and white in America." Furthermore, Cleaver said, he was personally insulted by James Baldwin's "flippant, schoolmarmish dismissal" of Mailer's essay. He found in Baldwin's work "the most grueling, agonizing, total hatred of the blacks, particularly of himself, and the most shameful, fanatical, fawning, sycophantic love of the whites that one can find in the writings of any black American writer of note in our time."

Having come up with this thesis—which must have astonished those white Americans who were still nursing the wounds inflicted by Baldwin's vigorous attacks on them over the previous twenty years—Eldridge Cleaver forced everything in Baldwin's work to prove his point. This approach was a politician's, not a writer's, a would-be spokesman, not a witness'. What Cleaver was apparently concerned about was the black image rather than the truth of the black experience, good and bad. Much of what Baldwin wrote was not good for the image; therefore he must hate blacks—it couldn't be that he respected and loved them enough to think they could survive even the truth. Cleaver suggested there was a decisive quirk in Baldwin's vision "which corresponds to his relationship to black people and to masculinity." It was this same quirk, Cleaver claimed, that compelled Baldwin to slander the character of Rufus Scott, the young black who commits suicide in *Another Country* (Rufus, based on a friend, was, in fact, drawn with great affection and insight), venerate André Gide (Cleaver should have read Baldwin's essay on Gide more carefully), repudiate "The White Negro" (for reasons Cleaver didn't deal with), and drive the blade of Brutus into the corpse of Richard Wright (a politician's oversimplification of a serious difference and very complex relationship between two major black writers). Between the lines of Cleaver's *Soul On Ice* he revealed a male chauvinist's attitude toward women, heterosexuality and bisexuality. He closely related sex and violence, and confused nonviolence with what was weak and, to him, womanish. Baldwin, according to Cleaver, embodied in his art "the self-flagellating policy of Martin Luther King."

The minister of information didn't succeed in proving his case against Baldwin, not even by making use of the very early work in which Baldwin confessed to a good deal of self-hatred and therefore hatred of being black, and toward the end of his onslaught, Cleaver became progressively wilder. Baldwin, according to Cleaver, despised Richard Wright's masculinity: "He cannot confront the stud in others—except that he must either submit to it or destroy it . . ." But what Cleaver did succeed in doing was to point out chinks in the armor of the Panthers. Their view of life, as laid down by Cleaver, contained the same machismo, winners-and-losers, survival-of-the-fittest attitude they condemned in the society they were struggling to reform. Many of their beliefs—and their ways of expressing them—seemed as narrow and intolerant as those of the white racists.

Baldwin took his time about replying. He was now in the position that Richard Wright had been in with him. Hadn't he written when Wright died: "I do not know how I will take it when my time comes." Now he knew—he was furious in private, cool in public. The first time he had met Cleaver in California with the Panther leader Huey Newton, he had been very much impressed, but he had sensed a certain constraint between them: "I felt that he didn't like me—or not exactly that: that he considered me a rather doubtful quantity." By the time Baldwin had read *Soul On Ice,* Cleaver had gone into exile abroad, on the run from the police. "All that toy soldier has done is call me gay," Baldwin told me. "I thought we'd gone through all that with the Muslims and were past it. All he wants is a gunfight at the OK Corral. He should go and make movies with John Wayne." The rage roared out of him, but in public, partly because Cleaver was in trouble, he was very cool, refusing to put down Cleaver when gossip columnists came after him.

Not surprisingly he did comment in his next book, *No Name in the Street,* that he hadn't liked what Cleaver had had to say about him "at all." But he had admired *Soul On Ice* as a whole and thought he could see why Cleaver had felt compelled to issue what was, in fact, a warning: "He seemed to feel that I was a dangerously odd, badly twisted, and fragile reed, of too much use to the Establishment to be trusted by blacks." Baldwin said sternly that he felt Cleaver used "my public reputation" against him both naively and unjustly, "and I also felt that I was confused in his mind with the unutterable debasement of the male—with all those faggots, punks, and sissies, the sight and sound of whom, in prison, must have made him vomit more than once . . ." Baldwin there seemed to be playing a machismo role himself, spiking Cleaver's guns. "Well," Baldwin went on, "I certainly hope I know more about myself, and the intention of my work than that, but I *am* an odd quantity. So is Eldridge, so are we all . . ."

Artists and revolutionaries, he warned Cleaver, are both odd and disreputable, but seldom in the same way; they were both driven by a vision and needed each other "and have much to learn from each other." With the utmost politeness, careful to give no comfort to Cleaver's enemies, he warned Cleaver of the bad habits of politicians (which Cleaver had displayed in *Soul On Ice*) of not respecting the individual and of assuming they knew better what the people wanted than the people themselves. Baldwin then went on to affirm his backing of the Panthers—alive, dead, active, in jail or in exile.

In its very different way, this exchange with Cleaver was as important to Baldwin's development as the quarrel with Richard Wright. It cleared his head. Until then his relations with the younger black generation had been too one-sided, putting him on a celebrity pedestal sometimes at the expense of King, who was called an Uncle Tom. The Cleaver attack came like a slap in the face bringing Baldwin to attention, making him reexamine his own situation. Coupled with the decline of interest in the civil rights movement and then finally the death of King, which was the climax of the whole trend of events, Cleaver helped to shape his racial attitudes in middle age.

Meanwhile the fate of his Malcolm X screenplay became like the whole civil rights drama in a Hollywood nutshell, a warning of what was to come. Another Hollywood group had taken on the life of another revolutionary, Cuba's romantic Ché Guevera, and turned out a safe package "for the consumer society." Baldwin was determined not to betray Malcolm that way. He "quite unscrupulously" intercepted an interoffice Columbia memo to the producer advising him to make it clear to the writer—Baldwin—"that the tragedy of Malcolm's life was that he had been mistreated early by some whites and betrayed later by *many* blacks." The writer was also "to avoid suggesting that Malcolm's trip to Mecca could have had any political implications or repercussions." Baldwin felt both fascinated and challenged, but obviously to make sure he kept to the studio's line he was assigned a collaborator under the disguise of being a "technical expert." Each week Baldwin would deliver several scenes, which the collaborator would then translate into cinematic language, shot by shot, camera angle by camera angle. "This seemed to me a somewhat strangling way to make a film," Baldwin commented. "My sense of the matter was that the screenwriter delivered as clear a blueprint as possible, which then became the point of departure for all the other elements involved in the making of a film." But it became clear to him as his "translated" scenes were returned to him that "all meaning was being siphoned out of them." Some of the collaborator's changes to create more action simply showed no knowledge of the Harlem hustler environment that Malcolm had lived in at one time. Baldwin realized he had fallen into a "trap" by accepting "technical" assistance and that when the long screenplay was cut, it would be shaped in the interest of perceived "entertainment" values rather than the truth.

There was a big row, but this time the setting wasn't the artistic Actors Studio as it had been with *Blues* but a tough commercial Hollywood company, and Baldwin was in a weak position. Columbia Pictures weren't really interested in filming his uncompromising view of Malcolm, and considering the changing mass market and the growing conservatism of America typified by Richard Nixon's running for president that year, many of the top executives were quite keen to drop the subject of Malcolm altogether. Baldwin finally walked out, taking his original script with him, which he then published in book form as *One Day, When I Was Lost—A scenario based on The Autobiography of Malcolm X*. After Malcolm was shot at the end, his voice was heard saying, "And if I can die, having brought any light, having helped expose the racist cancer that is malignant in the body of America . . . all of the credit is due to Allah. Only the mistakes have been mine." The "legal complexities" didn't allow Baldwin to use the names of either the Black Muslims' organization or its leaders, but he felt he had remained faithful to Malcolm's book and to "the truth of the stormy, much maligned, groping and very moving character of the man known as Malcolm X." More of the public than the private Malcolm was depicted in the crammed, fast-moving screenplay, but perhaps Billy Dee Williams would have been able to convey much of the personal side that Baldwin had left out. The "scenario" as published suggests rather a hurried first draft awaiting the writer's deeper touches to bring the private man behind the public figure more to life. It perhaps reflects the harried circumstances in which it was written with Baldwin struggling with Columbia, with the Tony Maynard case, and with the decline of the civil rights movement and the Cleaver attack. If the film had been made, it no doubt would have been as dramatic in production as *Blues* in rehearsals. Baldwin considered it "a gamble which I knew I might lose, and which I lost—a very bad day at the races." He thought he would "rather be horsewhipped, or incarcerated in the forthright bedlam of Bellevue [Hospital] than repeat the adventure." It remained "very painfully in my mind, and, indeed, was to shed a certain light for me on the adventure occurring through the American looking-glass."

He had no doubt not made a greater drama about his fight with Columbia Pictures—there were none of the round-by-round accounts in the media there had been with *Blues*—because of the tragedy that overshadowed everything for him that year and possibly for the remainder of his life. Billy Dee Williams and he were sitting having a few drinks by the swimming pool of the rented house in Palm Springs. The cook-chauffeur was about to prepare supper. The phone had been brought out to the pool and it rang while Billy Dee Williams was doing "what I took to be African improvisations" to a record of singer Aretha Franklin. Baldwin picked up the phone. A voice said: "Jimmy—? Martin's just been shot. He's not dead yet, but it's a head wound—so—" Baldwin didn't remember what he replied. He wept briefly, but it was "more in helpless rage than in sorrow." Malcolm, the aggressive threatening Malcolm, he had half-expected to be killed, but not Martin, the saintly apostle of nonviolence, the winner of the Nobel Prize for Peace, the man who, Martin Luther King, Sr., cried when he saw his son's body in the coffin, "never hated anybody." Baldwin had never got to know him really well—"circumstances, if not temperament, made that impossible, but I had much respect and affection for him." He remembered King as he had last seen him, so weary-looking, so philosophical, so much under pressure from all sides. Some of the younger militants had even dismissed him as an Uncle Tom—well, this Uncle Tom had been dangerous enough to be killed. If Martin was killed, then who was safe? He remembered striking a wall of the house in rage—in hatred. In his highly emotional state, Billy Dee Williams was a reminder of Malcolm X and that Martin Luther King had now met the same fate. His heart wasn't free of either hatred or despair that day. King's death, he told *Esquire*, signified "the abyss over which this country hovers now." He didn't any longer believe in what the white world said, he added angrily. The riots in the ghettoes across the country that greeted the news of King's murder seemed to reflect his own feelings.

295

The last time he had seen King at the New York fundraising event, he had had nothing suitable to wear and so had rushed out to buy a dark suit. It was this suit that he wore to King's funeral in Atlanta. He went alone, which was rare for him on any journey. A huge crowd blocked the way to the church, but someone on the church steps recognized him "and sort of lifted me over." Robert Kennedy had sent a private jet to Memphis to bring King's body home to Atlanta, and Baldwin saw him in the church. He told Esquire that Bobby Kennedy was "very shrewd, but I think he's absolutely cold. I think he may prove to be, well, very dangerous," and almost surely would be the next president. Harry Belafonte was sitting next to Coretta King. King's great friend and Man Friday, Ralph David Abernathy, sat in the pulpit. In a nearby pew was Marlon Brando, Sammy Davis, Eartha Kitt and Sidney Poitier. The tension, he wrote later, was "indescribable—as though something, perhaps the heavens, perhaps the earth, might crack. Everyone sat very still." Baldwin concentrated on controlling his feelings in public—"I did not want to weep for Martin; tears seemed futile." After the service, he walked in the funeral procession between Marlon Brando and Sammy Davis. As far ahead as he could see, every inch of ground seemed to be "black with black people." They stood in silence as the procession with famous black and white faces—John Kennedy's widow, Jacqueline, with Mrs. King—passed by behind the coffin. Baldwin lost control before the grieving silence of the vast crowd. "I started to cry, and I stumbled, and Sammy grabbed my arm."

A week later, when Baldwin was back in Hollywood having a drink with Billy Dee Williams in a fashionable bar, a young Hollywood producer came over to their table to insist that the Martin Luther King story should be filmed at once and that Baldwin should write it. Baldwin thought it was a terrible idea, but he had no wish to discuss Martin's death with a Hollywood producer. He merely said he wasn't free, he was working on his Malcolm X screenplay. But the young producer didn't take the hint and leave. If Baldwin couldn't do it, he said, what black writer could? He asked for some names and Baldwin politely gave him some. But the producer wasn't impressed, possibly he had never heard of them, and he insisted Baldwin was the only one who could do it. Billy Dee Williams, who had been listening in silence, then "got mad." He said, "You don't really mean any of that crap about Jimmy being the greatest, and all that. That's bullshit. You mean that Jimmy's a commercial name, and if you get that name on a marquee linked with Martin Luther King's name, you'll make yourself some bread. That's what you mean." Said Baldwin: "Billy spoke the truth, but it's hard to shame the devil."

After Baldwin's death I mentioned this scene to Billy Dee Williams, and he remarked with a grin, "Yes, I have a big mouth, too." dramatic Jimmy. When I said Baldwin seemed even more shocked by King's death than Malcolm's, Billy Dee Williams replied, "Well, Malcolm was much more of an aggressive character. I guess aggressive characters are always more likely to meet their demise. Martin Luther King's death was with Jimmy for a long time. I doubt if he ever got over it. It was unbelievable to him that anyone would go that far. Much of his hope died with King."

Shortly after King's death, Marlon Brando invited Baldwin to accompany him to the funeral of a Black Panther in San Francisco, but Baldwin was still too upset about King. Even three years later in 1971 he still felt deeply enough to write: "Since Martin's death in Memphis and that tremendous day in Atlanta, something has altered in me, something has gone away. Perhaps even more than the death itself, the manner of his death has forced me into a judgment concerning human life and human beings which I have always been reluctant to make— indeed, I can see that a great deal of what the knowledgeable would call my lifestyle is dictated by this reluctance. Incontestably, alas, most people are not, in action, worth very much; and yet every human being is an unprecedented miracle. One tries to treat them as the miracles they are, while trying to protect oneself against the disasters they've become." This was Baldwin close to despair.

As he looked back over King's years of marches and petitions he saw the same "act of faith," the same resistance to despair—and hatred. And look how it had ended, all King's hopes snuffed out by a gunshot. He told journalist Leonard Lyons that he would never be able to wear again the suit that he had on at King's funeral and promptly received a phone call from a black friend from junior high school days who was the same size and wanted the suit. "Now, for me, that suit was drenched in the blood of all the crimes of my country," Baldwin remarked. But his friend was only a postal worker and couldn't afford "my elegant despair." Baldwin accepted an invitation to dinner to present the suit and arrived in a rented car, a Cadillac limousine with a white chauffeur. "I was no longer the person my friend and his family had known and loved—I was a stranger now, and keenly aware of it, and trying hard to act, as it were, normal." The daughter, a militant, argued with him about the merits of Styron's *Nat Turner,* which he suggested that she read before condemning. "This rather shocked the child, whose militancy, like that of many, tends to be a matter of indigestible fury and slogans and quotations." It rather shocked the parents who had not imagined he and a black militant could possibly disagree about anything. Baldwin had "saved" the father when he was a teenage preacher and then he had betrayed him by giving up the church himself. Now he was seen as a celebrity—rich—a stranger, whereas, Baldwin told himself, he was merely "an aging, lonely, sexually dubious, politically outrageous, unspeakably erratic freak." Inevitably there was an argument about Vietnam. Baldwin became angry with his old friend, and saw the mother staring at him, "wondering what had happened to her beloved Jimmy"—the same look that suggested one took part in civil rights marches "to sell one's books." His friend tried on the suit and it was a perfect fit. Freedom to the friend seemed to mean the power to give away a suit like Baldwin or to rent a limousine or take what Baldwin saw as his own "increasingly terrifying transatlantic journeys." How could he tell his old friend of his schooldays that freedom was taken not given, and that no one was free until all were free, and that the price was high, as Martin Luther King's murder showed? He went home, feeling even more depressed after this trip back into his past.

Baldwin's self-dramatizing, which was part of his intense identification with the subjects that he wrote about, the way he played his role as a witness, was often misinterpreted by cooler characters with a different temperament. If such people had behaved like Baldwin, it would have been phony, but with James Baldwin it had become natural, his method of coping with enormous tensions. His growing fondness for words like "terrifying" and his emotional talk about "Martin" almost as if they had been brothers caused some of his critics to conclude his expression of his feelings was much exaggerated. Some were skeptical about the personal effect of King's death on him—for example, Norman Podhoretz, the editor of Commentary. Baldwin and Podhoretz had grown apart over the years, a genuine "estrangement," with Baldwin accusing Podhoretz of becoming a right-wing reactionary and Podhoretz convinced Baldwin had become "more radical, leftist, a black nationalist." After Baldwin's death, when I mentioned King's murder, Podhoretz said, "I think Jimmy exaggerated his relations with people like Martin Luther King. It grated on me when he referred to him as Martin. The world in which he really lived was the world of the New York literary intellectuals. He wasn't part of the civil rights movement or Harlem. He was a New York literary intellectual. That was his natural milieu. He was more a part of Greenwich Village than Harlem."

Other New York intellectuals have made more or less the same point, but people who knew Baldwin better in the civil rights milieu like Dr. Kenneth Clark and Bayard Rustin took almost an opposite view. "He was *very* affected by Dr. King's death," Kenneth Clark told me. "I think there was a change in him over the years. I had a feeling as time went on Jim became less and less hopeful about positive changes in America as far as race is concerned. He reminded me of William Du Bois in the later part of Du Bois' life. I think that feeling of mine is supported by the amount of time he spent away from the United States after Dr. King's death." Bayard Rustin said in a talk before his death, "Jimmy Baldwin lost much of his hope, his idealism about integration, after Dr. King was killed, as many other people did. Jimmy Baldwin's role in the civil rights movement was not a day-to-day involvement in the front line, but to use his fame to raise funds and make friends and bring us media publicity, which he did very well. In fact, he did a great job. He was one of the few who was well thought of by both Dr. King and the Black Panthers. Many critics of his writing have no practical experience of the civil rights movement in the front line and the great camaraderie among the people taking part. Martin and Jimmy in this way were Movement comrades, and though they didn't see a great deal of each other, I know from both of them they respected and were fond of each other. People sometimes didn't understand Jimmy's intense identification with people in the Movement. He often came off a platform after speaking trembling with emotion. It's a wonder to me such intensity didn't wear out that frail body long ago. I know after Martin's death, he wondered if he would be next to be killed."

He found he couldn't write. He had an immense writer's block even for personal letters. For months afterward, as he recalled at the end of his life, "I didn't think I could write at all. I didn't see any point to it. I was hurt . . . I can't even talk about it. I didn't know how to continue, didn't see my way clear." When I met Baldwin a few weeks after King's death at a hearing concerning the Tony Maynard case, he appeared much older, his face more somber and lined, with the first gray in his hair. "Martin," he said, "will turn out to be the most influential figure of the sixties, not the Kennedys or Lyndon Johnson." The revisionist histories published since King's death, notably Taylor Branch's study of the civil rights movement, suggest he was quite right.

When Robert Kennedy was shot, too, that summer, Baldwin saw it as yet more confirmation of the reactionary mood of the country. It was becoming dangerous to be liberal or radical. But he was changing, too. He had spent almost his whole life struggling against the feelings that his stepfather had planted in him. Martin Luther King's murder marked a turning point for him. From now on he would be a different Jimmy Baldwin.

17

Home at Last

It WAS no consolation to Baldwin that his face had become as famous as Ernest Hemingway's had been in the fifties. Hemingway's bearded, smiling figure had been better known than many a film star's, and Baldwin, so different in every way from the macho Hemingway, had attained the same kind of international recognition. "Aren't you James Baldwin?" someone was always likely to ask wherever he was—New York, Mississippi, London, Paris, Istanbul or the latest stopping place. His invariable answer was a friendly gap-toothed grin and a willingness to sign autographs unless he was hurrying to keep an appointment he was already very late for.

But when he left America after King's death, the fame, the recognition merely irritated his frayed nerves. He was popping tranquilizers into his mouth like candy, drinking scotch like water and chain-smoking endlessly, but none of it helped. He had an apartment in Paris now, but since his books were being translated into French and his face had appeared on the covers of popular French magazines, Paris was hopeless except as a stop on the way to somewhere else. But Istanbul was still far enough away in distance and also culture, though it was becoming increasingly westernized.

He tried to relax by directing a play starring his friend, Engin Cezzar—John Herbert's *Fortune and Men's Eyes*—about the bad conditions and homosexuality in some Canadian houses of correction. In Turkish it was called *Düsenin Dostu* ("Friend of the Fallen"). When Baldwin had been Elia Kazan's assistant on *Sweet Bird of Youth* ten years before he marveled at Kazan's patience. Kazan had told him if a director didn't have patience he might as well look for another line of work, and after hearing about Baldwin's impatient outburst over *Blues* he doubted Baldwin had the patience to direct a play or a movie. But Baldwin proved him wrong in Istanbul. He directed the play as a "Twentieth Century morality play," a "modern *Oliver Twist,*" and it was a success.

Even in Istanbul he could not escape the attention of the media. Asked why he had come to Istanbul, he told reporters he had wanted "a place where I can find out again where I am and what I must do. A place where I can stop and do nothing in order to start again." There were times, according to Ebony magazine, when he seemed like a joyful little boy up after dark, but there were other times when he seemed "infinitely older than anyone else one knows . . . immensely sadder . . . awash in a special sort of aloneness out of which the great eyes look past strangers for someone he knows." Asked if he was hopeful, he replied, "Hope is invented every day." He explained to an Associated Press interviewer what was on his mind. He was, he said, "in some ways the last unassassinated Negro of my generation," but his residence abroad didn't mean he had withdrawn from the civil rights struggle in America or lost hope for the future. Living in Istanbul was "preparation, not flight." He said he was writing a new civil rights analysis to be called *No Name in the Street* and he planned a lecture tour of American campuses in a few months. "What we called the civil rights struggle can be said to have been buried with Martin Luther King," he summed up. That event and the election of Richard Nixon as president showed that white Americans didn't want to hear the truth about the situation of the American black. How violent the situation became, how extreme, wasn't up to American blacks, but to whites. "If I were really pessimistic, a long time ago I would have found a cabin on some mountain and I would be sitting there." What happened now was anyone's guess—"I'm no prophet." But he doubted there was enough moral energy left in most white Americans to accomplish the miracle which was now demanded. "I hope I'm wrong."

For Architectural Digest he looked back over the places he had lived in. He mentioned the house he had bought in New York for his mother. "I did not live in this building for very long, but the manuscripts piling up in the basement of the house made the reality of my accelerating age something to be confronted." King's death "devastated my universe" and he "wandered around" visiting Istanbul, then London and Italy. "I collapsed physically several times, and when I came back to Paris I collapsed again. Friends then shipped me, almost literally, out of the American Hospital to St. Paul-de-Vence, a little lofty village near Nice in the south of France." There he recuperated and found a new determination to live.

Without knowing it he had found what was to be his home for the rest of his life. St. Paul-de-Vence goes back to medieval times, built on a mountain with ancient cobblestone streets and houses and a famous hotel and restaurant, the Colombe d'Or, where such well-known artists as Picasso, Braque, Bonnard and Matisse dined and left sketches in tribute to the cooking. Yves Montand and Simone Signoret held their wedding there, and after Baldwin became friendly with them, they helped to persuade him to buy a house and settle there. He lived at first at a hotel. "It was grief I had been avoiding," he said later, "which was why I had collapsed. A friend of mine came down from Paris to look after me, and was so outraged at my hotel bills that he packed my bags and moved me"—to what was then a rooming house up the hill. "Part of my family came to see me. Eventually, I looked around me and realized that I had rented virtually every room in the house. Then I thought, why not stay here?"

It was 1970 and he was forty-six. He had doubts about how long he would live, it was time to settle. He liked the house, a fine stone building with twelve rooms overlooking a magnificent valley at the foot of the village. He set up a studio and workroom—my "torture chamber"—on the first floor next to a terrace, once the studio of Georges Braque. There were several acres of garden. Being very old, the house always had something in need of repair, but Baldwin decided that was "good for the soul, for it means that one can never suppose one's work is done." Perhaps, too, he had reached the age at which "silence becomes a tremendous gift, and the vineyard in which one labors a rigorous joy." The decision to settle down there proved a good one. Friends like Lucien, Bernard Hassell and Beauford Delaney came to stay with him. American friends who were vacationing in France came to have lunch with him. From now on he would visit the U.S. but he would make his home there in St. Paul-de-Vence.

He and agent Robert Lantz had parted company after the Malcolm X Hollywood failure. "There was no real rift between Jimmy and me," remembered Lantz. "He moved to France and I think he had representation there. Any inquiries I received I forwarded to his brother David. There was no argument between Jimmy and me. I adored him and I visited him at his home at St. Paul-de-Vence. His house was gorgeous with a beautiful, unkempt garden. I have rarely seen such a beautiful garden in such need of a haircut. In France he had become a giant figure, a bigger celebrity than a movie star, a man generally admired."

The setting seemed perfect for his writing. When he was tired he could recuperate on the terrace, "an island of silence and peace." He ate lunch at a bamboo-shaded table with a view of the village, white and shining in the sun. Roses climbed over the back entrance leading to the kitchen. He had a sense of ownership he had never had before—it reminded him of what he had read about Henry James late in life when he bought a home called Lamb House in Rye outside London. That had been James' first real home, too.

Since King's death he had published only two books and both were non-books in a sense, simply transcripts of conversations with veteran white anthropologist Margaret Mead *(A Rap On Race)* and with young black poet, Nikki Giovanni *(A Dialogue)*, but he credited the Mead book with helping him "significantly" and his friendly relations with Giovanni prepared the way for a good post-Cleaver relationship with the new generation of black writers. He had finished a draft of his latest book, *No Name in the Street,* before he moved into his house. Recuperating from his stay in hospital, where he had feared he was going mad like his stepfather, he tried to get the book ready to be published. It had become a long continuous essay, almost like a stream of consciousness constructed around Martin Luther King's death and funeral. He had never been so unsure of any writing he had done. Had he maintained his self-control or was the whole thing too self-indulgent? Dial Press was waiting for a new book, he couldn't raise any more money until he gave them something new, but he wavered over letting his manuscript go. He sat in the sun reading and rereading what he had written. His brother David saved him. David phoned from New York and Jimmy told him, "I just can't finish this book. I don't know what to do with it." David flew over to see him and read the manuscript and immediately sent it on to Dial Press.

He now had a new editor, Don Hutter, who had taken over from E.L. Doctorow when he left to write a novel. "I edited *No Name in the Street,*" Hutter said, "which picked up from *The Fire Next Time.* It gave his view of the country in the time since *The Fire Next Time* from perhaps a slightly different point of view. Not as apocalyptic as *The Fire Next Time.* It was a good book, but it didn't do as well as *The Fire Next Time.* Jimmy had come back to quite a different America, changed in many positive ways. He had to recognize the changes, but still felt his own concern about what was wrong that still had to be redressed. It was not as urgent a book to the reading public, but it was a very good book. It didn't do better because of the times. There was not a great deal I suggested in the way of revisions, just fine-tuning. He was very easy to work with. He was living in France most of the time, so our work was largely by correspondence. He came to New York a couple of times. I found him a remarkable person. I thought he was an extraordinarily eloquent and sensitive person. The civil rights movement was not as prominent then, but he was very perceptive about what was happening, and then there were always his strong family concerns, an important part of anything he wrote. He was not so much a spokesman as an artist who voiced concerns that were important to people. He clearly felt he could no longer live in New York, though it was still his primary society."

No Name in the Street was scheduled to be published in May, 1972, but before then there was yet another change of editor at Dial. Hutter left to join another publishing company and was replaced by Richard

Marek. To make matters worse, Richard Baron, who had a long-standing relationship with Baldwin, also left. By then Baldwin must have felt the unsettled state of the company reflected his own unsettled state of mind too closely. He let it be widely known that he was seeking another publisher. When he met a friend who worked for one of the leading commercial publishers he announced he was leaving Dial, so the friend asked him if he would like an offer from his company. He said he would. As Baldwin was returning immediately to St. Paul-de-Vence, the friend phoned him there later that week with an offer of a $100,000 advance for his next novel. Baldwin could get more than that to change publishers but the advance could be negotiated upward; the first offer in such circumstances was almost never the last word. The friend arranged to call him the next week on a certain day at a certain time. When he did so a strange voice said Mr. Baldwin wasn't at home and he had no idea when he would return. Other calls for weeks obtained the same result. The friend never received a reply to the $100,000 offer. When he eventually wrote Baldwin snappily about such treatment, he received no reply, though he heard that sister Paula, whom he knew, was very annoyed at his writing her brother that way. Meanwhile he learned that a young agent in Paris had submitted to publishers a twenty-page chapter of a new, highly autobiographical novel entitled *No Papers for Mohammed,* written in the first person in the intense, dramatic style of *Giovanni's Room.* It was at this stage that Richard Marek found himself to be Baldwin's new editor at Dial.

"I was a young man at the time," recalled Marek, "and it seemed to me that it was my major job at Dial to keep James Baldwin at Dial. He was under contract for a novel. *No Name in the Street* was scheduled for May. *One Day, When I Was Lost,* his Malcolm X scenario, was for the fall or early in the new year. I wrote him virtually every day when I got there. He was in France. But he didn't reply to any of my letters. Finally there was a meeting with a lawyer representing him and it was quite a heated meeting. He was trying to wrest Jimmy from Dial, but we steadfastly refused to let him go. I was particularly unhappy because I thought Jimmy was not being fair. I think he was angry with Helen Meyer for some reason, probably over money. His agent, Tria French, announced she would see me in Paris that Wednesday. We were at an impasse so I flew over and met Tria for a drink in Paris. She was a black American. I thought she was just wonderful. We talked for a few hours and it went well. I had read everything Jimmy had written. I was told if I flew to Nice, Jimmy would meet me on Wednesday morning there. We did meet. Jimmy was extremely hostile. We met at the Negresco Hotel at lunchtime. He said something like 'This nigger ain't goin' to pick another bale of cotton . . .' I was furious. I had been jerked about a great deal. There were three months of not answering my letters and then that interview in Paris to check me out. I said impulsively, 'If you continue with this attitude, you will publish with Dial or never again in the United States.' That was instinctive. I was mad. And he believed me. He saw how angry I was and immediately changed his stance to one of friendship. We had a wonderful lunch. It remains one of the most memorable times of my life. We talked about Dostoevsky, politics— everything. By the end of that lunch I had a 'pass' from him which guaranteed me safe passage when blacks took over New York. 'If you get it out of your wallet in time, you may be all right,' he told me. I knew I was in the presence of somebody highly remarkable. He never again tried to get away from Dial, at least while I was there.

"We signed a two-book contract for two novels, which were to be *Just Above My Head,* which was in the works, and *No Papers for Mohammed,* but the way it worked out was I edited another novel, *If Beale Street Could Talk,* and *Just Above My Head,* though I had left Dial by the time that novel was published in 1979. There was also the non-fiction *The Devil Finds Work.* Jimmy found it increasingly difficult to write. It's very comfortable to be a hero with crowds of fans and to be invited to all the parties, to be lionized. He was always confused about his identity as a writer and his role in the civil rights movement, I think he didn't know whether he should be a political being or not. He was certainly a humanitarian and didn't believe in guns. The violence of Cleaver and that lot put a great deal of pressure on him and hurt him. It was hard to divorce himself from that particular time. The general civil rights movement had been cut short by the assassination of King. The assassination worked. Jimmy eventually was driven back much more on himself. His novels became more domestic, looking inside himself. Even the twenty pages of the unfinished novel, *No Papers for Mohammed,* are highly autobiographical.

"To me, he was a very great writer. He was obviously a genius. He was a very great force in American society. He was one of the most brilliant, if not the most brilliant man I have known, and surely one of the most delightful, challenging and stimulating. He was wonderful to argue with. He was almost always saying something provocative. Our politics were very close."

Marek had inherited *No Name in the Street,* he had not been involved in its editing, but he was in time to supervise its publication. Critical reactions to it tended to reflect the change in the country. Mrs. King, the Reverend Ralph Abernathy, Andrew Young, Jesse Jackson and the rest of Martin Luther King's team tried to carry on as usual, but obviously the heart had gone out of the civil rights movement, and demonstrations were held now in a largely indifferent country that was completely obsessed with ending the Vietnam War. Baldwin was treated by some reviewers like a record still playing the same old tune, others were annoyed by what they saw as a hardening of his attitude. Like many established writers, he was treated as a familiar brand-name product with friends and enemies among the critics. Liberal and black reviewers tended to be approving and middle-of-the-road and conservative critics were skeptical, disapproving or even downright hostile or dismissive. The new book was perfectly consistent with his past work in that it bore witness to his extremely unsettled, insecure, shocked state of mind. His viewpoint was a mixture of a black celebrity under pressure and a writer on the edge of a breakdown. It was the work of a man who had lost his belief in the American people's willingness to right the wrongs of the past. It began with one of his earliest memories at the age of five and ended with a reference to "the wrath to come."

Newsweek reported that "many critics thought his argument had coarsened and his language had deteriorated. Where once he had written, 'It is a terrible, an inexorable law that one cannot deny the humanity of another without diminishing one's own,' he now wrote, 'I have no compassion whatever for this country or my countrymen.' Here was his dilemma: on the one hand, Baldwin was a success, as much of a celebrity as writers ever get to be, yet on the other, he could never escape the snap of harassing fire. A sensitive man, he could never entirely disagree with his critics. With success, his famous noble rage had become a kind of truculent belligerence—it's difficult to sustain an apocalyptic style from the back seat of a chauffeured limousine. With the spark now fitfully flickering, his assaults on white Americans come to look like reflexive gestures, easily and constantly repeated from a lecture plat-form, an interview or an op-ed article. Many, perhaps most writers deliver their best books at the beginning, and Baldwin can't be blamed for feeling ill-at-ease as the black protest changed its tone; he was, after all, a professional exile." The Newsweek reviewer, Peter S. Prescott, concluded that "always he felt himself an exile: because he was black and ambivalent about his religion and his sexuality."

Time saw him differently: "Despite his credentials as an outsider, James Baldwin has been a middleman between black rights activists and white liberals. Finely written early novels like *Go Tell It on the Mountain* sensitized white readers to life under black skin. The moral essays *(Nobody Knows My Name, The Fire Next Time)* personalized the abstrac-tions of racism with passion and high intelligence. Yet a middleman runs the risk of being caught between both ends. Liberals eventually tired of having their noses rubbed in their own hypocrisy. Radical brothers like Eldridge Cleaver charged Baldwin with caring more about personal needs than black liberation. Indeed, the sad irony of Baldwin's success is that it is based on terms laid down by white society before many black leaders had redefined the terms of success with their blood." Time suggested "Baldwin seems particularly aware of his vulnerability in *No Name in the Street,* a collection of reminiscences raked from his private disasters and public disappointments." Baldwin, added Time, "seems to have an instinct for no-win situations. It is almost as if he needed them to fulfill a larger need for his incessant self-examinations, which often turn out to be self-deprecations." Baldwin "consistently main-lines on guilt, whose source appears to be an unreasonable sense of inadequacy. He seems truly tortured by the world as it is and by his inability as an artist to change it. The healing Christian love, so strongly preached in the earlier writings, proved inadequate but remains as a rhetorical echo. The righteous, cleansing fire he summoned for 'next time' is now only a vague and sinister 'shape of the wrath to come.' Time concluded that "Baldwin the complex artist too often succumbs to Baldwin the propagandist and fantasist. When he calls America the Fourth Reich, he sounds as if fascism were a completed fact rather than a terrifying possibility. And when he speaks of 'Martin' or 'Malcolm', there is a touch of envy in his reverence. It is almost as if Baldwin would rather break the apron strings of his beautiful prose style and become a martyr himself."

Mel Watkins, editor of Black Review, in reviewing *No Name in the Street* for the New York *Times Book Review,* gave a black view of Baldwin up to that time and related him directly to King—"Along with Martin Luther King, Jr., he helped shape the idealism upon which the sixties' civil rights protest was based. But Baldwin and King, while demonstrating that blacks were 'the conscience of the nation,' exposed the depth of American intransigence regarding the racial issue. They were instrumental in exhausting the dream of an effective moral appeal to Americans, and in effect set the stage for Malcolm X and the emergence of Stokely Carmichael, 'Rap' Brown, Huey Newton, Eldridge Cleaver and George Jackson—figures who reacted in a purely pragmatic (and therefore quintessentially American) manner to the blighted expectations of the sixties' failed idealism. Since he was a political leader, King's influence on the events of the sixties is readily understandable. The source of Baldwin's influence as a writer is less apparent, particularly since the ideological content of his essays was rarely new—among others, Frederick Douglass, W.E.B. Du Bois, and Richard Wright had previously dealt with many of the ideas that he presented. Aside from the accident of timing, it was the uniquely personal perspective and style in which Baldwin couched his ideas that set him apart. His essay style, in fact, set a literary precedent that would later develop into the 'new journalism.' "

David Brudnoy in the National Review damned Baldwin's new book with faint praise. He thought Baldwin had only once written "a totally dreadful book"—his play, *Blues for Mister Charlie*— "although portions of *Another Country* were unreadable" and "swatches" of his recorded conversation with Margaret Mead, *A Rap On Race,* were "ludicrous." *No Name in the Street* "is at once another example of James

Baldwin's enormous gift with words, and rather conclusive proof that he has finally crossed that street separating those who blame everything unhappy for his group—here, his race—on others, and those who don't." Much of the new book "bespeaks . . . that final lapse into hate-Americanism so damnably fashionable, and worse, so frighteningly debilitating to the spirit of those who succumb to it." Baldwin "gives vent to what has heretofore been rare in his books, bald hate. He expresses hatred of the white race, hatred of western civilization, which he rejects, hatred of America, the soul of which nation, he tells us, is in its South." The reviewer concluded that the book was unmistakably passionately written, bitterly argued; it was also fundamentally bitterly botched, a true cry of despair mingled fatally with a savage shriek of apocalyptic fury.

Benjamin DeMott in The Saturday Review was another critic who saw the new book as an occasion to sum up Baldwin's writing career, almost as if he were already an out-of-date classic. He saw him as a "spokesman," a role Baldwin had always rejected. "Difficulty in seeming to be your own man, rather than a knee-jerk reaction to events, is but one of many problems besetting spokesmen," wrote DeMott. "Another has to do with expense of spirit. Few Americans have been called on as frequently as has James Baldwin in the last decade to function as the public voice of rage or frustration or denunciation or grief." How now, asked DeMott, "does he conduct a hunt for language that hasn't been emptied out by repetition—how can he witness his own scramblings for freshness without coming in some sense to despise this self-involved fastidiousness? To function as a voice of outrage month after month for a decade and more strains heart and mind, and rhetoric as well; the consequence is a writing style ever on the edge of being winded by too many summonses to intensity." Then further, DeMott added, there was the problem of fame. "The spokesman becoming a celebrity among celebrities need not forsake his cause, isn't obliged to care less than before about his people. But his life circumstances must change. At the end of the book "hints of splendor rise from the words: 'New York, San Francisco, Hollywood, London, Istanbul, St. Paul-de-Vence, 1967–1971.'" Baldwin also seems "restless, rushes himself, seems bored with the drill of conventional dramatization." Yet, DeMott concluded, "despite the book's faults, despite the trials and afflictions of his spokesmanship," Baldwin "retains a place in an extremely select group: that composed of the few genuinely indispensable American writers. He owes his rank partly to the qualities of responsiveness that have marked his work from the beginning and that seem unlikely ever to disappear from it. Time and time over in fiction as in reportage, Baldwin tears himself free of his rhetorical fastenings and stands forth on the page utterly absorbed in the reality of the person before him." DeMott saw the new book as a spotty, discontinuous and "devastatingly despairing" view of recent times.

James Baldwin paid more attention to reviews than he admitted and he must have been startled to find himself accused by several critics of the very hatred and despair he felt he had succeeded in keeping at bay at the risk of a complete breakdown. "My own state of health is certainly precarious enough," he said at this time. He must also have been further depressed by the picture of himself as past his best, perhaps even a dated figure whose fire was now merely smoldering embers of belligerence that had little relevance to the new America of the seventies. The attitude of the Nixon administration toward the racial situation seemed to be "benign neglect," though often in practice the neglect wasn't so much benign as ruthless. But Baldwin refused to play the role some of the critics had given him, and, indeed, on the black side he was still one of the few public figures of the older generation that the younger militants even listened to. He also remained as active as he could, rushing, for example, to the defense of two of the most prominent militants, Stokely Carmichael ("This victimization has occurred over and over again . . .") and Angela Davis ("If they take you in the morning, they will be coming for us that night"). His open letter about Angela Davis is of particular interest because it reflects clearly the change in him. He mentioned "the enormous revolution in black consciousness" which meant the new black generation was completely different from his and his father's generation, and the change meant "the beginning or the end of America" depending on how the white American responded. "We cannot awaken this sleeper, and God knows we have tried. We must do what we can do, and fortify and save each other." He made the same point to a black reporter for the New York *Times*: "The tangible thing that happened to me—and to blacks in America—during that whole terrible time was the realization that our destinies are in our hands, black hands, and no one else's." He said he decided "I have no right nor reason to be despairing. But I do not believe in the promise of America in the same ways. There will be no moral appeals on my part to this country's moral conscience. It has none."

It was easy to understand why critics read rage and despair in such remarks because the tone was so different from the early essays in which the stress was always on waking up White America. Now he seemed to be saying, Sleep on, White America; we don't need you; we'll save ourselves. Was this close to Muslim thinking? Was he renouncing the decision he had come to in *The Fire Next Time*? To explain further what he meant, he put aside the two novels he had been working on—he would return in time to *Just Above My Head,* but not to *No Papers for Mohammed*—and began a short, straight-from-the-shoulder novel in which he would be a witness to the new generation and his own changed viewpoint. It would portray his faith in the possibility of "black survival and eventual triumph" in America. He already had a title for it—*If Beale Street Could Talk.*

18

Full Circle

SOON AFTER the publication of *No Name in the Street,* Baldwin met an old friend on Broadway near his mother's home on Seventy-first Street. With the friend was a young black man who had recently been released from prison. Baldwin invited them both back to his mother's, where the usual mixed crowd was filling the downstairs apartment he used. Several young black women writers were there, also Tony Maynard's sister, Valerie, and a young Frenchman who had come over with Baldwin. The friend had a copy of Henry James' essays, *The American Scene,* and as Baldwin hadn't read them, he gave him the book. Baldwin seized it with boyish enthusiasm and instructed the young Frenchman to be sure to pack it in his luggage, they were returning to France in a couple of days. Meanwhile the young man just out of jail had been regarding Baldwin with a look of astonishment. "Is that the writer of *The Fire Next Time* I read in prison—that *queen?*" he whispered indignantly. The friend was annoyed and snapped, "He's more of a man than most you know, I bet." It was a recurring reaction that Baldwin was well aware of, particularly since the Cleaver attack. He often wondered what his nephews thought of the stories about him. He would deal with it in his own time—in his last novel, *Just Above My Head,* which would sum up so much of his life. But first he had to finish *Beale Street.*

When the friend came by next day a magazine photographer was busy taking pictures of Baldwin from every angle. His mother, worried about her eldest son's health, thought such occasions should be limited to business hours—but what were Baldwin business hours? From noon to dawn? Mrs. Baldwin had once expressed the wish that Jimmy would get married so he would settle down. He seemed to be wearing himself out. But holding a copy of *No Name in the Street,* Baldwin gave one of his wide cheerful grins, which the magazine photographer immediately caught. "The drought is over," Baldwin said. "After *Beale Street,* I've got a play, *Brother Joe,* my version of the Gospels in blackface, and a novel entitled *In the Cross a Trembling Soul.* I'm also going to write a movie called 'The Inheritance' about an American woman of mixed parentage who goes to Germany to get what her rich white father has left her. I'm doing it for an interracial company, Kelly-Jordan Enterprises. I'll direct the movie and I'm hoping Diana Sands will be in it. Lucien may be my assistant director." It seemed to please him to have so many projects and talking about them dispelled his somber mood. But unless *In the Cross a Trembling Soul* was another title for *Just Above My Head,* none of these great plans except *Beale Street* resulted in published books or play or film productions in his lifetime. Every writer's career is filled with abandoned projects, and perhaps Baldwin at that period, when he was finding it hard to write, was just trying to boost his own confidence. The change in him, the disillusionment following King's death, certainly affected his viewpoint as a writer. The fierce idealism that had been so much a part of his writing had been largely lost with the decline of the civil rights movement. This probably explained why he found it so hard to write and flitted from project to project. *Beale Street* was his best hope of a new start, of expressing his lowered expectations.

Back in France, he was less open in interviews about King—perhaps he had talked about him too much. He told a Life reporter, "I just reeled after King's death. We had been young together, we had tramped all over the South together, we had even dared hope together." This was Baldwin in his dramatic "I picked your cotton" mood. "I was never the Christian that Martin was," he said, "but I sat behind him and was awed by his faith and I believed in him." He also told Life: "I am still one of the most possessed, confused, hung-up, terrified and perhaps crazy people I have ever known. But at least I am now listening to my own demons and no one else's, and I am going to keep working until they have all said what it is they are trying to tell me—and you. I am not going to stop until the last voice within me has been stilled. Then I may go home, take off my shoes, have spareribs and sit around with my brothers and sisters and cousins and nephews and listen to them tell me I never *did* make any sense."

He had trouble with *If Beale Street Could Talk.* At first he planned a bigger, more dramatically topical story, telling a reporter in 1972 that it concerned a black revolutionary in an American jail whose pregnant wife gave birth to their son at the instant the father was slain. The novel published two years later was slighter, more domestic and everyday, the revolutionary transformed into a young artist who is still alive at the end. But the final version made the same point about black survival— the answer lay not in a leader like King, a white ally like the Kennedys, but in oneself, in self-reliance—and perhaps the message was more effective delivered in an everyday setting. Once more, as in his preceding novel, *Tell Me How Long the Train's Been Gone,* published six years earlier, Baldwin wrote in the first person—from the viewpoint of a pregnant young black woman whose man is in prison for a rape he didn't commit. *If Beale Street Could Talk*—the very title is like the cry of someone seeking a witness to some important event, a witness whom Baldwin as the author then supplies, a witness to the self-reliance of the poor. His young narrator, with no money, no power, no influential friends, with only her family united behind her, sets out to get her man out of jail. Much of *Beale Street* obviously came from Baldwin's experiences in the Tony Maynard case. What had strongly impressed him, even though he had known it most of his life, was how much it cost to get a fair trial. If Maynard hadn't had famous, wealthy friends, he might not have won a retrial. But Baldwin's young woman reflects about her man, "Something travels from him to me, it's love and courage. Yes. Yes. We are going to make it, somehow." The novel ends with the crying of their baby—a cry of hope.

Just before the publication of *Beale Street* Baldwin became the third recipient after Tennessee Williams and dancer Martha Graham of the prestigious Centennial Medal awarded to "The Artist as Prophet" by New York's Cathedral of St. John the Divine (where thirteen years later his funeral would be held). He described *Beale Street* as about "the price we have to pay and the ways in which we help each other to survive." Even though he was no longer the fashionable figure he once was, he was invited on some of the top TV shows to be interviewed about *Beale Street.*

Some of the reviewers had obviously expected a more ambitious novel after six years; the deceptively modest story was seen by some as an example of declining talent rather than a changed Baldwin coping with a changed world. The dragged-out ending of the Vietnam War had been accompanied by disasters in Washington—the enforced resignation of Vice-President Spiro Agnew and then the anguished weeks over the Watergate scandal that finally brought down President Nixon himself. "All the chickens are coming home to roost" was Baldwin's attitude as he followed events from his terrace in St. Paul-de-Vence. *Beale Street*'s stoic message of self-reliance seemed very fitting for those insecure times, yet the reviews were very mixed, ranging from The New Republic's "His best novel yet" to the daily New York *Times'* dismissal of it as an "urbanized *Perils of Pauline.*" The Sunday New York *Times Book Review,* however, couldn't have been more different. On the front page novelist Joyce Carol Oates claimed *Beale Street* was "so vividly human and so obviously based upon reality, that it strikes us as timeless—an art that has not the slightest need of esthetic tricks, and even less need of fashionable apocalyptic excesses." The opposing views of the daily and Sunday editions of the New York *Times* also applied to the way they saw Baldwin himself. Anatole Broyard in the daily wrote, "He is a brand name by now. In fact, he is so dated—I think even

Richard Wright is more contemporary—that he might even qualify for our current nostalgia craze." Joyce Carol Oates in the Sunday *Book Review* was much more sympathetic: "James Baldwin's career has not been an even one, and his life as a writer cannot have been, so far, very placid. He has been both praised and in recent years denounced for the wrong reasons."

Time decided it was "not a success, being too sentimental and predictable by half. But it has the makings of a splendid opera." However, *Beale Street* was not opera but a form of social realism—"It is hard to speculate how a writer of Baldwin's quality succumbed to such timeless bathos. It is even more difficult to accept that a man capable of writing the dense, seductive prose of *Giovanni's Room* could turn out a slack bromide like 'trouble means you're alive.' " People magazine said that the reader knew the twenty-one-year-old heroine would survive—"It is this tone of optimism in Baldwin's work, despite the frequent darkness of his vision, that probably accounts both for his widespread inclusion on lists of required reading in schools and universities and for the disenchantment of black activists with him." People quoted him as saying he made a certain kind of "plea" in *The Fire Next Time* "I would not be able to make now." To whom would he make it now even if he wanted to? No, "it is now up to us."

Some critics decided that the novel proved Baldwin was out of touch and the reason was that he now lived in France. Even old friends like Elia Kazan made the same point: "When Jimmy lived on Seventy-first Street he was in a black and white world. He combined them both. Jimmy was the first guy I knew who had some feeling of love for everybody. He was the most affectionate man I have ever met. I remember his wonderful laugh—derisive, funny, and yet at the same time affectionate. But what happens to a lot of people when they become famous, they slowly pull away from a preoccupation with root concerns and live in another world. I don't see how you can come through life without confronting a lot of outrage and pain. But you can't save yourself living in the south of France—perhaps as a person, yes, but not as a writer. Jimmy's last books had nothing to do with real personal and social concerns. We had a very painful argument about it. I said he shouldn't settle in Europe. I know it's easy for a white man to say that. But painful as it was for Jimmy to stay in the United States, with the anger and the other intense feelings it aroused, he got more stimulation there as a writer. 'But when you go over to Europe, Jimmy,' I told him, 'you make up a story, it doesn't come from your deepest feelings.' I remember a novel he wrote about a young man and a young lady [*Beale Street*]. It was insipid. But Jimmy would tell me, 'Shit! I can't take it anymore!' He made fun of me and my argument. He felt he had to get away to Europe."

Unless people accepted that James Baldwin had changed with the times, they generally talked about the effect of living abroad or the influence of fame. Otto Friedrich had noticed a change even about the time of the Actors Studio adaptation of *Giovanni's Room*. Friedrich was "very poor with four children" and Baldwin invited him to lunch at the Blue Ribbon in Times Square. "He had become more affected, I thought. He always had a Bette Davis routine even when he was young, but later he was doing it as a self-image. And I remember those huge rings and how he batted his eyes. It seemed terribly campy. He always had a melodious voice, he always spoke well and rhetorically in long sentences with dependent phrases, the style of a preacher. With someone you once knew very well, there is nothing changed or everything has changed, usually the latter. Of course one changes oneself. Living in suburbia I probably regarded him with a chip on the shoulder. There is a tremendous class difference between the successful and the unsuccessful. Much of what I had written hadn't been published, yet my first novel had been published before his. We really had nothing to say to each other. We had become strangers. I met him several times in later years and we talked about the old days in Paris. But most of the fiction Jimmy wrote after he became famous lacked the passion of his younger years. That is part of the price of success."

Norman Podhoretz thought "his sensibility was coarsened as a writer" and he was "surrounded by a court of sycophants." He "developed a kind of self-importance as the years went on." For such a writer "to adopt a public posture and see himself as a public figure is to go against the grain of a natural talent." A publisher who knew him well said, "After his great success, Jimmy saw stars. Hollywood hurt him just as it did a great many other fine American writers. People began to recognize him on the street and such fame affected the quality of what he wrote. Jimmy finally left the country, so how could he write about what was happening? He insulated himself from the seamy side of life and protected himself from all the currents. He was a man who could absorb things and read a situation very fast, but not from such a great distance."

Dr. Kenneth Clark said, "Fame as far as I'm concerned was not influential in changing Jim. The suggestion is ridiculous. He was influenced by what was happening and not happening in the U.S. He was very, very concerned. I believe he became more and more pessimistic. The idea that he was changed by fame is absurd to me. At the peak of his fame he remained an intense advocate, pointing an accusing finger. The only thing I would say is that he escaped. All that time in Europe was an escape from the burdens, from the intense feelings. But perhaps he wouldn't have survived even as long as he did without that escape."

I remember at the peak of his fame when his face seemed to be on television every day and his name in the papers, I mentioned an old woman from Guyana who lived in Harlem on West 132nd Street, his old neighborhood. She was a great fan of his. Her name was Gertie Wood and in Guyana she had been awarded the Order of the British Empire for her work among children. When her parents died and then her sister, she couldn't stand to stay in Guyana with all its memories so she settled in the U.S., where she gave piano lessons and worked as a cleaning woman. She was forever talking about her beautiful dead sister and how she was the ugly one of the family, and it was true she had a big square jaw but her eyes and her smile transformed her. The mention of her feeling about her ugliness interested Baldwin, as did her refusal to become a U.S. citizen because, she said, that would make her "a nigger." I asked Baldwin if on his next visit to Harlem he could spare five minutes to meet her. I expected him to claim to be too busy, but he told me he was going to get his hair cut in Harlem the next day and he would meet her afterward.

A Harlem barbershop is a social center as well as a place of business, and so cutting Baldwin's hair was a whole afternoon's work, ten minutes of haircutting and several hours of exchanging stories and ideas about the state of the world. Baldwin was clearly enjoying himself; he was back in the past not even as an unknown young writer but as a boy to whom these streets had been the whole world. The next stop was Small's Paradise, where one of the other customers, a singer named Little Charles, sent Baldwin a drink. I kept phoning Gertie Wood that we were on our way, but by the time we made it, we were nearly two hours late and her dinner for Mr. Baldwin was past its best. Her small second-floor room was crowded with books everywhere, and her Baldwin collection was spread out on her bed. She had something of Albert Schweitzer's reverence for life and so found it impossible to kill anything, including cockroaches—consequently there were nearly as many roaches crawling about her room as there were books. I wondered how Baldwin, with his new haircut and dressed in a smart black suit, would take the roaches, but he sat down on one of her wooden chairs as easily as if he were in the lounge of the Waldorf-Astoria, ate her Guyanese dinner and when she wasn't looking occasionally flicked off the roaches that came crawling on him. They soon addressed each other as Gertie and Jimmy, and she told him about how she was the ugly one of her family and he told her about Frog Eyes. He sat chatting with her for over an hour among the roaches and later arranged for his mother to invite Miss Wood to visit her. It didn't seem like the action of a man who had been much changed by fame.

The change I noticed over the years was a gradual aging—more rapid after King's death and the decline of the civil rights movement—and the fieriness within him that could light up his eyes and set his finger wagging slowly growing less intense until he became almost mellow, the old fire still there but smoldering now. The boyish idealism, the belief in integration, the optimism about the future—all this changed into a kind of disillusionment, almost resignation. The chant of "Freedom now" was slowly replaced by a shrug and a "Well, Rome wasn't built in a day."

He celebrated his fiftieth birthday the same year—1974—that *Beale Street* was published, and with far less emotion than he had shown on his fortieth. He seemed to have a series of illnesses as if, having overspent his energy, he had become a temporary burnt-out case. Yet having at last established a settled home, he seemed unable to stay there for long before, restless again, he was off to the airport. And quite apart from his permanent attachments, he always seemed to have a new companion, progressively younger as he aged, as if he hoped to recapture some of his own lost youth by sharing theirs.

Over the years he had given several public performances entitled "An Evening with James Baldwin," with a solo act accompanied by jazz musicians. He even organized a tribute to Ray Charles, one of his favorite musicians, at New York's Carnegie Hall as part of the Newport Jazz Festival. "I come out of the church and so does he," Baldwin explained. The New York *Times* found the tribute "disappointing" and thought the blind Ray Charles responded to Baldwin's questions "in such a natural and engaging manner as to underline the pomposity of Mr. Baldwin's approach." But at least performing in public probably satisfied the would-be actor who was still very much alive in him.

He was in London for the publication of *Beale Street,* starting an exhausting round of interviews an hour after flying in at 8:35 A.M. Over lunch he told *The Guardian*'s interviewer, Hugh Hebert: "The older I get, the more I work, the less I understand about words. Your characters say: Here I am, I got to tell you this and you got to listen. Then they get you to listen and maybe you listen to a whole lot of shit. But you've got to listen. And then one day they say, Thanks, baby, goodbye—and they go out into the world." When Hebert suggested that in his books he was "working at a vast tragedy," he didn't like the word tragedy because of its closeness to despair, yet agreed that in achieving an optimism "you have to reach a certain level of despair to deal with your life at all." And was there anger as some critics had suggested? "I get angry with the universe, with myself, with my lover, but . . ." A shrug ended the remark.

One of his many engagements in 1975 was a farewell concert and reception for Syvilla Fort, the black dance teacher who had come out of the hospital after a cancer operation with only a few weeks to live.

All her show-business friends, led by Harry Belafonte, whose wife was one of her students, gathered to pay tribute. Baldwin didn't know her personally, but lent his name and presence to a black occasion, as he had in the civil rights days. "It is now up to us," he was fond of saying, quoting *Beale Street* as an example of what he meant.

Incredible as it seemed, during this busy international commuting he was long enough at home in St. Paul-de-Vence to complete another book. Admittedly he took the easiest form—an extended essay of reminiscences about the past, much of it about his childhood. He had trouble with it, however, probably because he could seldom give it his sustained attention. Richard Marek recalled that of the Baldwin books he edited, "the most work was on *The Devil Finds Work.* It just seemed to me that the ideas in a number of places were not clear. There were passages that needed clarifying. Jimmy was one of the easiest people to work with. I have used him as an example many times of how the better a writer is the easier he is to work with." While Baldwin was working on it, a friend sent him a quotation from William James, who had warned his brother, Henry, about the ill effects of exile on a writer: "Keep watch and ward, lest in your style you become too Parisian and lose your hold on the pulse of the great American public." The friend also quoted from Henry James' "Daisy Miller," in which a woman warns her nephew: "You have lived too long out of the country. You will be sure to make some great mistake." The friend had intended it as a joke, but Baldwin was not amused; it was obviously still a tender topic. He sent the friend a copy of his *Dialogue* with Nikki Giovanni with the following underlined: "It's very valuable to be forced to move from one place to another and deal with another set of situations and to accept that this is going to be—in fact it is—your life. And to use it means that you, in a sense, become neither white nor black. And you learn a great deal about— you're forced to learn a great deal about—the history out of which all these words and conceptions and flags and morals come."

The new book, *The Devil Finds Work,* dealt with his filmgoing from the age of about seven—when he saw Joan Crawford in "Dance, Fools, Dance" with his mother or an aunt, he couldn't remember which—up to "The Exorcist" ("The mindless and hysterical banality of the evil presented . . . is the most terrifying thing about the film"). Each movie reminded him of a period in his life, and he related his own experience to the way the movies depicted interracial life. "Guess Who's Coming to Dinner," for example, with his friend Sidney Poitier, moved him to comment: "The immense quantity of polish expended . . . is meant to blind one to its essential inertia and despair." This blend of movie criticism and autobiography encouraged several of his critics to see a further waning of his powers, a repetition of what he had said more forcefully before. Orde Coombs, a black critic, thought the book "teems with a passion that is all reflex, and an anger that is unfocused and almost cynical." His former editor, Christopher Lehmann-Haupt, wrote in the daily New York *Times,* "So James Baldwin is still here, still pursuing us, a ghost of '60's past. Even though he long ago became unfashionable, long ago wore out his welcome even in the black revolution (because he dared to believe that whites and blacks could love each other despite everything), he goes on jumping up and down and pointing like the man in the old Philadelphia *Inquirer* ads." It was better, he wrote, to ignore the two-thirds of the new book that was "wrong-headed" and concentrate on the one-third "that is right" where Baldwin was "testifying honestly to his own experience at the movies." He suggested that Baldwin, once overpraised, was now being underrated.

Meanwhile Baldwin acted as if he ignored the reviewers and kept on the move as usual, lecturing, making personal appearances and writing short pieces that didn't need any sustained concentration. He reviewed Alex Haley's *Roots* for the New York *Times* in 1976, The Bicentennial year, and watched the book become a huge bestseller and an equally popular TV miniseries, the kind of ultimate popular success that had eluded him even in his heyday. Haley had attempted to do in non-fiction through his own family what Baldwin had once planned in his novel, *The House Nigger*—a generational story about blacks from the first slaves through to the present. But whereas Baldwin had imagined a fiery testament to eternal rebellion, Haley's story was more one of courageous and ingenious survival and therefore more acceptable in the conservative America of the mid-seventies. To Baldwin, *Roots* suggested "with great power how each of us, however unconsciously, can't but be the vehicle of the history which has produced us. Well, we can perish in this vehicle, children, or we can move on up the road." The "children" was a new way of addressing the reader. Did it reflect a new note of resignation and an acceptance of age? Certainly in the little he published in this period, there seems to be the sadness, the pessimism, that Dr. Kenneth Clark had noticed.

Bad news came from Paris. Beauford Delaney, now in his mid-seventies, hadn't recovered from his latest breakdown, had developed an incurable mental illness and was drifting into senility, living in dreams of the past. Baldwin had had him down to stay at St. Paul-de-Vence, and he and Bernard Hassell had looked after him, but he now needed constant hospital care. Baldwin got him into a hospital in Paris, where most of the people he knew lived and could visit him. Although the artist was much older than he was, Beauford's decline was bad for Baldwin's spirits, and he tried to escape into work on his long novel, *Just Above My Head,* but ran into the same blocks he had been experiencing with it for the past two years, and so wrote *Little Man, Little Man,* a short book for children, thinking it would be less demanding and with the prospect of addressing children directly that pleased him. But it was merely like a footnote to his real work. Julius Lester, who had become a leading black voice of the new generation, wrote apologetically in the New York *Times Book Review,* "I wish I could love this book because I love James Baldwin. But it is a slight book, and that it was written by a man I will always honor cannot alter this assessment." At least the post-Cleaver generation was showing him more respect, even if they did make him feel like a classic of the past.

If he wanted any further confirmation that his market value was not what it used to be, Baldwin received it when he decided the book he should do was one about the Tony Maynard case that was over with Tony free at last. Surely it would be a good topical way of looking at the last decade of American life and it shouldn't be too difficult to write as he had rehearsed it in his account of the case in *No Name in the Street.* He would split the proceeds with Tony and the money would help Tony get started again. But when he proposed it to Dial Press with a big advance requested since there were two of them involved, no real enthusiasm was shown and the proposed advance was considered far too big. Ten years before Dial had been struggling to hold on to him, acting even as his banker and tax consultant, but the latest books hadn't been big bestsellers, his audience had shrunk and therefore his declining value as an investment gave him less power in the literary marketplace. Dial was even willing to let him offer the book to other publishers. "Jimmy wanted a lot of money," said Richard Marek, "and I thought that was a project that wouldn't get anywhere and it didn't." Edward J. ("Jay") Acton, an editor at Thomas Y. Crowell, signed up the book. "I thought Jimmy might do a longer account than what he wrote about the case in *No Name in the Street*," Acton said. "I signed up the book for Crowell and Ballantine." The two publishers, one hardcover, the other paperback, could then share the large advance. "I think Maynard had a piece of the advance. We signed it up rather than Dial because Jimmy wanted more than Dial was willing to pay." Baldwin had many earnest research sessions with Tony Maynard but eventually gave up work on the book. "He always had a lot to do and never enough time," Acton said. "It was a question of priorities. He wanted to finish *Just Above My Head*. There were contracts going back ten, twelve years in his active file!"

Baldwin told me that when he started writing the Maynard book, he realized he had said all he wanted to in *No Name in the Street*. But taken up by literary gossip, this merely further confirmed all the stories about his waning powers, as if he were a Samson steadily losing his strength—that is, his talent.

In the summer of 1977 he met Robert Coles, the author of *Children of Crisis* and other social studies, and told him he was returning to New York not for one of his frequent visits but to live, a sign of his impatience with all the remarks about his being out of touch. He said many times you might disapprove of your country, might be forced to leave it or "battle" with it, yet you couldn't escape it. In a single lifetime, you couldn't pull up your roots and put them down someplace else. If you pretended not to see the immediate reality that formed you, you would go blind. Wherever he lived, he'd always be an American—a black American. Talking about living in New York again perhaps came from the idea that it would help him to write more vigorously, but he kept his house in St. Paul-de-Vence, which presumably meant he wasn't really serious. He told Coles that as a young writer now, he wouldn't go to Paris but to Africa or Asia—the so-called Third World. "Exiles, wanderers, refugees find different havens, from generation to generation." In America, he said, he found more hope in the changed South— the black man and the white man "haven't yet become strangers"—but "it's too early to know whether that hope will turn out to be justified. I don't wish at this point in my life to turn into a southern romantic." But the note of hope *was* new. He found, however, little hope in northern slums, where nearly half the black young people could find no work—would America's white people stand for that? He had been reading Dostoevsky's *The Possessed* about Russian political activists of the nineteenth century and making parallels with the America of today. "The races are less obsessed with each other than was the case in the 1960s," he said as reported by Coles in the New York *Times Book Review*. "Many black students tell me they pay no attention to whites— though indifference may conceal many other emotions." He had also met many white students who seemed "bewildered, troubled, at a loss to know what to do, where to go." Inertia, even despair could be a stage in one's growth, a way of coming to terms "with what one has gone through and learned." Was he also talking about himself in the years since King's death?

He also mentioned *Just Above My Head* to Robert Coles. It took up where *Go Tell It On the Mountain* left off, though not with the same characters. He thought he had been skirting the subject all his writing years—the life and death of a male gospel singer. "I have a few more months of work on the novel," he said. He planned to finish it in France. "Then, I guess, I'll be able to come home." Maybe it would be "the end of more than the novel—a long apprenticeship, I sometimes think." It was as if his instincts were trying to tell him something, for this was to be his last novel, and as though he knew this, he had begun to cram into it so many memories he wanted to bear witness to and relive.

Jay Acton had left Crowell and set up as a literary agent. Baldwin became one of his clients, and Acton remained his agent until two years before he died. "We lasted longer than most of Jimmy's agents," Acton said wryly. The problem then was to get him to finish *Just Above My Head*. He seemed incapable of concentrating on it for long, as if writing had become even more difficult for any length of time. In 1978 he was in the middle of a controversy over a play about Paul Robeson. In January, just before the play starring James Earl Jones opened in New York, Baldwin was among fifty-six black writers, artists, educators and religious and political leaders who protested against the play's view of Robeson. In May he was in a forum at Hunter College in New York still objecting to how Robeson was portrayed. "The popular culture," said Baldwin, "has to find a way to make Robeson moving, charming, noble and innocent, and above all irrelevant."

He also had welcomed the election of southerner Jimmy Carter, friend of King's father, as president. In an open letter to him, Baldwin wrote that "You, in my lifetime, are the only President I would have written." He saw Carter, who had appointed King's assistant, Andrew Young, to be his United Nations ambassador, as the product of a similar regional experience as black southerners like Young and King.

But none of these public activities, backed up by his usual hectic personal life while in New York, was helping to finish *Just Above My Head*. Nor did the news that Beauford Delaney had died in the Paris hospital. It was a relief that Beauford wouldn't have to suffer anymore, but Baldwin felt the old artist had taken part of his life with him. It was as if a father had died—a father he hadn't "slayed" but had loved. He remembered their first meeting in the Village so long ago and how Beauford had opened his eyes to so much. Beauford's death seemed to bring his own death closer. He had the feeling that his life was shrinking as the ranks of his old friends slowly thinned. It thrust him back into the comforts of memory—into the world of *Just Above My Head*—and yet he couldn't shut himself away to finish it. There was always some-body to meet and he welcomed the distraction. Helen Meyer's remark that "Jimmy's only trouble really was to settle down and write" seemed truer than ever in those days. And Richard Marek was beginning to worry that he would never finish the novel. Agent Jay Acton decided something drastic was in order.

"In the summer of 1979 I literally kidnapped Jimmy to get him to finish *Just Above My Head,*" recalled Acton. "Dial had already announced it in their catalog, so there was a lot of pressure on Jimmy to finish and he still had one hundred pages from being closed out, but he had been at that stage for two or three years. I had a house at Brewster, Massachusetts, on the Cape. I rented a house two doors away belonging to a doctor we knew. I put Jimmy in the house with just a houseboy-help, a young man from North Carolina, to shop, drive, do the chores. We made sure Jimmy arrived alone and we set up the phone so Jimmy wouldn't be disturbed. We even took the number off the phone so he couldn't tell anyone the number. There were people who tried to come and visit him, but it was part of our job to make sure they didn't. We really had Jimmy in handcuffs. He stayed the whole summer from June to September. By September he had completed everything but the last twenty pages. I remember he had to fly out to keep a lecture date and on the way back he called me to say he was at the airport. I thought he meant Hyannis, not far away, so I said take a cab. He arrived in about two hours. He had come from Boston. The cab cost about $135. Being Jimmy, he said, 'Pay the guy, will you.'

"He was very accepting of the change in his fame. I had often said of him that if he wanted to teach, to lecture more and to go easier on writing, his legend was secure. He didn't need to write another word. But like all great writers, he lived to write, to get that next word out. He was always going to struggle against giving that up. I think there were two people. There was Jimmy, the guy you hung out with and laughed and told stories, and then there was James Baldwin with a certain kind of persona, which you could see when he went to universities to speak. He became then a fiery, impassioned preacher as he had been when he was a boy. He was my literary hero when I was in high school in Boston. The notion of meeting and working with him was a thrilling one. Like all of us, Jimmy had great points and weak points.

I have one friend who went five times to an airport in California to collect Jimmy and five times he didn't show up. There are certain people who say he wasn't a very good novelist. I happen to think he was very good. *Giovanni's Room* is almost a perfect book with perfect pitch. There hasn't been as good a first novel as *Go Tell It On the Mountain* written in this century. I think there are parts of *Just Above My Head* written on my porch that are a rare experience. He would come over to read aloud parts of *Just Above My Head* to make sure he got the voice right. It was an unforgettable author-reader experience. This man was very, very good. We all know the phases that literary fashion passes through. Mailer hasn't been in fashion all the time. Jimmy was on stage for an awful long time."

Richard Marek was delighted to receive the manuscript of *Just Above My Head* and to find "it was completely straightforward. I did no editing whatever on that." While Dial was rushing it through the printer's, Baldwin was on the West Coast for a series of lectures and speeches at several universities. He seemed to be strengthening his links with universities and the lecture circuit, almost as if he were thinking of how to earn a living in other ways. Mel Watkins, who was now an established black critic, interviewed him for the New York *Times Book Review* in Berkeley, California, during an especially hectic day that included several speeches, other interviews and appearances as guest of honor at two receptions. At night he was at a party at a private home in the Berkeley hills. The guests included Angela Davis, the civil rights activist, and Huey Newton, the former Black Panther leader, and the street outside was lined with police patrol cars. Watkins asked Baldwin about *Just Above My Head*. In a recent essay Baldwin had written that he suspected "every life moves full circle—toward revelation," so it seemed rather ominous when he told Watkins that he had experienced "absolute terror" in finishing the novel and that now he felt "I've finally come full circle." It sounded as if he was considering his life was completed, but ever the optimist when he could manage it, Baldwin added, "From *Go Tell It On the Mountain* to *Just Above My Head* sums up something of my experience—it's difficult to articulate—that sets me free to go someplace else." By "come full circle" was he referring to the return to the religious theme that had dominated *Mountain*? "In one sense, yes," he replied, "I guess it is the religious aspect. But in this book religion and salvation are part of a much vaster framework." He was also asked about the critics who said he was out of touch. "I never understood the criticism," he said firmly. He added he knew very well he couldn't live without his brothers and sisters, and he discovered "quite literally that you carry your home with you. There is no way you can escape from it—to think otherwise is simply an illusion." He also discussed some of the themes of *Just Above My Head* such as the civil rights movement. "You could hardly have found three more improbable people to be thrown together: Malcolm, Martin and me. First of all, they were exceedingly respectable in a way that I'm not, and the role I began to play was not a role I'd foreseen. In a sense, I was feeling my way—suppressing certain arguments I had, certain questions, because of the way things were going." Did he then believe a writer should become involved? "I certainly can't imagine art for art's sake . . . that's a European approach, which never made any sense to me. I think what you have to do, which is the difficult thing about a writer, is avoid slogans. You have to have the [guts] to protest the slogan, no matter how noble it may sound. It always hides something else; the writer should try to expose what it hides."

He was also asked about the theme of homosexuality in his new novel. "In the past," Baldwin replied, "this theme has been more self-conscious for me. I think in this novel it's less so. I'm less defensive perhaps than in *Giovanni's Room* or in *Another Country*. Less shrill, I'd like to say." Was this also the case with the racial issue? "Well, first, there are few white people in the novel." He thought the whole concept of race had had its day. This was an idea he was to repeat many times in his last years. According to Baldwin, we wasted our lives worrying about meaningless questions of color and dreams of security. "We're better than all that nonsense," he would say impatiently. He looked ahead instead to a world without narrow national identities and without wars over boundaries. His mother had told him as a boy that "You don't know where you're going to find yourself so you've got to treat everybody as long as you live as though they were your brothers and sisters. And," he said, "that seems very simple to me." He believed it was an idea that all human beings would eventually live by "or we shall perish." But he added: "I know this sounds remote now, and that I will not live to see anything resembling this hope come to pass." An interviewer asked him was he troubled by death and received the answer: "Not at all by death. I'm troubled over getting my work done and over all the things I've not learned. It's useless to be troubled by death, because then of course you can't live at all."

19

Just Above My Head

JUST ABOVE MY HEAD, published five years after *Beale Street* (which was published six years after *Train*), was to be James Baldwin's last published novel and his last book with Dial Press. A long association was coming to an end. Dial, as part of Dell Publishing Company, had been bought by Doubleday, a giant compared to Dial, and Baldwin was now just one celebrity author among many on the Doubleday lists. Gone for good were the days when he was the company's superstar with a close personal relationship with the publishers of both Dial and Dell, and with Helen Meyer at the top always ready to help in a personal emergency. Now there were committees and editorial boards to be consulted. To make the changeover even more difficult, he had to face yet another change of editors while he was finishing *Just Above My Head*. Richard Marek, with whom he had a friendly relationship, left to join another company with his own list. For Baldwin it was yet another sign of the growing insecurity, the increasing uncertainty, of his life as a writer. Friends pressed him to seek some sinecure in a university—writer-in-residence lecturing just occasionally on literature or civil rights—a chair—so that he could have a regular income and write only when he felt like it.

His new novel, which he had brought forth after an intense struggle, contained glimpses of his major personal concerns as he reached fifty-five. "Have Mercy" was the evocative title of the novel's first part, and under it he quoted the old traditional refrain, "Work: for the night is coming," another eerie suggestion of approaching death. No wonder he was knocking on wood for good luck more than ever. *Just Above My Head* was another novel in the first person like its two predecessors, *Beale Street* and *Train*. Its narrator was the elder brother of a famous gospel singer—in this story Baldwin was both elder brother and the star younger brother, for the gospel singer shared much of his own past. Here is the elder brother defending the younger brother's homosexuality: "I once heard myself shouting at some asshole white producer, who was giving me some mealy-mouthed crap about my brother's private life being a problem, *If he likes boys, then buy him a bathtubful, you hear? Buy him a boatload! What the fuck do you like?*"

There was also a revealing exchange between the elder brother and his nephew after the death of the younger brother, who shared Baldwin's middle name of Arthur.

"What was my uncle—Arthur—like?"

"Well—why do you ask? *You* knew him."

The nephew replied, "A lot of the kids at school—they talk about him."

The elder brother asked, "What do they say?"

"They say—he was a faggot."

The elder brother said, "Your uncle was my brother, right? And I loved him. Okay? He was a very—lonely—man. He had a very strange—life. I think that—he was a very great singer . . . I know a lot of men who loved my brother—your uncle—or who thought they did. I know two men—your uncle—Arthur loved . . . I know—before Jimmy [Arthur's young lover]—Arthur slept with a lot of people—mostly men, but not always. He was young, Tony. Before your mother *I* slept with a lot of women . . . mostly women, but—in the army—I was young, too—not always. You want the truth. I'm trying to tell you the truth—anyway, let me tell you, baby, I'm proud of my brother, your uncle, and I'll be proud of him until the day I die. You should be, too. Whatever the fuck your uncle was, and he was a whole lot of things, he was nobody's faggot . . . didn't I—we—tell you, a long time ago, not to believe in labels? . . . What did you think of your uncle?"

And the boy replied, "I thought he was a crazy, beautiful cat . . . I loved him—that's why—"

It is easy to imagine Baldwin behind this exchange, aware as he was of the rough, crude jokes about him ("Martin Luther Queen" and so on). He had often wondered how his young nephews and nieces might respond if they were teased about it by other children. There was sadness here, a need to defend himself, and there was sadness in much of the novel, but the nephew's reply, "I loved him," echoed through the story, too, holding the sadness at bay and giving these last Harlem memories a very special poignancy and glow. Baldwin returned to scenes and people he had described before, but his view was more mellow, more accepting, revealing the love, the warmth rather than stressing the dark side of the ghetto, of poverty, the need for change. This was the private, the personal Baldwin ever looking inward. "You began to see, and even rejoice to see, what you always saw. You can even tell anguish to sit down, and shut up, you're busy right now—and anguish, as you should certainly know by now, ain't to go nowhere. It might go around the corner, on a particularly bright day, and there *are* those days: but anguish has your number, knows, to paraphrase the song, where you live. It's a difficult relationship, but mysteriously indispensable. It teaches you." He wrote those words while he was working on the novel.

He tried for a last time to show what anguish teaches in *Just Above My Head.* He looked back over the life of the dead gospel singer, dead Arthur, a stand-in for himself. "I wouldn't be able to live, man, if I thought you were ashamed of me," was a key line. So was: "She had never wanted this, this rage and hatred. She had always wanted his love." Then there was this reminder of the loneliness so many people saw in Baldwin himself: "Arthur could bear solitude, had been born to it, and could never be surprised by it, however mightily he might be tormented." He described Solitude as he did Rage and Hatred and Love and Fear almost as if they were people haunting his imagination—his dreams when he was alone. The novel's fourth section is entitled "Stepchild." A key line there is: "You've got to depend on yourself"—Baldwin's favorite refrain since King's death. "I know that I smoke and drink too much. Whatever is going to kill me is already moving, is on the road, and I do not know, no more than anyone else does, how I will face that last intensity, when everything flames up for the last time and then the flame falters and goes out. I would like it to be swift: yet I know that this moment does not exist in time." At the end of the novel (". . . and then I wake up, and my pillow is wet with tears"), it seems as if one has been listening to Baldwin examining his life for a last time. No wonder he kept putting off finishing it. As he told Mel Watkins, he had "finally come full circle." There were other signs that he knew this was the real end of his writing career. He usually wrote at the end of a novel all the places where he had written it and the date when he finished it. This time he left it blank. He also dedicated it to his three brothers and five sisters and to Bernard Hassell, one of his oldest and most loyal friends, and to another friend, a photographer named Max Petrus, whose close-up of an aging, quizzical Baldwin was used on the jacket of the novel.

Baldwin's keen instincts about his own life, which usually guided him so well, must have known there would be no more, though a man with his sense of life and his great pride could not give up until he was completely worn down. All that he was to complete over the next eight years of declining health and vitality was an unsatisfactory rhetorical essay about a series of racial murders in Atlanta—an effort of will rather than talent—and his collected essays, for which he contributed merely a chatty introduction of yet more reminiscences. *Just Above My Head* was the end of his real *oeuvre,* his last appearance as a witness, and even in writing this last novel there were times when his energy flagged and the old fire, the old intensity and passion were not there.

His new editor at Dial, Juri Jurjevics, had inherited the novel from Richard Marek and wanted Baldwin to do more work on it, but he discovered "Jimmy couldn't take a lot of criticism. There were many changes I thought could have been made," Jurjevics recalled, "but he wasn't going to do it. It was thirty seven weeks on the Washington *Post* bestseller list, but I don't think it ever made the New York *Times* list. I think it sold about 40,000 to 50,000 copies. We printed 75,000 copies and bound 65,000. It was a featured alternate selection with the

Book-of-the-Month Club, and Dell paid $305,000 for the paperback rights in competition with other publishers.

Jurjevics remembered their first meeting. "He was exactly the way I had imagined him. He could get you in eighteen seconds, he was so totally charming, but not in any namby-pamby way. He got you in some way to identify with him if you only knew him for an hour. His family was very supportive of him. They had a real understanding of him. It was incredible the extent to which he was an object of adulation. I remember we were walking down a street and a bus driver pulled his bus over to recognize him. I've never seen a writer before in that role. It was really hard to live that way. In a restaurant you had to practically build a wall around him. The other customers, the busboys, people passing the window—they were all eyeing him. It was like going to lunch with someone like Jackie Kennedy, not a writer. Not even Mailer would get that kind of attention. I remember when he was signing books for the kids at City College. I had in mind it could be dangerous because he was so exposed. They were all the time stuffing notes to him into his coat. Remember at Dial Press, we received hate calls about him—the nineteenth call was a bomb threat. He was very conscious of that and it affected his mood. There was also the time factor—the past. He was sometimes rather sad, almost maudlin, and it was hard to shake him out of it. He had once chastised whites—the Establishment—the world—and they had listened, but not any more. He was out there doing it alone, growing angry and maudlin.

"I think in some ways he was paying the price for having been out of his own culture for so long in both his life and his writing. He tried to address himself to the same themes, but they just didn't connect any more. He didn't seem to realize that. Yet his speeches at City College were just unbelievable. They were totally extemporaneous. He seemed very nervous and almost shy in person. You never realized it of him that he would be able to take hold of an audience to such an extent until you witnessed it. He was quite brilliant. But it was very hard being such a celebrity because of all the added pressures. In his wildest dreams as a kid of being a famous writer, he couldn't have imagined such fame. He wasn't a famous writer so much as a famous person. He enjoyed it to some degree. Of course you've got to remember, too, the way he was always running short of money. The money paid to him, even large sums, he would just throw to the winds. It was almost as if it were too much and would alienate him from what he was. There was really a pathology there in his attitude toward money. He had to get rid of it. I remember his agent, Jay Acton, was very good and worked out a scheme that would help him to pay all his debts. Part of it involved a very fixed budget. Jimmy was to receive so much a month, not a great sum but very liberal. Jimmy was sitting listening to all this explained to him. His boyfriend of that time, a young black guy, was there and Jimmy kept smiling the delinquent smile he had when he had done something. I remember his agent left the room and Jimmy commented on his boyfriend's new boots. They were a spectacular pair of boots in rattlesnake or something. They had cost $5,000! Jimmy treated it like a big joke. But how could you get financially straight like that when you had debts to pay? He didn't live at such a high standard himself, but spent money for someone else. I know the French were always on him for taxes on his house in the South of France. Whatever money he was paid went straight to his agent, but it was very difficult to get Jimmy to budget in any way.

"He hadn't written anything for a while when *Just Above My Head* came out. I felt the novel was three-quarters there. It was the strongest writing he had done in years. It was very good but without much control, almost as if he had written it with a blotting pad instead of a typewriter. It wasn't very premeditated. It was like one hot draft. He was drinking a lot when he was writing it, perhaps in order to write it. I think he had had it in some way. The celebrity was terribly bothersome. It was hard to know, but he seemed at times to feel there would be some horrible judgment on his sexuality. That theme seemed to obsess him. He seemed to have come out of the closet so many times. Would that macho bus driver, for example, have pulled over his bus if he had known the kind of guy Jimmy was? That kind of question bothered him. And of course the bus driver did know—everyone knew. But half the time Jimmy couldn't see it and the other half he felt unsure. It was sometimes a torture to him. And then of course there was unhappiness over the direction the country had gone in. An unfortunate part of his power was some kind of pessimism that made people sit up and pay attention, but the attention had gone, and only the pessimism was left. He was really out of sync with the white audience he had once captured. He was left more with a black audience than a white audience. That was why I was so interested in all the weeks he was on the Washington *Post* bestseller list. He was the choice of middle-class blacks, but I don't think he ever really connected with that base he once had. If he had, he might have changed his writing and recaptured his audience. As it was, they treated him as some sort of historical figure. He found it creepy being a legend. There was always media attention without much substance. He was media-fodder. It gets you a table at a restaurant, but it's a pain. He had an amazingly strong personality and it was surprising how incredibly sweet he was in those last years."

Donna Schrader, once again in charge of publicity, also remembered the burdens of celebrity. "Everybody wanted to see him. He had me sending books to prisons. People's reaction on the street when they recognized him was almost like touching a god. It really moved him. I remember a little modest production of *The Amen Corner* on the west side in New York. I went with Jimmy and his mother and Gloria. Jimmy had such a good time laughing at the performances and I enjoyed just watching him. He might not have known the words. *Anna Karenina* was one of his favorite books, and when he found me reading it, he leaned over and read it, too. He laughed with enjoyment at it."

Schrader was also a witness of an emotional reminder of the distant past, the days he recaptured in the novel. When he was signing books at the Harvard Co-op in Boston, a young man asked him, "Do you remember Bill Miller?" Baldwin said he certainly did remember her. How could he possibly forget the teacher who had done so much to open his eyes and whose trips to the movies with him he had written about in *The Devil Finds Work*? "Well," said the young man, "I'm her son."

The reviews were predictably mixed for *Just Above My Head*. As Schrader noted, "He always got attention from reviewers, but it wasn't as exciting for the later books. Fashions had changed. There was definitely a change of attitude." The New York *Times Book Review* found the novel uneven with "veering, shifting forces" of inspiration and too much that was "unrealized." The consummation of Baldwin's art had not yet come to pass. The curious fact was that the novel was "so narrow, so tame." Baldwin's focus was still the private self—"he has given us another of his warm, melancholy, basically likable novels and hasn't really made use of his elaborate generational-historical scheme." There was a lack of passion, they said. The daily New York *Times* referred to Baldwin's attempt to find a prophetic role "while spending too much time in Turkey and France" and said that "he sat on and squashed his lyric impulse." People magazine commented: "As in the past, Baldwin powerfully evokes the ambience of bars, cafes, apartments, streets and the very weather of New York and Paris. His characters are funky, violent, crazed, worldly, innocent and wildly overdrawn. The style borrows from the excesses of black gospel hymns and preaching, but that is appropriate to the story. Reading it is an entrancing plunge into dark and melancholy waters." People also profiled him, noting that he lived and traveled openly with a "muscular, good-looking New Yorker in his late 20s" and yet became "visibly nettled" when his homosexuality was alluded to, remarking, "I love a few people; some are women and some are men." Of his writing, he said: "Thank God I didn't say anything I have to take back."

Some of the other reviews of *Just Above My Head* were more like comments on his celebrity life than on his book. It was the price a writer paid for being a public figure. Baldwin had written his last testament with flagging energy, struggling at last to complete it, but if he wasn't to be accorded the respect that deserved, then he wasn't going to let it bother him, at least not in public.

He concealed his ill health by staying at home in St. Paul-de-Vence, but guests from all over the world descended on him and he was continually busy playing host. He talked about novels and plays and film projects he was working on as if he were in the prime of his life. Simone Signoret noted in her autobiographical *Nostalgia Isn't What It Used to Be*: "It wasn't until yesterday's lunch with James Baldwin that I finally after seventeen years got a correct definition for this word [waiver] whose wandering etymology does, somewhere way back, have something to do with the waves of the sea and hand gestures." Herbert Gold also visited him. Arriving before Baldwin was up, he was given bulletins by a young black—"He's awake . . . He's up . . ." and so on. "I think he was Jimmy's lover at the time. He said he was originally from California. He had a street-hustler style. He told a story about getting on a Greyhound bus to go to New York and how he occupied three seats to sleep and people were standing up, afraid to ask him to move over. He thought it was pretty funny. Jimmy's brother and a nephew, about ten or twelve, were there. Jimmy was very nice to his nephew [Gloria's son]. I remember we all went on a walk. I got in an argument with his black friend and Jimmy told him, 'Baby, you have to remember Herb's Jewish and doesn't think the same way.'"

Jay Acton also came. "It was a beautiful setting with fascinating company," Acton said. "Simone Signoret would come for dinner— people like that. The garden wasn't one of Jimmy's interests. He wasn't a gardener. He didn't really seem interested in landscape or paintings. But he loved that house. He did everything to protect and keep that house. In the tributes paid to Jimmy, people rarely mentioned his humor. He was a wonderful mimic in a good way, not at all cruel to people. He understood people intuitively. He would go to a meeting and in five minutes Jimmy knew whether the person was genuine or full of bullshit." An assistant of Acton, a boxing writer and former middleweight contender named Fraser Scott, accompanied him on one visit. "Baldwin had a beautiful place there on a hillside," Scott recalled. "He was a friendly man, but very complicated and confusing. I didn't understand him." Helen Meyer, vacationing in France, arranged to meet him at a restaurant in Nice. He arrived so late with a group of friends that the restaurant had closed and they had to move to another, where hours later she left Baldwin still talking and drinking with his friends.

He soon grew restless again. He did his best to carry on as usual. In New York he told a friend he had had to have minor surgery because he had done someone "a favor," a reference apparently to a sexual encounter.

He seemed to be graying rapidly and shrinking into old age, the lines on his face deeper, with almost a wizened look. When he was drinking with three old friends he warned them that he wasn't well. He seemed nervously irritable, and when one friend began to argue about William Faulkner and the South, he snapped, "If you're going to argue, you better get up and go." This was so unusual for Baldwin, who could argue fiercely but generally ended good-humoredly, that the friend got up and left and Baldwin watched him do so without another word.

He was to have taken part in a Soviet-American writers workshop at a Black Sea resort, but illness upset his plans. He spoke at a conference at Rutgers University on literature, and John A. Williams, who met him, recalled: "The organizers had wanted the speeches in advance, but this proved impossible in Jimmy's case. He had a long reputation for not being dependable on that score. I don't think he ever spoke from notes, but off the cuff. I didn't often see him because I wasn't really involved in the literary circuit. It's the system to have just one leading black writer. I remember a couple of New York editors saying, 'You have got your choice of Ellison or Baldwin as your leader.' Ed Doctorow when he was at Dial asked me to come to Dial. But they had Gaines and Baldwin. That meant they had their share of black writers. I didn't feel I'd get their full effort if I joined the stable. It was nothing to do with Jimmy as an individual. It was just the way things worked."

The irony was that Baldwin no longer felt in a privileged position at Dial. They hadn't been interested in his Tony Maynard book proposal, and now they had rejected him for the first time, how did he know for sure his future books would be accepted? It was a question that worried him. A writer needed to feel secure with his publisher. He had been with Dial for twenty-four years, ever since *Giovanni's Room,* but for how long now? As if to reassure him, Dial established a James Baldwin Prize for "new or previously unrecognized black writers of unusual talent." The first Baldwin prize was awarded to Raymond Andrews for his novel, *Appalachee Red,* set in the black neighborhood of a small town in northern Georgia. "Young black writers are moving in some ways in a larger world than when I was growing up," Baldwin noted. "They have African and Latin American literature to refer to whereas I had to discover it for myself." The young prize-winner's agent, Susan Ann Protter, said that after the award ceremony they all went out for drinks and Baldwin was "just as I imagined he would be—very warm and friendly."

He spent a month as a lecturer in Afro-American Studies at the University of California, arriving late and being persistently late for most of his classes. "I'm having a little difficulty pulling myself together," he confessed. Much of what he said was gloomy. He made no point of integration. America and the Western world as we knew it were doomed; black people were America's only hope. But, as the Los Angeles *Times* noted, "it is his manner that disarms. Instant affection, admiration and a wild, fleeting desire to protect this gray-haired man who was wearing his face as naked as a child's. Anxiety, dread, panic—there for all to see and watch—gave way to relief, delight, anger, challenge. It was all in the eyes and mouth. The rest of him seemed to have been consumed by those two features."

He was still trying to maintain the same pace but it was becoming harder and harder. Yet he needed distraction. It was as if he couldn't ever bear to be alone. Even his succession of young lovers often seemed like just an insurance that he would have company when everybody else went home. But he worried about the difference in their ages. "You sure you want to hang out with an old man like me?" a character asks in *Just Above My Head,* and receives the reply from his young lover: "You don't look so old to *me.*"

When he talked about writing it was essays and articles, always journalism, and the subject was invariably related to the past, generally the civil rights movement. He wanted to write a piece for The New Yorker and considered the Supreme Court's decision ordering school desegregation and what had happened since. But he soon lost interest in it. "I'm wrestling with myself," he told several people. The effects of age continued to worry him. At times he wondered whether to dye his hair, but he had always made such a point of admitting to who and what he was. But he showed how he felt before one student audience when he said he was born on August 2, 1924, and there was a gasp as if he had said 1824. He tried to laugh it off. "Yes, there are people still alive who were born in 1924. Sometimes I'm amazed, too." He gave a forced laugh, but clearly wasn't amused. When he described himself as the grandson of a slave, a student said his voice sounded "different," and Baldwin replied quickly, "Oh, I've been around."

He was curiously impatient with some of the more recent movements. "All these movements—women's liberation, gay liberation—all these eruptions. Perhaps I'm old-fashioned, but I feel very dubious about all that. You don't have to prove you're a woman, and if you happen to be homosexual or whatever, you don't have to form a club in order to learn to live with yourself."

His next idea for The New Yorker was to revisit some of the main battlefields of the civil rights movement down South, interview the former leaders and tell what had happened to them and the racial scene in the meantime. It would need a lot of legwork and research. Did he really want to do it or was he just responding to a growing nostalgia for those movement days? He finally went south with a TV crew who wanted to make a film of his journey. The film, made by Dick Fontaine and Pat Hartley, was finished and shown, but Baldwin never wrote anything about it unless his long essay about the Atlanta murders included some of his observations. In the film he was shown meeting former civil rights leaders in Washington, Atlanta, Birmingham, Selma, New Orleans, Newark and St. Augustine. There was a reunion with Jerome Smith, and no doubt references to the famous Kennedy meeting. Some children patted Smith's bald head with delight as he and Baldwin were talking—a moment the film caught. At the other extreme was a flashback showing the young brother of James Chaney, a black civil rights worker beaten to death in Mississippi along with two white workers, Michael Schwerner and Andrew Goodman, in 1964, weeping at his brother's funeral and swearing to carry on his brother's work—if he could ever accept what had happened Baldwin knew how he felt. He discovered that later the brother was charged with allegedly killing a white man. "The movie leaves us to make the connections," noted The New York Times.

Although the film tried to give an impression of spontaneity, as if the camera just happened to be there, the general air of self-consciousness spoiled most of the exchanges. Baldwin was simply a better actor than most of the former Movement leaders. Probably the most telling point was the way they had all aged, it really looked like twenty years later, though most of them appeared in better shape than Baldwin. They were all fairly pessimistic about the progress made since King's death, but in some cases there was clearly, too, a case of middle-age blues and nostalgia for their youthful past. But it was a superficial, surface exchange; before their talk could really get anywhere the scene was over, the camera off somewhere else. It was an obvious release for Baldwin the would-be actor, but what was needed was some straight-from-the-shoulder observation and reflection from Baldwin the writer. The New York *Times* commented that the center of *I Heard It Through the Grapevine,* as the film was called, remained hidden inside the mind of James Baldwin, "who is a writer, not a performer or master of ceremonies." But the acting, the TV camaraderie were perhaps as much as he was able to do at that time. It was also a very emotional occasion for him, especially since the changes in the South gave him a sense of the King (and Baldwin) years having been left far behind. Down there he was a figure of the dim, distant past to the new generation, all his links were middle-aged, with their parents.

On his journey he encountered two very different black writers. He and LeRoi Jones, now Amiri Baraka, had a reunion with much more in common now that they were both older and arguments about black power were now almost academic without the Movement. Black striving was now much more at a local level electing black mayors, congressmen, managers, foremen, registering voters, sharing power in the unions, on school boards, in city halls. It wasn't a time for national demonstrations or exchanges on overall philosophies. In the film Baraka took Baldwin around his New Jersey hometown, Newark, to see where the riots of the sixties took place in the ghetto—the "rebellion," as Baraka called it. Whole blocks had been left to decay like a symbol of official indifference. Black youths mugged for the camera while Baldwin and Baraka, once rivals for attention with different philosophies, chatted like members of a mutual-admiration society.

Brother David acted as Baldwin's straight man in the film, and they both referred to the "Western world" as if they were not a part of it but could easily escape into an international black identity. On the subject of black Africa Baldwin was as uncritical as he was about black Americans, though he had continued to turn down every opportunity to go back there to write about it. A.L. Hart, an editor at Dial, recalled trying to persuade him to cover the civil war in Biafra, but, he said, Baldwin didn't see himself as a "war correspondent," but rather it seemed to be that, for whatever reason, he had decided to pay Africa the respect of not writing about it. But in the TV film he did meet a famous African—the Nigerian writer, Chinua Achebe. They were shown on a Florida beach that was formerly for whites only. As overheard in the film, their talk was cut to the easy simplifications that TV encourages, so different from the complexity of their books. Baldwin and Achebe both had black faces, but their physiques, poise and personalities reflected quite different cultures. A real encounter between two such different black writers might have been most telling, but not this playacting for TV.

One learns much more from Achebe's account of the meeting after Baldwin's death. He had been wanting to meet Baldwin for a long time, and when finally they did meet "in the jungles of Florida," he greeted him with "Mr. Baldwin, I presume." Achebe added: "You should have seen his eyes dancing, his remarkable face working in ripples of joyfulness. During the four days we spent down there, I saw how easy it was to make Jimmy smile; and how the world he was doomed to inhabit would remorselessly deny him that simple benediction." Achebe gave an example. He and Baldwin were invited to hold a public conversation at the African Literature Association's annual conference in Gainesville. As Baldwin, "in particularly high spirits," the old preacher in him reacting to the crowd, began his opening statement, "a mystery voice came over the public address system and began to hurl insults at him and me." Achebe said he would never forget that moment. "The happiness was brutally wiped off Baldwin's face; the genial manner gone; the eyes flashing in defiant combativeness; the voice incredibly calm and measured. And the words of remorseless prophecy began once again to flow." Achebe commented: "Principalities and powers do not tolerate those who interrupt the sleep of their consciences. That Baldwin got away with it for forty years was a miracle. Except of course that he didn't get away; he paid dearly every single day of those years, every single hour of those days. What was his crime that we should turn him into a man of sadness, this man inhabited by a soul so eager to be loved and to smile?"

A man of sadness—that was how the Nigerian writer saw him, and when Baldwin wrote a short piece for Esquire in which he made a brief reference to his trip south, he called it "Dark Days," for, he said, "we know how much there is to be done and how unlikely it is that we will have another sixty years."

20

"Professor Baldwin"

FIGURES FROM the distant past started reappearing. He was sitting in the Cafe de Flore in Paris when whom should he see but Elia Kazan, who invited him to dinner at Lipp's. Kazan found him "older, as plain as I am, bug-eyed to boot, and as adorable as ever." They spent almost the whole time reminiscing about *Blues for Mister Charlie* and, according to Kazan, Baldwin recounted the whole backstage drama of nearly twenty years ago, including his speech from the top of the thirty-foot ladder, as if it had only happened that week.

At a function at New York Public Library he met William Cole, who recalled: "Jimmy gave me a big kiss and described me as his oldest friend in publishing. He was always very friendly and talkative, but that night he was sparkling." At The Nation's 120th anniversary celebrations at the 167th Street Armory in New York, Ann Birstein from the Paris days found him talking at the bar to cartoonist Jules Feiffer. "Jimmy and I just laughed. We always did a lot of laughing. He could be so funny. He wrote down his phone number for me, but I never called."

E.L. Doctorow, his former Dial editor and now a well-known novelist himself, was also there. "We talked as if there had been no time lapse since our last meeting," said Doctorow, "and then something stopped him in mid-sentence, so I turned when his face broke into a big smile and standing there was Jesse Jackson." He had known Jesse Jackson since he was one of Martin Luther King's young assistants and now he was running for president, the first mainstream black candidate. He and Jesse Jackson had not always agreed any more than King had always approved of his young assistant's ideas, but Baldwin knew the importance of what Jesse Jackson was doing—"Nothing will ever again be what it was before . . . It changes the way the boy in the street and the boy on Death Row and his mother and his father and his sweetheart and his sister think about themselves." Jesse Jackson also had something approving to say of Baldwin, who was "honest and courageous and Dr. King had great respect for him. Jimmy and I did not always see eye to eye, but he was an important window on what it meant in America—and still means— to try to live, to survive as a persecuted minority when the majority is blind, indifferent or unequivocally your mortal enemy."

Otto Friedrich and his wife on the way to the opera in New York met Baldwin by chance at his favorite bar-restaurant near his mother's, The Ginger Man. "My wife got there ahead of me and she ran into Jimmy whom she hadn't seen since the Paris days. They had been really good friends. Back in New York she had invited him to dinner, but he never showed up. He called just before he was due to say he had missed the train, etc. She felt 'Damn him!' because she had all the meal ready. But they had a great old reunion at The Ginger Man. There was a middle-aged white guy with Jimmy to pay the bill and Jimmy kind of ignored him, and there was a black woman with a tape recorder trying to interview him. We barged in breaking everything up, though she tried to continue the interview for a time and then put her tape recorder away. We talked about the old days in Paris until we left to go to the opera. The woman trying to interview him was Alice Walker, whose novel, *The Color Purple,* had just come out."

He was also interviewed by Peter Manso for an oral biography of Norman Mailer: "Perhaps I expected something from my countrymen when I was twenty-five. No longer. Not even from Norman." He added that Mailer had become bored with the civil rights struggle "when the struggle came north," but he wasn't really talking about Mailer—

"Norman is as Norman does. It would be unfair of me to single him out. In order to be hurt, your confidence must be placed there, and, as I say, talking about Norman is very painful, very difficult for me."

His next move was back again to the university world in search of a more permanent position. In 1983 he was appointed Five College Professor in the W.E.B. Du Bois Department of Afro-American Studies at the University of Massachusetts at Amherst. His friends there, including former SNCC member Michael Thelwell, Julius Lester and Chinua Achebe, hoped that he would be able to come from his home in St. Paul-de-Vence to lecture for a few months a year. Much would depend on how the faculty and the students reacted to him, but as he was a revered figure with so many, that didn't seem to be a problem. At first Julius Lester helped him to settle in. "He came and had dinner with my family quite a bit," Lester recalled, "I often used to drive him to the airport when he was going somewhere." Lester also interviewed him for the New York *Times Book Review*. He was particularly interested in Baldwin's description of himself as a "witness" because that wasn't how he would describe himself as a writer. Baldwin replied that in the church in which he was raised, you were supposed to bear witness to the truth. What was the difference between a spokesman and a witness? "A spokesman assumes that he is speaking for others. I never assumed that—I never assumed that I could." Lester asked him what he saw as the task facing black writers at the time. "To make the question of color obsolete," replied Baldwin. But some black writers said their responsibility was to write about black people. "That is not a contradiction," answered Baldwin. "If our voices are heard, it makes the concept of color obsolete. That has to be its inevitable result."

One of Baldwin's lectures on "Blacks and Jews" disturbed Lester, a black American who had converted to Judaism. In his account of "becoming a Jew" entitled *Lovesong,* Lester referred to Jesse Jackson's attitude toward Jews as his "Achilles' heel" and so was not surprised, he wrote, when Jackson was quoted as calling Jews "Hymies." Said Lester: "Last Tuesday Jimmy devoted his lecture [as part of a course on the 'History of the Civil Rights Movement'] to the Jesse Jackson affair. He began with a diatribe, albeit an eloquent one, blaming the media for reporting it." Lester said he was shocked "when Jimmy referred to Jews as being nothing more than 'white Christians who go to something called a synagogue on a Saturday rather than church on Sunday.' " Lester continued: "I know he is not an anti-Semite, but his remarks in class were anti-Semitic, and he does not realize it." At question-time black students, according to Lester, mouthed "every anti-Semitic cliché they knew" while Baldwin "listened and said nothing." The Jewish students were "hurt and angry." Lester had lunch with Baldwin to discuss it. "He was surprised and distressed to hear how I and the Jewish students felt about his remarks."

"You know I'm not anti-Semitic," he said, and offered at the next lecture to apologize to the Jewish students. He never did, Lester said. But Baldwin's other friends in the Afro-American Studies department came to his defense, claiming that he didn't need to be defended if you read what he had said, all of it, and they published a little pamphlet with a transcript of his lecture, but the row was still continuing months after Baldwin's death.

Baldwin said he had hesitated over the offer to teach there because he wasn't a trained teacher, and some of the students, once they became used to having a celebrity in the classroom, criticized his disjointed style and compared it to that of a preacher or a jazz musician. He became notorious for arriving late to class and on two occasions never appeared. "He's a night person—if it was at ten P.M. when he had a stool and could smoke a cigarette, he would feel more comfortable," said an older student. His health also gave him trouble. On the way to a writing class at Hampshire College, one of the five colleges he was attached to, he became ill and had to be rushed to a hospital in Northampton. It was "a mild heart attack," and he was told to go easy on the drinking.

Michael Thelwell explained that Baldwin came as a professor for Five Colleges Inc., including the University of Massachusetts, Hampshire College, Mount Holyoke, Smith and Amherst. He was to give courses to groups of about twenty aspiring writers—one subject he lectured on was writers in exile and of course he used Henry James as an example.

351

Then he also gave a course to a much bigger group of over two hundred students about the civil rights movement (of which his "Blacks and Jews" lecture had been part).

"We had first discussed the possibility of his coming when the University of Massachusetts gave him an honorary degree in 1978," said Thelwell. "I hadn't seen him for about ten years and he seemed frailer than I remembered. His whole relationship to White America had changed. The assassinations and what had happened to the Movement had deeply affected him. When I first met him, he was talking about black and white coming together. One of the criticisms made against him that I thought very pointless was that Jimmy had talked too much about White America. He was talking about all of us. But toward the end he was talking more as a black person making a clear distinction between white and black Americans. This was a result of the rise of the Right, the decline of the Movement, the death of a dream. One critic suggested Jimmy had relapsed into racism. It was as ridiculous as the suggestion that fame and being a celebrity had affected him. If he was ever seduced by celebrity and for a brief moment he may have been, I think he saw through it very quickly.

"Jimmy was profoundly disturbed by the murders of Malcolm, King and Medgar Evers, and by the failures of American society in civil rights. I had been drinking often enough with him to know his feelings about this, but he never expressed any bitterness over the change since the sixties regarding him personally. He woke up one morning and saw that white people were no longer listening. You had to find an audience within the black community or be quiet. Jimmy understood that perfectly. He wasn't bitter but realistic. The whole consciousness of what he was, the whole man, didn't make such easy bitterness possible.

"I remember we were discussing some celebrity one night, some white celebrity, who had become a whore and a shell. It may have been Truman Capote, whom Jimmy had known in the early days. I said sometimes we don't really understand how much we have to be thankful for being born black, though black people can fall for it, too—there were collaborators with slavery just as there were with Nazi Germany. At this point Jimmy looked around to make his characteristic rap on a piece of wood. Some of the writers he had known had become 'monsters' after they became famous. Jimmy said to me, 'I feel blessed.' I think what he meant by that was what I saw on the few occasions I traveled with him to speaking engagements and the reception I saw, the affection and gratitude that a whole generation of black people felt for him. People went out of their way to approach him, including a good number of whites, and they testified in moving ways about the importance of his work in their lives. Jimmy's values were such that he knew that was worth more than the honors of the literary establishment. Sometimes he talked about former allies and what had happened to them, and then he would shake his head in sadness. 'Lord, Lord, Lord'— that was his phrase. His anger was really reserved for social injustice and hypocrisy and immorality.

"When he first came, he was living among the students and didn't like it. Privacy was difficult. His heart started acting up. He had rapid palpitations and went in the hospital to be examined. He was exhausted and had to have rest and was put on medication. He had to keep away from drink. There was a fundraising party for Jesse Jackson and we asked him to come and speak. It got later and later, and he still didn't show up. A car was sent to get him. Jimmy at last arrived and said, 'I feel I have been hijacked.' He made a brief speech. I don't think he and Jesse Jackson knew each other that well. He would say, 'I know Jesse too well,' but that was his dramatic way of talking about some people. He expressed grave dissatisfaction with his housing situation. We found him a place in the home of the poet James Tate, who was away on sabbatical."

The Tate home was a peaceful white house in Pelham, set off the road among trees and with its own driveway. It looked to be an ideal refuge for an ailing writer. Michael Thelwell recalled: "He brought a secretary with him, a young man who lived in Washington and who saw to it that Jimmy got to his appointments. He rented a car and drove Jimmy around. He was a responsible person and took care of Jimmy. He was paid and was not a lover. But then a young Afro-American turned up. He was a very destructive young man. Jimmy was apparently emotionally involved so life became a series of melodramas and I sometimes had to serve as referee. He would disappear all night with a rented car and Jimmy wouldn't be able to sleep. He would sit up all night and look all haggard next day. He'd be worried the fellow would be in jail or had killed himself in the car. The combination of Jimmy's fame coupled with an atmosphere of vulnerability about Jimmy was irresistible to a certain type of person. They always wanted to take over and run his life, protect and take care of him. 'What should I do?' Jimmy would sometimes ask as if he were genuinely in need of guidance. People with him were advised to watch his drinking and, as soon as he appeared tired, to put him in the car and get him home. But I don't think Jimmy was ever as vulnerable as he would appear or at a loss. He had a quality of toughness, but not in a pejorative way. He didn't need instruction in how to live his life.

"He was helped in various ways. Cynthia Packard from our department came over to clean up one day a week and she eventually took Jimmy away. She thought Jimmy needed looking after and someone to make sure he got his rest and took his medication and went for checkups. She bought a house and Jimmy went to live there."

Baldwin came back again the next year for a semester. "I had many late night drinking sessions with Jimmy, sessions at my house, sometimes at Cindy Packard's," Thelwell said. "Jimmy wasn't doing a heck of a lot of work. He was drinking too much. He said he was going to write a love story. He told me about his first love affair. It was with somebody called Arthur when Jimmy was fifteen or sixteen. He said he was going through difficulties at home with his father. It promised to be an extraordinary narrative if he ever got it written. In one scene he was walking down Lenox or some other avenue. He had walked all the way from downtown on a very cold day. He noticed a big older guy kept watching him, seeing him at different places. The guy said cryptic things and so he would run away. He was coming back to Harlem this particular night and didn't want to go home. There was a church in session and he walked in, as much for the warmth as for anything else. He stood inside the church with his hand on a railing and suddenly a much larger hand came over his hand and there was Arthur standing there. He said something dramatic like, 'I have been waiting for you. I have been looking for you.' He felt a sense of confusion, but also of protection. I think he followed Arthur home, walking behind him. Soon after that, without knowing why, he was drawn back there—to Arthur's."

"He once wrote about a Harlem racketeer he had had a love affair with at that age," I said.

"It's the same person," Thelwell replied. "It meant a great deal to him."

Thelwell remembered that "Jimmy was drinking a good deal. He was lonely. Sometimes late at night when I was drinking with him, he talked about being lonely. Sometimes we saw the dawn in, and my wife got restless at my staying out so much. But I felt Jimmy needed it. He was getting old and he was still always attracted to young men. He was still capable of great acts of irresponsibility. He would fall in love or tell himself he had. He would show up with some young man traveling with him. I had the sense he really wanted or thought he wanted to be passionately involved with somebody who would love him and take care of business. He needed someone stable and competent to be always there. I heard references to Lucien, his great friend, but I never figured out why that separation came. I never really asked questions. I just let Jimmy talk. I don't think he was able to do much writing. His lifestyle wasn't conducive to writing at that stage. He was going out on speaking engagements, taking classes, drinking, staying up late. I had heard him speak when he was young. He had become a real shadow of himself as a public speaker. The eloquence and the precision were not there in the same way. Sometimes when he got up to speak, he had had too much to drink. He was always hurrying to get to classes and stay abreast. But it was a continual struggle. He liked to stay up late at night, have a leisurely late meal with drinks and good conversation and then go on drinking and talking even though he had to get up to go to classes. He simply had no time for writing. I recommended he should have staff to look after all day-to-day arrangements. It was one way in which celebrity affected his writing. His lifestyle and other people did interfere with his work.

"He had a persistent cough those last months at Amherst. He took medicine for it. We understood he had to stop smoking, stop drinking and rest more and stay on his medication. He and I used to talk a lot about the civil rights movement and the sixties. We knew so many people in common. We often returned to Martin, his views and experience, and to Malcolm and Medgar Evers and people like Harry Belafonte."

There was also a memory of Michael Thelwell's mother. She had considered Baldwin ugly from his pictures, but when she met him, she told him, "Oh, Mr. Baldwin, you should sue your publisher for those pictures because you're not ugly at all!" Baldwin laughed, and they talked together for hours and he took a bracelet off his wrist and gave it to her. He also somehow found the time to write an introduction to Thelwell's collected essays, *Duties, Pleasures and Conflicts*. "Incredible pressures combined to delay these notes," he apologized for being late for the book's deadline. "I was working on the road in America, and it is simply not possible to concentrate on writing anything between planes, lectures, classes and the public pressures surrounding publication." He saw Thelwell's book that covered the march on Washington and the King period as "the record of a monumental betrayal." He thought "Martin's Dream" was "manipulated, as were we, and that it was never intended that any promise made would be kept." We were no better off now, twenty-three years later, than at the time of the march on Washington. He ended with a reference to the "limitless potential of every human being in the world." The level of despair seemed to rise, but then he pushed it down again.

Cynthia Packard recalled when he lived in her house. "I had known him through his books since I was sixteen, and I found him to be extraordinary as a person—warm, kind, generous, open, simply a wonderful human being. His presence seemed to take over the household. Living with him was perhaps disruptive to an ordinary daily schedule, but I'm not one who needs to keep to that. My son was old enough to know who Jimmy was and to read some of his writing. Jimmy was still Jimmy to him, but he knew he was also a famous man and why. They had conversations together. Jimmy and I saw eye to eye on most things. I talked to him about his real father, but some of it I don't want to talk about because it was confidential. He talked about [his stepfather] David Baldwin and how he didn't come to understand him until much later in life. The last years were difficult for Jimmy. He needed to find stable conditions, peace of mind, to write. He was living at an unbelievable pace, lecturing all over the place, wearing himself out. It was almost as if he was driven. Perhaps he knew he didn't have many years left. Writing was what he wanted to do most, but more and more it had to be put on the back burner to make way for some other crisis. He never really got a big financial break ever. So money was always a big issue."

One of the big occasions for "Professor Baldwin" was his sixtieth birthday party. Sitting beside his mother, he was seen frequently to wipe away tears during tributes to him as a writer and his contribution to racial harmony. Lerone Bennett, editor of Ebony and a black historian, said Baldwin "rose to spiritual heights attained by few mortals." Patrick Murphy, director of Five Colleges, Inc., announced Baldwin's reappointment and said he was "fully as good as a professor in the classroom as he is in the written word." The guests included Maya Angelou and Sol Stein. In response to the tributes, Baldwin said, "I've learned one thing, which is not ever to avoid the truth about yourself."

21

The Last Tug on the Handkerchief

HE WENT home to St. Paul-de-Vence for a rest between teaching sessions and perhaps to work on *No Papers for Mohammed,* the next novel to be published, he hoped. He told one interviewer that it was to be a very long novel that he knew a great deal about a few years ago, but "now that I'm working on it, I don't know much about it any more." The characters, he said, were walking up and down in his house talking to him, but he didn't yet know some of their names. He was soon interrupted, however—a welcome interruption, it seemed—by a letter from Walter Lowe, a Playboy editor, suggesting he go to Atlanta to write a story about the series of murders of young blacks.

Baldwin had read about the murders in French newspapers. He knew Atlanta and he immediately wondered if this was some new racist plot. One rumor was that the Ku Klux Klan was involved, then a young black man named Wayne Bertram Williams was arrested and subsequently convicted of two of the murders. The Atlanta police then closed twenty-three other cases involving the deaths of young blacks. It was as if Williams had been found guilty of these, too, without being charged. Claiming that prosecutors withheld critical evidence, Williams asked for a new trial, and Baldwin flew to Atlanta to take part in a news conference to publicize his petition.

It was more a story for an investigative reporter than an aging witness, as Baldwin soon found out. He couldn't get into the prison to talk to Williams, and none of the jury would talk to him—he was soon in the position of a witness with nothing to witness. As Norman Podhoretz of Commentary put it, "Jimmy's writing about race had to come from his own experience." Like a reporter with no real fresh story, he padded out his article for Playboy with an impression of Williams from television, speculating about his character as a spoiled only child. Andrew Young, whom he had known since the King days, had recently become mayor and he had met Williams as a brilliant youth, so Baldwin added "Andy Young's" impressions. He tried to relate the case to his own past and to the history of racial injustice, but it seemed to take him a long way from Atlanta. The rhetorical language left a vagueness, a sense of a familiar sermon preached with few new facts or revelations. For any reader who knew Baldwin's old precision and force, the Playboy article was worrying—worrying not so much for Williams' fate or the unsolved murders as Baldwin had intended, but worrying because of Baldwin's slight incoherence and falling back on familiar material (he even brought in Mrs. Ayer, his first black teacher, again). When he set out to expand the Playboy article into a short book, he couldn't find much more to write.

His Dial editor, Juri Jurjevics, found the short book "unintelligible" and turned it down. This was a shock for Baldwin and further confirmed his insecurity about Dial. As his ex-agent Robert Lantz said, "The people who had unconditionally adored him at Dial had left or lost much of their power, and his position was much harder." For years he had wanted to publish a collection of his poetry; Dial was not interested. Eventually Michael Joseph in Britain published a very slim collection entitled _Jimmy's Blues,_ which included "The Giver," dedicated to his mother—"For Berdis." It was free verse, almost conversational and sometimes so cryptic as to be like shorthand notes to the author. Few of Baldwin's great qualities as a writer were present in his poetry. Dial obviously classed the Atlanta book with the poetry as being unpublishable.

Baldwin next offered the Atlanta book to Richard Marek, who now had his own list at Putnam's; Marek also rejected it. "I didn't think the book worked," he said. "I thought it was fuzzy. I didn't ask him if he was willing to do any more work. I told him I didn't like it and I think he sold it very quickly to Doubleday, but then the editor left so Holt eventually did it." Baldwin discovered that even Jay Acton was not keen on the book, which led to the end of their business relationship. "I urged him not to publish it," said Acton. "He needed to do more work on it. I thought it would be a disservice to him if I advised him to go ahead with it. It had an unfortunate critical reception and didn't do well. It was the right subject for him, but there wasn't a lot more than there had been in the Playboy piece. We could have got him research help to collect all the evidence. But he wanted to do the kind of epistolary book that was his strength as we knew from *The Fire Next Time*. Bob Loomis at Random and Dick Marek also turned it down, and they're very substantial guys who knew Jimmy. It facilitated our break."

But before they parted, Acton suggested another idea for a much bigger, more ambitious book—a triple biography of King, Malcolm and Medgar Evers, "a mix of history, autobiography and biography." Baldwin liked the idea and typed out a short outline, Acton put a price of $300,000 to $400,000 on it and sent it out. Jurjevics at Dial turned that down, too, because they "wanted so much money" and because, added Jurjevics, "I couldn't see him researching anything of that kind and it would become some sort of personal declaration, and also it was becoming a most difficult thing for him to make the time to write." McGraw-Hill signed it up for reportedly a $400,000 advance, though for a six-month period after Baldwin's death the company would nei- ther confirm nor correct this figure, various officials saying only that it was "in the hands of our lawyers." Jay Acton estimated that probably Baldwin had completed no more than one hundred pages—"It may be Jimmy's *Answered Prayers,*" a reference to Truman Capote's last novel that he claimed to have finished and yet only a few chapters were found after his death. Baldwin never claimed to have made that much progress, but he frequently mentioned the triple biography in interviews. As he told Peter Manso for his *Mailer* biography, "I'm now doing a book about three friends of mine who were murdered. They were not friends of the white intellectual community. They were symbols, an opportunity to wash your conscience and nothing more." The book was to have been called *Remember This House.*

He called the Atlanta book *The Evidence of Things Not Seen,* from St. Paul's "Faith is the substance of things hoped for, the evidence of things not seen," and he dedicated it: "For David Baldwin, the father and the son." The reviews were not only probably the poorest he had ever had, but sometimes small and obscurely positioned in the publication, further evidence of his decline in prestige. The New York *Times Book Review* gave it merely a fat paragraph on an inside page: "This slim volume" would not satisfy many readers "nor, one suspects, does it satisfy the author himself." There was far too much sermonizing and not enough digging. "This lackluster account of a complex, nightmarish event" demanded "more thorough treatment."

As always, he got on well with the publicity people at the new publisher. Blanche Ingrid Brann, publicity director for Henry Holt, formerly Holt, Rinehart and Winston, said that Holt obtained *The Evidence of Things Not Seen* at the Frankfurt Book Fair through Baldwin's French publisher, Stock, who by that time held the U.S. rights to what they called *Meurtres à Atlanta* ("Murders in Atlanta"). "I met Jimmy first at The Ginger Man," she recalled. "We had drinks and dinner and it lasted all night long. I finally dropped him in a cab at David's on Ninety-sixth Street, where he was staying. At that first meeting I was absolutely in awe of him, but then after a couple of scotches we really seemed to understand each other real well. Jimmy could be so extraordinarily trusting initially, but there was really a combination of trust and caution in him. He sang me old gospel songs in the cab. He had great difficulty in getting organized. You tried to work through David, but I think David came to dislike me because I put too much pressure on Jimmy. They nicknamed me the 'Dragon Lady' because I was always trying to get Jimmy to get some sleep, things like that. It always took Jimmy a long time to wake up and get ready.

"I went down to Atlanta with Jimmy and David to the news conference about the retrial. It was a horrible thing to see twelve mothers of murdered children. It was an extremely stressful situation. I wanted Jimmy to get his rest because we had a strenuous tour publicizing the book ahead. 'Let's all go to sleep,' I'd say, but we'd still be there for the last call at the bar. I'd fly up to get Jimmy, rent a car and pick him up, and then drive him to the airport. The porters would say, 'Are you Mr. Baldwin?' He was always really open and wonderful with them. But he tipped too heavily. 'Don't tip that guy a twenty,' I'd say, and he'd reply, 'Blanche, I want to do it.' In Chicago we met a group who wanted to do *The Amen Corner* on TV. I suddenly saw my hand and said, 'I'm white.' I had completely forgotten. Jimmy turned to me and said, 'I have never forgotten what color my hand was.' I could be color-blind, but Jimmy could never be. There was one woman who was attracted to Jimmy, and when he died she was really shaken. She said, 'I wanted to have that man's baby.' It was astonishing the way women reacted toward Jimmy. We knew Jimmy was gay, but we still responded to him, were still attracted."

About Baldwin's men friends, she recalled: "There was this one guy in Toronto. Jimmy had just got off the stage with some other writers, including William Golding. Jimmy had given a reading. When he came off, there was this man standing in the back toward one of the exits waiting for Jimmy to come by. Jimmy saw him. He was an old lover from Turkey whom he hadn't seen for a long time. The Turkish guy looked very hungry. Jimmy came over to me and said, 'Is it okay if he stays in my room?' I said, 'That's fine. Don't worry about it.' I was only twenty-six years old and here was Jimmy asking my permission. The Turkish guy couldn't get into the U.S. Jimmy told me what had happened to the guy. He was a stowaway. Jimmy seemed to have no one person in his life. There was a very lonely quality about him. It was that kind of loneliness where he didn't want to go to sleep. He wanted to stay up all night. At three A.M. you'd still be in a bar with him. He was taking a lot of vitamins at that time. I tried to make sure he ate well when I was with him. I took really good care of him. He drank so much sometimes that when we changed planes, I had to carry him almost physically. He said, 'I've got to take it easy.'

"He talked about other writers—Richard Wright, James Jones. He had mellowed about Wright and about Julius Lester, who had been in disagreement with him at Amherst. He mentioned Henry James, Manuel Puig (he liked *Kiss of the Spider Woman*). Interviewers would mention

The Fire Next Time and ask him if things had changed in twenty years. Not much, he'd say. He wasn't being pessimistic, he was naturally optimistic, but he was also realistic. Could things change? Yes, it wasn't a black problem, it was a white problem."

Ms. Brann recalled "a big party at Cindy Packard's at Amherst. We still were dancing at 5:00 A.M. Jimmy was singing his lungs out. Old gospel tunes. He had given the commencement address at Hampshire College. He brought down the place. It was wonderful. He was really proud of his mother, really proud of the fact that he was able to buy her a house, but even happier that years before he could buy her a coat she wanted—I think it was a green coat. I remember when we went to Princeton to publicize the book, Jimmy said to remind him he was nearly lynched in Trenton when he was young. I was keen Jimmy should get his affairs sorted out, his money, his taxes, and prepare for the next phase of his life. He could then just live and do what he wanted to do. He had the financial capacity to do what he wanted, he didn't *have* to do anything just for money. But he had to get his act together. It never happened before he died. He seemed to have an inability to get himself together even with professional outside help. I wondered if he had a fear they would find out something, perhaps that he was making payments to something, somebody. People gave Jimmy so many things. We often came away with shopping bags full of gifts—cards, flowers."

Richard Seaver, Baldwin's editor at Holt, held a dinner at the Fifth Avenue Hotel in New York to launch the book. Mitchel Levitas, the editor of the New York *Times Book Review* and son of one of Baldwin's first editors, Sol Levitas of the New Leader, remembered that this was the last time he saw Baldwin. "I don't remember if our review of the Atlanta book had appeared, but Jimmy was warm and cordial and, as always, loved to remember the old days. Since I knew his history with my father, it was a very lovely evening. He drank as he always did. I always found him easy to argue with, assertive as anyone is who is lively and uninhibited as Jimmy was, but never unpleasant."

An adaptation of *Go Tell It On the Mountain,* starring Paul Winfield, was shown on television and touched him deeply. "I still see myself there," he said. "I was the character John once in some ways." He imagined himself once more helping his stepfather, David Baldwin, "get

363

dressed, brush the lint off his suit, as I used to do, help him into his coat, hand him his hat—and his walking cane!—and take him to see *Go Tell It On the Mountain.*"

He heard of another figure in his past—Floyd Patterson, the boxer. "I just feel that no writer today has anything for me," Patterson told journalist Gay Talese. "I mean, none of them has felt any more deeply than I have, and I have nothing to learn from them. Although Baldwin to me seems different from the rest." Patterson said Baldwin seemed like a wonderful guy. You met him on the street and you said, "Who's this poor slob?" But he thought he and Baldwin had a lot in common," and someday I'd just like to sit somewhere for a long time and talk to him."

Jay Acton, no longer Baldwin's agent, recalled "the novel he really wanted to write was—and like so many of Jimmy's titles, it was biblical—*I John Saw a Number.* I think it's from Matthew. It would have concerned his relations with David and his mother." He also talked at this time about a novel concerning a woman—that was all he said about the plot—which would be the first volume of a trilogy set in the U.S., France and Jamaica and would be entitled *A Higher Place Than I Have Found.* Another projected novel! All those talked-about novels, non-fiction books, plays and films of the last few years suggested a writer who was trying even more desperately to convince himself that he was industrious and productive and therefore all was well. The more writers talk about their works in progress, the less actual work they seem to do, and James Baldwin apparently was no exception. But the seemingly ceaseless traveling continued, making the writing harder than ever. Just a year before he died he was in Moscow with ten other writers, including Arthur Miller and Peter Ustinov, meeting Mikhail S. Gorbachev in the Kremlin. But even then he was feeling unwell, his strength steadily sapped by the disease that hadn't yet been diagnosed.

But one final publishing event pleased him. With Richard Marek, he put together a huge 690–page volume of his collected essays in chronological order, beginning with "Harlem Ghetto," which was published in Commentary in 1948 and ending with "Here Be Dragons," which appeared in Playboy in 1985. He gave it the title *The Price of the Ticket,* but much as he enjoyed dedicating his books, this last one he didn't dedicate to anyone, an ominous sign that he knew it was the end. The collection was the closest that he would ever come now to an autobiography, though no doubt he saw it as a vast Book of Witness, almost biblical in style and intention. But when it was published—not by Dial Press but by St. Martin's/Marek—*The Price of the Ticket* received little more attention than *The Evidence of Things Not Seen.* The tone of the reviews was more favorable, of course—it was almost like commenting on established classics—but not much space was devoted to the book. In Baldwin's heyday, it no doubt would have been on the literary front pages, but the New York *Times Book Review,* for example, gave it only a large paragraph inside, and some leading papers and magazines didn't notice it at all.

Richard Marek was angry about the reception. "The collected essays was something I had wanted to do for as long as I can remember," he said. "All of his books of essays were in it except the Atlanta murders. We left out one or two individual essays in consultation that were topical at the time and perhaps dated now. The chronology was sometimes difficult to work out, but we did it. The New York *Times Book Review* gave the collection only a long paragraph inside. I thought that was a disgrace."

Asked about the coverage, Mitchel Levitas, the editor of the *Times Book Review,* said that by the time the essays appeared in the collection, "Jimmy's views had become so familiar and, in fact, unchanged that to have discussed them again in a long review would have risked paining Jimmy even more than his pain at what had happened to civil rights in America. There was so little that was fresh in the text or opinions. For a reviewer to have made that point would have been very unpleasant for Jimmy. I didn't want to dismiss him at length. America had come to know Jimmy Baldwin's views on civil rights quite well by that time and the tendency of readers is to say, 'I have heard that before.' It doesn't make it any less valid, but less inviting for readers who have heard it before. I see the objection to our review and I think it's arguable, but I think we made the right decision."

Christopher Lehmann-Haupt, his former editor who reviewed and still does for the daily New York *Times,* had a similar reaction. "On the daily, no one wanted to do it. There was a feeling it was a lot of rehash stuff—disappointing . . ."

When *The Price of the Ticket* was published in Britain a few months later, *The Guardian* commented about the American reception: "It was a taste of failure late in life that must have been very bitter for that 'abnormally ambitious' black cat. It is greatly to Mr. Baldwin's credit that he has persisted along his now unpopular course as the messenger with bad news, for it has probably cost him a Nobel Prize." *The Guardian* also noted his lifelong achievement in keeping the hatred and despair under control. "The level of his anger—and his self-indulgence —rises as he sees how much of the battle has been in vain, and he begins to write of 'Whites' from the viewpoint of 'Blacks' in a way he never used to allow himself. But at every low point he calls himself to attention with a reminder that, as he puts it on the final page of his collection, 'We are a part of each other,' and by that he means male and female as well as black and white, for he is refreshingly honest about his bisexual experience and quite unsentimental about homosexuality."

It was as if the final curtain had come down on a lifetime's drama and *The Price of the Ticket* was a last curtain call. When he read the reviews, he must have felt a little like the comedian in Chaplin's "Limelight" when the audience no longer laughed at his jokes. No wonder he insisted in the later years that writers couldn't be judged by their contemporaries but only by posterity. He had been fond of comparing life to a pocket handkerchief, which you slowly pulled out by the intensity of your experiences. If you lived a full life and didn't play safe, all the handkerchief should be out before you died. James Baldwin had lived his life so intensely from the beginning that *The Price of the Ticket* must have been like the last tug on the handkerchief.

22

This Morning, This Evening, So Soon

HE HAD always lived as if he never expected to make old age. He was unsparing—reckless, some would have said—in the treatment of his slight, frail body, continually driving himself as if he had little time left even when he was a young man and the years still stretched ahead. Now, as the year 1987 began, he could count the time left him in months, though he did not know it yet.

"Jimmy, you're no longer twenty-one," his mother had kept warning him. The strain of all those sleepless nights, of half-starving in the early days, of all the drinking and smoking, the love affairs, and above all his many draining roles as a witness—it was all beginning to tell on him at last. The persistent cough that his friend Michael Thelwell had noticed, the nervous ailments that he attributed to exhaustion, probably even his "heart palpitations" were all signs of the breakdown of his body.

He had often made grim jokes about his chain-smoking giving him lung cancer or his drinking cancer of the liver, but the first symptoms showed up in his throat. His famous baritone grew weak and husky, and swallowing was difficult. Cancer of the esophagus was diagnosed. An operation was arranged late in April at a medical institute outside Nice that specialized in cancer cases. He was on the operating table for several hours—nine altogether, he said that the doctors told him. Afterward, the doctors presented a cheerful front to *Monsieur* Baldwin. They sent him home to convalesce in the sun, apparently to get well. He canceled all his trips and engagements and planned to remain in St. Paul-de-Vence for the summer and fall, expecting to have recovered by the end of the year.

But the doctors gave a very different report to David Baldwin. When they operated to remove the esophagus they had found the cancer had spread—his liver was finished. They gave him about nine months if he was lucky. Let him think he was going to get better, light drugs would keep the pain at bay. Let him enjoy the summer.

It was a difficult decision for David Baldwin. He and Jimmy had always leveled with each other and shared secrets, and Jimmy as a man had always been so straight from the shoulder in his dealings with the world. But why not let him enjoy the summer? He would know soon enough, when he needed to. David Baldwin had the backing of three of Jimmy's closest friends—Lucien Happersberger, Bernard Hassell and David Leeming. They formed a team to make the last months as cheerful, contented and painless as possible. They also decided to tell few people outside the family so there would be no invasion of friends and lovers that would alert Jimmy. Let old friends drop by naturally as they usually did when it was known he was in residence.

Herbert Gold heard he was "sick" and came by to see him quite late, in October, just a few weeks before he died. "He was quite sick when I saw him," Gold recalled. "People in the village said he was dying, but I spent the afternoon chatting with him. I arranged the visit through Bernard Hassell, who was then acting as his cook and general factotum. I went to the house at the time arranged. I was staying nearby at a hotel. I went at his invitation because since he wasn't well, I wasn't going to just drop in on him. I knew where the house was because I had been there eight or nine years ago. The first time I went, there was no answer at the door and I was kind of annoyed because nobody was there when I had a definite appointment. Ever since I had first known Jimmy, he was very unreliable about appointments. He was late or he didn't show up and then there would be an apology and a sort of shrug. I thought then he couldn't be so ill, this seemed to be the old Jimmy. The door was open so I walked in. Nobody was there. The door to his bedroom was closed. It occurred to me he might be in there so I called out. No one answered. I left him a note. I got a call that night. He had been there, but asleep. So I went back.

"He seemed to think he was going to get well. He even explained how long it was going to take him. He had been on the operating table for nine hours and a doctor had told him he would need a month of recovery for every hour on the table. I think I even asked him directly had he AIDS and he laughed. It was cancer of the esophagus. But I thought that would affect his speech and he spoke normally, though he seemed very tired. His French maid told me, 'I have been working for him for seventeen years' and she was convinced he was getting better. He was so tired it was hard for him to write, but he talked fine. No sign of illness in his voice. His voice was totally normal. But he looked very thin and weak. Yet he could move around. He was dressed, and when I left, he walked me to the door. He was very frail and I put my arms around him to say goodbye and he seemed to weigh no more than about ninety pounds.

"It was the nicest talk I ever had with him. There were the fewest defenses or offenses. We reminisced a lot about the days in Paris in 1949–51, about the Hotel Verneuil, Saul Bellow, my first wife, Otto Friedrich of Time. Jimmy and I were born in the same year. We had a lot in common. He was pleased that the production of one of his plays, *The Amen Corner,* was about to be done in London. One of his books *(Just Above My Head)* had just come out in France. He talked about old lovers, using first names.

"At this last meeting he seemed sure he was going to live. He seemed to have mellowed, was more generous, more genuinely interested in others. He talked about Saul Bellow who he thought had never liked him. He spoke with sadness, not animosity. Previously he had sometimes seemed indifferent toward people or was generous in a way that didn't seem to matter. I remember a meeting at Cyrano's in Los Angeles. He was involved with Marlon Brando, I think, in trying to make a movie of *Another Country.* A banker recognized him, rushed to a bookstore and came back with a pile of his books to sign. Jimmy signed the books and then said sweetly, 'This is my friend, Herb Gold. He's a writer, too.' It was sweet, but it was also a dismissal.

"I think he had been depressed in the last years. He hadn't written much fiction for a long time. In relation to other writers, he was no longer *the* black writer, the successor to Richard Wright and Ralph Ellison. He wasn't forgotten, but it was assumed he had done his work. The last book about the killings in Atlanta was a real failure. And he was not an old man. He continued to try to write, but he was a blocked writer in the most important ways. But at that last meeting, he was different, a changed Jimmy. He was much more mellow, more generous."

Michael Thelwell, who admired Baldwin so much he had modeled himself as a writer on him, hadn't cared for the Atlanta book either—"It lacked Jimmy's clarity and precision and didn't go deeply enough. I tried to avoid talking to Jimmy about it. Much of it had been written when he was drinking." Thelwell was looking forward to seeing him again back at Amherst when he heard he was ill. One report said he was dying. "I wanted to call him, but I was told he mustn't be bothered. Finally I ignored this advice and phoned him in St. Paul-de-Vence. He came to the phone. His voice sounded weak, but he was glad to hear from me. We talked for a little while for a last time."

Almost to the end, he tried to write or talked about the writing he was doing—the triple biography of Martin, Malcolm and Medgar; *No Papers for Mohammed* (was *Any Bootlegger Can* that he talked about the same novel with a new title or a different one—perhaps the novel about his first Harlem lover that he had mentioned to Michael Thelwell?); a screenplay based on an old Turkish novel entitled *The Swordfish*; and a play, *The Welcome Table,* which David Leeming said was "about people similar to those Jimmy knew, set in a town in the South of France in a house like Jimmy's." When the two Davids, Baldwin and Leeming, took turns sitting up with him at night, David Leeming said, "When Jimmy awoke during the night he sometimes liked to have something read to him from the screenplay for *The Swordfish*. He was interested in it up to the end. He wrote off and on until close to his death." Leeming said, "We never talked about him dying because he didn't want that. He wanted to keep things positive, cheerful. He was only on light drugs. He was down to nothing, very thin." What was so extraordinary was that although Baldwin had often talked about his fears and about being terrified throughout the dramas of his life, now that he faced death it was as if these words of alarm had been dropped from his vocabulary. He had said not long before this last illness: "It seems to me that one ought to rejoice in the *fact* of death—ought to decide, indeed, to earn one's death by confronting with passion the conundrum of life." And that he had done.

Inevitably the news of his condition reached writer and journalist friends in New York, and some flew over for last meetings, last interviews. David Baldwin usually arranged to meet them at Nice's Côte d' Azur airport to tell them Jimmy had terminal cancer and to keep an upbeat manner. But as Jimmy began to decline in the last weeks, these precautions hardly seemed necessary. He probably guessed the truth by now. In the early days he had sat outside on the terrace and received visitors there. Even, with Herbert Gold, he had been able to accompany him to the door. But in the final days he moved from his own bedroom on the ground floor that received the most brilliant sunlight to a much darker bedroom at the back. He became too weak to get in and out of bed himself, and David Baldwin or one of his three friends lifted him. Mementos of his extraordinary life were visible everywhere in the house in those last days to lift his spirits. Awards and citations in Latin were displayed in honor, as they put it, of *Jacobus Arturus* Baldwin. David Baldwin had assembled a brilliant collage about his life. The jacket of *The Price of the Ticket* was pinned up prominently so that he could see it.

His time was obviously running out. He had to end some last conversations abruptly because of the pain. In his prime he had appeared so passionate, so fiery that at times he might almost have been on fire with emotion. Now it seemed as if he had been reduced to a single flickering flame of life that could go out at any moment.

A publishing friend in New York phoned his mother—"I asked her if she was going over to St. Paul-de-Vence to see him but she said she

371

just couldn't fly." Mother and eldest son had a last talk on the phone two days before he died. They had always been very close since the days of Frog Eyes, and he had shared all his successes with her. She had expected to die before him, but those who saw how much he depended on her being there when he needed her strength and inspiration were content that he was going first. It would have greatly increased his loneliness to be without her backing. "I was happy I was able to talk with him before he passed," Mrs. Baldwin said. "David was with him to the last. I don't know if I will ever get over it."

The day before he died he told David Leeming, "I'm bored."

The next day was December 1, 1987.

David Leeming had to go away on business for him, but David Baldwin, Lucien and Bernard were there with him at the end. He was conscious when he died. Bernard Hassell said, "Jimmy had a quiet and painless death. That is to say, he died with great dignity and the world will never be quite the same without him. You know he encouraged and inspired so many people. I had a serious problem a couple of years ago and I was depressed. He said, 'I have seen you go through a lot, but I have never seen you in despair. You are going to be all right.' I will never forget that."

When the last moments came, Bernard Hassell said, Jimmy indicated that he wanted to be lifted up in the bed. It was typical of the way he had lived his life not to want to be lying down when he confronted death. He had said he didn't know how he would face "that last intensity when everything flames up for the last time and then the flame falters and goes out." He had said he would like it to be "swift" yet he knew that the moment didn't "exist in time."

Yet it was swift. He sighed and breathed his last. The flame faltered and then slowly went out.

The life of James Baldwin was over.

It was big news around the world. In his native land the New York *Daily News* announced across a whole page: *A Flame Extinguished: James Baldwin Dies.* In France, his adopted second home, *Liberation* was typical in announcing that *L'Auteur de "La Prochaine Fois Le Feu" Est Mort* ('The Author of *The Fire Next Time* is Dead').

After his huge funeral that became "a celebration" of his life and the last drive through Harlem, he was buried in Ferncliff Cemetery in Hartsdale, about a half hour's drive from New York City. The cemetery is famous as the last resting place for celebrities ranging from Jerome Kern to Judy Garland. There are no gravestones. It looks like a peaceful park with well-trimmed lawns and neat pathways. The graves are under the lawns, and along the paths are bronze plaques with the names. James Baldwin did not yet have a plaque so a man trimming the lawns indicated where he lay—in Number 1203. Next to him was a plaque for Toots Shor, the New York bar-restaurant owner who was famous for his celebrity customers. Being next to Toots Shor would have amused Baldwin—"They're making sure I can always get a drink," he would probably have laughed.

Across the lawn only a few yards away was Paul Robeson's grave, and not far away was Malcolm X and Diana Sands and the black comedienne, Moms Mabley. He was among friends.

It was customary to sum up a person's life with a quotation on the plaque. One quotation would convey Baldwin's triumph—*It now had been laid to my charge to keep my own heart free of hatred and despair.* He had succeeded in doing so both as a man and as a writer, but oh, what it had cost him.

A life was a journey, he was fond of saying, and you had to pay the price of the ticket. He had paid with his life, but what an incredible journey it had been. Many people would have liked to be the public James Baldwin, but few would have paid the price the private man did. He had been a dedicated witness to a way of life that the rest of the world had been ignorant of and needed to know about. He created out of his memories and imagination a multitude of living people like John and Arthur and Ida and Rufus to bear witness for him. To hold back his fears, his anger and his despair, to avoid the madness of his stepfather, he wore himself out. He knew his strengths and weaknesses better than any of his critics, but as he once told a friend, "I'm very sound at the bottom." And so he proved in all the dramatic storms he traveled through right to the end. As Roy Innis of CORE said after his death, there was no one left on the American scene who spoke in the same straight-from-the-shoulder way that he did.

The man had passed, but the writer had joined the company of the immortals whom he read as a young boy. Perhaps even now there is a boy in Harlem deep in one of his books imagining that one day he will be a famous writer like James Baldwin, just as Baldwin used to dream of being another Charles Dickens—or Richard Wright. "At my death," he once said, "I will pass on the torch to the young. They are all my children." And now he has.

_____ *Acknowledgments*

No BIOGRAPHY is the work of a single writer. It is a tapestry of memories from as many sources as possible. Only the overall view is the writer's alone. Unlike the majority of biographers, I am fortunate in having known the subject well personally, and I am grateful to James Baldwin for our many conversations over the years, which I have quoted from extensively in describing the complex course of his life. We had many arguments, and he said during one heated exchange that really we should not get on because we were too much alike, by which he meant we were both obstinate in expressing what we thought rather than being diplomatic. But when he was at his most fiery, he was sometimes at his most revealing.

Occasionally, however, when he expressed the same thought or memory in his writings, I have preferred to quote from there, assuming it was the more precise version and the one he would have wished to be used. But this is copyrighted material, and so I wish to express my appreciation to his publishers. The main works referred to are *Notes of a Native Son,* published by Beacon Press, and the following all published by Dial Press, now absorbed into the Bantam Doubleday Dell group: *Go Tell It on the Mountain* (originally published by Alfred A. Knopf, Inc.), *Giovanni's Room, Nobody Knows My Name,*

Another Country, The Fire Next Time, Tell Me How Long the Train's Been Gone, Going to Meet the Man, No Name in the Street, The Amen Corner, Blues for Mister Charlie, If Beale Street Could Talk, The Devil Finds Work, Just Above My Head. Henry Holt, formerly Holt, Rinehart and Winston, published *The Evidence of Things Not Seen,* and St Martin's/Marek were the publishers of his collected essays, *The Price of the Ticket,* which essentially brought together the non-fiction books originally published by Beacon Press and Dial Press. The transcripts of two conversations were also published by J.B. Lippincott Company, now part of Harper & Row—*A Rap on Race,* by James Baldwin and Margaret Mead, and *A Dialogue,* by James Baldwin and Nikki Giovanni.

I have also found in some accounts of other lives another version of incidents that he described to me—for example, the description of a visit to Norman Mailer given in *Mailer,* by Peter Manso (Simon & Schuster, Inc. 1985, reprinted by Penguin Books 1986), which James Baldwin told me about a little differently and without the sense of loneliness noted by Adele Morales Mailer.

Before I begin the long list of acknowledgments of people who have helped me to piece together James Baldwin's life, I wish to thank the Baldwin family for conversations over the years. I have known best David Baldwin and Gloria Karefa-Smart, but all James Baldwin's eight brothers and sisters seem remarkable people headed by their great matriarch, Mrs. Berdis Baldwin, who contributed so much to her eldest son's extraordinary life as I have tried to show in my book. I have not, however, requested any interview with any member of the Baldwin family since I began the research for this portrait, as they might disagree with my portrayal of his life, though I hope not.

I also wish to make special mention of James Baldwin's old friends, Lucien Happersberger and Bernard Hassell, who were with him when he died. I am indebted to Mr. Happersberger for several conversations over the years and to Mr. Hassell for describing his long friendship and the final months. Even a year after James Baldwin's death, he broke down in describing the last moments, and at such times a biographer feels too intrusive.

David Adams Leeming generously discussed his first meeting with James Baldwin in Istanbul and their many Henry James exchanges as well as the final months, even though he is at work on the authorized biography. Similarly Otto Friedrich shared his James Baldwin memories although he planned to write an account himself in a collection of essays. Aronald Rampersad was also generous enough while completing the second volume of his *Life of Langston Hughes* to have an exchange about the prickly relationship of Langston Hughes and James Baldwin.

I am grateful, too, to such old friends of James Baldwin as Jerome Smith, Tony Maynard and Lorenzo Hail for conversations long ago that helped me to understand him better, though they may not agree always with the conclusions I have drawn.

There were so many aspects to James Baldwin that I am particularly appreciative of Michael Thelwell's insight and frankness in discussing his experience of James Baldwin over more than twenty years as a fellow writer, a comrade in the civil rights movement and a fellow professor at the University of Massachusetts.

I was lucky enough to interview Dr. Kenneth B. Clark at a time when his shrewd common sense and extensive experience of the American racial scene helped to balance the judgments of some other acquaintances of James Baldwin. I am grateful, too, to both Arthur Schlesinger, Jr, and Harry Belafonte for sharing with me their differing views of the famous meeting with Robert Kennedy, but the way they both see Kennedy in the years after the meeting now seems remarkably close. I also owe thanks to all the people involved in the Actors' Studio Theater's Broadway production of *Blues for Mister Charlie* for helping me to sort out that complicated drama as far as possible, including Elia Kazan, Rip Torn, Frank Corsaro, David Baldwin (at the time he was appearing in the play), and the late Lee and Paula Strasberg.

The following people I interviewed during the research ranged from James Baldwin's former editors to his old school friends, but all were busy in their professions and personal lives so I am indebted to them for sparing the time to go over their memories with me. They are in alphabetical order: Edward J. (Jay) Acton, Joseph Attles, Richard Baron, Virginia Baron, Burton Bendow, Ann Birstein, Blanche Ingrid Brann, Emile Capouya, William Rossa Cole (who also loaned me an early photograph of James Baldwin), Harold Conrad, Carver Davis, Lee Eisenheimer, Donald I. Fine, Eileen Finletter, Joseph M. Fox, Anne Freedgood, Herbert Gold, Paul Gorman, Herbert Hannum, A.L. Hart, Don Hutter, Roy Innis, Gloria Jones (who also loaned me a picture), Juri Jurjevics, Elia Kazan, Alfred Kazin, Mrs. John Killens, Judge Theodore Kupferman, William Koshland, Robert Lantz, Christopher Lehmann-Haupt, Julius Lester, Mary Lyons, Richard Marek, Helen Meyer, Cynthia Packard, William Phillips, Norman Podhoretz, Susan Ann Protter, James Purdy, Karen Benta Rodriguez, Raymond B. Rosenthal, Barney Rosset, Philip Roth, Donna Schrader, James B. Silberman, Terry Southern, Sol Stein, Roslyn Targ, Raleigh Trevelyan, Billy Dee Williams, John A. Williams.

Two important figures in James Baldwin's career I was fortunate enough

Acknowledgments _____

to interview with many long follow-up talks before they died should also be mentioned here: Robert Mills, one of James Baldwin's most devoted agents, and Bayard Rustin, a great cavalier of the civil rights movement and a wise man with a profound understanding of James Baldwin.

I must also mention my Harlem friends of many years for helping me to understand where James Baldwin came from, including the late Mr. and Mrs. James Martin, the late Kenneth Hendrix, whose eulogy I spoke at a funeral parlor on 125th Street, and the late Gertie Wood, whose meeting with James Baldwin I describe in the book. There were also friends in the South who helped me to understand the North-South relationship that was important in James Baldwin's life, notably Drucilla C. Parker, the late Abner Parker, Sr, and some of the civil rights leaders I interviewed, including Martin Luther King, Sr, and Jr., Andrew Young, Jesse Jackson, Julian Bond, James Forman, the late Slater King, and Malcolm X.

I am grateful to the staff of the Schomberg Center for Research in Black Culture for helping me to trace books and clippings relating to James Baldwin and for showing me the unpublished letters, copyrighted by the James Baldwin estate, which are part of its collection. I hope when James Baldwin's own files are available there that a special James Baldwin Room will house everything pertaining to his life and work. Another of the New York Public Library's branches, the newspaper library on West Forty-third Street, also deserves a tip of my hat as do the French Embassy's Cultural Services and the University of Massachusetts Photographic Services.

I am indebted to Cathy Henderson, research librarian, and the Harry Ransom Humanities Research Center, the University of Texas at Austin, for providing me with copies of documents from the Alfred A. Knopf archives concerning the company's publication of James Baldwin's first novel, *Go Tell It on the Mountain*. My thanks, too, to Ashbel Green and William Koshland of Knopf for arranging for me to obtain these copies.

Arthur Gelb, managing editor of The New York *Times,* kindly arranged for me to consult the *Times'* files on James Baldwin, and Robert Medina and his staff were very helpful in providing files and copying facilities. I am grateful, too, to Mitchel Levitas, editor of The New York *Times Book Review,* for sharing his memories of James Baldwin and the professional reasons for the the *Review*'s coverage of James Baldwin's collected essays.

Ray Cave, editorial director of Time, Inc., kindly arranged for me to consult Time, Life and People clippings on James Baldwin, and Elaine Felsher, head of Time, Inc.'s archives, and her assistant were most helpful.

378

I interviewed William Styron for *The Guardian* of Britain when James Baldwin was still alive, and after my questions relating to Styron's life and work, I asked him about his experiences with James Baldwin and he described some of their meetings in Paris and when James Baldwin was his house guest. I am also indebted to another novelist friend of James Baldwin's, E.L. Doctorow, who was one of his editors at Dial. Doctorow informed me of a tribute he was giving at City College, and although the microphone was rather crackly, I found his recollections very revealing, and also he was kind enough to answer follow-up questions by letter. I had, moreover, kept my notes of a conversation I had with him about James Baldwin when he was at Dial and I was American editor of Penguin Books.

William F. Buckley, Jr., Editor of National Review and James Baldwin's opponent in several public debates, wrote me "I know nothing about James Baldwin that I didn't write at the time," and he was kind enough to provide me with copies of all his columns about James Baldwin.

I am also grateful for the helpfulness of George Plimpton, who felt he did not know James Baldwin well enough to be interviewed, but referred me to the 1984 Paris Review interview with James Baldwin by Jordan Elgrably. In the interview James Baldwin said many things that he had mentioned to me twenty years before, a nice example of the consistency of his opinions and his memory, and so I have quoted briefly from the Paris Review interview to make this point.

I would like to pay tribute to the speed, efficiency and sensitivity with which Donald I. Fine, the publisher and editor, and his team have produced this book. And thanks to Bob Silverstein, the agent for this book, for professional and personal encouragment and for accompanying me to look at James Baldwin's final resting place.

Other names I would also like to mention because they helped my research in various ways are: Zahra Belkadi; Richard Gott, feature editor, *The Guardian*; John Harland, manager of the New York office of the Manchester Guardian; Emil P. Moschella, chief Freedom of Information-Privacy Acts Section, Records Management Division, United States Department of Justice, Federal Bureau of Investigation; Thomas and Sheila Weatherby; Edith Whiteman; Victor and Rosemary Zorza.

To the informants who did not wish to be named for personal or professional reasons, I can only say: thank you.

Source Notes

As WILL be clear from the foregoing acknowledgments, the main sources are my own experiences with James Baldwin, especially the conversations in which he talked about his past; interviews with people who knew him; and his writings. Where an important source is not listed in detail, the information came directly from James Baldwin in conversation.

1. Blues for Mister Baldwin

page 1

"mystical view": This was clear in both his conversations and his writings.

"Turkish silver ring": See Chapter 10, *Discovering Istanbul*.

"little stone from India": sent to me.

"I suspect": "Every Good-bye ain't Gone," New York Magazine, Dec. 19, 1977, reprinted in *The Price of the Ticket*, (St Martin's/Marek 1985).

page 2

"Witness to whence": "James Baldwin: Reflections of a Maverick," interview by Julius Lester, New York *Times Book Review,* May 27, 1984.

"you begun to see": "Every Good-bye ain't Gone" (see above).

"Take no one's word": "My Dungeon Shook," *The Fire Next Time* (Dial Press 1963) Copyright © 1962, 1963 by James Baldwin. Reprinted by permission of Doubleday.

"life to a handkerchief": conversations with author.

"One writes": Publicity statement for Knopf, reprinted as "Autobiographical Notes" in *Notes of a Native Son* Copyright © 1955, renewed 1983 by James Baldwin. Reprinted by permission of Beacon Press.

pages 2–5

Funeral details: Interviews with Karen Benta Rodriguez of Benta's Funeral Home, and with Paul Gorman of the Cathedral of St John the Divine; Baldwin family's funeral message; WJW reportage on the route to Ferncliff Cemetery.

page 4

"Frog Eyes": author interviews with bystanders; also see *Go Tell It on the Mountain* Copyright © 1952, 1953 by James Baldwin, originally published by Knopf, reprinted by Dial Press, now Doubleday.

page 5

"We never lived beyond": "Fifth Avenue Uptown," *Nobody Knows My Name* Copyright © 1954, 1956, 1958, 1959, 1960, 1961 by James Baldwin.

"like a thousand blinded eyes": *Go Tell It on the Mountain.*

2. "Frog Eyes"

page 6

"I really have": *Into Eternity: The Life of James Jones, American Writer* by Frank MacShane, Houghton Mifflin 1985. Interviews with Gloria Jones, New York, 1988. James Baldwin conversations with me.

"He talked about": A series of interviews with Emile Capouya, New York, 1988.

"Even after he became well-known": Interviews with David Adams Leeming, Donna Schrader, Cynthia Packard and others, New York, 1988.

page 7

"He had assumed": James Baldwin with me, with other friends and various references in *The Price of the Ticket* (St Martin's/Marek 1985).

"did not arrive on *my* scene": *No name in the Street* Copyright © 1972 by James Baldwin.

"No matter": TV Guide, Jan. 12, 1985.

"No doubt": *The Devil Finds Work* (Dial Press 1976).

"In talks": James Baldwin with me, also with young lover in mid-60s who does not wish to be named.

"Baldwin's first memory": *No Name in the Street.*

page 8

"He also remembered": *Notes of a Native Son.*

"His stepfather once gave him": "Here be Dragons," originally published as "Freaks and the American Ideal of Manhood," *Playboy,* January 1985, reprinted in *The Price of the Ticket.*

"My mother used to say": *The Furious Passage of James Baldwin* by Fern Maria Eckman (M. Evans 1965).

"I just know I have an English name": *A Rap on Race* by James Baldwin and Margaret Mead, J.P. Lippincott 1971.

page 9

"A friend in publishing": Interview with Donna Schrader, New York, 1988.

"there are old friends": Two in Harlem who didn't wish to be named concerning such a controversial matter.

page 10

"It is easy to be unfair": James Baldwin to me and to various newspaper and magazine interviewers, also in *Notes of a Native Son* and *Go Tell It on the Mountain.*

page 11

"They got cans of corned beef": "Here be Dragons" (see above).

"The Harlem he had been": James Baldwin to me and such essays as "Fifth Avenue Uptown," *Nobody Knows My Name,* and "Dark Days," published in Esquire, October 1980, reprinted in *The Price of the Ticket.*

page 12

"The first home": "Fifth Avenue Uptown."

"At first his home": *No Name in the Street.*

"His stepfather's son": *No Name in the Street.*

page 13

"The taunts": James Baldwin to me, also "Here be Dragons," etc.

page 14

"Mrs Baldwin told": *The Furious Passage of James Baldwin.*

page 15

"Much later": Interview with Blanche Ingrid Brann, publicity director, Henry Holt, June 27, 1988.

page 16

"bravura": "Autobiographical Notes," *Notes of a Native Son.*

page 17

"Help arrived": James Baldwin to me, also referred to in *The Devil Finds Work,* reprinted in *The Price of the Ticket.*

page 19

"He began to write": TV Guide.

page 21

"I would improvise": *The Paris Review* 91, interview with Jordan Elgrably, 1984.

page 22

"He said of his Douglass years": James Baldwin to me, he also read me notes from an old school diary.

page 29

"a Harlem racketeer": "Here be Dragons," also James Baldwin to me, also see Michael Thelwell interview reported in Chapter 20.

3. Baptism of Fire

page 36

"I had scarcely arrived": *Notes of a Native Son* Copyright © 1955, renewed 1983 by James Baldwin. Reprinted by permission of Beacon Press.

page 38

"By then all the pressures": James Baldwin to me, also described in *Notes of a Native Son.*

page 40

"The day of the funeral": James Baldwin to me, also described in *Notes of a Native Son.*

page 42

"He went back to work": James Baldwin to me, he also read passages from an old school diary.

page 46

"An introduction to another new friend": "Alas, Poor Richard," *Nobody Knows My Name*. Also *The Unfinished Quest of Richard Wright* by Michel Fabre Copyright © 1973 by William Morrow and Company Inc. Reprinted by permission of William Morrow and Company, Inc.

page 48

"When Harper's president": "Here be Dragons."

page 55

"The Harlem Ghetto": reprinted in *Notes of a Native Son*.

page 56

"Wright had moved from Brooklyn": "Alas, Poor Richard," *Nobody Knows My Name*.

4. Exile in Paris

page 65

"dashed to death": "Every Good-bye ain't Gone."
"They took him": "Alas, Poor Richard," *Nobody Knows My Name*.

page 69

"Baldwin told Julius Lester": Interview in New York *Times Book Review* already mentioned.

page 74

"On the day Zero": "Alas, Poor Richard," *Nobody Knows My Name*.

page 75

"Many Thousands Gone": this essay was also reprinted in *Notes of a Native Son*.

page 78

"Young Truman Capote": Author interview with Capote 1974.

page 81

"Equal in Paris": this essay was also reprinted in *Notes of a Native Son*.

page 82

"This Morning, This Evening, So Soon": this short story was collected in *Going to Meet the Man.*

page 85

"James, Baldwin decided": "An Interview with James Baldwin on Henry James" by David Adams Leeming, *The Henry James Review,* Fall 1986.

page 87

"Actress Simone Signoret": Interview with Simone Signoret by me in London, 1963. She also described the scene in her autobiography, *Nostalgia Isn't What It Used to Be.*

"It was about this time": Interview with Dr Kenneth B. Clark, Hastings-on-Hudson, 1988.

5. *Getting* Mountain *Published*

page 89

"One of James Baldwin's friends": "Every Good-Bye Ain't Gone."

page 91

"By now Baldwin's": "Stranger in the Village," *Notes of a Native Son.* Copyright © 1955, renewed 1983 by James Baldwin. Reprinted by permission of Beacon Press. Also James Baldwin to me.

page 95

"Unknown to him": Alfred A. Knopf Archives, Harry Ransom Humanities Research Center, The University of Texas at Austin.

page 97

"Baldwin credited Cole": Introduction, *The Price of the Ticket.*

page 98

"Bernard Hassell": Letter from Hassell, 1988.

page 99

"The first reports": Knopf Archives, Harry Ransom Humanities Research Center, The University of Texas at Austin.

page 102

"Hassell remembered": Letter from Bernard Hasell, 1988.

"Another arrival in Paris": James Baldwin to me, also Chester Himes' autobiography, *The Quality of Hurt* (Doubleday 1972), and interview with Chester Himes, 1972.

page 104

"Donald Barr": "Guilt was Everywhere" by Donald Barr, The New York *Times Book Review,* May 17, 1953; Orville Prescott, The New York *Times,* May 19, 1953; Time, May 18, 1953.

"One of the more negative comments": *The Life of Langston Hughes* Volume II by Arnold Rampersad (Oxford University Press 1988).

6. Giovanni's *Rejection*

page 106

"He also applied": Knopf Archives, Harry Ransom Humanities Research Center, The University of Texas at Austin.

page 113

"Time's review": Time, December 5, 1955; "From Harlem to Paris" by Langston Hughes, The New York *Times Book Review,* Feb. 28, 1956.

"He awaited": New York *Times Book Review,* March 29, 1959.

page 116

"Just how insecure": James Baldwin and Langston Hughes to me; also *The Life of Langston Hughes* Volume II by Arnold Rampersad (Oxford University Press 1988).

page 117

"To Langston Hughes": Rampersad's biography of LH, Volume II, see above.

7. *Paying Dues*

page 125

"Faulkner and Desegregation": reprinted in *Nobody Knows My Name.*

page 127

"They met": James Baldwin to me, "The Black Boy Looks at the White Boy," *Nobody Knows My Name; Mailer* by Peter Manso (Simon & Schuster 1985, Penguin Books 1986).

page 130

"A sign of his rising confidence": "Princes and Powers," *Nobody Knows My Name.*

8. Down South

page 135

"When Dr Kenneth Clark": Interview with Dr Clark, Hastings-on-Hudson, 1988

page 137

"He went first to Charlotte": "A Fly in Buttermilk," "Nobody Knows My Name: A Letter from the South," *Nobody Knows My Name*. Also "The Dangerous Road Before Martin Luther King," originally published in *Harper's Magazine,* Feb. 1961, and reprinted in *The Price of the Ticket*. Plus many conversations I had with James Baldwin about King. And *No Name in the Street*.

page 141

"He was among the first": Several conversations with Bayard Rustin in the 60s and 70s, Washington, Montgomery and New York.

page 142

"Harry Belafonte": Telephone conversation with Belafonte, 1988.

page 143

"Roy Innis": Interview, CORE Manhattan office, 1988.

"It was astonishing": James Baldwin to me, also *The Furious Passage of James Baldwin,* and "Sweet Lorraine", an introduction by James Baldwin to *To Be Young, Gifted and Black* by Lorraine Hansberry (Prentice-Hall 1969).

page 144

"Another writer": Interview with Gloria Jones, *Into Eternity: The Life of Jzmes Jones* by Frank MacShane (Houghton Mifflin 1985), and *Mailer* by Peter Manso (Simon & Schuster 1985, Penguin Books 1986).

page 146

"One night": Interview with John A. Williams, 1988.

"Working on the production": James Baldwin to me, Interview with Elia Kazan (who sometimes referred to his autobiography, *A Life,* Knopf 1988).

page 148

"I don't remember": Interview with Rip Torn, Greenwich Village, 1988.

page 149

"Another play": "Sweet Lorraine" and *To be Young, Gifted and Black* (see above).

page 150

"Baldwin also got to know": James Baldwin to me; "Sidney Poitier" by James Baldwin, Look Magazine, July 28, 1968.

page 151

"He also received": "The Black Boy Looks at the White Boy," *Nobody Knows My Name.*

9. Going to Meet the Man

page 157

"Ingmar Bergman": James Baldwin to me; "The Northern Protestant," *Nobody Knows My Name.*

page 160

"Alas, Poor Richard": reprinted in *Nobody Knows My Name.*

page 162

"Baldwin was becoming": Interview with Michael Thelwell, Amherst, Mass., 1988, also Thelwell's tribute at a service of respect and appreciation held at the University of Massachusetts, Dec. 16, 1987.

10. Discovering Istanbul

page 163

"The Joneses' home": *Into Eternity: The Life of James Jones; James Jones: A Friendship* by Willie Morris; interviews with Gloria Jones, William Styron; conversations with James Baldwin.

page 165

"Back home Norman Mailer": James Baldwin to me; "The Black Boy Looks at the White Boy," *Nobody Knows My Name; Advertisements for Myself* by Norman Mailer (Putnam's 1961); *Mailer* by Peter Manso (Simon & Schuster 1985, Penguin Books 1986).

page 167

"The way Baldwin described it": "The Black Boy Looks at the White Boy," *Nobody Knows My Name.*

page 173
"The news had now spread": Interview with William Styron for *The Guardian,* 1980; "Jimmy in the House" by William Styron, New York *Times Book Review,* Dec. 20, 1987; conversations with James Baldwin.

page 177
"He liked Istanbul": Interview with David Adams Leeming.

11. At the White House

page 183
"In Schlesinger's *A Thousand Days*": *A Thousand Days: John F. Kennedy in the White House* by Arthur M. Schlesinger, Jr. (Houghton Mifflin 1965).

page 184
"Baldwin had also been selected": I covered the Prix Formentor meetings for *The Guardian.*

page 189
"Baldwin arrived early": Baldwin's Look article about Sidney Poitier, see above.

page 193
"Maya Angelou": "A Brother's Love" by Maya Angelou, New York *Times Book Review,* Dec. 20, 1987.

page 194
"On magazine assignments": James Baldwin to me; "The Fight" by James Baldwin, Nugget, February 1963; Interview with Harold Conrad.

12. The Fire Next Time

page 198
"The Honorable Elijah Muhammad": *The Fire Next Time.*

page 203
"As always with a long journey": James Baldwin to me; interview with the late Robert Mills; *The Furious Passage of James Baldwin.*

page 204
"Time put him on its cover": Time, May 17, 1963.

page 209

"Calling him": Jane Howard, Life, November 1962.

page 211

"At a dinner": I was one of the guests.

13. Educating Robert Kennedy

page 218

"William Goldsmith": *A Thousand Days: John F. Kennedy in the White House* and *Robert Kennedy and His Times* both by Arthur M. Schlesinger, Jr, and both published by Houghton Mifflin. Interviews with Schlesinger, Dr Kenneth B. Clark, Rip Torn, Harry Belafonte, Jerome Smith, and conversations with James Baldwin. *Robert Kennedy in His Own Words* edited by Edwin O. Guthman and Jeffrey Shulman (Bantam Books 1988). *To Be Young, Gifted and Black* by Lorraine Hansberry.

page 228

"Baldwin told": "James Baldwin Rejects Despair Despite Race 'Drift and Danger'" by M.S. Handler, The New York *Times,* June 3, 1963.

page 229

"Baldwin had a reunion": James Baldwin to me; *Nothing Personal* (Atheneum 1964).

page 231

"Baldwin claimed": James Baldwin to me; *Dangerous Dossiers* by Herbert Mitgang (Donald I. Fine, Inc. 1987); interview with Rip Torn.

page 233

"In early October": James Baldwin to me.

14. Baldwin on Broadway

page 236

"Elia Kazan gave": Interview with Elia Kazan, who sometimes referred to his autobiography, *A Life* (see above) to save time.

page 237

"When Medgar Evers was killed": Introduction to *Blues for Mister Charlie.*

page 241

"Cheryl Crawford": *One Naked Individual: My Fifty Years in the Theater* by Cheryl Crawford (Bobbs-Merrill, 1977).

page 246

"Baldwin continued to claim": "James Baldwin . . . in Conversation," a collage of statements by Dan Georgakas in *Black Voices* (New American Library 1968), reprinted from Arts in Society (Summer 1966), the publication of the University Extension of the University of Wisconsin.

page 248

"Baldwin waited up": The New York *Times,* April 24, 1964.

15. The Price of Fame

page 257

"They had had many arguments": "Sweet Lorraine" (see above).

page 262

"Malcolm, too, showed Baldwin respect": Interview with Dr Kenneth B. Clark and with the late Malcolm X in 1963–64. *King, Malcolm, Baldwin,* three interviews by Kenneth B. Clark (Wesleyan University Press 1985).

page 263

"The news reached Baldwin": *No Name in the Street.*

16. The Turning Point

page 288

"It was to take a long time": I followed the Maynard case through attending court sessions and talks with James Baldwin and Tony Maynard. But James Baldwin also wrote about the case in *No Name in the Street.*

page 290

"attacked him in a book": *Soul on Ice* by Eldridge Cleaver (McGraw-Hill 1968).

page 293

"Meanwhile the fate": James Baldwin to me, also *The Devil Finds Work* and interview with Billy Dee Williams.

page 296
 King funeral: James Baldwin to me, my own observation, *No Name in the Street.*

page 298
 "Baldwin accepted an invitation": James Baldwin to me, *No Name in the Street.*

17. Home at Last

page 302
 "He tried to relax": James Baldwin to me, interview with David Adams Leeming, "A Love Affair: James Baldwin and Istanbul", *Ebony* March 1970.

page 303
 "For Architectural Digest": Architectural Digest Visits James Baldwin, text by James Baldwin, Architectural Digest, August 1987.

page 308
 "Baldwin was treated by some reviewers": Newsweek (Peter S. Prescott), May 29, 1972; Time (R.Z. Sheppard), May 29, 1972; New York *Times Book Review* (Mel Watkins), May 28, 1972; National Review (David Brudnoy), July 7, 1972; Saturday Review (Benjamin DeMott) May 27, 1972

page 312
 "He made the same point": "For James Baldwin, A Rap on Baldwin," The New York *Times,* June 26, 1972.

page 315
 "He told a Life reporter": Life (William A. McWhirter), July 1971.

18. Full Circle

page 326
 "In the summer of 1977": New York *Times Book Review* (Robert Coles), July 31, 1977.

page 330
 "Mel Watkins": New York *Times Book Review* (Mel Watkins), September 23, 1979.

page 332

"An interviewer": He said almost exactly the same to me in the 70s and to Jordan Elgrably in the 80s (Paris Review 1984).

19. Just Above My Head

page 334

"His new novel": *Just Above My Head* (Dial Press 1979). Copyright © 1978, 1979 by James Baldwin.

page 335

"You began to see": "Every Good-bye Ain't Gone," see above.

page 344

"The movie leaves us": The New York *Times,* March 3, 1982.

page 346

"One learns much more": Chinua Achebe's tribute at the service of respect and appreciation, University of Massachusetts, the Five College community, December 16, 1987.

page 347

"A man of sadness": "Dark Days," Esquire, October 1980, reprinted in *The Price of the Ticket.*

20. Professor Baldwin

page 349

"He and Jesse Jackson": *Thunder in America: The Improbable Presidential Campaign of Jesse Jackson in 1984* by Bob Faw and Nancy Skelton (Texas Monthly Press 1986, PaperJacks 1988). Tributes after Baldwin's death, December 1987.

page 357

"One of the big occasions": Interview with Sol Stein; Springfield *Morning-Union,* Sept. 24, 1984 ("James Baldwin honored at 60th birthday party" by Sarah Van Arsdale).

21. The Last Tug on the Handkerchief

page 363

"An adaptation": "James Baldwin reflects on 'Go Tell It' PBS Film" by Leslie Bennetts, New York *Times,* Jan. 10, 1985; TV Guide, Jan. 12, 1985.

page 364

"He heard of another figure": "The Loser," *Fame and Obscurity* by Gay Talese (Dell 1986).

22. This Morning, This Evening, So Soon

This last chapter describing James Baldwin's final months is largely based on interviews with David Leeming, Bernard Hassell, Herbert Gold and a few other people.

Index